Equilibrium and Efficiency in Production Economies
Second Edition

Springer
Berlin
Heidelberg
New York
Barcelona
Hong Kong
London
Milan
Paris
Singapore
Tokyo

Antonio Villar

Equilibrium and Efficiency in Production Economies

Second Revised and Enlarged Edition

With 34 Figures

 Springer

Prof. Dr. Antonio Villar
University of Alicante & IVIE
Department of Economics
03071 Alicante
Spain

ISBN 3-540-66396-7 Springer-Verlag Berlin Heidelberg New York

Library of Congress Cataloging-in-Publication Data
Die Deutsche Bibliothek – CIP-Einheitsaufnahme
Equilibrium and efficiency in production economies, 2. ed. / Antonio Villar. – Berlin; Heidelberg;
New York; Barcelona; Hong Kong; London; Milan; Paris; Singapore; Tokyo: Springer, 2000
  ISBN 3-540-66396-7

© Springer-Verlag Berlin · Heidelberg 2000
Printed in Germany

The use of general descriptive names, registered names, trademarks, etc. in this publication does
not imply, even in the absence of a specific statement, that such names are exempt from the relevant protective laws and regulations and therefore free for general use.

Hardcover-Design: Erich Kirchner, Heidelberg

SPIN 10734562   43/2202-5 4 3 2 1 0 – Printed on acid-free paper

FOREWORD

This book is a substantially revised and enlarged version of the monograph **General Equilibrium with Increasing Returns**, published by Springer-Verlag as a *Lecture Notes* volume in 1996. It incorporates new topics and the most recent developments in the field. It also provides a more systematic analysis of the differences between production economies with and without convex production sets. Five out of twelve chapters are new, and most of the remaining ones have been reformulated. An outline of contents appears in chapter 1.

As its predecessor, this book contains a formal and systematic exposition of the main results on the existence and efficiency of equilibrium, in production economies where production sets need not be convex. There is an explicit attempt at making of it a suitable reference both for graduate students and researchers interested in theory (not necessarily specialists in mathematical economics).

With this twofold purpose in mind, the work has been written according to three key principles:

(i)   To provide a **unified approach** to the problems involved. For that we construct a basic model that is rich enough to encompass the different models appearing throughout, and to derive all the results as corollaries of a reduced number of general theorems.

(ii)   To maintain a relatively **low mathematical complexity**. Thus, when the estimated cost of generality exceeds the benefit of simplicity, we shall state and prove the theorems under assumptions that need not be the most general ones.

(iii)   To offer a highly **self-contained exposition**. In particular, detailed proofs of the results and explanations of the main concepts are provided.

Foreword

Ana B. Ania, Carlos Alós, Subir Chattopadhyay, Luis Corchón, Ana Guerrero, Thorsten Hens, Carmen Herrero, Javier López Cuñat, Martine Quinzii, Walter Trockel and Rajiv Vohra made comments and remarks to different parts of this and the former work. I'm most grateful for their generosity. Needless to say that the remaining errors are my own. I'll be pleased in receiving the reader's comments, suggestions or criticisms.[1]

Financial support from the *Dirección General de Enseñanza Superior e Investigación Científica*, under project PB97-0120, is gratefully acknowledged.

A. Villar

Alicante, May 1999

---

[1] E-mail address: villar@merlin.fae.ua.es

Contents

Chapter 1

PRELIMINARIES

1.1 Introduction

1.1.1 Motivation

Most societies organize their economic activity through the functioning of markets. Myriads of individual economic agents make decisions according to their private interests, whose interaction results in an allocation of resources. The production and exchange of commodities is at the centre of the picture: consumers demand commodities and supply labour services, firms produce commodities according to their technological knowledge, and commodities flow among agents by means of an exchange process which is realized through markets and prices.

General equilibrium models try to capture the logic of this complex network of interactions viewing the economic system as a whole, that is, taking all the simultaneous interdependencies established among economic agents into account (as opposed to partial equilibrium models, that typically concentrate on the analysis of specific markets or decision units). The first concern of general equilibrium theory is the analysis of conditions ensuring that all the actions taken independently by economic agents are simultaneously feasible. An *equilibrium* is a situation in which all the agents are able to realize their plans; in other words, agents do not find it beneficial to change their actions. Needless to say that the nature of such an equilibrium depends on the behaviour of economic agents, and that the feasibility of the collective action may not correspond to a socially desirable state of affairs.

The analysis of the social desirability of equilibrium outcomes comes next in the agenda of general equilibrium theory. Suppose that the economy is arranged in such a way that all agents are simultaneously realizing their plans. Can the economy do better? If this were the case, there would be scope for the intervention of some authority (the Government, say), because changing the spontaneous allocation of resources would result in a better state. The key questions are, of course, what "better" means, and whether such an authority will be able to improve the social situation.

There are many ways of ranking the outcomes of an economy, but there is a simple principle which seems difficult to object: no resource allocation can be considered satisfactory, if it were possible to improve the situation of all the members of the society with the available resources. This is the Pareto principle, which is to be understood as a minimal test of economic *efficiency*. Note that there may well be allocations passing this test which can be deemed socially undesirable. To be clear: We are not saying that the Pareto principle ensures good outcomes; what we are saying is that one should be worried about those outcomes which do not pass such a simple test.

1.1.2 Production economies and increasing returns

This book analyzes the existence and efficiency of equilibrium allocations in production economies, under the maintained assumption that markets are complete, commodities are perfectly divisible, and the numbers of agents and commodities are finite and given. The standard competitive model of a production economy with convex firms will be presented first. It will be shown that, under a set of quite general and reasonable axioms, an equilibrium exists and yields an efficient allocation. Therefore, competitive markets are institutions that permit the spontaneous coordination of economic agents, and do it efficiently: decentralization is neither chaotic nor wasteful. This summarizes the *Invisible Hand Theorem*, according to Adam Smith's poetic expression.

The Invisible Hand Theorem is based on two key axioms about the nature of the economy (apart from the maintained assumption mentioned above): *the convexity assumption* and *price taking behaviour*. The convexity assumption says that agents choose actions within convex sets, guided by a convex criterion (a quasi-concave objective function). Price taking behaviour means that those variables conditioning agents' choices are independent on individual actions. The combination of these two features has a number of implications, among which we would like to emphasize the following:

(i) The mappings describing the behaviour of economic agents (demands and supplies) are upper hemicontinuous correspondences, with non-empty, closed and convex values. This permits to apply a fixed point argument, in order to prove the existence of an equilibrium.

(ii) The local properties that characterize the maximization of individual objective functions imply global maximization. This entails that marginal conditions are sufficient for the efficiency of equilibrium outcomes.

(iii) The maximization of all individual objective functions on individual choice sets implies the maximization of aggregate values on the aggregate choice set. As a consequence, the number of agents does not matter for the analysis of existence and efficiency of equilibrium (as long as this is a finite number).

From these features it follows that the set of competitive equilibria of a given economy is non-empty and coincides with the set of efficient allocations (the two welfare theorems). And also that production economies do not differ substantially from pure exchange economies, when production activities are carried out by convex competitive firms. This is so because, from a an analytical standpoint, a production economy with these characteristics is equivalent to a pure exchange economy, in which the initial endowments vary with prices (within a well defined compact set determined by the available technology).

Things are really different when production sets are not assumed to be convex and/or firms do not behave competitively. Here production decisions really matter, and the results obtained with respect to pure exchange economies do not translate into the world of production economies. The analysis of economies with firms that may exhibit increasing returns to scale will be the focus of this book. Different equilibrium models will be analyzed, and their efficiency properties discussed.

Increasing returns is a topic which many economists find it to be simultaneously *important, difficult* and *discouraging*. It is important because it refers to a well established technological phenomenon, related to some common features such as indivisibilities, fixed costs, internal economies of scale or externalities. It is difficult because the standard concepts and tools for the analysis of these economies fail: increasing returns are essentially incompatible with the functioning of competitive markets. In particular, the supply mappings are not well defined, and alternative rules of behaviour are hard to handle in a general equilibrium framework. It is discouraging because the available models do not seem to solve the basic questions. *Normative* models, where nonconvex firms follow marginal pricing, do not achieve efficient outcomes. And *positive* models cannot properly incorporate monopolistic competition, as a way of defining the behaviour of those firms with increasing returns to scale.

Even though the last assessment is not false, I would like to think that this book will contribute to show that "the increasing returns question" is neither too difficult nor too discouraging. Concerning the difficulty, it will be shown that the analysis can be carried out with essentially the same tools as those applicable to the standard competitive model. As for the relevance of the results available, let us advance that: (i) There are abstract existence results for general equilibrium models with increasing returns, under very weak assumptions; and (ii) Negative results abound, concerning the efficiency of market equilibria when there are increasing returns. These results, however, provide a sound understanding of the difficulties involved in the allocation of resources through a market mechanism with nonconvex technologies. And this knowledge provides clues which are precise enough to allow for positive results in specific models.

1.2   Overview

1.2.1   Outline of contents

The book consists of 12 chapters, all of which share the setting presented later in this one.

Chapter 2 describes competitive consumers. Each consumer is characterized by a choice set, a preference relation and a wealth restriction. All these elements are discussed in detail, and conditions are given in order to represent preferences by continuous utility functions. Rational behaviour is identified with the choice of the best affordable alternatives, at given prices. Namely, the demand mapping associates to each given price vector the solutions of a program consisting of maximizing utility, under the associated wealth restriction. Under general assumptions the demand mapping is shown to be an upper hemicontinuous correspondence, with non-empty, compact and convex values.

Chapter 3 deals with production and supply. The basic properties of production sets are considered first, discussing aspects such as productive efficiency, additivity, divisibility and returns to scale. Then we analyze the behaviour of competitive firms when production sets are convex. In particular, we discuss the conditions under which supply is an upper hemicontinuous correspondence with non-empty, compact and convex values. We also consider the inverse supply correspondence, as an alternative representation of firms' behaviour. This will serve as an introduction to the pricing rule approach, that is applied to model the behaviour of non-convex firms in most of later chapters.

Chapter 4 analyzes the existence and efficiency of competitive equilibria in a standard convex world. We consider a private ownership market economy made of m consumers and n firms, and discuss the existence of equilibrium, using the standard fixed-point argument. Then we move towards the normative analysis, and present the two welfare theorems (all equilibria are efficient and viceversa, under suitable assumptions). We also review the equivalence between equilibrium and optimum, in terms of their marginal properties (marginal rates of substitution and transformation).

Chapter 5 extends the analysis on the existence of equilibrium to the case of non-convex firms. In order to do so, we introduce the notion of *pricing rules*, as a suitable way of modelling the behaviour of non-convex firms. A pricing rule is a generalization of the inverse supply mapping; it associates, to each efficient production plan, those prices that the firm finds "acceptable" in order to carry out such a production. Specifying which prices are "acceptable" means to define a particular mapping that links production and prices. We offer in this chapter a general result on the existence of equilibrium when firms' behaviour is defined by means of abstract pricing rules. This provides a reference model that encompasses the alternative economic scenarios that are discussed in the following chapters.

Chapter 6 is devoted to the study of marginal pricing (a pricing rule satisfying the necessary conditions for optimality), and the efficiency of the associated equilibrium allocations. It starts by presenting a self-contained analysis of Clarke normal cones (the generalization of supporting prices when production sets are neither smooth nor convex). Next we analyze the key properties of marginal pricing, and the existence of marginal pricing equilibria. Then we take up the efficiency problem. We show that every efficient allocation can be decentralized as a marginal pricing equilibrium, but also that marginal pricing equilibria are not generally Pareto optimal. Hence a sort of "impossibility result" obtains: efficiency and non-convexities are incompatible with decentralized decision, under general conditions.

Chapter 7 analyzes economies in which those firms with increasing returns can be associated with natural monopolies. We study first the regulation of these monopolies in terms of two-part tariffs. This is a regulation policy by which those consumers who buy positive amounts of the goods produced by non-convex firms, are charged an entrance fee plus a proportional one (which corresponds to marginal pricing). Therefore, by using a system of non-linear prices one can meet both the necessary conditions for optimality and a break-even constraint. Besides proving the existence of two-part tariffs equilibria, and finding again that these equilibria need not be Pareto optimal, we identify a particular family of economies for which this regulation policy yields efficient outcomes (pure fixed cost economies). We also consider the case of unregulated monopolies, when they apply perfect price discrimination to sell their output.

Chapter 8 deals with market economies in which firms follow *loss-free* pricing rules (those in which the equilibrium of firms involves nonnegative profits). Mark-up pricing is analyzed first (including average cost pricing, as a particular case). Next we present a model in which non-convex firms behave as constrained profit maximizers. This model is applicable to situations in which there are some elements of fixed capital that restrict firms production possibilities and generate non-convexities in production. Constrained profit maximization is to be understood as an application of the *profit principle* to this setting: no firm will willingly admit a prices-production combination if there are feasible alternatives that, at these prices, yield higher profits.

Chapter 9 applies the results in chapter 8 to the study of competitive markets, when there are increasing returns to scale. Two alternative notions of competition are discussed. The first one, called *competitive pricing*, corresponds to a situation in which firms behave as constrained profit maximizers but obtain no extra profits (so here the profit principle is coupled with the scarcity principle, that require firms to pay for those inputs that limit capacity, the highest prices compatible with their incentives). The second, termed *classical equilibria*, corresponds to a scenario in which the equilibrium of firms is associated with the combination of constrained profit maximization and equal profitability.

Chapter 10 extends the analysis of equilibria with non-linear pricing to the case in which economic decisions involve the choice of a public environment, that may generate non-convexities in agents' choice sets. We explore here suitable extensions of the notions of *public competitive equilibrium* and *valuation equilibrium* to show that the two welfare theorems hold in this context.

Chapter 11 refers to input-output analysis. We present here some generalizations of the standard linear model (linear and non-linear joint production models). Three topics are considered. First, the solvability of the equation systems describing equilibrium of quantities and prices, for given values of the parameters of final demands and added values. Second, the non-substitution theorem in the context of joint production. And third, the existence of equilibrium in the different models considered.

Finally, chapter 12 deals with the analysis of the set of attainable allocations (the closedness of aggregate consumption and production sets, and the compactness of the set of attainable allocations). Even though there is little new in this chapter, it includes detailed proofs of these key results, that are not so easy to find in the literature.

All chapters conclude with some references to the literature, that aim at providing "useful links" for the interested reader. Therefore, more detailed references are usually provided in those chapters that refer to models with non-convex technologies.

There is no "Mathematical Appendix" in this book. K. Border's (1985) book, *Fixed Point Theory with Applications to Economics and Game Theory*, is well suited for most of the mathematics that are required. We refer to this text for those formal concepts and results which are to be known. More specific references are given along the text.

1.2.2 Conventions

Mathematical notation is standard. Nevertheless, let me clarify some points.

Let $\mathbb{R}$ stand for the real line, and $\mathbb{R}^n$ for the n-vector space of real numbers. Points in $\mathbb{R}$ (scalars) will be written in *italics*, whereas points in $\mathbb{R}^n$ will be **boldfaced**. For any two points $\mathbf{x}, \mathbf{y} \in \mathbb{R}^n$, the scalar product $\sum_{i=1}^n x_i y_i$ will be denoted by $\mathbf{xy}$, without distinguishing between row and column vectors. Similarly, if $\mathbf{A}$ is a matrix, the expression $\mathbf{Ax}$ implies that $\mathbf{x}$ is a column vector, whereas the expression $\mathbf{pA}$ implies that $\mathbf{p}$ is a row vector.

If K is a subset of $\mathbb{R}^n$, we denote by ∂K the *boundary* of K, by $intK$ the *interior* of K, and by $co\{K\}$ the *convex hull* of K (the intersection of all convex sets that contain K). Let K, M stand for two subsets of $\mathbb{R}^n$; then $K \setminus M$ (or $K - M$) denote the set of points that are in K but are not in M.

Concerning vector inequalities, we adopt the following convention: for all $\mathbf{x}, \mathbf{y} \in \mathbb{R}^n$,

(i) $\mathbf{x} \geq \mathbf{y} \Longleftrightarrow x_i \geq y_i$ for all $i = 1, 2, ..., n$.

(ii) $\mathbf{x} > \mathbf{y} \Longleftrightarrow \mathbf{x} \geq \mathbf{y}$, and $\mathbf{x} \neq \mathbf{y}$.

(iii) $\mathbf{x} >> \mathbf{y} \Longleftrightarrow x_i > y_i$ for all $i = 1, 2, ..., n$.

We denote by $\mathbb{R}^n_+$ the set of points in $\mathbb{R}^n$ with non-negative components (i.e. the set of points $\mathbf{x}$ in $\mathbb{R}^n$ with $\mathbf{x} \geq \mathbf{0}$). The set of points $\mathbf{x} \in \mathbb{R}^n$ with $\mathbf{x} \leq \mathbf{0}$ will be denoted by $-\mathbb{R}^n_+$, rather than by $\mathbb{R}^n_-$ (because it turns out to be easier to identify within the text).

Definitions, axioms, remarks, propositions, theorems, etc. are numbered independently within each chapter, according to the following principle: Definition (i, j) is the jth definition within the ith chapter; axiom (i, j) is the jth axiom within the ith chapter, etc.

The proofs of the theorems, propositions, etc. conclude with the expression $\boxed{\textbf{Q.e.d.}}$ (the abbreviation of the Latin expression *Quod eram demostrandum* –what we were demonstrating).

1.3   The setting

We are concerned here on economic problems that involve consumption and production decisions, relative to goods and services that are traded in the market. Consumers choose commodity bundles that include the demand for some goods and services as well as the supply of labour. Firms choose input-output combinations that are feasible, according to the available technology. Market prices affect these decisions, via budget restrictions and firms' profits. The study is carried out from a general equilibrium approach, focusing on the existence and efficiency of equilibrium allocations in production economies.

Let us now briefly describe the background of the analysis, that is, the specification of those elements defining the basic framework of the modelling:

(i) *Commodities and prices*, which are the variables of the problem.

(ii) *The agents*, which are the relevant decision units.

The specification of these elements provides the implicit assumptions under which the whole book is constructed.

1.3.1   Commodities and prices

It will be assumed throughout the book that there is a fixed number ℓ of commodities (where ℓ is a natural number, with $1 \leq \ell < +\infty$). Let us stress from the very beginning that commodities are here very specific objects, whose nature and interpretation may depend on the type of model considered. In general, commodities are goods or services that can be distinguished according to their **characteristics** and their **availability**. By "characteristics" we mean aspects such as physical properties, design, quality, functioning, etc. Hence, a used car, a new TV set or a lesson of a foreign language are different commodities. The "availability" refers to the specification of the conditions under which commodities are delivered. It is customary to consider three of these conditioning variables: *Location, time* and *state of the world.*

"Location" refers to the place where the commodity is delivered. When the model includes more than one place, the definition of a commodity must specify *where* the good or service is made available. Buying here a commodity that is delivered somewhere else, most likely requires incurring in some transportation costs. Therefore two goods with identical characteristics represent two different objects for a given agent, when available at different places.

"Time" refers to the date in which the good or service is to be delivered. If there are several time periods, the definition of a commodity must specify *when* is it available. Note that in this case decisions over commodity bundles involve choices about present and future consumption and production.

The "state of the world" refers to the *circumstances* under which goods and services are made available. This corresponds to an economy in which there is a number of alternative states of the world that can occur, and agents have to take decision without knowing in advance which one will happen. In this context the definition of a commodity must specify the event that conditions delivery, and commodities can be considered as *contingent commodities*. Note that, when there is uncertainty, the choice of commodity bundles involves implicit insurance decisions.

In short: A commodity is a good or service fully specified in terms of its characteristics and its availability. Consequently, two goods or services which are identical with respect to their characteristics, but are available in different locations, at different dates, or in different circumstances, will be considered as two different commodities. Observe that taking $\ell < +\infty$ implies that the number of conditioning aspects contemplated in the model, dates, locations and events, are finite.

The quantity of a commodity will be represented by a real number. This amounts to saying that we assume that commodities are perfectly divisible. This is certainly an over-simplification of the real world economies: objects such as computers, refrigerators or lorries are indivisible, so that 0.34 or $\pi/2$ of one of these commodities makes little sense. Yet this is partly an interpretative issue. One may well consider that the commodities are not the goods themselves, but the *services* provided by these goods (i.e., time of computing or refrigeration facilities, or transport capacity measured in Tons per Km.). This way of looking at commodities makes the divisibility assumption more palatable. Yet, note that this interpretation implies that we may be transforming the indivisibility problem in a problem of non-convexities: The firm which produces "computing facilities", say, will hardly have a convex production set.

The above specifications can be summarized by saying that we take $\mathbb{R}^\ell$ (the vector space obtained by replicating ℓ times the real numbers) as the *commodity space*.[1]

Each commodity $h = 1, 2, \ldots, \ell$ will have associated with it a real number p_h representing its price. The number p_h is to be interpreted as the amount to be paid here and today by a good or service, with precise characteristics, which will be delivered under well specified date, location and circumstances.

---

[1]Note that taking $\mathbb{R}^\ell$ as the commodity space is a convenient assumption, since it exhibits very good operational properties. In particular, it provides both a vector space structure and a suitable topology (e.g., the scalar product is a well defined and continuous operation).

If the kth commodity refers to a good or service to be delivered in a future period, its price is to be interpreted as its present value. When there is also uncertainty, the price of a commodity is the amount paid here today for a unit of a good or service, that will be available at a future date under specific circumstances. When the state of the world does not correspond to the conditioning event, no delivery takes place (though the price might have actually been paid).

In principle prices may be positive, zero or negative. Positive prices indicate that the corresponding commodity is "desirable". Zero prices may be interpreted as the definition of "free-goods": nobody is willing to pay a positive amount for the right to enjoy these goods. Finally, negative prices are to be interpreted as the cost of disposing off unwanted commodities (these commodities are "bads", rather than "goods"). We shall concentrate on the case of nonnegative prices. This can be derived in most cases from the "free-disposal" assumption about production sets, to be discussed later on. Thus, a *price system* will be typically represented by a vector $\mathbf{p} \in \mathbb{R}^{\ell}_{+}$.

Observe that $\mathbf{p}$ is a point in $\mathbb{R}^{\ell}$, which is precisely the commodity space. This introduces an implicit assumption which is essential: there is a price for each commodity. That is, commodities that will be available at future dates, different locations or alternative states of the world, have a well defined price. Therefore, the costs and benefits of those actions concerning production and consumption can be properly evaluated. This is usually expressed by saying that *markets are complete*.

1.3.2   Agents

Economic agents are the decision units of the model (the "actors" of the story told in the next pages). There will be three types of agents: *consumers, firms* and *the Government*. Of these three categories, only the first two will be explicitly modelled, while "the Government" will appear as a central agency imposing some regulation policies (such as taxes or pricing schemes), and enforcing the property rights.

Consumers are the agents making consumption plans, that is, deciding the demand for goods and services and the supply of labour, under the restriction of their available wealth. It is assumed that there is a given number m of them. The ith consumer's choice set is represented by a subset X_i of $\mathbb{R}^{\ell}$, called her consumption set, whereas u_i describes her way of ranking the available alternatives (called her utility function). A function r_i stands for the ith consumer's wealth mapping.

Firms decide about production and pricing policies, under the restriction of their technological knowledge and the nature of the markets. By assumption, there is a given number n of firms. The jth firm's choice set is represented by a subset Y_j of $\mathbb{R}^\ell$, called production set, while ϕ_j describes the way it chooses alternatives (called pricing rule).

All agents are assumed to make their decisions under a system of complete markets.

In summary, we introduce the following:

Preliminary Axiom: $\mathbb{R}^\ell$ *is the commodity space, with* $0 < \ell < +\infty$. *A price system is a point* $\mathbf{p} \in \mathbb{R}^\ell$ *(complete markets). There are* m *consumers and* n *firms.*

1.3.3 Economies

We call *economy* to a specification of the m consumers, the n firms, with their choice sets and choice criteria, and a vector $\omega \in \mathbb{R}^\ell$ which describes the initial resources. These are to be interpreted as those commodities which are available before production takes place, and will usually be referred to as the *initial endowments*. An economy can thus be presented as:

$$E = \{(X_i,\ u_i,\ r_i)_{i=1}^m; (Y_j,\ \phi_j)_{j=1}^n; \omega\}$$

The functioning of an economy can be thought of as a process through which the initial endowments are transformed in nature, composition, availability and distribution among agents. The outcome of this process will depend not only on the specifics of the economy (as described by the elements in E), but also on the institutional framework (in particular concerning the property rights and the nature of the interactions between economic agents). This is why the outcome of economic activity is usually considered as a *resource allocation* process, and each of the different institutional frameworks (the different ways of organizing the economic activity) for the economies under study, is considered as a *resource allocation mechanism*.

1.4 References to the literature

Arrow (1974), Debreu (1984), Mas-Colell (1987) and Cornet (1988a) are excellent introductory readings for some of the problems that will be analyzed later.

Many relevant results on the existence and efficiency of equilibrium in economies with non-convex technologies are gathered in vol. 17 of the *Journal of Mathematical Economics* (edited by Bernard Cornet in 1988). Interesting collections of readings on this subject appear in the books edited by Buchanan & Yoon (1994) and G. Heal (1999).

Chapter 2

CONSUMERS

2.1 Introduction

A **consumer** is an individual agent (a single household or a family) who takes consumption decisions, that is, decisions referring to the demand for goods and services and the supply of different types of labour. It will be assumed that there is a fixed number m of consumers, indexed by $i = 1, 2, ..., m$.

This chapter is devoted to modelling the consumer's decisions as *a problem of choice under restrictions*. The consumer's rational behaviour will be identified with the choice of best options within the set of alternatives that are affordable. There are three elements that define this problem:

(a) The *choice set*, that describes the universe of alternatives on which the consumer's choice problem is formulated.

(b) The *choice criterion*, that reflects the way in which the consumer evaluates alternative options.

(b) The *restrictions*, that limit the consumer's effective opportunities of choice.

We call *consumption set* the universe of alternatives. Each of these alternatives is a combination of goods and services that the individual can consume, as well as the amounts of different types of labour she can realize. The consumer's choice criterion will be modelled in terms of the binary relation "to be at least as good as", that expresses her tastes. In a market economy the effective consumption possibilities are determined by commodity prices and the consumers' wealth. It will be assumed that prices are independent on individual consumers' actions, so that they are taken as given.

The consumer's rational behaviour consists of choosing a best alternative among those that she can afford, depending on prices and wealth. We call *demand* to the mapping that associates the chosen options with the different

values of prices and wealth. In order to facilitate the analysis of consumers'
behaviour, we shall formulate the choice problem as the maximization of a
continuous function (the utility function) on a convex set (the budget set).
This permits an easier derivation of the key properties of demand mappings.

2.2   Consumption sets

The choice set for the ith consumer is given by a subset X_i of $\mathbb{R}^\ell$ that describes those consumption vectors that can be realized, given the individual's
abilities and biological constraints. A **consumption plan** for the ith consumer is an ℓ-dimensional vector $\mathbf{x}_i \in X_i$. A consumption plan specifies some
amounts of goods and labour which the ith consumer is able to realize. Those
goods and services that the consumer demands will be denoted by positive
numbers, whereas her supply of productive factors (different types of labour)
will be denoted by negative ones.[1] The ith consumer's **consumption set**
$X_i \subset \mathbb{R}^\ell$, is the set of all these consumption plans.

The next figure illustrates a consumption set in $\mathbb{R}^2$, where commodity 1
corresponds to a consumption good (corn) while commodity 2 is a productive
factor (labour). Point $\mathbf{x}_i = (-1, 2)$ represents a consumption plan, while the
set $X_i \subset \mathbb{R}^2$ gives us the ith consumer's consumption set.

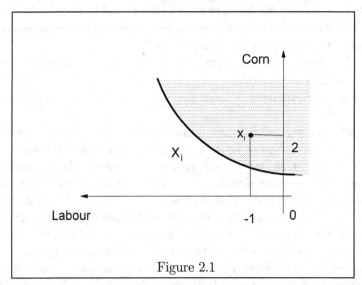

Figure 2.1

Note that consumption sets inform about things such as the different

---

[1]One can also take $X_i \subset \mathbb{R}^\ell_+$, by properly specifying the productive factors that might
be supplied by the ith consumer [on this see Arrow & Hahn (1971, ch. 3)].

types of labour a consumer is able to perform, the minimum requirements of goods and services needed in order to survive, and the consumption-labour combinations that are biologically feasible. They thus contain relevant information about the possibilities of the economy.

Concerning consumption sets we shall assume the following:

Axiom 2.1 *For every $i = 1, 2, \ldots, m$, X_i is a non-empty closed and convex subset of $\mathbb{R}^\ell$, bounded from below (that is, there is $\mathbf{c}_i \in \mathbb{R}^\ell$ such that $\mathbf{c}_i \leq \mathbf{x}_i$, $\forall \mathbf{x}_i \in X_i$).*

Besides non-emptiness, the first part of this assumption is partly technical (closedness simply says that if $\{\mathbf{x}_i^\nu\}$ is a sequence in X_i converging to a point $\mathbf{x}_i' \in \mathbb{R}^\ell$, then $\mathbf{x}_i' \in X_i$). It also says that if two consumption plans are feasible, so will be any intermediate combination (that is, if $\mathbf{x}_i, \mathbf{x}_i'$ are in X_i, then $[\lambda \mathbf{x}_i + (1 - \lambda)\mathbf{x}_i']$ is also in X_i, for any scalar λ in the closed interval $[0, 1]$). It is also assumed that X_i is bounded from below; this is a natural assumption, because demands are denoted by nonnegative numbers, and the amount of labour a consumer can supply cannot exceed 24 hours a day. Note that if one takes $X_i = \mathbb{R}_+^\ell$ axiom 1 is automatically satisfied (even though in this case one usually substitutes labour by leisure in the commodity space).

2.3 Preferences

In order to model the way in which a consumer ranks different consumption plans, we shall assume that there is a binary relation $\succsim_i$ defined over X_i. Let $\mathbf{x}_i, \mathbf{x}_i'$ be points in X_i; then $\mathbf{x}_i' \succsim_i \mathbf{x}_i$ means that $\mathbf{x}_i'$ is *at least as good as* $\mathbf{x}_i$, from the ith consumer's viewpoint. We shall refer to $\succsim_i$ as the ith consumer's **preference relation**.

Concerning this preference relation we postulate a number of properties that provide a suitable basis for the modelling of consumers' behaviour. These properties will be gathered into three different groups. The first group (completeness and transitivity) refers to order properties; they ensure that the preference relation is a complete preorder. The second group (continuity and convexity) introduces a rich analytical structure. The reader will observe that the first group of axioms is independent of the assumptions on X_i established in axiom 1, whereas the second one is not. Finally, the third group refers to alternative notions of non-satiation.

2.3.1 Order properties

Let us start by presenting and discussing the first group of properties:

Definition 2.1 (Completeness) *The ith consumer's preferences are complete if, for all* $\mathbf{x}_i, \mathbf{x}_i' \in X_i$,

$$[\mathbf{x}_i \succsim_i \mathbf{x}_i' \, or \, \mathbf{x}_i' \succsim_i \mathbf{x}_i]$$

Definition 2.2 (Transitivity) *The ith consumer's preferences are transitive if, for all* $\mathbf{x}_i, \mathbf{x}_i', \mathbf{x}_i'' \in X_i$,

$$[\mathbf{x}_i \succsim_i \mathbf{x}_i' \quad \& \quad \mathbf{x}_i' \succsim_i \mathbf{x}_i''] \Longrightarrow \mathbf{x}_i \succsim_i \mathbf{x}_i''$$

Completeness discards the presence of alternatives that the ith consumer cannot compare. Observe that the way in which is defined implies that $\succsim_i$ is also *reflexive* (as $\mathbf{x}_i = \mathbf{x}_i'$ is permitted). The transitivity property is to be understood as a property of "consistency in the evaluation". Nevertheless, even under certainty, transitivity can be violated in some cases; the best known examples are those in which the ith consumer has imperfect discriminatory power (inaccurate perception), or when the ith agent is actually a family and takes decisions by majority voting.

These properties imply that $\succsim_i$ is a *complete preference preorder*. This preorder reflects the ith consumer's evaluation of alternative consumption plans. From this preference preorder we can deduce a new binary relation, called **indifference relation** and denoted by $\sim_i$, which is defined as follows: Given $\mathbf{x}_i, \mathbf{x}_i'$ in X_i,

$$\mathbf{x}_i \sim_i \mathbf{x}_i' \Longleftrightarrow [\mathbf{x}_i \succsim_i \mathbf{x}_i' \quad \& \quad \mathbf{x}_i' \succsim_i \mathbf{x}_i]$$

to be read as $\mathbf{x}_i$ is *indifferent* to $\mathbf{x}_i'$, meaning that both consumption plans are equally satisfactory from the ith consumer's point of view.[2]

The indifference relation is obviously reflexive, symmetric (i.e. $\mathbf{x}_i \sim_i \mathbf{x}_i'$ implies $\mathbf{x}_i' \sim_i \mathbf{x}_i$), and transitive. It is thus an *equivalence relation* whose classes are called *indifference classes* (later called also *curves*). Let $\mathbf{x}_i'$ be a

---

[2]Note that "being indifferent" and "being non-comparable" are two logically distinct statements. The first one says $\mathbf{x}_i \succsim_i \mathbf{x}_i'$ and $\mathbf{x}_i' \succsim_i \mathbf{x}_i$, while the second one asserts that *neither* $\mathbf{x}_i \succsim_i \mathbf{x}_i'$ *nor* $\mathbf{x}_i' \succsim_i \mathbf{x}_i$.

point in X_i. Call $\mathcal{I}_i(\mathbf{x}'_i)$ the set of points in X_i which are indifferent to $\mathbf{x}'_i$, that is,

$$\mathcal{I}_i(\mathbf{x}'_i) = \{\mathbf{x}_i \in X_i \ / \ \mathbf{x}_i \sim_i \mathbf{x}'_i\}$$

When $\succsim_i$ is complete and transitive, $\sim_i$ is an equivalence relation. Hence, it generates a partition over X_i, that is:

$$\mathcal{I}_i(\mathbf{x}'_i) \neq \emptyset \text{ for each } \mathbf{x}'_i \in X_i$$

$$\bigcup_{x_i \in X_i} \mathcal{I}_i(\mathbf{x}'_i) = X_i$$

$$\mathcal{I}_i(\mathbf{x}'_i) \bigcap \mathcal{I}_i(\mathbf{x}''_i) \neq \emptyset \Longrightarrow \mathcal{I}_i(\mathbf{x}'_i) \equiv \mathcal{I}_i(\mathbf{x}''_i)$$

We can define now a third binary relation, called **strict preference** and denoted by $\succ_i$, as follows: for any two consumption plans $\mathbf{x}_i, \mathbf{x}'_i \in X_i$

$$\mathbf{x}_i \succ_i \mathbf{x}'_i \Longleftrightarrow [\mathbf{x}_i \succsim_i \mathbf{x}'_i \ \& \ \mathbf{x}'_i \notin \mathcal{I}_i(\mathbf{x}_i)]$$

The expression $\mathbf{x}_i \succ_i \mathbf{x}'_i$ is to be read as $\mathbf{x}_i$ *is preferred to* $\mathbf{x}'_i$ *by the ith consumer*. The properties of completeness and transitivity of $\succsim_i$ imply that $\succ_i$ is *irreflexive* ($\mathbf{x}_i$ cannot be preferred to itself) and *asymmetric* (that is, $\mathbf{x}_i \succ_i \mathbf{x}'_i$ implies that $\mathbf{x}'_i$ cannot be preferred to $\mathbf{x}_i$). Therefore, this relation induces a complete and strict ordering over the indifference classes [the elements of the quotient set $(X_i/ \sim_i)$].

Summing up: The completeness and transitivity of the preference relation $\succsim_i$ enable to partition the consumption set into classes which gather consumption bundles which are indifferent for the ith consumer, and are completely ordered by $\succ_i$. The consumer's choice problem thus consists of selecting a consumption bundle which is maximal in the subset of the affordable ones (i.e., a bundle in the "highest" indifference class attainable).

2.3.2 Analytical properties

Hereinafter we assume that X_i is a connected subset of $\mathbb{R}^\ell$. The first analytical property considered is that of continuity:

Definition 2.3 (Continuity) *The ith consumer's preferences are continuous if, for every $\mathbf{x}_i \in X_i$, the sets:*

$$\mathcal{B}_i(\mathbf{x}_i) \equiv \{\mathbf{x}'_i \in X_i \ / \ \mathbf{x}'_i \succ_i \mathbf{x}_i\}$$

$$\mathcal{W}_i(\mathbf{x}_i) \equiv \{\mathbf{x}_i' \in X_i \; / \; \mathbf{x}_i \succ_i \mathbf{x}_i'\}$$

are open in X_i.

$\mathcal{B}_i(\mathbf{x}_i)$ is the set of consumption plans that are *better than* $\mathbf{x}_i$, whereas $\mathcal{W}_i(\mathbf{x}_i)$ is the set of options that are *worse than* $\mathbf{x}_i$. The continuity axiom says that these sets are open. The intuition is clear: Let $\mathbf{x}_i$, $\mathbf{x}_i'$ be points in X_i such that $\mathbf{x}_i' \succ_i \mathbf{x}_i$; points that are "close enough" to $\mathbf{x}_i'$ will also be preferred to $\mathbf{x}_i$. More formally, $\succsim_i$ is continuous if for any $\mathbf{x}_i, \mathbf{x}_i' \in X_i$ with $\mathbf{x}_i' \succ_i \mathbf{x}_i$ there are neighbourhoods $\varepsilon(\mathbf{x}_i')$ and $\delta(\mathbf{x}_i)$ such that, for each $\mathbf{z} \in \varepsilon(\mathbf{x}_i')$ we have $\mathbf{z} \succ_i \mathbf{x}_i$, and for each $\mathbf{z} \in \delta(\mathbf{x}_i)$, $\mathbf{x}_i' \succ_i \mathbf{z}$.

Consider now the following sets:

$$\mathcal{BE}_i(\mathbf{x}_i) \equiv \{\mathbf{x}_i' \in X_i / \mathbf{x}_i' \succsim_i \mathbf{x}_i\}$$

$$\mathcal{WE}_i(\mathbf{x}_i) \equiv \{\mathbf{x}_i' \in X_i / \mathbf{x}_i \succsim_i \mathbf{x}_i'\}$$

These are the *better or equal than* and the *worse or equal than* sets. By complementarity, the continuity of $\succsim_i$ can equally be defined by requiring these sets to be closed in X_i. Observe that this implies that *indifference classes are closed*, as $\mathcal{I}_i(\mathbf{x}_i) \equiv \mathcal{BE}_i(\mathbf{x}_i) \bigcap \mathcal{WE}_i(\mathbf{x}_i)$. Furthermore, it is clear by completeness that $\mathcal{BE}_i(\mathbf{x}_i) \bigcup \mathcal{WE}_i(\mathbf{x}_i) = X_i$, for all $\mathbf{x}_i \in X_i$.

It is interesting to note that the order axioms are not independent from the continuity axiom. In particular, Schmeidler (1971) proves the following result:

Proposition 2.1 *Let $\succsim_i$ be a preference relation defined over a connected subset X_i of a topological space. Suppose that $\succsim_i$ is transitive and continuous in X_i, and that there are elements $\mathbf{x}_i$, $\mathbf{x}_i'$ in X_i such that $\mathbf{x}_i \succ_i \mathbf{x}_i'$. Then, $\succsim_i$ is also complete.*

Proof. (We drop subscripts to make notation simpler)
Let us show first that for all $\mathbf{x}, \mathbf{x}' \in X$ such that $\mathbf{x} \succ \mathbf{x}'$ one has

$$T = \left\{ \{\mathbf{z} \; / \; \mathbf{z} \succ \mathbf{x}'\} \; \bigcup \; \{\mathbf{z} \; / \; \mathbf{x} \succ \mathbf{z}\} \right\} = X \qquad [1]$$

By definition, $T \subset T' = \{\{\mathbf{z} \; / \; \mathbf{z} \succsim \mathbf{x}'\} \; \bigcup \; \{\mathbf{z} \; / \; \mathbf{x} \succsim \mathbf{z}\}\}$. To see that the converse inclusion also holds, let $\mathbf{r} \in \{\mathbf{z} \; / \; \mathbf{z} \succsim \mathbf{x}'\}$, and suppose that $\mathbf{r}$ does not belong to $\{\mathbf{z} \; / \; \mathbf{z} \succ \mathbf{x}'\}$. Hence, $\mathbf{x}' \succsim \mathbf{r}$. Since $\mathbf{x} \succ \mathbf{x}'$, it follows from transitivity that $\mathbf{x} \succ \mathbf{r}$, so that $\mathbf{r} \in \{\mathbf{z} \; / \; \mathbf{x} \succ \mathbf{z}\}$. The same reasoning applies for the case $\mathbf{x} \succsim \mathbf{r}$.

Therefore, $T = T' \neq \emptyset$ (since $\mathbf{x} \succ \mathbf{x}'$ by assumption). But X being a connected set, T open and T' closed (by continuity), it follows that $T = T' = X$, which proves the equality postulated in [1].[3]

Let us suppose now that preferences are not complete. Let then $\mathbf{v}, \mathbf{w} \in X$ non-comparable. According to [1], if $\mathbf{x} \succ \mathbf{x}'$,

$$\{\mathbf{z} / \mathbf{z} \succ \mathbf{x}'\} \bigcup \{\mathbf{z} / \mathbf{x} \succ \mathbf{z}\} = X$$

so that, either $\mathbf{v} \succ \mathbf{x}'$, or $\mathbf{x} \succ \mathbf{v}$. Without loss of generality, let $\mathbf{v} \succ \mathbf{x}'$. We would then have:

$$\{\mathbf{z} / \mathbf{z} \succ \mathbf{x}'\} \bigcup \{\mathbf{z} / \mathbf{v} \succ \mathbf{z}\} = X$$

Hence, $\mathbf{w} \succ \mathbf{x}'$ or $\mathbf{v} \succ \mathbf{w}$. $\mathbf{w}, \mathbf{v}$ being non-comparable, it follows that

$$\mathbf{w} \succ \mathbf{x}' \;\&\; \mathbf{v} \succ \mathbf{x}'$$

Thus, the open sets $\{\mathbf{z} / \mathbf{v} \succ \mathbf{z}\}$, $\{\mathbf{z} / \mathbf{w} \succ \mathbf{z}\}$ have a non-empty and open intersection. Furthermore, $\{\mathbf{z} / \mathbf{v} \succ \mathbf{z}\} \bigcap \{\mathbf{z} / \mathbf{w} \succ \mathbf{z}\}$ is not X (by construction). We can now show the following equality:

$$\{\mathbf{z} / \mathbf{v} \succ \mathbf{z}\} \bigcap \{\mathbf{z} / \mathbf{w} \succ \mathbf{z}\} = \{\mathbf{z} / \mathbf{v} \succsim \mathbf{z}\} \bigcap \{\mathbf{z} / \mathbf{w} \succsim \mathbf{z}\}$$

Let $\mathbf{v} \succsim \mathbf{z}, \mathbf{w} \succsim \mathbf{z}$. The fact that $\mathbf{z} \succsim \mathbf{v}$ together with the transitivity of the preference relation implies that $\mathbf{w} \succsim \mathbf{v}$, which goes against the assumption. On the other hand, $\mathbf{z} \succsim \mathbf{w}$ and transitivity would imply $\mathbf{v} \succsim \mathbf{w}$. Thus, the only possibility would be $\mathbf{v} \succ \mathbf{z}$ and $\mathbf{w} \succ \mathbf{z}$, so that the previous inequality holds. But then we have a non-empty and open set on the left-hand side, which is equal to a non-empty and closed one in the right-hand side. This can only be so if both are equal to X, which they are not by hypothesis. Then the relation $\succsim$ must be complete. $\boxed{\textbf{Q.e.d.}}$

The case of a preference relation that satisfies completeness and transitivity but it is not continuous is the **lexicographic ordering**. For $X_i = \mathbb{R}_+^2$ this ordering can be defined as follows: given $\mathbf{x} = (x_1, x_2), \mathbf{z} = (z_1, z_2) \in X_i$,

$$\mathbf{z} \succ \mathbf{x} \text{ if } \begin{cases} \text{(i) } z_1 > x_1, \text{ or} \\ \text{(ii) if } z_1 = x_1, \; y \; z_2 > x_2 \end{cases}$$

The next figure shows clearly that the set $\mathcal{B}_i(\mathbf{x})$ is neither open nor closed.

---

[3]Let us recall here that a nonempty subset T of a connected topological space X can only be open and closed in X if it is precisely X.

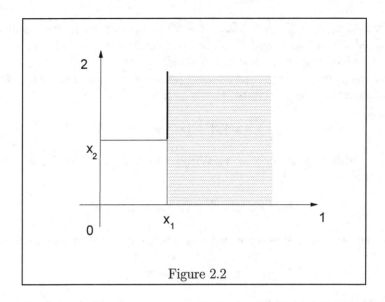

Figure 2.2

We consider next a series of alternative axioms on the *convexity of preferences*. They are presented in decreasing order of generality. Convexity is a postulate on the *liking of variety*: intermediate combinations of consumption bundles tend to be more appreciated. The particularities of the different axioms will be clear along the discussion.

Definition 2.3 (Weak convexity) *Let X_i be convex. The ith consumer's preferences are weakly convex if, for all $\mathbf{x}_i, \mathbf{x}'_i \in X_i$, every scalar $\lambda \in [0, 1]$,*

$$\mathbf{x}_i \succsim_i \mathbf{x}'_i \Longrightarrow [\lambda \mathbf{x}_i + (1 - \lambda)\mathbf{x}'_i] \succsim_i \mathbf{x}'_i$$

In words: a preference relation is weakly convex if any convex combination of two consumption plans is at least as good as the less preferred one. Thus, the convexity of preferences pictures a consumer who likes variety: a combination of any two consumption bundles, equally appreciated, never makes the consumer worse off. When preferences are complete, transitive, continuous and weakly convex, the "better than" sets $\mathcal{B}_i(\mathbf{x}_i)$ are open convex sets (and the "better or equal than" sets are closed convex sets). These axioms are compatible with the presence of *thick* indifference curves (that is, curves with non-empty interior).

A slightly more demanding notion is the following:

Definition 2.4 (Convexity) *Let X_i be convex. The ith consumer's preferences are convex if, for all $\mathbf{x}_i, \mathbf{x}'_i \in X_i$, every scalar $\lambda \in (0,1)$,*

$$\mathbf{x}_i \succ_i \mathbf{x}'_i \Longrightarrow [\lambda \mathbf{x}_i + (1-\lambda)\mathbf{x}'_i] \succ_i \mathbf{x}'_i$$

It can be shown that, under completeness, transitivity and continuity, convexity implies weak convexity (see below). Moreover, it follows from convexity that if $\mathbf{x}'_i$ is not a *bliss point* (a maximum of $\succsim_i$ over X_i), then the set $\mathcal{I}_i(\mathbf{x}'_i)$ has an empty interior.

The next figure shows the class of indifference curves that are compatible with the axioms established so far, in the simplified world of two goods (labour and corn).

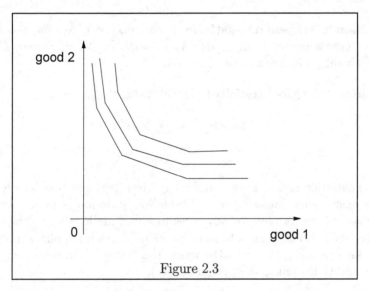

Figure 2.3

This figure illustrates that the convexity of preferences is still a relatively mild assumption, which permits the presence of *segments* in the indifference curves. A stricter assumption which eliminates this possibility is the following:

Definition 2.5 (Strict convexity) *Let X_i be convex. The ith consumer's preferences are strictly convex if, for all $\mathbf{x}_i, \mathbf{x}'_i \in X_i$, any $\lambda \in (0,1)$,*

$$\mathbf{x}_i \succsim_i \mathbf{x}'_i \Longrightarrow [\lambda \mathbf{x}_i + (1-\lambda)\mathbf{x}'_i] \succ_i \mathbf{x}'_i$$

This property says that if $\mathbf{x}_i$ is at least as good as $\mathbf{x}'_i$, then every intermediate bundle will be preferred to $\mathbf{x}'_i$. This obviously excludes the possibility of indifference curves with segments.

2.3.3 Properties of non-satiation

These properties introduce the idea that, in any relevant economic problem, the available commodities are always *scarce*, relative to the needs and desires of consumers. Some would postulate that this is the essence of economic problems. The following definitions, presented in a decreasing level of generality, provide alternative formalizations of this general idea:

Definition 2.6 (Non-satiation) *For every* $\mathbf{x}_i \in X_i$ *there exists* $\mathbf{x}'_i \in X_i$ *such that* $\mathbf{x}'_i \succ_i \mathbf{x}_i$.

Definition 2.7 (Local non-satiation) *For every* $\mathbf{x}_i \in X_i$, *and every scalar* $\alpha > 0$, *there exists* $\mathbf{x}'_i \in B(\mathbf{x}_i, \alpha) \bigcap X_i$ *such that* $\mathbf{x}'_i \succ_i \mathbf{x}_i$ *(where* $B(\mathbf{x}_i, \alpha)$ *denotes a ball of centre* $\mathbf{x}_i$ *and radius* α*).*

Definition 2.8 (Monotonicity) *For all* $\mathbf{x}_i, \mathbf{x}'_i \in X_i$,

$$\mathbf{x}_i >> \mathbf{x}'_i \Longrightarrow \mathbf{x}_i \succ_i \mathbf{x}'_i$$

Non-satiation simply says that for any given consumption bundle, there always exists some preferred one. Local Non-Satiation is more precise: it says that *arbitrarily close* to any consumption bundle, there always exists a better one. Finally, monotonicity provides a much simpler specification of the idea of non-satiation: "the more, the better" (the consumer always prefers additional amounts of commodities).[4]

The following claims summarize some immediate interconnections between these concepts:

Claim 2.1 *When* X_i *is not bounded above, monotonicity implies local non-satiation which in turn implies non-satiation. Note that non-satiation and local non-satiation are incompatible with compact consumption sets, whereas monotonicity is not.*

---

[4]There is a weaker version, known as **weak monotonicity**, which says that $\mathbf{x}_i \geq \mathbf{x}'_i$ implies $\mathbf{x}_i \succsim_i \mathbf{x}'_i$. And there is also a stronger version, called **strong monotonicity**, which says that $\mathbf{x}_i > \mathbf{x}'_i$ implies $\mathbf{x}_i \succ_i \mathbf{x}'_i$.

Claim 2.2 *None of these properties prevents the possibility that the ith consumer gets satiated with respect to some good; what certainly precludes is the possibility of satiation with respect to all commodities simultaneously. Moreover, monotonicity implies that commodities cannot be "bads".*

Claim 2.3 *Local non-satiation directly implies that indifference curves have an empty interior, and that the maximal elements cannot be interior points of the feasible set. It can be easily seen that these properties also derive from the combination of convexity and non-satiation.*

Claim 2.4 *When preferences are continuous, convex and non-satiable, indifference curves are closed with empty interior and consist precisely of the boundary of the convex better than sets.*

The following result is also of interest:

Proposition 2.2 *Let $\succsim_i$ be a transitive, complete and continuous preference relation, defined on a closed convex set $X_i \subset \mathbb{R}^\ell$. Then, $\succsim_i$ is convex and non-satiable if and only if it is weakly convex and locally non-satiable.*

Proof. ($\Longrightarrow$) Let us first show that convexity implies weak convexity. To prove this property amounts to showing that given any two points $\mathbf{x}_i$, $\mathbf{x}'_i \in X_i$, with $\mathbf{x}_i \succsim_i \mathbf{x}'_i$, the set Z of points in the segment $[\mathbf{x}_i, \mathbf{x}'_i]$ that are worse than $\mathbf{x}'_i$ is empty. For suppose not; the set Z cannot consist of a single point, because its complement in $[\mathbf{x}_i, \mathbf{x}'_i]$ must be closed (by continuity). Then, let $\mathbf{z}, \mathbf{z}'$ be two points in $[\mathbf{x}_i, \mathbf{x}'_i]$ that are worse than $\mathbf{x}'_i$. Without loss of generality, suppose that $\mathbf{z}$ is between $\mathbf{x}_i$ and $\mathbf{z}'$. As $\mathbf{x}_i \succ_i \mathbf{z}'$, convexity implies that $\mathbf{z} = \lambda \mathbf{x}_i + (1-\lambda)\mathbf{z}' \succ_i \mathbf{z}'$, for $\lambda \in (0,1)$. Moreover, $\mathbf{x}'_i \succ_i \mathbf{z}$ implies (we use convexity again) $\mathbf{z}' = \alpha \mathbf{x}'_i + (1-\alpha)\mathbf{z} \succ_i \mathbf{z}$. But this contradicts the previous conclusion, and the result follows.

Now take an arbitrary point $\mathbf{x}_i \in X_i$. By non-satiation, there exists $\mathbf{x}'_i \in X_i$ such that $\mathbf{x}'_i \succ_i \mathbf{x}_i$, and by convexity, $\lambda \mathbf{x}'_i + (1-\lambda)\mathbf{x}_i \succ_i \mathbf{x}_i$, for all $\lambda \in (0,1)$. Therefore, for all $\varepsilon > 0$, there exist points in $B(\mathbf{x}_i, \varepsilon)$ that are preferred to $\mathbf{x}_i$ (those in the interior of $[\mathbf{x}'_i, \mathbf{x}_i] \bigcap B(\mathbf{x}_i, \varepsilon)$), and local non-satiation is satisfied..

($\Longleftarrow$) Local non-satiation trivially implies non-satiation. Let us show now that local non-satiation and weak convexity imply convexity.

Let $\mathbf{x}_i, \mathbf{x}'_i \in X_i$ be such that $\mathbf{x}_i \succ_i \mathbf{x}'_i$. We have to show that $\lambda \mathbf{x}_i + (1-\lambda)\mathbf{x}'_i$ is better than $\mathbf{x}'_i$, for all $\lambda \in (0,1)$. By assumption, $\mathbf{x}_i \in int\mathcal{B}_i(\mathbf{x}'_i) = \mathcal{B}_i(\mathbf{x}'_i)$, that is a convex open set (by weak convexity and continuity). Moreover,

$\mathbf{x}'_i$ is a point in the closure of $\mathcal{B}_i(\mathbf{x}'_i)$ (we apply here continuity and local non-satiation). Therefore,[5]

$$\lambda \mathbf{x}_i + (1 - \lambda)\mathbf{x}'_i \in int\mathcal{B}_i(\mathbf{x}'_i) = \mathcal{B}_i(\mathbf{x}'_i)$$

This completes the proof. $\boxed{\textbf{Q.e.d.}}$

Remark 2.1 *We shall generally assume in the sequel that preferences are complete, transitive, continuous, convex and non-satiable.*

2.4 The utility function

2.4.1 Generalities

We have seen that when $\succsim_i$ is complete and transitive, it generates a partition over the consumption set via the indifference relation. The following question arises naturally in this context: Can we associate a real number to each indifference class, so that the order induced by the relation $\succsim_i$ translates into an order over real numbers? Or, more formally: is there any real-valued function which permits a numerical representation of the preference relation? If such a mapping exists, the ith consumer's choice problem can be formulated as the maximization of a real-valued function (rather than as the search for maximal elements of a binary relation). This formulation is usually easier to handle, as one can apply a number of well-established mathematical results, when such a function is continuous.

Definition 2.9 *A real-valued function* $u_i : X_i \to \mathbb{R}$ ***represents*** *a preference relation* $\succsim_i$ *over* X_i *if, for all* $\mathbf{x}_i, \mathbf{x}'_i \in X_i$,

$$u_i(\mathbf{x}_i) \geq u_i(\mathbf{x}'_i) \iff \mathbf{x}_i \succsim_i \mathbf{x}'_i$$

Function u_i *is called a **utility function**.*

Three remarks are in order:
(i) By definition, for any increasing function $f : \mathbb{R} \to \mathbb{R}$, we have:

$$f[u_i(\mathbf{x}_i)] \geq f[u_i(\mathbf{x}'_i)] \iff u_i(\mathbf{x}_i) \geq u_i(\mathbf{x}'_i) \iff \mathbf{x}_i \succsim_i \mathbf{x}'_i$$

so that u_i simply *represents* $\succsim_i$, and its actual values are not relevant magnitudes.

---

[5]We apply here a standard property of convex sets, known as the *Accessibility Lemma*, that says the following: "Let K be a convex non-empty subset of $\mathbb{R}^n$, $\mathbf{x} \in intK$, $\mathbf{x}' \in clK$. Then, $\lambda \mathbf{x} + (1 - \lambda)\mathbf{x}' \in intK$, for all $\lambda \in (0,1)$."

(ii) Note also, that for such a representation to be a useful tool (in the sense of allowing for the formulation of the consumer's choice problem as a maximization problem), the utility function should be continuous.

(iii) The existence of such a function is far from trivial when X_i is not countable and not all the elements in X_i are indifferent.

It turns out that the continuity of the preference relation is the key assumption for the existence of a continuous utility function, when X_i is taken to be a connected subset of $\mathbb{R}^\ell$. The next result is a powerful tool in the analysis of consumer choices, and will be presented without proof [see Debreu (1959, 4.6)]. A detailed proof of a slightly less general result, which is nevertheless adequate for our purposes, is presented later in this chapter.

Proposition 2.3 *Let X_i be a connected subset of $\mathbb{R}^\ell$, and $\succsim_i$ a preference relation satisfying completeness, transitivity and continuity. Then, there exists a continuous function $u_i : X \to \mathbb{R}$ which represents this preference relation.*

The following result is obtained:

Theorem 2.1 *Let $\succsim_i$ be a preference relation defined over a connected subset X_i of $\mathbb{R}^\ell$. Suppose furthermore that there are at least two elements $\mathbf{x}_i, \mathbf{x}'_i \in X_i$ such that $\mathbf{x}_i \succ_i \mathbf{x}'_i$. Then, $\succsim_i$ can be represented by a continuous utility function if and only if it is transitive and continuous.*

Proof. ($\Longrightarrow$) Follows directly from Propositions 2.1 and 2.3.

($\Longleftarrow$) If $u_i : X_i \to \mathbb{R}$ is continuous over X_i, then it is a single-valued mapping defined for all $\mathbf{x}_i$ (hence $\succsim_i$ is complete); furthermore, since it applies over $\mathbb{R}$, it preserves the natural order of the real numbers (so that $\succsim_i$ is transitive). Finally, continuity implies that the inverse image of open sets are open; in particular, the sets of points $\mathbf{x}_i \in X_i$ such that $u_i(\mathbf{x}_i) > u_i(\mathbf{x}'_i)$ [resp. $u_i(\mathbf{x}_i) < u_i(\mathbf{x}'_i)$], are open (and hence the "better than" and "worse than" sets are open, so that $\succsim_i$ is continuous). $\boxed{\text{Q.e.d.}}$

Therefore, every non-trivial preference relation defined over a connected subset of $\mathbb{R}^\ell$ that satisfies transitivity and continuity, can *equivalently* be described by a real-valued function. We shall use the utility representation in the sequel, as it makes the presentation easier. The search for maximal elements will then be formulated as the maximization of a continuous real valued function (let us recall here, that Weierstrass' theorem ensures that such a maximum will exist over any compact non-empty subset of X_i).

Let us now consider the following definitions:

Definition 2.10 *A function* $F : \mathbb{R}^n \to \mathbb{R}$ *is* **quasi-concave** *if, for all* $\mathbf{x}, \mathbf{y} \in \mathbb{R}^n$, *all* $\lambda \in [0, 1]$, $F[\lambda \mathbf{x} + (1 - \lambda)\mathbf{y}] \geq \min\{F(\mathbf{x}), F(\mathbf{y})\}$.

Definition 2.11 *A function* $F : \mathbb{R}^n \to \mathbb{R}$ *is* **quasi-concave$^+$** *if, for all* $\mathbf{x}, \mathbf{y} \in \mathbb{R}^n$, *all* $\lambda \in [0, 1]$, $F(\mathbf{x}) \neq F(\mathbf{y})$ *implies* $F[\lambda \mathbf{x} + (1 - \lambda)\mathbf{y}] > \min\{F(\mathbf{x}), F(\mathbf{y})\}$.

Definition 2.12 *A function* $F : \mathbb{R}^n \to \mathbb{R}$ *is* **strictly quasi-concave** *if, for all* $\mathbf{x}, \mathbf{y} \in \mathbb{R}^n$, *all* $\lambda \in [0, 1]$, $F[\lambda \mathbf{x} + (1 - \lambda)\mathbf{y}] > \min\{F(\mathbf{x}), F(\mathbf{y})\}$.

These definitions are obviously linked to the alternative notions of convex preferences presented above. In particular, the weak convexity of $\succsim_i$ is equivalent to the quasi-concavity of u_i, the convexity is equivalent to the quasi-concavity$^+$ of u_i, and the strong convexity is equivalent to the strict quasi-concavity of u_i. Observe that when we maximize a quasi-concave$^+$ function over a convex set, any maximum turns out to be a *global maximum* (by the Local-Global theorem).[6] This is important because usual methods that enable us to find extremal points only allow us to identify local extrema. It follows from Proposition 2.2, that if F is continuous and quasi-concave$^+$, then it is also quasi-concave. It is easy to see that if one maximizes a strictly quasi-concave function over a convex set and a solution exists, it will be unique.

Similarly, we say that F is **monotone** if $\mathbf{x} >> \mathbf{x}'$ implies $F(\mathbf{x}) > F(\mathbf{x}')$. F satisfies **local non-satiation** if, for all $\mathbf{x}$ in the domain of F all $\varepsilon > 0$, $\mathbf{x}'$ exists in the intersection of $B(\mathbf{x}, \varepsilon)$ with the domain of F, such that $F(\mathbf{x}') > F(\mathbf{x})$. And F is **non-satiable** if for all $\mathbf{x}$ in the domain of F there exists $\mathbf{x}'$ in such domain, such that $F(\mathbf{x}') > F(\mathbf{x})$.

The following result gives us the additional properties derived from the convexity assumption:

Corollary 2.1 *Let* $\succsim_i$ *be a nontrivial preference relation, defined on a convex subset* $X_i \subset \mathbb{R}^\ell$ *that satisfies transitivity, continuity, convexity and non-satiation. Then, there is a continuous, quasi-concave$^+$ and non-satiable utility function* $u_i : X_i \to \mathbb{R}$ *that represents* $\succsim_i$.

---

[6]The Local-Global theorem can be stated as follows: Let $U : D \to \mathbb{R}$ be a continuous and quasi-concave$^+$ function, where D is a convex subset of $\mathbb{R}^n$. Then, any maximum of U over D is a global maximum.

2.4.2 The existence of a continuous utility function

The next result is a particular case of Proposition 2.3. Yet, it is general enough for our purposes, and has a rather intuitive proof (that will be developed in detail).

Proposition 2.4 *Let $X_i \subset \mathbb{R}^\ell$ be a convex set, and let $\succsim_i$ be a binary relation on X_i that satisfies completeness, transitivity, continuity and local non-satiation. Then, $\succsim_i$ can be represented by a continuous utility function, $u : X_i \to \mathbb{R}$.*

    Proof. The proof will be divided into three parts, to make things easier. First an explicit utility function will be proposed. We shall see then that this function actually represents the preference relation. Finally, we shall show that this is a continuous function. Subscripts will be omitted in order to simplify notation.

    (i) Let $\mathbf{x}^0$ be an arbitrary point in X (which will be taken as a reference point), and let $d : X \to \mathbb{R}$ be a function given by $d(\mathbf{x}) = \|\mathbf{x} - \mathbf{x}^0\|$ (that is, for each $\mathbf{x} \in X$ it gives us the euclidean distance between $\mathbf{x}$ and $\mathbf{x}^0$). For any subset $T \subset X$, the expression $d(T)$ denotes the distance between $\mathbf{x}^0$ and T (that is, $d(T) = \min d(\mathbf{x})$ with $\mathbf{x} \in T$). Define now $u : X \to \mathbb{R}$ as follows:

    (a) $u(\mathbf{x}^0) = 0$.
    (b) For $\mathbf{x} \in X$ such that $\mathbf{x} \succsim \mathbf{x}^0$, $u(\mathbf{x}) = d[\mathcal{BE}(\mathbf{x})]$.
    (c) For $\mathbf{x} \in X$ such that $\mathbf{x}^0 \succsim \mathbf{x}$, $u(\mathbf{x}) = -d[\mathcal{WE}(\mathbf{x})]$.

    The utility of a consumption bundle $\mathbf{x} \in X$ is thus defined as the distance between the reference point $\mathbf{x}^0$ and the set of alternatives which are better than or equal to $\mathbf{x}$ (resp. worse than or equal to $\mathbf{x}$, depending on the ranking of $\mathbf{x}$ versus $\mathbf{x}^0$). The continuity of the preference relation and the distance function ensure that u is well defined for all $\mathbf{x} \in X$.

    (ii) To show that this function u actually *represents* the preference relation $\succsim$, it suffices to show that the following relations hold:

$$\mathbf{x} \sim \mathbf{x}' \Longrightarrow u(\mathbf{x}) = u(\mathbf{x}') \qquad [1]$$
$$\mathbf{x} \succ \mathbf{x}' \Longrightarrow u(\mathbf{x}) > u(\mathbf{x}') \qquad [2]$$

This is so because $[u(\mathbf{x}) > u(\mathbf{x}')\ \&\ \mathbf{x} \sim \mathbf{x}']$ is not compatible with [1], whereas $[u(\mathbf{x}) = u(\mathbf{x}')\ \&\ \mathbf{x} \succ \mathbf{x}']$ is not compatible with [2].

    Implication [1] follows trivially from the definition of u, because completeness and transitivity imply that $\mathcal{BE}(\mathbf{x}) = \mathcal{BE}(\mathbf{x}')$, whenever $\mathbf{x} \sim \mathbf{x}'$.

    Let us check whether [2] also holds. To see this let us assume that $\mathbf{x} \succ \mathbf{x}'$, and consider the following cases:

    a) $\mathbf{x} \succ \mathbf{x}' \succsim \mathbf{x}^o$. Transitivity implies that $\mathcal{BE}(\mathbf{x}) \subset \mathcal{BE}(\mathbf{x}')$, so that $u(\mathbf{x}) \geq u(\mathbf{x}')$.

b) $\mathbf{x}^o \succsim \mathbf{x} \succ \mathbf{x}'$. By transitivity $\mathcal{WE}(\mathbf{x}') \subset \mathcal{WE}(\mathbf{x})$, hence $d[\mathcal{WE}(\mathbf{x})] \le d[\mathcal{WE}(\mathbf{x}')]$, that is, $u(\mathbf{x}) \ge u(\mathbf{x}')$.

c) $\mathbf{x} \succ \mathbf{x}^o \succsim \mathbf{x}'$ (or $\mathbf{x} \succsim \mathbf{x}^o \succ \mathbf{x}'$). In this case, we have: $u(\mathbf{x}) \ge 0$ and $u(\mathbf{x}') \le 0$.

Therefore, $\mathbf{x} \succ \mathbf{x}'$ implies $u(\mathbf{x}) \ge u(\mathbf{x}')$. It remains to be shown that these numbers are different. Looking for a contradiction, let us suppose that $u(\mathbf{x}) = u(\mathbf{x}')$ with $\mathbf{x} \succ \mathbf{x}'$. Observe first that $u(\mathbf{x}) = 0$ implies $\mathbf{x} \sim \mathbf{x}^o$. To see this, notice that completeness ensures that $\mathbf{x} \succsim \mathbf{x}^o$ or $\mathbf{x}^o \succsim \mathbf{x}$. Suppose that $\mathbf{x} \succsim \mathbf{x}^o$ and $u(\mathbf{x}) = 0$. It follows that $d[\mathcal{BE}(\mathbf{x})] = 0$, so $\mathbf{x}'' \in \mathcal{BE}(\mathbf{x})$ exists such that $d(\mathbf{x}'') = 0$. But this is possible only if $\mathbf{x}^o \in \mathcal{BE}(\mathbf{x})$, and we would have $\mathbf{x}^o \succsim \mathbf{x}$ (hence: $\mathbf{x} \sim \mathbf{x}^o$). The same reasoning applies in the case of $\mathbf{x}^o \succsim \mathbf{x}$. This proves that $\mathbf{x} \succ \mathbf{x}'$ implies $u(\mathbf{x}) \ne 0$ (otherwise the transitivity of the indifference relation would imply $\mathbf{x} \sim \mathbf{x}'$). Therefore, $\mathbf{x} \succ \mathbf{x}'$ and $u(\mathbf{x}) = u(\mathbf{x}') = 0$ cannot hold simultaneously.

Consider now the case $u(\mathbf{x}) = u(\mathbf{x}') > 0$, and let $\widetilde{\mathbf{x}} \in X$ be a point such that $d(\widetilde{\mathbf{x}}) = u(\mathbf{x})$. As $\widetilde{\mathbf{x}} \in \mathcal{BE}(\mathbf{x})$, we know that $\widetilde{\mathbf{x}} \succsim \mathbf{x} \succ \mathbf{x}'$. The continuity of preferences ensures that we can find a scalar $\alpha \in (0,1)$ small enough so that $[(1-\alpha)\widetilde{\mathbf{x}} + \alpha\mathbf{x}^o] \succsim \mathbf{x}'$, that is $[(1-\alpha)\widetilde{\mathbf{x}} + \alpha\mathbf{x}^o] \in \mathcal{BE}(\mathbf{x}')$. We can then write:

$$u(\mathbf{x}') \le d[(1-\alpha)\widetilde{\mathbf{x}} + \alpha\mathbf{x}^o] = \|(1-\alpha)\widetilde{\mathbf{x}} + \alpha\mathbf{x}^o - \mathbf{x}^o\|$$

$$= (1-\alpha)\|\widetilde{\mathbf{x}} - \mathbf{x}^o\| = (1-\alpha)d(\widetilde{\mathbf{x}}) = (1-\alpha)u(\mathbf{x})$$

That is, $u(\mathbf{x}') = u(\mathbf{x}) \le (1-\alpha)u(\mathbf{x})$, which can only occur if $u(\mathbf{x}) = 0$. But we had already discarded this possibility, hence $\mathbf{x} \succ \mathbf{x}'$ implies $u(\mathbf{x}) > u(\mathbf{x}')$.

The case of $u(\mathbf{x}) = u(\mathbf{x}') < 0$ can be analyzed along the same lines, by taking $\widetilde{\mathbf{x}} \in \mathcal{WE}(\mathbf{x}')$ such that $-d(\mathbf{x}') = u(\mathbf{x}')$.

Therefore, function u represents $\succsim$.

(iii) To prove that u is a continuous function we have to show that, for any scalar $a \in \mathbb{R}$, the sets $U(a^+) = \{\mathbf{x} \in \mathbf{X} \, / \, u(\mathbf{x}) \ge a\}$, $U(a^-) = \{\mathbf{x} \in \mathbf{X} \, / \, u(\mathbf{x}) \le a\}$ are closed.

Let us show firs that $U(a^+)$ is a closed set. Let $\{\mathbf{x}^n\} \to \mathbf{x}$ be a sequence in X such that $u(\mathbf{x}^n) \ge a$ for all n, and let $\mathbf{x}'$ be such that $d(\mathbf{x}') = u(\mathbf{x}) > 0$ (that is, we assume $\mathbf{x} \succ \mathbf{x}^o$). By local non-satiation there exists $\mathbf{z} \in X$, arbitrarily close to $\mathbf{x}'$ such that $\mathbf{z} \succ \mathbf{x}'$. By transitivity $\mathbf{z} \succ \mathbf{x}$. Now continuity implies that from a large enough n onwards, $\mathbf{z} \succsim \mathbf{x}^n$. Hence, $u(\mathbf{z}) \ge u(\mathbf{x}^n) \ge a$. But $\mathbf{z}$ can be chosen as close to $\mathbf{x}'$ as we wish. As $\mathbf{z} \succ \mathbf{x}^o$, $d(\mathbf{z}) \ge u(\mathbf{z}) \ge a$, and $d(.)$ is continuous, it follows that $d(\mathbf{x}') \ge a$. Thus, $u(\mathbf{x}) = u(\mathbf{x}') = d(\mathbf{x}') \ge a$, because $\mathbf{x}' \sim \mathbf{x} \succ \mathbf{x}^o$.

Now let $\{\mathbf{x}^n\} \to \mathbf{x}$ be a sequence in X such that $u(\mathbf{x}^n) \ge a$ for all n, with $\mathbf{x}^o \succsim \mathbf{x}$. By transitivity $\mathbf{x}^o \succsim \mathbf{x}^n$, for all n. By definition, $u(\mathbf{x}^n) =$

$-\min\{d(\mathbf{z}) \ / \ \mathbf{z} \in \mathcal{WE}(\mathbf{x}^n)\} = -d(\widehat{\mathbf{x}}^n)$, with $\mathbf{x}^n \sim \widehat{\mathbf{x}}^n$ for all n. As $u(\mathbf{x}^n) = -d(\widehat{\mathbf{x}}^n) \geq a$, we can therefore write: $d(\widehat{\mathbf{x}}^n) \leq -a$ for all n, so that the sequence $\{\widehat{\mathbf{x}}^n\}$ is bounded from above. Let $\{\widehat{\mathbf{x}}^{n_k}\}_k$ be a subsequence converging to $\widehat{\mathbf{x}}$. The continuity of the distance function implies that $u(\widehat{\mathbf{x}}) = -\min\{d(\mathbf{z}) \ / \ \mathbf{z} \in \mathcal{WE}(\widehat{\mathbf{x}})\} \geq -d(\widehat{\mathbf{x}}) \geq a$. By continuity $\mathbf{x} \sim \widehat{\mathbf{x}}$ and hence $u(\mathbf{x}) = u(\widehat{\mathbf{x}}) \geq a$, according to part (ii) above.

This proves that $U(a^+)$ is a closed set.

Let us now show that the set $U(a^-)$ is also closed. Let $\{\mathbf{x}^n\} \to \mathbf{x}$ be a sequence such that $u(\mathbf{x}^n) \leq a$, and $\mathbf{x} \succsim \mathbf{x}^o$. Let $\mathbf{x}'^n$ be such that $d(\mathbf{x}'^n) = u(\mathbf{x}^n)$ for each n. By construction $u(\mathbf{x}'^n) \leq a$. The sequence $\{\mathbf{x}'^n\}$ is bounded so it converges to a point $\mathbf{x}'$ such that $u(\mathbf{x}') \leq a$. According to part (ii), $\mathbf{x}'^n$ is indifferent to $\mathbf{x}^n$ for all n, and $\mathbf{x}^n \to \mathbf{x}$. Consider now the sequence $\{\mathbf{x}'^n\} \to \mathbf{x}'$; by continuity we conclude that $\mathbf{x}'$ is indifferent to $\mathbf{x}$, so that $u(\mathbf{x}') = u(\mathbf{x}) \leq a$.

Take now $\{\mathbf{x}^n\} \to \mathbf{x}$, with $u(\mathbf{x}^n) \leq a$, and $\mathbf{x}^o \succ \mathbf{x}$. If $\mathbf{z} \succsim \mathbf{x}$ for all $\mathbf{z} \in X$, then we would have $\mathbf{x}^n \succsim \mathbf{x}$ and, by (ii), $a \geq u(\mathbf{x}^n) \geq u(\mathbf{x})$ (which proves the result). Suppose then that there is some $\mathbf{z}$ in X such that $\mathbf{x} \succ \mathbf{z}$. If there is some n for which $\mathbf{x}^n \succsim \mathbf{x}$ we would again have that $u(\mathbf{x}) \leq a$. Consider the last possible alternative: $\mathbf{x} \succ \mathbf{x}^n$ for all n. From some n onwards we shall have $\mathbf{x}^o \succ \mathbf{x} \succ \mathbf{x}^n \succ \mathbf{z}$, by continuity. Let $\{\widetilde{\mathbf{x}}^n\}$ be a sequence such that $\widetilde{\mathbf{x}}^n \sim \mathbf{x}^n$, with $u(\mathbf{x}^n) = -d(\widetilde{\mathbf{x}}^n)$. By (ii) we know that $u(\mathbf{z}) < u(\mathbf{x}^n) = -d(\widetilde{\mathbf{x}}^n)$, so that $d(\widetilde{\mathbf{x}}^n) < -u(\mathbf{z})$ for all n. Thus $\{\widetilde{\mathbf{x}}^n\}$ is bounded and we can find a subsequence $\{\widetilde{\mathbf{x}}^{n_k}\}_k$ converging to some $\widetilde{\mathbf{z}}$. By continuity $\widetilde{\mathbf{z}} \sim \mathbf{x}$, so: $u(\mathbf{x}) = u(\widetilde{\mathbf{z}}) = -d(\widetilde{\mathbf{z}}) \leq a$, because $d(.)$ is continuous, $\{\widetilde{\mathbf{x}}^{n_k}\}_k \to \widetilde{\mathbf{z}}$, and $-d(\widetilde{\mathbf{x}}^n) = u(\mathbf{x}^n) \leq a$ for all n. That is, $u(\mathbf{x}) \leq a$.

This proves that $U(a^-)$ is a closed set.

In this way the proof is complete. $\boxed{\textbf{Q.e.d.}}$

The next figure, where we take $X_i = \mathbb{R}^2_+$ and $\mathbf{x}^0_i = \mathbf{0}$ illustrates the construction of the utility function:

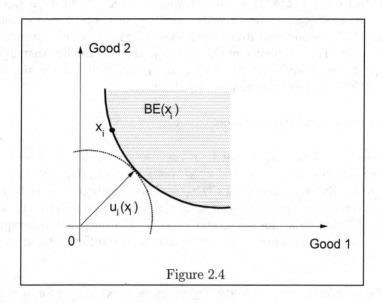

Figure 2.4

2.5   Wealth restrictions

In a market economy, the ith consumer's economic problem consists of choosing a best consumption plan among those that are *affordable* in X_i (note that this is something different from being physically realizable). We have already modelled the ith consumer's consumption set and preferences (i.e. her universe of alternatives and her way of ranking them). In order to analyze the ith consumer's behaviour we also have to model the restrictions that limit her choices within her consumption set (budget restrictions). The main result in this section refers to the properties of the budget correspondence when it is defined over a compact choice set. It will be seen later that this is not a relevant restriction.

Let $\mathbf{p} \in \mathbb{R}^\ell$, be a price vector, and $\mathbf{x}_i \in X_i$ a consumption plan. The ith consumer's expenditure is given by the scalar product

$$\mathbf{p}\mathbf{x}_i = \sum_{k=1}^{\ell} p_k x_{ik}$$

Note that, according to the sign convention introduced in section 2.2, $\mathbf{p}\mathbf{x}_i$ actually describes the difference between the cost of goods and services demanded (those commodities with positive entries), and the revenue obtained by selling factors (those commodities with negative ones).

A scalar $r_i \in \mathbb{R}$ will denote the ith consumer's wealth, to be understood as the net worth of the ith consumer's assets. For the time being r_i will be considered as a given magnitude, even though later on it will be treated as a function dependent on market prices. Note that r_i can be positive or negative, depending on the ith consumer's "financial position" (a negative r_i simply means that debts exceed the worth of the assets).

The ith consumer's wealth constraint, which determines what is affordable to her, can be expressed as the set of consumption plans $\mathbf{x}_i$ in X_i satisfying $\mathbf{p}\mathbf{x}_i \leq r_i$. More formally,

Definition 2.13 *The ith consumer's **budget correspondence** is a mapping* $\beta_i : \mathbb{R}^\ell \times \mathbb{R} \to X_i$ *given by:*

$$\beta_i(\mathbf{p}, r_i) = \{\mathbf{x}_i \in X_i \ / \ \mathbf{p}\mathbf{x}_i \leq r_i\}$$

Observe that:

(i) β_i is homogeneous of degree zero in $(\mathbf{p}, r_i)$, that is, for every $\lambda > 0$, $\beta_i(\lambda\mathbf{p}, \lambda r_i) = \beta_i(\mathbf{p}, r_i)$.

(ii) Under axiom 2.1, $\beta_i(\mathbf{p}, r_i)$ is a closed convex set, for all $(\mathbf{p}, r_i)$ in $\mathbb{R}^\ell \times \mathbb{R}$.

(iii) Nothing ensures that $\beta_i(\mathbf{p}, r_i)$ is non-empty.

For any given $\mathbf{p} \in \mathbb{R}^\ell$, let $\min \mathbf{p}X_i$ denote the minimum of the scalar product $\mathbf{p}\mathbf{x}_i$ over X_i. The number $\min \mathbf{p}X_i$ gives us the minimum worth at prices $\mathbf{p}$ of a feasible consumption bundle, for the ith consumer. Observe that this minimum exists whenever X_i is closed and bounded from below, as $\mathbf{p}\mathbf{x}_i$ is a continuous function.

Now let $D_i \subset \mathbb{R}^\ell \times \mathbb{R}$, describe the set of price-wealth pairs such that $r_i > \min \mathbf{p}X_i$. By definition, if $(\mathbf{p}, r_i) \in D_i$ then $\beta_i(\mathbf{p}, r_i) \neq \emptyset$; moreover, the ith consumer's wealth is above the cheapest consumption bundle at prices $\mathbf{p}$. The reader should understand clearly that such a set D_i can always be found (provided X_i is non-empty).

The main result on the budget correspondence is as follows:

Theorem 2.2 *Let $X_i \subset \mathbb{R}^\ell$ be compact and convex, and let $D_i \subset \mathbb{R}^\ell \times \mathbb{R}$ denote the set of points $(\mathbf{p}, r_i)$ such that $r_i > \min \mathbf{p}X_i$. Then, the budget correspondence β_i is continuous in D_i.*

Proof. Let $(\mathbf{p}^o, r_i^o)$ be an arbitrary point in D_i. In order to prove that β_i is continuous at $(\mathbf{p}^o, r_i^o)$ we have to show that it is both upper and lower hemicontinuous at this point.

(i) Let us first show that β_i is upper hemicontinuous at $(\mathbf{p}^o, r_i^o)$. Let $\{\mathbf{p}^q, r_i^q\}$ be a sequence in D_i converging to $(\mathbf{p}^o, r_i^o)$, and let $\{\mathbf{x}_i^q\}$ be a sequence in X_i converging to $\mathbf{x}_i^o$, such that $\mathbf{x}_i^q \in \beta_i(\mathbf{p}^q, r_i^q)$ for all q. One has to show that $\mathbf{x}_i^o \in \beta_i(\mathbf{p}^o, r_i^o)$ (because β_i is compact valued), that is, $\mathbf{p}^o\mathbf{x}_i^o \leq r_i^o$.

We know by assumption that $\mathbf{p}^q\mathbf{x}_i^q \leq r_i^q$ for all q. Taking limits as $q \to \infty$ (and bearing in mind that the continuity of the scalar product enables us to write the limit of the product as the product of the limits), one gets:

$$\lim_{q\to\infty} \mathbf{p}^q\mathbf{x}_i^q = \mathbf{p}^o\mathbf{x}_i^o \qquad\qquad \lim_{q\to\infty} r_i^q = r_i^o$$

Suppose, by way of contradiction, that $\mathbf{p}^o\mathbf{x}_i^o > r_i^o$. Then there will exist some q' such that, $\mathbf{p}^q\mathbf{x}_i^q > r_i^q$, for all $q > q'$. But this contradicts the hypothesis that $\mathbf{x}_i^q \in \beta_i(\mathbf{p}^q, r_i^q)$ for all q. Hence $\mathbf{x}_i^o \in \beta_i(\mathbf{p}^o, r_i^o)$, that is, β_i is upper hemicontinuous at this point.

(ii) We shall now show that β_i is lower hemicontinuous at $(\mathbf{p}^o, r_i^o)$.

Consider a sequence $\{\mathbf{p}^q, r_i^q\}$ in D_i converging to $(\mathbf{p}^o, r_i^o)$, and let $\mathbf{x}_i^o$ be a point in $\beta_i(\mathbf{p}^o, r_i^o)$ (that is, $\mathbf{x}_i^o \in X_i$ and $\mathbf{p}^o\mathbf{x}_i^o \leq r_i^o$). We have to show that there is a sequence $\{\mathbf{x}_i^q\}$ in X_i such that $\mathbf{x}_i^q \to \mathbf{x}_i^o$ and, for all q, $\mathbf{x}_i^q \in \beta_i(\mathbf{p}^q, r_i^q)$ (that is, $\mathbf{p}^q\mathbf{x}_i^q \leq r_i^q$).

There are two possible cases:

a) $\mathbf{p}^o\mathbf{x}_i^o < r_i^o$. Then, for all $q > q'$, for q' is large enough, $\mathbf{p}^q\mathbf{x}_i^o < r_i^q$. We can then define the following sequence: For $q \leq q'$, take $\mathbf{x}_i^q$ to be an arbitrary point in $\beta_i(\mathbf{p}^q, r_i^q)$; for $q > q'$, take the constant sequence $\mathbf{x}_i^q = \mathbf{x}_i^o$. It is immediate to check that this sequence satisfies the lower hemicontinuity conditions.

b) $\mathbf{p}^o\mathbf{x}_i^o = r_i^o$. Choose a point $\mathbf{x}_i' \in X_i$ such that $\mathbf{p}^o\mathbf{x}_i' < r_i^o$ (which exists by assumption). As $(\mathbf{p}^q, r_i^q) \to (\mathbf{p}^o, r_i^o)$, there exists a large enough q' so that, for all $q > q'$ one has: $\mathbf{p}^q(\mathbf{x}_i' - \mathbf{x}_i^o) < 0$. The straight line through $(\mathbf{x}_i', \mathbf{x}_i^o)$ has the following equation: $\mathbf{x}_i = \mathbf{x}_i^o + \lambda(\mathbf{x}_i' - \mathbf{x}_i^o)$, with $\lambda \in \mathbb{R}$. The hyperplane $H^q = \{\mathbf{z} \in \mathbb{R}^\ell \ / \ \mathbf{p}^q\mathbf{z} = r_i^q\}$ intersects this line at the point:

$$\mathbf{z}^q = \mathbf{x}_i^o + \frac{r_i^o - \mathbf{p}^q\mathbf{x}_i^o}{\mathbf{p}^q(\mathbf{x}_i' - \mathbf{x}_i^o)}(\mathbf{x}_i' - \mathbf{x}_i^o)$$

which is well defined for all $q > q'$, and satisfies $\mathbf{z}^q \to \mathbf{x}_i^o$ (see the figure below). Let us now define a sequence $\{\mathbf{x}_i^q\}$ as follows:

(1) For $q \leq q'$ take $\mathbf{x}_i^q$ as an arbitrary point in $\beta_i(\mathbf{p}^q, r_i^q)$.

(2) For $q > q'$:

(2.1) $\mathbf{x}_i^q = \mathbf{z}^q$, if $\mathbf{z}^q$ belongs to the segment $[\mathbf{x}_i^o, \mathbf{x}_i']$, which is contained in X_i, a convex set (that is, $\mathbf{x}_i^q = \mathbf{z}^q$ if and only if $0 \leq \frac{r_i^o - \mathbf{p}^q\mathbf{x}_i^o}{\mathbf{p}^q(\mathbf{x}_i' - \mathbf{x}_i^o)} \leq 1$).

(2.2) $\mathbf{x}_i^q = \mathbf{x}_i^o$ otherwise.

It is obvious that $\{\mathbf{x}_i^q\} \subset X_i$ and that $\mathbf{x}_i^q \in \beta_i(\mathbf{p}^q, r_i^q)$ for all q, with $\{\mathbf{x}_i^q\} \to \mathbf{x}_i^o$ (note that as $q \to \infty$, $H^q \to H^o = \{\mathbf{z} \in \mathbb{R}^\ell / \mathbf{p}^o \mathbf{z} = r_i^o\}$, so that $\mathbf{x}_i^o \in H^o$). Therefore, β_i is lower hemicontinuous in this case as well.

That completes the proof. $\boxed{\textbf{Q.e.d.}}$

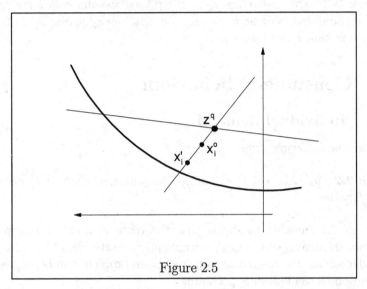

Figure 2.5

Concerning the assumptions of Theorem 2.2, the next figure illustrates the difficulties that emerge when $\min \mathbf{p}^o X_i = r_i^o$:

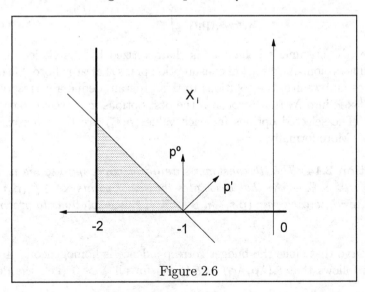

Figure 2.6

Let $(\mathbf{p}, r_i) \rightarrow (\mathbf{p}^o, r_i^o) = [(0,1), 0]$ in Figure 2.6, so that the wealth hyperplane rotates over the point $\mathbf{x}_i = (-1, 0)$. While $\mathbf{p} \neq \mathbf{p}^o$, the budget set $\beta_i(\mathbf{p}, r_i)$ (the shaded area in the figure) moves towards the segment $[-1, -2]$. Yet, $\beta_i(\mathbf{p}^o, r_i^o) = [0, -2]$.

Remark 2.2 *The restriction $r_i > \min \mathbf{p} X_i$ is usually called the "cheaper point" requirement, because it requires the existence of points in X_i that cost strictly less than r_i, at prices $\mathbf{p}$.*

2.6 Consumers' behaviour

2.6.1 Individual demand

Consider the following axiom:

Axiom 2.2 $u_i : X_i \rightarrow \mathbb{R}$ *is a continuous, quasi-concave$^+$ and non-satiable utility function.*

Axiom 2.2 amounts to saying that the ith consumer's preferences are complete, transitive, continuous, convex and non-satiable.

Under axiom 2.2, the ith consumer's choice problem can be expressed as the solution to the following program:

$$\left. \begin{array}{c} Max \ u_i\left(\mathbf{x}_i\right) \\[2mm] s.t. \\[2mm] \mathbf{x}_i \in \beta_i(\mathbf{p}, r_i) \end{array} \right\} \qquad [P]$$

The ith consumer's behaviour is characterized by the choice of a best affordable option. As the set of consumption plans that are affordable depend on prices and wealth, the solutions to this program define a correspondence from $\mathbb{R}^\ell \times \mathbb{R}$ into X_i that associates the best options in $\beta_i(\mathbf{p}, r_i)$ to each pair $(\mathbf{p}, r_i)$. The selected options for each value $(\mathbf{p}, r_i)$ are the ith consumer's *demand.* More formally,

Definition 2.14 *The ith consumer's **demand correspondence** is a mapping $\xi_i : \mathbb{R}^\ell \times \mathbb{R} \rightarrow X_i$ that associates the set of points $\mathbf{x}_i \in \beta_i(\mathbf{p}, r_i)$ that maximize u_i, to each pair $(\mathbf{p}, r_i)$ in $\mathbb{R}^\ell \times \mathbb{R}$ (i.e. the solutions to program [P] above).*

Observe that since the budget correspondence is homogeneous of degree zero, it follows that $\xi_i(\lambda \mathbf{p}, \lambda r_i) = \xi_i(\mathbf{p}, r_i)$ for all $\lambda > 0$ (i.e., the demand correspondence inherits the zero homogeneity property of the budget correspondence). This means that only relative prices and "real wealth" actually matter for consumers' decisions.

In order to analyze further properties of the demand mapping, let us first consider a result that gives sufficient conditions for the upper hemicontinuity of the solutions of a maximization problem [Berge (1963, III.3)]:

Theorem 2.3 (Maximum Theorem) *Let $D \subset \mathbb{R}^k$ and $X \subset \mathbb{R}^\ell$ compact. Let $\beta : D \to X$ be a non-empty valued continuous correspondence, $u : X \to \mathbb{R}$ a continuous function, and $\xi : D \to X$ be given by: $\xi(\mathbf{d}) = \{\mathbf{x} \in \beta(\mathbf{d}) \,/\, u(\mathbf{x})$ is maximum}. Then, ξ is upper hemicontinuous in D. Furthermore, the function $v(\mathbf{d}) = u(\mathbf{x})$ for $\mathbf{x} \in \xi(\mathbf{d})$ is continuous.*

Proof. As X is compact, it suffices to show that for all sequences $\{\mathbf{d}^n\} \subset D$, $\{\mathbf{x}^n\} \subset X$, converging to $\mathbf{d}^o$ and $\mathbf{x}^o$, respectively, and such that $\mathbf{x}^n \in \xi(\mathbf{d}^n)$ for all n, it follows that $\mathbf{x}^o \in \xi(\mathbf{d}^o)$.

Hence, let $\{\mathbf{d}^n\} \subset D$ be a sequence converging to $\mathbf{d}^o$, and $\{\mathbf{x}^n\} \subset X$ a sequence converging to $\mathbf{x}^o$ such that $\mathbf{x}^n \in \xi(\mathbf{d}^n)$ for all n. As $\mathbf{x}^n \in \beta(\mathbf{d}^n)$ for all n, and β is upper hemicontinuous, it follows that $\mathbf{x}^o \in \beta(\mathbf{d}^o)$. Moreover, as β is lower hemicontinuous, for any $\mathbf{z} \in \beta(\mathbf{d}^o)$ there exists a sequence $\{\mathbf{z}^n\} \subset X$ converging to $\mathbf{z}$ such that $\mathbf{z}^n \in \beta(\mathbf{d}^n)$, for all n. Thus, $u(\mathbf{x}^n) \geq u(\mathbf{z}^n)$ for all n [because $\mathbf{x}^n$ maximizes u over $\beta(\mathbf{d}^n)$], and in the limit $u(\mathbf{x}^o) \geq u(\mathbf{z})$]. As this inequality holds for every $\mathbf{z} \in \beta(\mathbf{d}^o)$, we have shown that $\mathbf{x}^o \in \xi(\mathbf{d}^o)$.

Now let $\{\mathbf{d}^n\} \to \mathbf{d}^o$, with $\mathbf{x}^n \in \xi(\mathbf{d}^n)$ for all n. As X is compact, we can take $\{\mathbf{x}^n\} \to \mathbf{x}^o \in X$. We have $v(\mathbf{d}^n) = u(\mathbf{x}^n)$. As u is continuous, by applying the former reasoning we conclude: $v(\mathbf{d}^n) = u(\mathbf{x}^n) \to u(\mathbf{x}^o) = v(\mathbf{d}^o)$. $\boxed{\textbf{Q.e.d.}}$

The following theorem tells us the key properties of the demand correspondence, as an application of theorems 2.2 and 2.3 above. To do this we need to restrict the ith consumer choice set to an arbitrarily large but compact subset of X_i. We do so in the following way: Let $\mathbf{e} = (1, ..., 1)$ stand for the unit vector in $\mathbb{R}^\ell$, and let $k > 0$ be an arbitrarily large scalar. Define then:

$$X_i(k) = \{\mathbf{x}_i \in X_i \,/\, \mathbf{x}_i \leq k\mathbf{e}\}$$

where k is chosen so that this set is non-empty. Under axiom 1, this is clearly a compact and convex subset of $\mathbb{R}^\ell$.

Associated to each of these sets $X_i(k)$, we can define the **restricted budget correspondence** $\widehat{\beta}_i$ as $\widehat{\beta}_i(\mathbf{p}, r_i) = \beta_i(\mathbf{p}, r_i) \bigcap X_i(k)$ for all $(\mathbf{p}, r_i) \in \mathbb{R}^\ell \times \mathbb{R}$. Similarly, we define the **restricted demand correspondence** $\widehat{\xi}_i$ as a mapping such that $\widehat{\xi}_i(\mathbf{p}, r_i)$ is the set of solutions to the program:[7]

$$\left. \begin{array}{c} Max \ u_i(\mathbf{x}_i) \\ s.t. \\ \mathbf{x}_i \in \widehat{\beta}_i(\mathbf{p}, r_i) \end{array} \right\} \qquad [\widehat{P}]$$

The following result is obtained:

Theorem 2.4 *Suppose that axioms 2.1 and 2.2 hold. Let k be an arbitrarily large scalar such that $X_i(k) \subset X_i$ is non-empty, and let $D_i \subset \mathbb{R}^\ell \times \mathbb{R}$ denote the set of points $(\mathbf{p}, r_i)$ such that $r_i > \min \mathbf{p} X_i$. Then, for all $(\mathbf{p}, r_i)$ in D_i, the restricted demand correspondence $\widehat{\xi}_i$, is upper hemicontinuous, with non-empty compact and convex values.*

Proof. First observe that, under the assumptions established, Theorem 2.2 applies. Hence $\widehat{\beta}_i$ is a continuous correspondence and Theorem 2.3 ensures that $\widehat{\xi}_i$ is upper hemicontinuous.

Observe now that $[\widehat{P}]$ has a solution, since $\widehat{\beta}_i(\mathbf{p}, r_i)$ is non-empty and compact-valued, and u_i is a continuous function (Weierstrass' Theorem). Moreover, the set $\widehat{\xi}_i(\mathbf{p}, r_i)$ of solutions to $[\widehat{P}]$ can be expressed as the intersection of the two following sets: $\widehat{\beta}_i(\mathbf{p}, r_i)$ (which is compact and convex, by construction), and

$$\{\mathbf{x}_i \in X_i \ / \ u_i(\mathbf{x}_i) \geq \max u_i(\mathbf{x}'_i), \ \text{with } \mathbf{x}'_i \in \widehat{\beta}_i(\mathbf{p}, r_i)\}$$

which is compact (because $X_i(k)$ is compact, and u_i is continuous), and convex (because u_i is quasi-concave). $\boxed{\textbf{Q.e.d.}}$

The next figure illustrates the equilibrium of an individual consumer,

---

[7]Precision would require to label the mappings $\widehat{\beta}_i$, $\widehat{\xi}_i$ differently, to make the dependence of the chosen parameter k explicit. However, we use this notation that is simpler and sufficiently descriptive for our purposes.

taking $X_i = \mathbb{R}_+^2$.

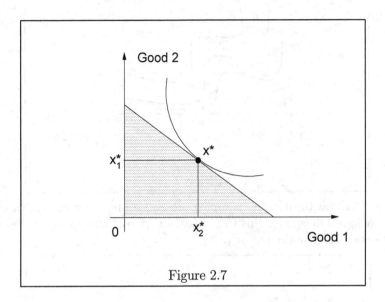

Figure 2.7

It is interesting to analyze the role of the convexity of preferences (the quasi-concavity of u_i) in the demand mapping. Note that if we drop this assumption the demand mapping will still be an upper hemicontinuous correspondence with non-empty, compact values (neither the maximum nor Weierstrass theorems depend on this property). Yet in this case the demand may present "jumps". This is illustrated in the next figures, for $\ell = 2$. The first one represents a consumer with non-convex preferences. The lack of convexity may derive from the presence of some "indivisibilities" in consumption, in the sense that some commodities may exhibit particular features that impede their combination with others (wine and milk, say). The figure shows how the ith consumer's equilibrium changes with prices, for a given wealth.

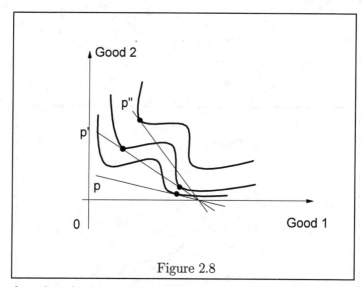

Figure 2.8

It is clear that the demand mapping presents a jump at a critical value $\mathbf{p}'$. The next figure illustrates this (note that, in spite of the jump, the demand is still upper hemicontinuous at $\mathbf{p}'$):

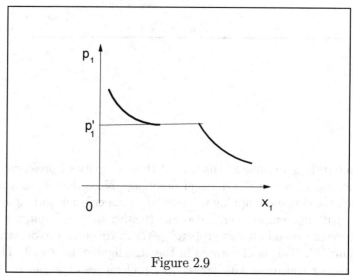

Figure 2.9

The next results tell us about the relationships between expenditure minimization and utility maximization. Proposition 2.5 establishes that the consumer expends all her wealth, and that those consumption plans which are preferred to her demand are more expensive. Proposition 2.6 in turn gives us sufficient conditions for expenditure minimization to imply utility maximization.

Proposition 2.5 *Let* $u_i : X_i \to \mathbb{R}$ *be a locally non-satiable utility function, and let* $\mathbf{x}_i^* \in \xi_i(\mathbf{p}, r_i)$. *Then:*

(a) $\mathbf{px}_i^* = r_i$

(b) $u_i(\mathbf{x}_i') \geq u_i(\mathbf{x}_i^*)$ *implies* $\mathbf{px}_i' \geq \mathbf{px}_i^*$ *(with* $\mathbf{px}_i' > \mathbf{px}_i^*$ *if the inequality is strict).*

Proof. (a) Suppose $\mathbf{px}_i^* < r_i$. Then $\mathbf{x}_i^*$ is an interior point of $\beta_i(\mathbf{p}, r_i)$, and we can find a ball $B(\mathbf{x}_i^*, \delta)$ contained in $\beta_i(\mathbf{p}, r_i)$. By local non-satiation, there will exist $\mathbf{x}_i' \in B(\mathbf{x}_i^*, \delta)$ that is better than $\mathbf{x}_i^*$, against the assumption.

(b) Suppose now that $u_i(\mathbf{x}_i') \geq u_i(\mathbf{x}_i')$ with $\mathbf{px}_i' < \mathbf{px}_i^* = r_i$. Then $\mathbf{x}_i' \in int\beta_i(\mathbf{p}, r_i)$, so that cannot be at least as good as a maximizer $\mathbf{x}_i^* \in \xi_i(\mathbf{p}, r_i)$. In particular, if we assume that $u_i(\mathbf{x}_i') > u_i(\mathbf{x}_i^*)$ and $\mathbf{px}_i' \leq \mathbf{px}_i^*$, then $\mathbf{x}_i' \in \beta_i(\mathbf{p}, r_i)$ and $\mathbf{x}_i^*$ would not be a maximizer of the preference relation over $\beta_i(\mathbf{p}, r_i)$. $\boxed{\textbf{Q.e.d.}}$

Proposition 2.6 *Let* $u_i : X_i \to \mathbb{R}$ *be a continuous utility function, and let* $\mathbf{x}_i^* \in X_i$ *be such that* $\mathbf{x}_i^*$ *minimizes* $\mathbf{p}^*\mathbf{x}_i$ *over* $\mathcal{BE}(\mathbf{x}_i^*)$, *with* $\mathbf{p}^*\mathbf{x}_i^* > \min \mathbf{p}^* X_i$, *for a given* $\mathbf{p}^* \in \mathbb{R}^\ell$. *Then,* $\mathbf{x}_i^*$ *maximizes* u_i *over the set* $A_i(\mathbf{p}^*, \mathbf{x}_i^*) = \{\mathbf{x}_i \in X_i \: / \: \mathbf{p}^*\mathbf{x}_i \leq \mathbf{p}^*\mathbf{x}_i^*\}$.

Proof. Let $\mathbf{x}_i' \in A_i(\mathbf{p}^*, \mathbf{x}_i^*)$. If $\mathbf{p}^*\mathbf{x}_i' < \mathbf{p}^*\mathbf{x}_i^*$, then $\mathbf{x}_i' \notin \mathcal{BE}(\mathbf{x}_i^*)$. Suppose then that $\mathbf{p}^*\mathbf{x}_i' = \mathbf{p}^*\mathbf{x}_i^*$. By assumption, there is some $\mathbf{z} \in X_i$ such that $\mathbf{p}^*\mathbf{z} < \mathbf{p}^*\mathbf{x}_i^*$. Define then $\mathbf{x}_i(\alpha) = \alpha \mathbf{x}_i' + (1 - \alpha)\mathbf{z}$, for α in $[0, 1]$. For every $\alpha < 1$ one has $\mathbf{p}^*\mathbf{x}_i(\alpha) < \mathbf{p}^*\mathbf{x}_i' = \mathbf{p}^*\mathbf{x}_i^*$, with $u_i(\mathbf{x}_i^*) > u_i[\mathbf{x}_i(\alpha)]$ [that is, $\mathbf{x}_i(\alpha)$ is not in $\mathcal{BE}(\mathbf{x}_i^*)$]. As α goes to 1, $\mathbf{x}_i(\alpha)$ tends to $\mathbf{x}_i'$, and $u_i(\mathbf{x}_i^*) \geq u_i[\mathbf{x}_i(\alpha)]$, for all α in $[0, 1)$. The continuity of the utility function implies that, in the limit, $u_i(\mathbf{x}_i^*) \geq u_i[\mathbf{x}_i(1)] = u_i(\mathbf{x}_i')$. $\boxed{\textbf{Q.e.d.}}$

What happens if $\mathbf{x}_i^*$ minimizes $\mathbf{p}^*\mathbf{x}_i$ over $\mathcal{BE}_i(\mathbf{x}_i^*)$ should be understood. The following figure illustrates that in such a case, expenditure minimization does not imply utility maximization.

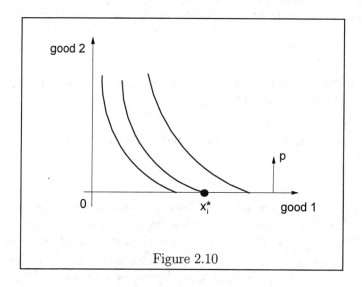

Figure 2.10

2.6.2   Aggregate consumption

Given a consumption set $X_i \subset \mathbb{R}^\ell$ for each consumer $i = 1, 2, \ldots, m$, the **aggregate consumption set** X, is given by:

$$X = \sum_{i=1}^{m} X_i$$

Under axiom 1 X is a non-empty and convex set (it is also closed, even though this is hard to prove).

The **aggregate demand correspondence** can be defined as a mapping ξ from $\mathbb{R}^\ell \times \mathbb{R}^m$ into X, such that, for every $(\mathbf{p}, \mathbf{r}) \in \mathbb{R}^\ell \times \mathbb{R}^m$ (where $\mathbf{r}$ is the vector representing the *wealth distribution*), it gives us:

$$\xi(\mathbf{p}, \mathbf{r}) = \sum_{i=1}^{m} \xi_i(\mathbf{p}, r_i)$$

This is again a zero homogeneous mapping.

Under axiom 1, we can choose a large enough scalar $k > 0$, so that *all* restricted consumption sets $X_i(k)$ are non-empty. For each of these scalars we can define $X(k) = \sum_{i=1}^{m} X_i(k)$. This is clearly a non-empty, compact and convex set. We can define the **restricted aggregate demand correspondence** as $\widehat{\xi}(\mathbf{p}, \mathbf{r}) = \sum_{i=1}^{m} \widehat{\xi}_i(\mathbf{p}, r_i)$.

Now call D that subset of $\mathbb{R}^\ell \times \mathbb{R}^m$ where $r_i > \min \mathbf{p}X_i$ for all i simultaneously (that is, $D = \bigcap_{i=1}^m D_i$). The following properties follow immediately from the above results:

Corollary 2.3 *Under axioms 1 and 2, for all $(\mathbf{p}, \mathbf{r})$ in D, the restricted aggregate demand correspondence $\widehat{\xi}$, is upper hemicontinuous, with non-empty, compact and convex values.*

2.7 References to the literature

This chapter is a summary of the standard theory, as in Debreu (1959), Arrow & Hahn (1971). See Deaton & Muellbauer (1980), Barten & Böhm (1982), Mas-Colell, Whinston & Green (1995) or Villar (1999a) for further developments (in particular with respect to the analysis of duality, uncertainty and the properties of the aggregate demand).

A different way of modelling the consumer's choice problem would be to use choice functions rather than preference relations. Yet, if one imposes minimal consistency properties, both approaches essentially coincide. See Suzumura (1983, ch. 2) for a discussion on this.

When one introduces the convexity and continuity assumptions, the transitivity and completeness of the preference relation can be dispensed with in order to ensure the existence of maximal elements. On this see Shafer (1974), Mas-Colell (1974), Shafer & Sonnenschein (1975), Walker (1977), Llinares (1998), and the discussion in Florenzano (1981) and Border (1985, Ch. 7).

Concerning the modelling of consumers' behaviour as an optimization problem, let us refer to Takayama (1985,ch.I) for a detailed discussion [see Bazaraa & Shetty (1979) for a guide on convexity and optimization]. The classic works of Kuhn and Tucker (1951), Arrow, Hurwicz and Uzawa (1961), and especially Arrow and Enthoven (1961) are still worth reading.

Chapter 3

PRODUCTION AND SUPPLY

3.1 Introduction

Production refers to a process by which certain commodities (inputs) are *transformed* into different ones (outputs). Input commodities may include raw materials, elements of fixed capital (land, machinery, buildings), energy, other produced commodities, and different types of labour. Outputs are produced commodities that can be consumed, stored or used as new inputs. Note that "transformation", here, has to be interpreted according to the notion of commodities adopted in chapter 1. In particular, transporting a commodity to a different place, or keeping it until another period, constitute transformations. Also, an element of fixed capital that is not totally used up in the production process appears as an additional commodity among the outputs (hence joint production is the rule).

In a market economy, these transformation processes are carried out within *firms*, which are the decision units concerning production. As in the case of the individual consumer, a firm can be regarded as a decision unit that makes choices on a subset of the commodity space $\mathbb{R}^\ell$, according to some choice criterion. Yet, a firm is a much more complex entity. On the one hand, the firm's choice set results from the combination of different elements: the *production technology*, and the *internal organization* (and possibly from the existence of quantity restrictions). On the other hand, its choice criteria usually depend on the structure of *property rights* (who owns the firm) and the *nature of the markets* in which the firm operates (competitive markets, oligopoly, etc.).

Technology describes the available means of transforming inputs into outputs, and reflects the state of the scientific and technological knowledge available. It can be understood as a "book of blue-prints", that is, a collection of engineering specifications that describe how to transform commodities. *Internal organization* refers to aspects like the coordination of the different phases of each technological process, the design of a hierarchy and a communication system to implement production decisions, the choice of the number of production units (*plants*) to carry out production, etc. Note that all this implies collective choices, information asymmetries, incentive problems, etc. Moreover, a firm's choice set may be subject to some *commodity restrictions*, when we consider the economy at a given point in time. This is the case of inputs or outputs already committed, or when there are capital goods that cannot be easily modified, or when the firm has limited access to some input market. In short: technology and the organization structure determine the firm's (notional) choice set, whereas the available resources may limit the firm's effective options.

The firm's choice criteria reflect its objectives (e.g. profit maximization or the achievement of larger market shares). As mentioned before, they typically depend on the structure of property rights and the nature of the markets in which the firm operates. Note that the variables that determine the choice sets and the choice criteria are interdependent. For example, the organization of the firm may depend on both the market regime (e.g. an oligopolistic firm may require a commercial division), and on the technology (decreasing returns to scale may call for several plants). The nature of the technological process can also affect the structure of the market and hence the firm's goals (e.g. natural monopolies in firms with increasing returns to scale). The organization may well influence the firm's goals (e.g. managers can incorporate their own goals into the decision process).

We shall drastically simplify this complex world, as follows:

(i) It will be assumed, throughout, that there is a given number n of firms, indexed by $j = 1, 2, \ldots, n$. These can be interpreted as potential firms, that only become real ones if they produce something.

(ii) Each of these n firms will be considered as a single production unit (that is, we assume that a firm consists of one plant). This permits us to carry out the analysis without having to distinguish between plants (the natural units of reference in production theory) and firms.

(iii) Each firm j will be identified with *a production possibility set Y_j*, that summarizes both the technological knowledge and the organizational alternatives, and *a criterion of choice ϕ_j*.

3.2 Production sets

3.2.1 Individual production

A **production plan** for the jth firm, denoted by $\mathbf{y}_j \in \mathbb{R}^\ell$, is a vector that specifies the amounts of (net) inputs that are required in order to obtain some given amounts of (net) outputs. Outputs will be represented by positive numbers and inputs by negative ones. A simple illustration of this way of describing production, for $\ell = 2$, is the following: Suppose that we can produce 300 Tons of corn using 50 Tons of corn and 1,000 hours of labour time. The corresponding production plan will be given by $\mathbf{y} = (-1,000, \ 250)$, meaning that we obtain 250 net Tons of corn (that is, 300 Tons of gross output minus 50 Tons which is used up as input) by means of 1,000 hours of labour.

A **production set** for the jth firm, denoted by $Y_j \subset \mathbb{R}^\ell$, is a set made of all the production plans that are possible for the jth firm, according to the technological knowledge available to it.

The key assumptions on production sets, that will be maintained throughout, are the following:

Axiom 3.1 $Y_j \subset \mathbb{R}^\ell$ *is closed.*

Axiom 3.2 $Y_j - \mathbb{R}^\ell_+ \subset Y_j$.

Axiom 3.1, sometimes called "continuity", is a technical requirement. It amounts to saying that any production plan that can be approximated by a sequence of elements $\{\mathbf{y}_j^\nu\} \subset Y_j$ will also be in Y_j.

Axiom 3.2 states that Y_j is a **comprehensive** set, that is: if $\mathbf{y}_j \in Y_j$ and $\mathbf{y}_j'$ is a vector in $\mathbb{R}^\ell$ satisfying $\mathbf{y}_j' \le \mathbf{y}_j$, then $\mathbf{y}_j'$ will also be in Y_j. In words: If a production plan is possible, any production plan which uses more inputs or obtains less outputs is also possible. The chief implication of axioms 1 and 2, on the shape of production sets, is that the boundary of Y_j is "downward sloping" (see Proposition 3.2 below).

There are other standard axioms that will be used here and there, when modelling specific scenarios. These are the following:

Axiom 3.3 $\mathbf{0} \in Y_j$.

Axiom 3.3 establishes that producing nothing (meaning obtaining no outputs and using no inputs) is always an alternative available to the jth firm (i.e., $\mathbf{0}$ belongs to Y_j). This trivially implies that Y_j is non-empty. When we interpret Y_j as a production set *strictu sensu* (that is, as a collection of technological specifications), this is a rather natural assumption. Yet, when we identify Y_j with a given firm's choice set, it discards the presence of "sunk costs". Together, axioms 3.2 and 3.3 imply that the jth firm can freely dispose of any amount of commodities (a property known as "free-disposal").

Axiom 3.4 $Y_j \cap \mathbb{R}^\ell_+ \subset \{0\}$.

Axiom 3.4 says that the intersection of Y_j with the positive orthant is either empty or reduces to the origin. The message is clear: "There is no such a thing as a Free Lunch", that is, any production plan involving strictly positive outputs has to use up some inputs (i.e. it has to contain strictly negative numbers as well). In some cases axioms 3.3 and 3.4 are presented together as $Y_j \cap \mathbb{R}^\ell_+ = \{0\}$.

Axiom 3.5 Y_j *is convex.*

Axiom 3.5 says that for all $\mathbf{y}_j, \mathbf{y}'_j \in Y_j$, all $\lambda \in [0, 1]$, $\lambda \mathbf{y}_j + (1 - \lambda)\mathbf{y}'_j \in Y_j$. That is, any convex combination of two feasible production plans defines a feasible production plan. Under axioms 3.1, 3.2 and 3.3, the convexity of Y_j implies the presence of decreasing returns to scale, as will be discussed later on.

The following figure depicts four production sets, all of which satisfy axioms 3.1 and 3.2. We represent a technology that produces corn (as a net output) by using labour (as a net input). Figure 1(a) presents a production set that satisfies all five axioms discussed above. Figure 1(b) satisfies all axioms except axiom 3.3. Figure 1(c) satisfies all axioms except axiom 3.4. Finally, figure 1(d) describes a production set that satisfies axioms 3.1, 3.2, 3.3 and 3.4, but does not satisfy axiom 3.5.

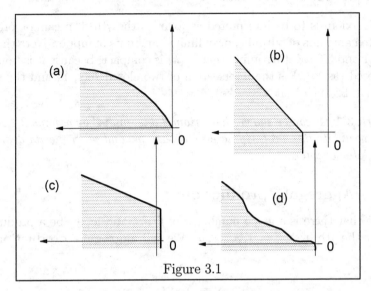

Figure 3.1

Let $\mathbf{e} = (1, 1, ..., 1)$ represent the unit vector in $\mathbb{R}^{\ell}_+$. For a given positive scalar $k > 0$, consider the set $Y_j(k) = \{\mathbf{y}_j \in Y_j \ / \ \mathbf{y}_j \geq -k\mathbf{e}\}$. Due to the sign convention, the point $-k\mathbf{e}$ can be interpreted as a given amount of inputs that can be used. Hence, $Y_j(k)$ describes the set of production plans that do not use more inputs than those in $-k\mathbf{e}$. The next figure illustrates one of these sets:

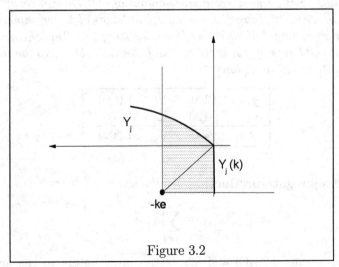

Figure 3.2

Consider now the following axiom:

Axiom 3.6 *For any given scalar $k > 0$ the set $Y_j(k)$ is bounded.*

This axiom is to be interpreted as follows: the jth firm cannot produce unlimited amounts of outputs out of limited amounts of inputs. Note that axioms 3.1 and 3.6 together imply that $Y_j(k)$ is compact, because it is bounded and closed (as $Y_j(k)$ is the intersection of two closed sets, Y_j and the set of points $\mathbf{t} \in \mathbb{R}^\ell$ such that $\mathbf{t} \geq -k\mathbf{e}$).

Remark 3.1 *It can be shown that axiom 3.6 is implied by axioms 3.1 to 3.4; yet we postulate this property here as an axiom, and postpone its deduction until a later chapter.*

3.2.2   Aggregate production

Assume that there is a given number n of firms, and let $\mathbf{y}_j$ be a production plan for the jth firm, $j = 1, 2, \ldots, n$. We call **aggregate production** the vector

$$\mathbf{y} = \sum_{j=1}^{n} \mathbf{y}_j$$

Note that when we add up all the firms' production plans, all trading among firms cancels out. The following example illustrates this:

Example 3.1 *Consider an economy with two firms with the following production plans. Firm 1 produces a gross output of 600 Tons of corn, by using 280 Tons of corn, 12 Tons of iron and 1,000 hours of labour time. Firm 2 produces a gross output of 20 Tons of iron, by using 120 Tons of corn, 8 Tons of iron and 600 hours of labour time. The following table gives the individual and aggregate production plans*

$\mathbf{y}_1 =$	(320,	-12,	-1.000)
$\mathbf{y}_2 =$	(-120,	12,	-600)
$\mathbf{y} =$	(200,	0,	-1.600)

We call **aggregate production set** the set:

$$Y = \sum_{j=1}^{n} Y_j$$

Clearly, axioms 3.2, 3.3 and 3.5 extend immediately to the aggregate production set. Yet this is not the case for axioms 3.1, 3.4 and 3.6. Even if all production sets satisfy axiom 3.1, the aggregate production set may fail to satisfy this axiom (the sum of a finite number of closed sets need not be closed). Similarly, even if all production sets satisfy axiom 3.4 (resp. axiom 3.6), the aggregate production set may fail to satisfy this axiom. The following example illustrates this:

Example 3.2 *Suppose that the economy consists of two firms, whose production sets satisfy axioms 3.1 to 3.6, and are given by: $Y_1 = \{\mathbf{y}_1 \in \mathbb{R}^\ell \ / \ \mathbf{y}_1 \leq \lambda(-1,1), \forall \lambda \geq 0\}$, $Y_2 = \{\mathbf{y}_2 \in \mathbb{R}^\ell \ / \ \mathbf{y}_2 \leq \lambda(2,-1), \forall \lambda \geq 0\}$. Therefore, $Y = (Y_1 + Y_2)$ is the set of points $\mathbf{y} \in \mathbb{R}^\ell$ such that $\mathbf{y} \leq \lambda(1,0)$. Clearly, $Y(k)$ is not bounded for any k (as Y is able to produce without using up inputs). Hence, Y satisfies neither axiom 3.4 nor axiom 3.6.*

Consider now the following axioms:

Axiom 3.7 $Y \cap (-Y) \subset \{\mathbf{0}\}$.

Axiom 3.8 *For all $k > 0$, the set $Y(k)$ is compact.*

Axiom 3.7, called **irreversibility**, states that if an aggregate production $\mathbf{y} \in Y$ is different from $\mathbf{0}$, the aggregate production $-\mathbf{y}$ cannot be in Y (that is, reversing the role of inputs and outputs in an aggregate production plan is not possible). Axioms 3.2, 3.3 and 3.7 together imply that $Y \cap \mathbb{R}_+^\ell \subset \{\mathbf{0}\}$ (because axioms 3.2 and 3.3 imply that $-\mathbb{R}_+^\ell \subset Y$, so that for any $\mathbf{y}$ in $\mathbb{R}_+^\ell - \{\mathbf{0}\}$ the point $-\mathbf{y}$ belongs to Y, contradicting irreversibility). It is much more difficult to show that, under axioms 3.1, 3.2, 3.3, 3.5 and 3.7, Y is also closed.

Axiom 3.8 postulates the compactness of the aggregate production set directly, when restricted to a given amount of inputs. This is a rather intuitive and realistic assumption; it establishes that it is not possible to obtain unlimited amounts of outputs when resources are limited. Under axioms 3.1 and 3.2, axiom 3.8 implies axiom 3.6 (i.e. $Y_j(k)$ is compact for all j). It can also be shown that axioms 3.1, 3.2, 3.3, 3.5 and 3.7 imply axiom 3.8.

Remark 3.2 *The results concerning the closedness of the aggregate production set and the boundedness of $Y(k)$, rely on a rather technical argument on the properties of asymptotic cones, which are discussed in chapter 12 of the book.*

3.3 Efficiency, additivity, divisibility

In this section we analyze three concepts that are pertinent in the theory of production: efficiency, additivity and divisibility. Efficiency refers to production plans: a production plan is efficient when it uses the minimal amount of inputs required in order to obtain some given amount of outputs. Additivity and divisibility refer to production sets. Additivity says that the sum of two feasible production plans is also feasible. Divisibility establishes that any feasible production plan can be scaled down without leaving the production set.

Consider the following definition:[1]

Definition 3.1 *A production plan* $\mathbf{y}_j^o \in Y_j$ *is **efficient** (resp. **weakly efficient**), if there is no* $\mathbf{y}_j' \in Y_j$ *such that* $\mathbf{y}_j' > \mathbf{y}_j^o$ *(resp.* $\mathbf{y}_j' >> \mathbf{y}_j^o$*).*

In words: An efficient production plan is an input-output combination such that it is not possible to increase the amount produced of a commodity, without decreasing the production of another or increasing the use of some inputs. Clearly, efficiency implies weak efficiency. By definition, if $\mathbf{y}_j$ is an efficient production plan, so it must be in ∂Y_j (the boundary of the jth firm's production set); yet, in general, the converse is not true.

Efficient production plans satisfy a very general and interesting property which can be formalized as follows:

Proposition 3.1 *Let* $Y_j \subset \mathbb{R}^\ell$ *be a production set, and let* $\mathbf{q}$ *be a vector in* $\mathbb{R}^\ell$ *such that* $\mathbf{q} >> \mathbf{0}$ *(resp.* $\mathbf{q} > \mathbf{0}$*). Suppose that, for some* $\mathbf{y}_j^o \in Y_j$*, we have:* $\mathbf{q}\mathbf{y}_j^o \geq \mathbf{q}\mathbf{y}_j, \forall \mathbf{y}_j \in Y_j$*. Then* $\mathbf{y}_j^o$ *is an efficient (resp. weakly efficient) production plan.*

(The proof is trivial and so it is omitted)

Remark 3.2 *Note that if we interpret* $\mathbf{q}$ *as a price vector, then this property can be read as follows: Profit maximization at given prices implies selecting efficient production plans. We should point out that none of the axioms presented in section 3.1 are required for this outcome.*

The next result serves to illustrate a key implication of axioms 1 and 2:

Proposition 3.2 *Under axioms 3.1 and 3.2, a production plan* $\mathbf{y}_j$ *in* Y_j *is weakly efficient if and only if* $\mathbf{y}_j \in \partial Y_j$*.*

Proof. (i) $\mathbf{y}_j$ weakly efficient $\Longrightarrow \mathbf{y}_j \in \partial Y_j$.

Suppose not. Then $\mathbf{y}_j \in int Y_j$ and there exists a neighbourhood of $\mathbf{y}_j$ contained in Y_j with points $\mathbf{y}_j' >> \mathbf{y}_j$, against the assumption.

(ii) $\mathbf{y}_j \in \partial Y_j \Longrightarrow \mathbf{y}_j$ weakly efficient.

---

[1]Let us recall here that notation for vector comparisons is: $\geq, >, >>$.

Suppose not. Then $\exists\ \mathbf{y}'_j \in Y_j$ with $\mathbf{y}'_j >> \mathbf{y}_j$. As Y_j is comprehensive, *all* points below $\mathbf{y}'_j$ are in Y_j, so that $\mathbf{y}_j \in intY_j$, which is a contradiction.
$\boxed{\text{Q.e.d.}}$

One way of interpreting this proposition is as follows: under axioms 3.1 and 3.2, the jth firm's relevant information about production possibilities is contained in the frontier of its production set.

Consider now the following properties, that will allow us to link axioms 3.3 and 3.5:

Definition 3.2 *A production set Y_j satisfies **additivity** if, for all $\mathbf{y}_j, \mathbf{y}'_j \in Y_j$, it follows that $(\mathbf{y}_j + \mathbf{y}'_j) \in Y_j$.*

Definition 3.3 *A production set Y_j satisfies **divisibility** if, for all $\mathbf{y}_j \in Y_j$, all $\lambda \in (0, 1)$, $\lambda\mathbf{y}_j \in Y_j$.*

The additivity property states that if two production plans are technologically feasible, a new production plan consisting of the sum of these two will also be feasible. Divisibility states that if a production plan is possible for the jth firm, then any production plan consisting of a reduction in its scale will also be feasible. Note that when Y_j is closed, divisibility implies that $\mathbf{0} \in Y_j$.

The next result shows that the convexity of production sets can be derived from the combination of the primitive properties of additivity and divisibility. Formally:

Proposition 3.3 *A closed production set Y_j satisfies additivity and divisibility if and only if it is a convex cone with vertex $\mathbf{0}$.*

Proof. (i) Y_j is a convex cone $\Longrightarrow Y_j$ satisfies additivity and divisibility.
If Y_j is a cone, $\mathbf{y}_j \in Y_j \Longrightarrow \lambda\mathbf{y}_j \in Y_j$ for all $\lambda > 0$. Hence divisibility holds. Now let $\mathbf{y}_j, \mathbf{y}'_j \in Y_j$. To show that $\mathbf{y}_j + \mathbf{y}'_j \in Y_j$ take some $\lambda \in (0, 1)$ and let $\mathbf{z}_j, \mathbf{z}'_j \in Y_j$ be such that $\lambda\mathbf{z}_j = \mathbf{y}_j$, $(1 - \lambda)\mathbf{z}'_j = \mathbf{y}'_j$ (this can always be done because Y_j is a cone). The convexity of Y_j implies that $\lambda\mathbf{z}_j + (1 - \lambda)\mathbf{z}'_j \in Y_j$, so that $\mathbf{y}_j + \mathbf{y}'_j \in Y_j$.
(ii) Y_j satisfies additivity and divisibility $\Longrightarrow Y_j$ is a convex cone.
Let $\mathbf{y}_j, \mathbf{y}'_j \in Y_j$. By divisibility $\lambda\mathbf{y}_j \in Y_j$, $(1 - \lambda)\mathbf{y}'_j \in Y_j$, for all $\lambda \in [0, 1]$. By additivity $\lambda\mathbf{y}_j + (1 - \lambda)\mathbf{y}'_j \in Y_j$. Hence, Y_j is convex.
Let $\mathbf{y}_j \in Y_j$. For all $\lambda \in (0, 1)$ divisibility implies $\lambda\mathbf{y}_j \in Y_j$. Moreover, for any natural number $\lambda \geq 1$ the same conclusion obtains from additivity (adding up λ times $\mathbf{y}_j$). Finally, if $\lambda > 1$ is not a natural number, we can

write $\lambda = K + \varepsilon$, where K is a natural number and $\varepsilon \in (0,1)$, so that $\lambda \mathbf{y}_j = K\mathbf{y}_j + \varepsilon \mathbf{y}_j$. But $K\mathbf{y}_j \in Y_j$, by additivity and $\varepsilon \mathbf{y}_j \in Y_j$ by divisibility. Applying additivity again, $K\mathbf{y}_j + \varepsilon \mathbf{y}_j \in Y_j$. Hence, Y_j is a cone. $\boxed{\textbf{Q.e.d.}}$

Remark 3.3 *Note that, when Y_j is a convex cone, if $\mathbf{y}_j \in Y_j$ is an efficient production plan, $\alpha \mathbf{y}_j$ is also efficient for all $\alpha \geq \mathbf{0}$.[2]*

3.4　Returns to scale

3.4.1　Definitions

A key technological aspect in the modelling of firms refers to the nature of the *returns to scale*. These describe how the productivity evolves with the scale of operations. Roughly speaking, constant returns to scale means that productivity does not change with the scale of operations; and increasing (resp. decreasing) returns means that productivity increases (resp. decreases) with the scale. The following definitions make these ideas precise, in a context where production typically involves several inputs and outputs.

Definition 3.4 *Let $\mathbf{y}_j \in Y_j$ be given. To **change the scale of operations** consists of multiplying $\mathbf{y}_j$ by a scalar $\lambda > 0$. When $\lambda > 1$ (resp. $\lambda < 1$) we speak of **increasing** (resp. **decreasing**) the scale.*

A change in the scale of operations, relative to a given $\mathbf{y}_j \in Y_j$, is simply another production plan proportional to $\mathbf{y}_j$.

Definition 3.5 *Y_j exhibits **increasing returns to scale** when, for all $\mathbf{y}_j \in Y_j$, we can arbitrarily increase the scale of operations.*

A production set exhibits increasing returns to scale if and only if, for all $\mathbf{y}_j \in Y_j$ and all $\lambda > 1$, it follows that $\lambda \mathbf{y}_j \in Y_j$.

Definition 3.6 *Y_j exhibits **decreasing returns to scale** when, for all $\mathbf{y}_j \in Y_j$, we can arbitrarily decrease the scale of operations.*

Decreasing returns to scale hold if and only if, for all $\mathbf{y}_j \in Y_j$ and all $\lambda \in (0,1)$, $\lambda \mathbf{y}_j \in Y_j$. Note that decreasing returns and divisibility are equivalent concepts.

---

[2]To see this suppose that this is not the case. Then, $\mathbf{y}'_j > \alpha \mathbf{y}_j$, for some $\mathbf{y}'_j \in Y_j$. This is not possible for $\alpha = 0$. For $\alpha > 0$ we would have $\frac{1}{\alpha}\mathbf{y}'_j \geq \mathbf{y}_j$, with $\frac{1}{\alpha}\mathbf{y}'_j \in Y_j$, contradicting the assumption that $\mathbf{y}$ is efficient. The result follows.

Definition 3.7 Y_j *exhibits* **constant returns to scale** *when, for all* $\mathbf{y}_j \in Y_j$, *we can arbitrarily change the scale of operations.*

A production set with constant returns to scale is thus characterized by the following property: $[\mathbf{y}_j \in Y_j \ \& \ \lambda > 0] \implies \lambda\mathbf{y}_j \in Y_j$. Given the definitions given above, Y_j exhibits constant returns to scale if and only if it exhibits both increasing and decreasing returns to scale.

Remark 3.4 *Under axioms 3.1, 3.2 and 3.3, a production set exhibits constant returns to scale if and only if it is a closed convex cone with vertex zero.*

The next figure shows three production sets in $\mathbb{R}^2$, satisfying axioms 3.1, 3.2 and 3.3. Case (a) corresponds to constant returns to scale (in this case the production set is a convex cone with vertex zero). Case (b) illustrates a convex production set with (strictly) decreasing returns to scale. Case (c) depicts a firm with (strictly) increasing returns to scale; observe that in this case the production set is not convex (that is why it is customary to refer to increasing returns as to the presence of non-convexities in production).

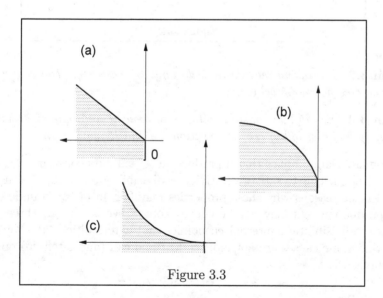

Figure 3.3

Needless to say, production sets may not satisfy any of the above definitions of returns to scale (as in Figure 3.1d); in particular, a non-convex production set need not exhibit increasing returns to scale.

3.4.2   Additivity, divisibility and returns to scale

The relationships between the additivity and divisibility properties and the different types of returns to scale can be summarized as follows:

Claim 3.1 *If Y_j is convex with $0 \in Y_j$, it satisfies divisibility (decreasing returns to scale). The converse is not true, as the following figure shows.*

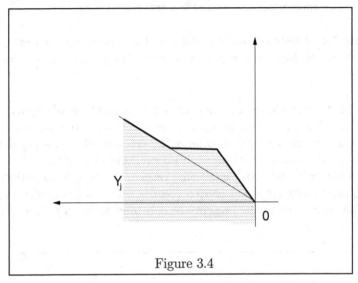

Figure 3.4

Claim 3.2 *Increasing returns to scale implies additivity. The converse is not true (see figure 3.5 below).*

Claim 3.3 *Y_j exhibits constant returns to scale if and only if it satisfies additivity and divisibility (see Proposition 3.3 and Remark 3.2).*

The last claim implies that a production set exhibits constant returns to scale, or else it fails to satisfy additivity or divisibility (or both). Let us now consider the reasons why these properties may fail, in order to understand why production sets may not be convex cones. We single out three main causes: indivisibilities, internal economies and externalities. It should be clear that these causes are not independent and can (and often do) operate simultaneously.

Indivisibilities

Consider the case in which there are commodities whose production or use takes place only in fixed amounts. In this case the divisibility property does

not hold, but the production set may well satisfy additivity, as illustrated
in the next figure. Note that even though Y_j satisfies additivity it does not
exhibit increasing returns to scale.

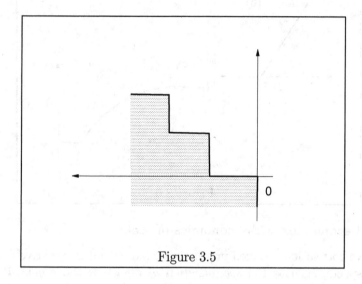

Figure 3.5

A particular case of special relevance is that of fixed costs: There is a
fixed amount of some input that has to be used before any positive production takes place. This typically occurs when production involves the use
of elements of *fixed capital* (buildings, land, machinery, etc.), or when the
technology involves the use of *information* (the information required for a
production process may well take the form of a fixed cost, independent of
the number of times this process is used).

The following figures illustrate this case. The first one describes a technology with a constant marginal rate of transformation with some installation
costs. The production set does not satisfy divisibility but satisfies additivity
(indeed, here we have a technology with strictly increasing returns to scale,
because producing more permits the division of the fixed cost among more
units, so that the "average cost" is decreasing). In the second one, the production set is made of a fixed cost plus a strictly convex set (we can think
that there is a production level beyond which the productivity of the fixed
input decreases). Here neither divisibility nor additivity hold.

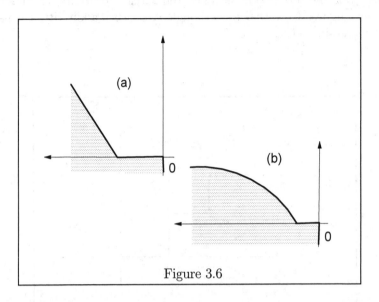

Figure 3.6

Internal economies or diseconomies of scale

A positive correlation between productivity and output may derive from internal aspects, such as the *specialization of inputs* or the *organization of productive factors*. This correlation was first pointed out by Adam Smith, who established a connection between the "division of labour" and the "extent of the market". His classical example on "the pin factory" provided a first insight into how the division of labour can enhance productivity. This is even clearer when machinery is involved. "In the use of machinery and the adoption of indirect processes there is a further division of labour, the economies of which are again limited by the extent of the market. It would be wasteful to make a hammer to drive a single nail..." [C.f. A. Young (1928)].

Internal economies of scale may also be a consequence of physical laws. As an illustration, consider the well known example of the transport of oil through a pipe-line (the inputs required per inch of pipe-line vary with the radius of the pipe, whereas output —volume of oil transported per inch, varies with the square of such a radius). In these cases production sets typically exhibit increasing returns to scale; the divisibility property fails whereas additivity holds.

A negative correlation between output and productivity emerges when the production process makes use of a fixed amount of an implicit factor, that cannot be replicated. Particular "talents" or specific "managerial abilities", are examples of these singular factors which are not listed in the set of commodities.[3] Here additivity fails but divisibility holds. In particular, the organizational aspects of the firm seem to be subject to decreasing returns, for large scales.

Figures 3.3(b,c) serve to illustrate these cases.

Externalities

So far we have taken the jth firm's production possibilities as a fixed given set. There are situations, however, where these possibilities may be affected by some other firms' production activities. In such a case we say that the jth firm's production set is subject to *externalities*. These external economies can be positive or negative. Examples of the first class are network externalities (communication systems, say), public goods provided by the public sector (roads, airports), or research activities. The typical example of negative externalities is that of pollution. Both types of externalities may generate non-convexities in production sets, and may well be incompatible with additivity and/or divisibility.

It may be that, for each given production decision of all the other firms, the jth firm's conditional production set is a convex cone; and the unconditional production still fails to satisfy additivity and/or divisibility.[4]

3.5 The behaviour of competitive firms

3.5.1 Competitive firms

The standard notion of firms' competitive behaviour can be described by two key postulates:

(A) Each firm takes market prices as given data and assumes that, at these prices, there are no quantity restrictions. In other words, the firm can sell all the outputs it produces and buy all the input it required.

(B) The jth firm's choice criteria consist of selecting those production plans that maximize profits at given prices.

From (A) it follows that jth firm takes the production set as the *effective* choice set. This reflects the idea that the individual firm is very small with respect to the available resources and the size of the markets in which it operates, so that there are practically no external limits on the firm's choices. The absence of quantity restrictions can be regarded as the counterpart of

---

[3]Note that when production sets are engeneering specifications on what transformations are possible, they cannot include (explicit) input restrictions.

[4]This corresponds, roughly speaking, to Alfred Marshall's treatment of increasing returns: they are internal to the industry but external to the firm.

price-taking behaviour: individual actions have a negligible effect on market prices. From (A) and (B) it follows that all the information a firm needs to be able to choose a production plan is its production set and market prices. Hence, there is no need to take what other firms do, or the demand side into account; in particular, there is no place for strategic considerations.[5]

In this section we shall assume that individual firms satisfy axioms 3.1 to 3.6. Namely, (a) Y_j is a closed set; (b) $Y_j - \mathbb{R}_+^\ell \subset Y_j$; (c) $\mathbf{0} \in Y_j$; (d) $Y_j \cap \mathbb{R}_+^\ell \subset \{\mathbf{0}\}$; (e) Y_j is convex; and (f) For all $k > 0$, the set $Y_j(k) = \{\mathbf{y}_j \in Y_j \ / \ \mathbf{y}_j \geq -k\mathbf{e}\}$ is bounded.

3.5.2 Supply

Let $\mathbf{p} \in \mathbb{R}^\ell$ be a given price vector, and $\mathbf{y}_j \in Y_j$ a given production plan for the jth firm. According to the sign convention, the profit associated with this production plan at these prices is given by the scalar product

$$\mathbf{p}\mathbf{y}_j = \sum_{h=1}^{\ell} p_h y_{jh}$$

The notion of competitive behaviour presented above implies that the jth firm will agree to produce a vector $\mathbf{y}_j^* \in Y_j$ at prices $\mathbf{p} \in \mathbb{R}^\ell$, if and only if

$$\mathbf{p}\mathbf{y}_j^* \geq \mathbf{p}\mathbf{y}_j, \quad \forall \mathbf{y}_j \in Y_j$$

Note that there might be price vectors for which no production plan maximizes profits. Under axioms 3.1 to 3.3, such will be the case when $\mathbf{p} \in \mathbb{R}^\ell$ contains negative entries.[6] We can therefore eliminate negative prices from the price space without loss of generality. Moreover, when $\mathbf{p} = \mathbf{0}$ *all* production plans are profit maximizers (that is, the firm's choice problem is irrelevant). Hence we can take the set $\mathbb{R}_+^\ell - \{\mathbf{0}\}$ as the relevant price space. Nothing ensures, however, the existence of profit maximizing production plans for all $\mathbf{p} \in \mathbb{R}_+^\ell - \{\mathbf{0}\}$. When the jth firm exhibits constant returns to scale and $\mathbf{p}\mathbf{y}_j > 0$ for some $\mathbf{p} \in \mathbb{R}_{++}^\ell$, for example, there is no profit maximizing production plan at these prices (we can always increase profits by increasing the

---

[5] Joan Robinson pointed out that it was sort of funny calling "competitive" to those firms that actually do compete at all among them. Yet, as we shall discuss later, this behaviour can be regarded as an outcome rather than as an assumption.

[6] Suppose that $p_1 < 0$, for some $\mathbf{p} \in \mathbb{R}^\ell$, and consider production plans with the form $\mathbf{y}_j = \lambda(y_{1j}, 0, ..., 0)$, with $y_{1j} < 0$ (this is possible under axioms 3.1, 3.2 and 3.3 because $-\mathbb{R}_+^\ell \subset Y_j$). As λ grows $\mathbf{p}\mathbf{y}_j$ increases, so that there is no profit maximizing production plan at thse prices.

scale of operations).[7]

The behaviour of the competitive firm is summarized in the supply mapping, defined as follows:

Definition 3.8 *The jth firm's* **supply correspondence** *is a mapping* $\eta_j :$ $\mathbb{R}^\ell_+ - \{\mathbf{0}\} \to Y_j$ *given by*

$$\eta_j(\mathbf{p}) \equiv \{\mathbf{y}_j \in Y_j \ / \ \mathbf{py}_j \geq \mathbf{py}'_j, \ \forall \ \mathbf{y}'_j \in Y_j\}$$

Note that, under axiom 3.1, if $\mathbf{y}_j \in \eta_j(\mathbf{p})$, then $\mathbf{y}_j$ is a point in the boundary of Y_j (this follows from Propositions 3.1 and 3.2). Moreover, for all $\lambda > 0$, $\eta_j(\lambda\mathbf{p}) = \eta_j(\mathbf{p})$, that is, the supply correspondence is homogeneous of degree zero in prices.

We can also define the jth firm's **profit function** as a single-valued mapping $\pi_j : \mathbb{R}^\ell_+ - \{\mathbf{0}\} \to \mathbb{R}$ such that $\pi_j(\mathbf{p}) = \max_{\mathbf{y}_j \in Y_j} \mathbf{py}_j$. This function is homogeneous of degree one in prices, that is, $\pi_j(\lambda\mathbf{p}) = \lambda\pi_j(\mathbf{p})$, for all $\lambda > 0$.

The following figure illustrates the geometry of profit maximization. The point $\mathbf{y}_j$ maximizes profits at prices $\mathbf{p}$, and appears as the intersection between Y_j and the hyperplane $\mathbf{py} = \alpha$ with the highest α for which this intersection is non-empty [that is, for $\alpha = \pi_j(\mathbf{p})$].

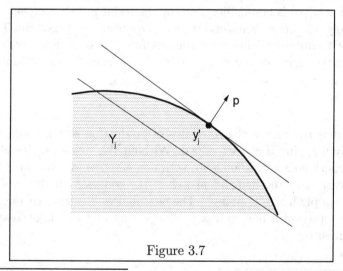

Figure 3.7

---

[7]We take a price vector $\mathbf{p} >> \mathbf{0}$ in this example, in order to emphasize that, contrary to the case of consumers, strictly positive prices do not ensure the existence of optimal choices.

For a given $k > 0$, we define $Y_j(k) = \{\mathbf{y}_j \in Y_j \; / \; \mathbf{y}_j \geq -k\mathbf{e}\}$. Associated with this set, we can define the jth firm's **restricted supply correspondence** as a mapping $\widehat{\eta}_j : \mathbb{R}^\ell_+ - \{\mathbf{0}\} \to Y_j(k)$, given by $\widehat{\eta}_j(\mathbf{p}) \equiv \{\mathbf{y}_j \in Y_j(k) \; / \; \mathbf{p}\mathbf{y}_j \geq \mathbf{p}\mathbf{y}'_j, \; \forall \, \mathbf{y}'_j \in Y_j(k)\}$.

The following result gives us the main properties of the supply mapping:[8]

Proposition 3.4 *Let $\mathbf{p}$ be a point in $\mathbf{p} \in \mathbb{R}^\ell_+ - \{\mathbf{0}\}$, and suppose that axioms 3.1 to 3.6 hold. Then:*

(a) $\eta_j(\mathbf{p})$ is a closed convex set, with $\mathbf{p}\mathbf{y}_j \geq 0$ for all $\mathbf{y}_j \in \eta_j(\mathbf{p})$.

(b) For all $k > 0$, the restricted supply correspondence $\widehat{\eta}_j$ is upper hemi-continuous, with non-empty, compact and convex values.

Proof. Under the axioms established, $\eta_j(\mathbf{p})$ is a closed convex set (possibly empty), because it is the intersection of two sets with these properties. Clearly, $\mathbf{p}\mathbf{y}_j \geq 0$ for all $\mathbf{y}_j \in \eta_j(\mathbf{p})$, as $\mathbf{0} \in Y_j$. Moreover, $Y_j(k)$ is compact, convex and non-empty; as $\mathbf{p}\mathbf{y}_j$ is a continuous function, Weierstrass' theorem ensures that $\eta_j(\mathbf{p})$ is non-empty; and, by the result in (a), compact and convex. Finally, the upper hemicontinuity derives from the Maximum Theorem, because we are maximizing a continuous function on a fixed compact set which can be regarded as a constant correspondence (trivially continuous).
Q.e.d.

Note that the role of the convexity of production sets is to ensure that the supply mapping is convex-valued. Without this axiom, $\widehat{\eta}_j$ is still an upper hemicontinuous correspondence with non-empty and compact values. As was the case with the demand mapping, the convex valuedness of η_j prevents the supply from "jumping". The next figures illustrate this possibility, where we represent a non-convex production set and the associated supply correspondence.

---

[8] As it was the case with consumers' restricted correspondences, precision would require to name the mappings $\widehat{\eta}_j$, $\widehat{\pi}_j$ differently, to make explicit the dependence of the parameter k. Here again we use this simpler notation.

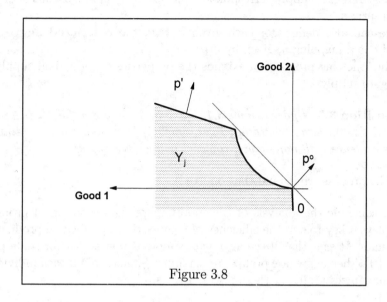

Figure 3.8

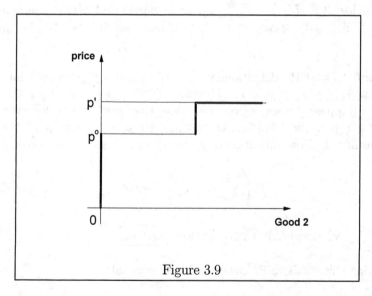

Figure 3.9

Let us now consider the aggregate behaviour of competitive firms.

Definition 3.9 *The **aggregate supply correspondence** is a mapping* $\eta :$
$\mathbb{R}_+^\ell - \{0\} \to Y$ *given by* $\eta(\mathbf{p}) \equiv \sum_{j=1}^n \eta_j(\mathbf{p})$.

The aggregate supply correspondence is obviously homogeneous of degree zero in prices.

We can also define, for each given $k > 0$, the **restricted aggregate supply** as a mapping $\widehat{\eta}$, given by $\widehat{\eta}(\mathbf{p}) = \sum_{j=1}^{n} \widehat{\eta}_j(\mathbf{p})$.

The following proposition extends the properties of individual supply to aggregate supply.

Proposition 3.5 *Under axioms 3.1, 3.2, 3.3, 3.5 and 3.6, for all* $\mathbf{p} \in \mathbb{R}_{+}^{\ell} - \{\mathbf{0}\}$, *all* $k > 0$, *the restricted aggregate supply* $\widehat{\eta}$ *is an upper hemicontinuous correspondence with non-empty, compact and convex values.*

(The proof is trivial and thus omitted).

To conclude the analysis of the supply mapping we present a property that plays a key role in the efficiency of competitive equilibria in production economies. It says that if the aggregate supply is non-empty for some $\mathbf{p}^* \in \mathbb{R}_{+}^{\ell} - \{\mathbf{0}\}$, then aggregate profits are maximized if and only if each individual firm maximizes profits at these prices. Formally:

Proposition 3.6 *Let* $Y = \sum_{j=1}^{n} Y_j$, *and suppose that* $\eta(\mathbf{p}^*)$ *is non-empty, for* $\mathbf{p}^* \in \mathbb{R}_{+}^{\ell} - \{\mathbf{0}\}$. *Then,* $\mathbf{y}^* \in \eta(\mathbf{p}^*)$ *if and only if* $\mathbf{p}^*\mathbf{y}^* \geq \mathbf{p}^*\mathbf{y}$, *for all* $\mathbf{y} \in Y$.

Proof.   ($\Longrightarrow$) By definition, $\mathbf{y}^* \in \eta(\mathbf{p}^*)$ implies $\mathbf{y}_j^* \in \eta_j(\mathbf{p}^*)$ for all j, that is, $\mathbf{p}^*\mathbf{y}_j^* \geq \mathbf{p}^*\mathbf{y}_j, \forall \mathbf{y}_j \in Y_j$. Therefore, $\mathbf{p}^*\mathbf{y}^* \geq \mathbf{p}^*\mathbf{y}$, for all $\mathbf{y} \in Y$.

($\Longleftarrow$) Suppose, by way of contradiction, that $\mathbf{p}^*\mathbf{y}^* \geq \mathbf{p}^*\mathbf{y}$ for all $\mathbf{y} \in Y$, with $\mathbf{y}^* \notin \eta(\mathbf{p}^*)$. By definition, there will exist $\mathbf{y}_h' \in Y_h$ with $\mathbf{p}^*\mathbf{y}_h' > \mathbf{p}^*\mathbf{y}_h^*$, for some firm h. Now substituting $\mathbf{y}_h^*$ by $\mathbf{y}_h'$ in the aggregate vector $\mathbf{y}^*$ we get:

$$\mathbf{p}^* \left(\sum_{j \neq h} \mathbf{y}_j^* + \mathbf{y}_h' \right) > \mathbf{p}^*\mathbf{y}^*$$

with $\left(\sum_{j \neq h} \mathbf{y}_j^* + \mathbf{y}_h' \right) \in Y$. Contradiction. $\boxed{\text{Q.e.d.}}$

Linking this result to Proposition 3.1 we conclude:

Corollary 3.2 *Let* $\mathbf{y}^* \in \eta(\mathbf{p}^*)$. *Then* $\mathbf{y}^*$ *is efficient in* Y.

This corollary gives an important property of competitive markets: It ensures that when individual firms maximize profits at given prices, the resulting aggregate production is efficient in the aggregate production set. This is not a general property. The reader is kindly requested to prove the following:

Claim 3.4 *Suppose that Y_j satisfies axioms 3.1 to 3.6, for all $j = 1, 2, ..., n$, and let $(\mathbf{y}_j)_{j=1}^n$ stand for a collection of production plans, each of which belongs to the boundary of Y_j (and is thus efficient, according to Proposition 3.2). It may be the case that $\sum_{j=1}^n \mathbf{y}_j$ is a point in the interior of $\sum_{j=1}^n Y_j$.*

This is to be interpreted as a warning: when firms do not behave as profit maximizers at given prices, aggregate production efficiency is not guaranteed, even if each firm chooses an individually efficient production plan. Hence Pareto efficiency is at stake.

Neither the last Proposition nor its Corollary depend on the axioms established above, as we only require each individual supply mapping to be non-empty at prices $\mathbf{p}^*$. Yet it should be noted that it is implicitly assumed that the supply mappings depend *only* on market prices. We are therefore discarding the presence of externalities, input restrictions or other conditioning variables. When these are present, the efficiency of aggregate production may not hold.

3.5.3 The inverse supply mapping

The preceding analysis is based on the idea that a competitive firm j will agree to produce a vector $\mathbf{y}_j^* \in Y_j$ at prices $\mathbf{p} \in \mathbb{R}^\ell - \{\mathbf{0}\}$ provided $\mathbf{p}\mathbf{y}_j^* \geq \mathbf{p}\mathbf{y}_j$, for all $\mathbf{y}_j \in Y_j$. We have identified this behaviour as "profit maximization at given prices". Let us approach that idea from a different perspective.

We know that profit maximization implies the selection of efficient production plans. Moreover, under axioms 3.1 and 3.2 the set of efficient production plans coincides with the boundary of Y_j. The supply mapping therefore is actually a correspondence from the price space $\mathbb{R}^\ell - \{\mathbf{0}\}$ into ∂Y_j. Taking this into account, we can define the inverse supply mapping as follows:

Definition 3.10 *The **inverse supply correspondence** is a mapping $\Phi_j : \partial Y_j \rightarrow \mathbb{R}^\ell - \{\mathbf{0}\}$, given by:*

$$\Phi_j(\mathbf{y}_j) = \{\mathbf{p} \in \mathbb{P} \ / \ \mathbf{p}\mathbf{y}_j \geq \mathbf{p}\mathbf{y}_j', \ \forall \ \mathbf{y}_j' \in Y_j\}$$

For each point $\mathbf{y}_j$ in the boundary of Y_j, the inverse supply correspondence $\Phi_j(\mathbf{y}_j)$ selects those prices that support $\mathbf{y}_j$ as a profit maximizing production plan. Under axioms 3.1 and 3.2, ∂Y_j coincides with the set of weakly efficient production plans. Moreover, if Y_j is also convex, $\Phi_j(\mathbf{y}_j)$ is non-empty, closed and convex. That is, under axioms 3.1 to 3.4, any efficient production plan can be supported as a competitive supply by a price system. It can also be shown that this is an upper hemicontinuous correspondence (we discuss this point later on).

Note that the inverse supply correspondence is a more flexible way of describing the behaviour of competitive firms. This behaviour is now characterized by those pairs $(\mathbf{y}_j, \mathbf{p}) \in \partial Y_j \times \mathbb{R}_+^\ell - \{\mathbf{0}\}$ such that $\mathbf{p} \in \Phi_j(\mathbf{p})$ (i.e. there is no other $\mathbf{y}_j' \in Y_j$ that yields higher profits at prices $\mathbf{p}$). Hence, one does not have to assume price taking behaviour. Instead, the jth firm can be viewed as setting prices and taking quantities as given. Or, more generally, as choosing pairs of production plans and price vectors that satisfy the profit maximization principle. What makes this criterion of choice specific to competitive firms, as opposed to other market regimes, is that the jth firm takes the whole Y_j as its opportunity set. That is, the competitive nature of the firm derives from the fact that it applies the profit principle *unconditionally*, whereas price taking behaviour is not an essential feature.

To understand the relevance of this point, note that competitive behaviour implies a very specific relationship between production and prices. Indeed, $\Phi_j(\mathbf{y}_j)$ is the normal cone to Y_j at the boundary point $\mathbf{y}_j$ (i.e. the set of vectors that are perpendicular to Y_j at $\mathbf{y}_j$). This means, from an economic viewpoint, that commodities are priced according to their "marginal contributions", as the slope of the hyperplane tangent to Y_j at $\mathbf{y}_j$ describes the jth firm's marginal rates of transformation at this point. Hence, competitive behaviour induces firms to pay the "real worth" of the inputs they use, and to sell their outputs according to their relative costs. In particular, when production sets exhibit constant returns to scale profit maximization implies zero profits (otherwise increasing the scale of operations would yield higher profits). When the returns to scale are strictly decreasing, equilibrium profits may be positive. Let us recall here that, in the absence of externalities, the lack of additivity was related to the existence of some implicit limiting factors (implicit inputs that cannot be replicated). Hence the firm's profits can be interpreted as the price of these scarce factors.

This suggests that unconditional profit maximization at given prices can be regarded as the outcome of market competition, in the sense that the individual firm has no bargaining power so that it cannot appropriate any rent derived from the use of the available technology. Therefore, choosing a production plan that maximizes profits unconditionally has the effect of reducing the profits to the minimum value that is compatible with the firms' incentives. This is a vague statement for the time being. We shall see later that it can be given a precise content.

Summarizing: The inverse supply mapping allows us to have further insights into the nature of competitive equilibria; namely, profit maximization at given prices is a reduced model that expresses more primitive notions on the nature of competitive markets. This conclusion emerges from two interdependent ideas. The first is that price taking behaviour is not an essential feature of competitive equilibrium. The second is that (unconditional) maximum profits implies no extra profits.

Remark 3.4 *The inverse supply mapping is a particular case of what will be called, in chapter 5, a "pricing rule". Allowing for different ways of choosing pairs* $(\mathbf{y}_j, \mathbf{p})$ *(i.e. different mappings* Φ_j*) we can describe alternative rules of behaviour. This flexibility is required when production sets are not convex.*

3.6 References to the literature

The reader is referred to the classical works of Koopmans (1957), Debreu (1959), Arrow & Hahn (1971), the survey by Nadiri (1982), and Mas-Colell *et al.* (1995) for a more detailed study of production theory. Varian (1992) provides a detailed analysis of production and cost functions.

The work of Sraffa (1926) is still an interesting reading, on the nature of returns to scale in a competitive economy. Ichiishi (1993) studies the strategic nature of the firm. The reader can also consult the monograph of Bobzin (1998), dealing with the presence of indivisibilities.

Chapter 4

COMPETITIVE EQUILIBRIUM

4.1 Introduction

This chapter is devoted to the analysis of *competitive markets*, that is, markets in which consumers and firms behave as payoff maximizers at given prices. The next sections provide a positive answer to the old question concerning the capability of prices and markets to coordinate economic activity in a decentralized framework. It will be shown that, under a set of well specified assumptions, markets are in themselves adequate institutions for the efficient allocation of resources. This may be called the *Invisible Hand Theorem*, which summarizes the most relevant features of competitive markets: competitive equilibria constitute a non-empty subset of the set of efficient allocations.

A competitive equilibrium is a situation in which all agents are simultaneously realizing their plans, for a given vector of market prices. The *existence* of a competitive equilibrium will be obtained by applying a fixed point argument. The strategy of the proof consists of identifying the set of competitive equilibria with the set of fixed points of a suitable mapping, and making use of Kakutani's fixed point theorem. For this approach to work, one has to be able to ensure that the set of attainable allocations of the economy is non-empty (and bounded), and that the excess demand mapping is an upper hemicontinuous correspondence, with non-empty, compact and convex values. The convexity of preferences and of consumption and production sets allows one to obtain an excess demand mapping with such properties, when agents behave as payoff maximizers at given prices.

An efficient allocation is a situation in which it is not feasible to make all consumers better off. It will be shown that competitive equilibria yield efficient allocations (First Welfare Theorem), and also that efficient allocations can be realized as competitive equilibria (Second Welfare Theorem). The *efficiency* of competitive equilibrium derives from two basic features. The first one refers, again, to the fact that agents behave as payoff maximizers at given prices, so that each agent equates her marginal rates of transformation to the relative prices (and hence, in equilibrium, they become equal for *all agents*). The second one is that *each variable that affects the payoff function of an individual is associated with a price, and belongs to her choice set*, so that prices turn out to be sufficient information, enabling the exploitation of all benefits derived from production and exchange.[1] The equalization of prices and marginal rates of transformation is a necessary condition for optimality, which under the assumption of convex preferences and choice sets, turns out to be sufficient as well.

Remark 4.1 *Note that if* **p** *is a candidate for an equilibrium price vector, then all agents' payoff functions must be well-defined at these prices. Under the assumptions on consumers and firms established before, which we shall also use here, we know that: (a)* **p** $= \mathbf{0}$ *cannot be an equilibrium price vector, because individual demands are not defined in this case; and (b) If* **p** $\in \mathbb{R}^\ell$ *contains some negative entry, then the firms' supplies will not be defined (as firms would be able to increase profits without limits). Hence, we shall take the set* $\mathbb{R}^\ell_+ - \{\mathbf{0}\}$ *as the largest price space in which to look for equilibrium prices.*

4.2   The model

4.2.1   Economies and allocations

We have presented, in chapters 2 and 3, the consumption and production sets as the relevant choice sets for consumers and firms, respectively. In order to fully describe the economic possibilities of a society, we have to introduce an additional element: the initial endowments. This is a vector of commodities $\omega \in \mathbb{R}^\ell$ which describes the resources that are already available: land, buildings, machinery, natural resources, commodities already produced and stored, etc. This is the inheritance of the past and the basis for present production and exchange. A society's economic possibilities can be regarded as the combination of three different types of resources: material resources

---

[1]Note that this condition calls for the absence of externalities, the existence of complete markets and the presence of well informed agents.

(the collection of commodities ω already available), technological resources (summarized by firms' production sets), and human resources (implicit in consumers' consumption sets).

An **economy** is composed of the following elements:

(i) m consumers, characterized by their consumption sets X_i and their utility functions u_i.

(ii) n firms, characterized by their production sets Y_j.

(iii) The available resources $\omega \in \mathbb{R}^\ell$.

This can be summarized as

$$E = [(X_i, u_i)_{i=1}^m, (Y_j)_{j=1}^n, \omega]$$

Now consider the following definitions:

Definition 4.1 *An **allocation** is a point $[(\mathbf{x}_i)_{i=1}^m, (\mathbf{y}_j)_{j=1}^n]$ in the set $\prod_{i=1}^m X_i \times \prod_{j=1}^n Y_j$.*

An allocation is a collection of actions, one for each agent, within their respective choice sets (hence a point in $\mathbb{R}^{\ell(m+n)}$).

Definition 4.2 *A point $[(\mathbf{x}_i)_{i=1}^m, (\mathbf{y}_j)_{j=1}^n] \in \mathbb{R}^{\ell(m+n)}$ is an **attainable allocation** if:*
(a) $[(\mathbf{x}_i)_{i=1}^m, (\mathbf{y}_j)_{j=1}^n]$ is an allocation.
(b) $\sum_{i=1}^m \mathbf{x}_i \le \sum_{j=1}^n \mathbf{y}_j + \omega$.

We say that an allocation is attainable (or *feasible*) for an economy, if the aggregate consumption does not exceed the sum of the aggregate production plus the available resources.

We say that a consumption plan $\mathbf{x}_i$ is **attainable for the ith consumer** if there is a feasible allocation $[(\mathbf{x}_i)_{i=1}^m, (\mathbf{y}_j)_{j=1}^n]$ containing $\mathbf{x}_i$ as its ith co-ordinate vector. Similarly, we say that a production plan is **attainable for the jth firm** if there is an attainable allocation $[(\mathbf{x}_i)_{i=1}^m, (\mathbf{y}_j)_{j=1}^n]$ containing $\mathbf{y}_j$ as its jth coordinate. The set of attainable allocations will be denoted by Ω, that is:

$$\Omega = \left\{ [(\mathbf{x}_i)_{i=1}^m, (\mathbf{y}_j)_{j=1}^n] \in \Pi_{i=1}^m X_i \times \Pi_{j=1}^n Y_j \ / \ \sum_{i=1}^m \mathbf{x}_i \le \sum_{j=1}^n \mathbf{y}_j + \omega \right\}$$

The projection of Ω on X_i, Y_j gives us the ith consumer's set of **attainable consumptions**, denoted by X_i^A, and the jth firm's set of **attainable productions**, denoted by Y_j^A, respectively.

Remark 4.2 *It can be shown that, under standard assumptions, the set Ω is compact. We analyze this point in detail in chapter 12.*

4.2.2   Private ownership economies

We refer to *private ownership economies* as those in which consumers own both the available resources and the firms, and the public sector plays no role in the allocation of resources (other than ensuring the property rights). In order to model this family of economies, let $\omega_i \in \mathbb{R}^\ell$ denote the ith consumer's initial holdings, with $\omega = \sum_{i=1}^m \omega_i$. And let θ_{ij} stand for the fraction of the jth firm owned by the ith consumer. This represents an entitlement to, precisely, that share of the jth firm's profits. By definition, $0 \leq \theta_{ij} \leq 1$ for all i, j, with $\sum_{i=1}^m \theta_{ij} = 1$, for all j.

A private ownership economy can be summarized as:

$$E_{pp} = \left[(X_i, u_i, \omega_i)_{i=1}^m, (Y_j)_{j=1}^n, (\theta_{ij}) \right]$$

Let E_{pp} be a private ownership economy. For a given $\mathbf{p} \in \mathbb{R}_+^\ell - \{\mathbf{0}\}$, the jth firm determines its supply $\eta_j(\mathbf{p})$ by choosing those production plans that maximize profits. The associated profits are $\pi_j(\mathbf{p}) = \mathbf{p}\mathbf{y}_j$, for $\mathbf{y}_j \in \eta_j(\mathbf{p})$, $j = 1, 2, ..., n$. Then, the ith consumer's wealth at prices $\mathbf{p}$ is given by:

$$r_i(\mathbf{p}) = \mathbf{p}\omega_i + \sum_{j=1}^n \theta_{ij}\pi_j(\mathbf{p})$$

that is, the ith consumer's wealth is given by the sum of the worth of her initial endowments plus the fraction of total profits determined by the numbers (θ_{ij}).

Given these prices and wealth, the ith consumer selects consumption plans that maximize utility within the budget set:

$$\beta_i(\mathbf{p}) = \{\mathbf{x}_i \in X_i \ / \ \mathbf{p}\mathbf{x}_i \leq \mathbf{p}\omega_i + \sum_{j=1}^n \theta_{ij}\pi_j(\mathbf{p})\}$$

Clearly $\beta_i : \mathbb{R}_+^\ell \to X_i$ is homogeneous of degree zero in prices, because the supply mappings have this property..

The **demand correspondence** is now defined as a mapping

$$\xi_i : \mathbb{R}_+^\ell - \{\mathbf{0}\} \to X_i$$

such that, for each $\mathbf{p} \in \mathbb{R}_+^\ell - \{\mathbf{0}\}$, selects the points in $\beta_i(\mathbf{p})$ that maximize utility. This is also a correspondence homogeneous of degree zero.

Remark 4.3 *Note that rigor would require us to rename the budget correspondence and the demand correspondence differently. This is so because* *these are mappings that now apply $\mathbb{R}_+^\ell - \{0\}$ into X_i, whereas in chapter 2 they were defined as mappings that apply $\mathbb{R}_+^\ell - \{0\} \times \mathbb{R}$ into X_i (the wealth was taken to be a parameter). Yet, we prefer to keep the same symbols in order to minimize notation.*

The aggregate behaviour of the economy can be summarized by an excess demand, a mapping defined as follows:

Definition 4.3 *The **excess demand correspondence** is a mapping $\zeta :$ $\mathbb{R}_+^\ell - \{0\} \to \mathbb{R}^\ell$ given by:*

$$\zeta(\mathbf{p}) = \sum_{i=1}^m \xi_i(\mathbf{p}) - \sum_{j=1}^n \eta_j(\mathbf{p}) - \{\omega\}$$

Let $\mathbf{z}$ be a point in $\zeta(\mathbf{p})$. Then $z_k > 0$ tells us that the aggregate demand for the kth commodity, at prices $\mathbf{p}$, exceeds the sum of the associated supply plus the available resources (and viceversa, if $z_k < 0$). A value $z_k = 0$ expresses the equality between (net) demand and supply for this commodity, that is, the market for the kth commodity is in equilibrium at these prices.

Note that the excess demand is homogeneous of degree zero, i.e. $\zeta(\lambda \mathbf{p}) = \zeta(\mathbf{p})$ for all $\lambda > 0$, because all demand and supply mappings have this property. Hence, for any price vector $\mathbf{p} \in \mathbb{R}_+^\ell - \{0\}$, one can always take $\lambda = 1/\sum_{k=1}^\ell p_k$ (a positive number as $\sum_{k=1}^\ell p_k > 0$), and define $\mathbf{p}' = \lambda \mathbf{p}$ (a price vector that satisfies $\sum_{k=1}^\ell p'_k = 1$, by construction). This allows us to substitute the price space $\mathbb{R}_+^\ell - \{0\}$ by the set:

$$\mathbb{P} = \{\mathbf{p} \in \mathbb{R}_+^\ell \ / \ \sum_{k=1}^\ell p_k = 1\}$$

This is the *normalized price set* (also called the *price simplex*), a non-empty compact and convex set.

We take the simplex $\mathbb{P}$ as the price space in the sequel.

4.2.3   Equilibrium

An equilibrium is a situation in which all agents are simultaneously realizing their plans at given prices. Namely, every consumer chooses the best consumption plan she can afford, all firms select production plans that maximize profits, and all these actions are compatible with the available resources.

Formally:

Definition 4.4 *A **competitive equilibrium** for a private ownership economy,* $E_{pp} = \left[(X_i, u_i, \omega_i)_{i=1}^m, (Y_j)_{j=1}^n, (\theta_{ij}) \right]$, *is a price vector* $\mathbf{p}^* \in \mathbb{P}$ *and an allocation* $\left[(\mathbf{x}_i^*)_{i=1}^m, (\mathbf{y}_j^*)_{j=1}^n \right]$ *such that:*
(α) For all $i = 1, 2, ..., m$, $\mathbf{x}_i^* \in \xi_i(\mathbf{p}^*)$.
(β) For all $j = 1, 2, ..., n$, $\mathbf{y}_j^* \in \eta_j(\mathbf{p}^*)$.
(γ) $\sum_{i=1}^m \mathbf{x}_i^* \le \sum_{j=1}^n \mathbf{y}_j^* + \omega$, *with* $p_k^* = 0$ *when the inequality is strict.*

A competitive equilibrium is a situation in which: (a) All consumers maximize utility within their budget sets at prices $\mathbf{p}^*$; (b) All firms maximize profits at $\mathbf{p}^*$ within their production sets; and (c) All markets clear (i.e. $\left[(\mathbf{x}_i^*)_{i=1}^m, (\mathbf{y}_j^*)_{j=1}^n \right]$ is an attainable allocation with $\mathbf{p}^* \mathbf{z}^* = 0$, for $\mathbf{z}^* = \sum_{i=1}^m \mathbf{x}_i^* - \sum_{j=1}^n \mathbf{y}_j^* - \omega$). Note that we implicitly assume that those amounts of commodities that nobody wants can simply be ignored; this is allowed by the free-disposal assumption (namely, the economy can get rid off those goods in excess supply at no cost).

4.3   Assumptions and consequences

Now let us consider the following axioms, which we shall discuss in the inverse order in which they are presented:

Axiom 4.1 *For all* $i = 1, 2, ..., m$,
(i) $X_i \subset \mathbb{R}^\ell$ *is a non-empty, closed convex set, bounded from below.*
(ii) $u_i : X_i \to \mathbb{R}$ *is continuous, quasi-concave$^+$ and non-satiable utility function.*
(iii) $\omega_i \in X_i$, *and there exists* $\mathbf{x}_i^0 \in X_i$ *with* $\mathbf{x}_i^0 << \omega_i$.

Axiom 4.2 *For all* $j = 1, 2, ..., n$,
(i) Y_j *is a closed subset of* $\mathbb{R}^\ell$.
(ii) $Y_j - \mathbb{R}_+^\ell \subset Y_j$.
(iii) $\mathbf{0} \in Y_j$.
(iv) Y_j *is convex.*

Axiom 4.3 *The set of attainable allocations* Ω *is compact.*

Axiom 4.3 directly postulates that the set of attainable allocations is closed and bounded. This is a property that can be derived from axioms 4.1 and 4.2, together with the irreversibility assumption $Y \cap -Y = \{0\}$, as will be discussed later on. It conveys the idea that the economy is bounded, in the sense that it is not possible to obtain unlimited amounts of commodities from limited resources.

Axiom 4.2 corresponds to the modelization of competitive firms in chapter 3. It is assumed that production sets are closed, convex and comprehensive subsets of $\mathbb{R}^\ell$, and that $\mathbf{0} \in Y_j$ (i.e. inactivity is possible at no cost). From this it follows that firms' equilibrium profits are always non-negative ($\pi_j(\mathbf{p}) \geq 0$ for all j, all $\mathbf{p} \in \mathbb{P}$). Moreover, axioms 4.2 and 4.3 imply that there exists a scalar $k > 0$, such that every attainable production set Y_j^A belongs to the interior of the "square" $[-k\mathbf{e}, k\mathbf{e}]$ (where $\mathbf{e}$ is the unit vector in $\mathbb{R}_+^\ell$).

Define $\widehat{Y}_j = Y_j \cap [-k\mathbf{e}, k\mathbf{e}]$, a non-empty, compact and convex set, with $Y_j^A \subsetneq \widehat{Y}_j$. Let $\widehat{\eta}_j(\mathbf{p})$ denote the **restricted supply correspondence**, that is, $\widehat{\eta}_j(\mathbf{p})$ is the set of production plans that maximize profits at prices $\mathbf{p}$ in $\widehat{Y}_j$. Call $\widehat{\pi}_j$ the associated (restricted) profit function. It was proven in Proposition 3.5 that, for all $\mathbf{p} \in \mathbb{P}$, the restricted supply mapping $\widehat{\eta}_j$ is an upper hemicontinuous correspondence, with non-empty, compact and convex values. Hence, $\widehat{\pi}_j$ is a continuous function for all $\mathbf{p} \in \mathbb{P}$, with $\widehat{\pi}_j(\mathbf{p}) \geq 0$.

Parts (i) and (ii) of axiom 4.1 correspond to the standard modelization of consumers, developed in chapter 2: a closed and convex choice set bounded from below, and a preference relation that satisfies completeness, transitivity, continuity, convexity and non-satiation. Part (iii) is sometimes called the *survival axiom*. The basic idea is that the ith consumer is able to survive without participating in production or exchange activities, because $\omega_i \in X_i$ means that she can always consume her initial endowments. Indeed, it says more: the ith consumer can survive even if her initial holdings were slightly decreased.

Part (iii) of axiom 4.1 is a very strong assumption. Yet it plays a relevant role when combined with other axioms. In particular:

(a) Under axioms 4.1 and 4.2, $r_i(\mathbf{p}) = \mathbf{p}\omega_i + \sum_{j=1}^n \theta_{ij}\pi_j(\mathbf{p}) > \min \mathbf{p}X_i$ for all $\mathbf{p}$ in $\mathbb{P}$ (as $r_i(\mathbf{p}) \geq \mathbf{p}\omega_i \geq \min \mathbf{p}X_i$, because $\pi_j(\mathbf{p}) \geq 0$).

(b) From this it follows that, if $\mathbf{x}_i^*$ is a point in the demand set, then $u_i(\mathbf{x}_i^*) \geq u_i(\omega_i)$; hence, in equilibrium, no consumer can be worse-off than with her initial endowments.

(c) $\Omega \neq \emptyset$, because the allocation $[(\omega_i)_{i=1}^m, (\mathbf{0})_{j=1}^n]$ is attainable.

Note that quasi-concavity[+] and non-satiation imply that $\mathbf{p}\mathbf{x}_i = \mathbf{p}\omega_i + \sum_{j=1}^n \theta_{ij}\pi_j(\mathbf{p})$. Summing over i, and taking into account that $\sum_{i=1}^m \omega_i = \omega$, and that $\pi_j(\mathbf{p}) = \mathbf{p}\mathbf{y}_j$, for $\mathbf{y}_j \in \eta_j(\mathbf{p})$, we obtain:

$$\mathbf{p}\sum_{i=1}^m \mathbf{x}_i = \mathbf{p}\omega_i + \sum_{i=1}^m \sum_{j=1}^n \theta_{ij}\mathbf{p}\mathbf{y}_j$$

As $\sum_{i=1}^m \theta_{ij} = 1$, for all j, it follows that $\mathbf{p}\sum_{i=1}^m \mathbf{x}_i = \mathbf{p}\omega_i + \sum_{j=1}^n \mathbf{p}\mathbf{y}_j$.

Or, writing this equality differently, $\mathbf{p}\left[\sum_{i=1}^{m}\mathbf{x}_i - \sum_{i=1}^{m}\omega_i - \sum_{j=1}^{n}\mathbf{y}_j\right] = 0$, where the expression in brackets is the excess demand mapping associated with these prices. It follows therefore that $\mathbf{pz} = 0$, for all $\mathbf{p} \in \mathbb{P}$, all $\mathbf{z} \in \zeta(\mathbf{p})$. This property is known as the **Walras Law** and tells us that the worth of the excess demand is always equal to zero. When $\mathbf{p} >> \mathbf{0}$ and $z_k < 0$ for some commodity k, there must be some other commodity t for which $z_t > 0$. The Walras Law also says that if $z_k = 0$ for $k = 1, 2, ..., \ell - 1$, then $z_\ell = 0$. In words: $\ell - 1$ markets clear if and only if the whole set of ℓ markets does so. Then, a competitive equilibrium results when there is a price vector $\mathbf{p}^* \in \mathbb{P}$ such that $\mathbf{z}^* \leq \mathbf{0}$, for some $\mathbf{z}^* \in \zeta(\mathbf{p}^*)$, with $\mathbf{p}^*\mathbf{z}^* = 0$.

Under axioms 4.1 and 4.3, we can find a scalar $k > 0$ such that the ith consumer's set of attainable consumption plans, X_i^A, belongs to the interior of the square $[-k\mathbf{e}, k\mathbf{e}]$, for all i. Without loss of generality, we can take this number k to be the same as that which was used for production sets previously. Define then $\widehat{X}_i = X_i \cap [-k\mathbf{e}, k\mathbf{e}]$. By construction $\widehat{X}_i$ is a non-empty compact and convex set, with $\omega_i \in \widehat{X}_i$, and $X_i^A \subsetneq \widehat{X}_i$. Call $\widehat{\xi}_i(\mathbf{p})$ the correspondence that associates the solutions to the following problem to each price vector $\mathbf{p} \in \mathbb{R}_+^\ell - \{\mathbf{0}\}$:

$$Max \quad u_i(\mathbf{x}_i) \\ s.t. \quad \mathbf{px}_i \leq \mathbf{p}\omega_i + \sum_{j=1}^{n} \theta_{ij}\widehat{\pi}_j(\mathbf{p}) \\ \mathbf{x}_i \in \widehat{X}_i \left.\right\}$$

that is, $\widehat{\xi}_i$ is the **restricted demand correspondence** for the ith consumer. Then the following result is obtained:

Proposition 4.1 *Suppose that axioms 4.1, 4.2 and 4.3 hold. Then, for all $\mathbf{p} \in \mathbb{P}$, the ith consumer's restricted demand $\widehat{\xi}_i$, is an upper hemicontinuous correspondence, with non-empty compact and convex values.*

(The proof can be easily derived from the results in chapter 2).

We leave the proof of following claims to the reader. Claims 4.1 and 4.2 refer to the restricted demand correspondence (and are formulated in the understanding that axiom 4.3 holds). Claim 4.3 refers to the demand correspondence defined on the whole set X_i.

Claim 4.1 *Suppose that parts (i) and (ii) of axiom 4.1 hold, but ω_i belongs to the boundary of X_i. Then, for all $\mathbf{p} \in \mathbb{R}_+^\ell - \{\mathbf{0}\}$, $\widehat{\xi}_i(\mathbf{p})$ is non-empty compact and convex. Yet $\widehat{\xi}_i$ may not be upper hemicontinuous.*

Claim 4.2 *Suppose that axiom 4.1 holds. Then, for all* $\mathbf{p} \in \mathbb{R}_+^\ell$, $\widehat{\xi}_i(\mathbf{p})$ *is non-empty compact and convex. Yet* $\widehat{\xi}_i$ *is not upper hemicontinuous at* $\mathbf{p} = 0$.

Claim 4.3 *Suppose that axiom 4.1 holds. Then, for all* $\mathbf{p} \in int\mathbb{R}_+^\ell$, ξ_i *is an upper hemicontinuous correspondence with non-empty, compact and convex values.*

We can define the **restricted excess demand correspondence** as a mapping $\widehat{\zeta} : \mathbb{P} \to \sum_{i=1}^m \widehat{X}_i - \sum_{j=1}^n \widehat{Y}_j - \{\omega\}$, given by:

$$\widehat{\zeta}(\mathbf{p}) = \sum_{i=1}^m \widehat{\xi}_i(\mathbf{p}) - \sum_{j=1}^n \widehat{\eta}_j(\mathbf{p}) - \{\omega\}$$

The properties discussed above with respect to demand and supply mappings, together with the Walras Law, induce the following result:

Proposition 4.2 *Under axioms 4.1, 4.2 and 4.3, the restricted excess demand correspondence* $\widehat{\zeta}$ *is upper-hemicontinuous, with non-empty, compact and convex values, with* $\mathbf{pz} = 0$, *for all* $\mathbf{p} \in \mathbb{P}$, $\mathbf{z} \in \widehat{\zeta}(\mathbf{p})$.

4.4 The existence of equilibrium

From a mathematical viewpoint, an equilibrium corresponds to the existence of a "zero" in the excess demand mapping; or, more precisely, to the existence of points $\mathbf{p}^* \in \mathbb{P}$, $\mathbf{z}^* \in \zeta(\mathbf{p}^*)$, such that $\mathbf{z}^* \leq \mathbf{0}$, with $\mathbf{p}^*\mathbf{z}^* = 0$ (which is equivalent to saying that $p_k^* = 0$ whenever $z_k^* < 0$). Thus we have to find appropriate values for a vector of ℓ variables, out of ℓ unknowns. The variables $\mathbf{z}$ describe the excess demand of each commodity, and the unknowns $\mathbf{p}$ are the market prices. Observe that there are only $\ell - 1$ independent variables, because the aggregate net demand is homogeneous of degree zero. But it is also the case that there are only $\ell - 1$ independent "equations" as the Walras Law asserts that $\mathbf{pz} = 0$ for all $\mathbf{p} \in \mathbb{P}$, $\mathbf{z} \in \zeta(\mathbf{p})$ (this means that one of these equations is a linear combination of the remaining $\ell - 1$).

Note that our objective is rather ambitious. We want to analyze the solvability of this system, without knowing the specifics of the excess demand mapping ζ. The only properties of this mapping that we can establish, from axioms 4.1, 4.2 and 4.3, are: (a) The restricted excess demand correspondence $\widehat{\zeta}$ is upper hemicontinuous, with non-empty, compact and convex values; and (b) ζ satisfies the Walras Law. Not surprisingly, this problem calls for the use a powerful mathematical technique: the fixed point theorem.

4.4.1   A preliminary result

The next theorem gives us the key result for the existence of equilibrium. It states that when the excess demand is an upper hemi-continuous correspondence with non-empty, compact and convex values, and satisfies the Walras Law, there exists a price vector that induces a feasible allocation in which all agents maximize their payoff functions at given prices. This theorem, however, is not directly applicable to our model, because the required properties of demand and supply mappings are not guaranteed. We shall see later on how this difficulty can be overcome.

Theorem 4.1 *Let $Z \subset \mathbb{R}^\ell$ be a compact convex set, and $\zeta : \mathbb{P} \to Z$ an upper hemi-continuous correspondence, with non-empty, compact and convex values. Suppose furthermore that for all $\mathbf{z} \in \zeta(\mathbf{p})$, all $\mathbf{p} \in \mathbb{P}$, $\mathbf{p}\mathbf{z} = 0$. Then, there exist $\mathbf{p}^* \in \mathbb{P}$, $\mathbf{z}^* \in \zeta(\mathbf{p}^*)$ such that $\mathbf{z}^* \leq \mathbf{0}$, with $p_k^* = 0$ if $z_k^* < 0$.*

Proof.   Define a mapping $g : Z \to \mathbb{P}$ as follows:

$$g(\mathbf{z}) = \{\mathbf{p} \in \mathbb{P} \;/\; \mathbf{p}\mathbf{z} \geq \mathbf{p}'\mathbf{z}, \; \forall \, \mathbf{p}' \in \mathbb{P}\}$$

This correspondence satisfies:

(a) $g(\mathbf{z})$ is non-empty, compact and convex, for all $\mathbf{z} \in Z \neq \emptyset$. Non-emptiness derives from Weierstrass' theorem (because $\mathbb{P}$ is compact and $\mathbf{p}\mathbf{z}$ is a continuous function). Boundedness is trivial as $\mathbb{P}$ is compact; closedness follows from the very definition of g. Finally, convexity is easily derived from the definition, as $\mathbb{P}$ is a convex set (i.e. $\mathbf{p}, \mathbf{p}' \in g(\mathbf{z})$ implies $\lambda\mathbf{p} + (1 - \lambda)\mathbf{p}' \in g(\mathbf{z})$, for all $\lambda \in [0, 1]$).

(b) g is upper hemi-continuous. To see this note that $\mathbf{p}\mathbf{z}$ is a continuous function in $\mathbb{P} \times Z$. Take now a correspondence $\delta : Z \to \mathbb{P}$, given by $\delta(\mathbf{z}) = \mathbb{P}$, for all $\mathbf{z} \in Z$. This is a constant correspondence and hence trivially continuous. Making use of the Maximum Theorem, we conclude that g is an upper hemicontinuous correspondence.

Now define a new mapping $\mu : Z \times \mathbb{P} \to Z \times \mathbb{P}$ as follows: For all $(\mathbf{z}, \mathbf{p}) \in Z \times \mathbb{P}$,

$$\mu(\mathbf{z}, \mathbf{p}) = \zeta(\mathbf{p}) \times g(\mathbf{z}).$$

Note that $Z \times \mathbb{P}$ is a non-empty, compact convex set, since both Z and $\mathbb{P}$ do have these properties. Moreover, μ is an upper hemicontinuous correspondence with non-empty, compact and convex values, as both g and ζ do have these properties. We can apply Kakutani's fixed point theorem[2] which

---

[2]Kakutani's Theorem: "Let K be a non-empty, compact and convex subset of $\mathbb{R}^\ell$, and $\Gamma : K \to K$ an upper hemicontinuous correspondence, with non-emtpy, compact and convex values. Then, there exists a fixed-point $\mathbf{x}^* \in \Gamma(\mathbf{x}^*)$."

ensures the existence of a point $(\mathbf{z}^*, \mathbf{p}^*) \in \mu(\mathbf{z}^*, \mathbf{p}^*)$. By construction this means that $\mathbf{p}^* \in g(\mathbf{z}^*)$ and $\mathbf{z}^* \in \zeta(\mathbf{p}^*)$; in particular,

$$0 = \mathbf{p}^*\mathbf{z}^* \geq \mathbf{p}\mathbf{z}^*, \forall \, \mathbf{p} \in \mathbb{P}$$

(because $\mathbf{p}\mathbf{z} = 0$ for all $\mathbf{z} \in \zeta(\mathbf{p})$, all $\mathbf{p} \in \mathbb{P}$, by assumption). As $\mathbf{p} \geq \mathbf{0}$ for all $\mathbf{p}$ in $\mathbb{P}$ and $\mathbf{0} \notin \mathbb{P}$, it follows that $\mathbf{z}^* \leq 0$ (take simply the canonical vectors). Moreover, $z_k^* < 0$ implies $p_k^* = 0$ (otherwise $\mathbf{p}^*\mathbf{z}^* = 0$ would not hold). $\boxed{\text{Q.e.d.}}$

4.4.2 The existence result

Next, we shall prove the existence of equilibrium under axioms 4.1, 4.2 and 4.3. Observe that these axioms do not ensure the excess demand mapping to have the suitable properties that permit the use of a fixed point argument. For instance, the excess demand mapping may not be defined for all price vectors in the boundary of $\mathbb{P}$ (which will be the case when $p_k = 0$ corresponds to a commodity that is desirable for some consumer). To transform Theorem 4.1 into an equilibrium existence theorem, applicable under our axioms, we proceed as follows: Given an economy E_{pp} with m consumers and n firms, that satisfies axioms 4.1, 4.2 and 4.3, we construct an *artificial* economy $\widehat{E}_{pp}$ which is identical to the original one, except in that we restrict agents' choice sets to suitable compact subsets of $\mathbb{R}^\ell$. The excess demand correspondence associated with this artificial economy is an upper hemicontinuous correspondence, with non-empty, compact and convex values. Hence, we can apply Theorem 4.1 to this economy. We shall now show that the equilibrium so obtained is actually an equilibrium for the original economy E_{pp}.

Theorem 4.2 *Let E_{pp} be a private ownership economy satisfying axioms 4.1, 4.2 and 4.3. Then, a competitive equilibrium exists.*

Proof. Under axioms 4.1 to 4.3, there exists a large enough scalar $k > 0$ so that every attainable consumption and production set is contained in the interior of the square $[-k\mathbf{e}, k\mathbf{e}]$. We now construct now an artificial economy $\widehat{E}_{pp}$ as follows. For all $i = 1, 2, ..., m$, all $j = 1, 2, ..., n$, define $\widehat{X}_i = X_i \cap [-k\mathbf{e}, k\mathbf{e}]$, $\widehat{Y}_j = Y_j \cap [-k\mathbf{e}, k\mathbf{e}]$. These are compact convex sets, under the assumptions of the model. Call $\widehat{\xi}_i : \mathbb{P} \to \widehat{X}_i$, $\widehat{\eta}_j : \mathbb{P} \to \widehat{Y}_j$ the restricted demand and supply mappings, respectively; that is, $\widehat{\eta}_j(\mathbf{p})$ is the set of production plans that maximize profits at prices $\mathbf{p}$ in $\widehat{Y}_j$, and $\widehat{\xi}_i(\mathbf{p})$ is the set of consumption plans that maximize utility in $\widehat{X}_i$ subject to $\mathbf{p}\mathbf{x}_i \leq$

$\mathbf{p}\omega_i + \sum_{j=1}^{n} \theta_{ij}\widehat{\pi}_j(\mathbf{p})$. Let $\widehat{\zeta}$ stand for the associated restricted excess demand correspondence. As discussed above, under these axioms $\widehat{\zeta}$ is an upper hemi-continuous correspondence, with non-empty, compact and convex values, that satisfies the Walras Law. Note also that $Z = \sum_{i=1}^{m} \widehat{X}_i - \sum_{j=1}^{n} \widehat{Y}_j - \{\omega\}$ is a non-empty, compact convex set. Hence Theorem 4.1 applies; namely, there exists a competitive equilibrium $\{\mathbf{p}^*, [(\mathbf{x}_i^*)_{i=1}^{m}, (\mathbf{y}_j^*)_{j=1}^{n}]\}$ for this economy $\widehat{E}_{pp}$.

We now have to show that this equilibrium is actually an equilibrium for the original economy E_{pp}, that is, that parts $(\alpha), (\beta)$ and (γ) of the definition are satisfied.

First note that $[(\mathbf{x}_i^*)_{i=1}^{m}, (\mathbf{y}_j^*)_{j=1}^{n}]$ is an attainable allocation for the original economy, so that condition (γ) is satisfied. In particular, this implies that all $\mathbf{x}_i^*, \mathbf{y}_j^*$, for $i = 1, 2, ...m$, $j = 1, 2, ..., n$, are in the *interior* of the square $[-k\mathbf{e}, k\mathbf{e}]$.

Let us check now condition (β). We know that $\mathbf{y}_j^*$ maximizes profits at prices $\mathbf{p}^*$ in $\widehat{Y}_j$. Suppose, by way of contradiction, that $\mathbf{y}_j^*$ is not a profit maximizing production plan in Y_j. Then, there exists $\mathbf{y}_j' \in Y_j$ such that $\mathbf{p}^*\mathbf{y}_j' > \mathbf{p}^*\mathbf{y}_j^*$. As $\mathbf{y}_j^* \in \widehat{Y}_j$ is a point in the interior of $[-k\mathbf{e}, k\mathbf{e}]$, we can find a scalar $\lambda \in (0,1)$ large enough so that $\mathbf{y}_j'' = \lambda\mathbf{y}_j^* + (1 - \lambda)\mathbf{y}_j'$ belongs to the square $[-k\mathbf{e}, k\mathbf{e}]$. As Y_j is convex, it follows that $\mathbf{y}_j'' \in \widehat{Y}_j$ and also that $\mathbf{p}^*\mathbf{y}_j'' > \mathbf{p}^*\mathbf{y}_j^*$, a contradiction. Hence, $\mathbf{y}_j^*$ maximizes profits at prices $\mathbf{p}^*$ in Y_j.

To see that (α) also holds, note that $\mathbf{x}_i^*$ maximizes u_i over the set:

$$\widehat{\beta}_i(\mathbf{p}^*) = \{\mathbf{x}_i \in \widehat{X}_i \;/\; \mathbf{p}^*\mathbf{x}_i \leq \mathbf{p}^*\omega_i + \sum_{j=1}^{n} \theta_{ij}\mathbf{p}^*\mathbf{y}_j^*\}$$

where, as we have just shown, $\mathbf{p}^*\mathbf{y}_j^* = \pi_j(\mathbf{p}^*) = \widehat{\pi}_j(\mathbf{p}^*)$. Suppose that there exists $\mathbf{x}_i' \in X_i$ such that $u_i(\mathbf{x}_i') > u_i(\mathbf{x}_i^*)$ with $\mathbf{p}^*\mathbf{x}_i' \leq \mathbf{p}^*\omega_i + \sum_{j=1}^{n} \theta_{ij}\mathbf{p}^*\mathbf{y}_j^*$. As $\mathbf{x}_i^*$ is a point in the interior of $[-k\mathbf{e}, k\mathbf{e}]$, there exists $\lambda \in (0,1)$ such that $\mathbf{x}_i'' = \lambda\mathbf{x}_i^* + (1 - \lambda)\mathbf{x}_i'$ is a point in $[-k\mathbf{e}, k\mathbf{e}]$. As X_i is convex, $\mathbf{x}_i'' \in \widehat{X}_i$. Moreover, the convexity of preferences implies that $u_i(\mathbf{x}_i'') > u_i(\mathbf{x}_i^*)$. A contradiction. Hence $\mathbf{x}_i^*$ is a point in the ith consumer's demand of the original economy.

That concludes the proof. $\boxed{\text{Q.e.d.}}$

The existence of equilibrium establishes that competitive markets are institutions that are able to ensure that the production and exchange process, carried out by price taking agents, can be consistently realized in a decentralized way. Note, however, that from this result one cannot deduce that market forces *drive* the economy towards an equilibrium. Indeed, we know rather well *when* the existence of an equilibrium can be ensured, and know very little about *how* this happens (if indeed it happens) and how fast it does.

Remark 4.4 *When the behaviour of competitive firms is described in terms of inverse supply mappings (see the discussion in chapter 3), a competitive equilibrium is a price vector $\mathbf{p}^* \in \mathbb{P}$ and an allocation $[(\mathbf{x}_i^*)_{i=1}^m, (\mathbf{y}_j^*)_{j=1}^n]$ such that: (α') For all $i = 1, 2, ..., m$, $\mathbf{x}_i^* \in \xi_i(\mathbf{p}^*)$; (β') $\mathbf{p}^* \in \bigcap_{j=1}^n \Phi_j(\mathbf{y}_j^*)$; and (γ') $\sum_{i=1}^m \mathbf{x}_i^* \leq \sum_{j=1}^n \mathbf{y}_j^* + \omega$, with $p_k^* = 0$ when the inequality is strict. Parts (α') and (γ') coincide with (α) and (γ) in the previous definition. Part (β'), says that each firm chooses a competitive pair $(\mathbf{y}_j^*, \mathbf{p}^*)$, and that all firms "agree" on the prices at which commodities are sold.*

4.4.3 Equilibrium with abstract wealth functions

Consider an economy with m consumers and n competitive firms, similar to that in former sections, except in that the ith consumer's wealth is now given by an abstract function $r_i : \mathbb{P} \to \mathbb{R}$, that describes the ith consumer's wealth as a function of market prices. This extension permits one to treat market economies with a different system of property rights, or private ownership economies with taxes and transfers. It also allows us to relax the survival axiom.

An economy of this type can be summarized as:

$$E = [(X_i, u_i, r_i)_{i=1}^m, (Y_j)_{j=1}^n, \omega]$$

Consider now the following axioms:

Axiom 4.1' *For all $i = 1, 2, ..., m$: (i) $X_i \subset \mathbb{R}^\ell$ is a non-empty closed convex set bounded from below; (ii) $u_i : X_i \to \mathbb{R}$ is continuous, quasi-concave$^+$ and locally non-satiable; (iii) r_i is continuous with $r_i(\mathbf{p}) > \min \mathbf{p} X_i$. Moreover, $\sum_{i=1}^m r_i(\mathbf{p}) = \mathbf{p}\omega + \sum_{j=1}^n \pi_j(\mathbf{p})$.*

Axiom 4.1' generalizes axiom 4.1 above. Parts (i) and (ii) are identical, and part (iii) is an extension of the corresponding requirement there. Finally, it is also assumed that total wealth equals the worth of the aggregate endowments plus total profits at prices $\mathbf{p}$. This ensures that the Walras Law holds. Two examples of wealth mappings satisfying this restriction are the following:

Example 4.1 $r_i(\mathbf{p}) = \lambda_i [\mathbf{p}\omega + \sum_{j=1}^n \pi_j(\mathbf{p})]$, *with $\lambda_i > 0$, $\sum_{i=1}^m \lambda_i = 1$ (the ith consumer gets a constant fraction of the worth of aggregate resources plus total profits).*

Example 4.2 $r_i(\mathbf{p}) = \mathbf{p}\omega_i + \sum_{j=1}^{n} \theta_{ij}\pi_j(\mathbf{p}) + \tau_i(\mathbf{p})$, where $\mathbf{p}\omega_i + \sum_{j=1}^{n} \theta_{ij}\pi_j(\mathbf{p})$ describes the ith agent's private wealth, and $(\tau_i)_{i=1}^{m}$ is a tax-subsidy system satisfying $\sum_{i=1}^{m} \tau_i(\mathbf{p}) = 0$.

For every given price vector $\mathbf{p} \in \mathbb{P}$ the ith consumer chooses consumption bundles that maximize utility within the budget set $\beta_i'(\mathbf{p}) = \{\mathbf{x}_i \in X_i \ / \ \mathbf{p}\mathbf{x}_i \leq r_i(\mathbf{p})\}$. It is routine to show that, under axioms 4.1', 4.2 and 4.3, the restricted demand and supply mappings are upper hemicontinuous correspondences with non-empty, compact and convex values. The associated excess demand inherits these properties. Moreover, it is immediate that the Walras Law also holds.

Therefore:

Proposition 4.3 *Let E be an economy that satisfies axioms 4.1', 4.2 and 4.3. Then an equilibrium exists.*

4.5   Equilibrium and efficiency

4.5.1   The Pareto principle

An equilibrium selects a particular point within the set of attainable allocations, at which all agents realize their plans simultaneously, given their choice restrictions. How good is this allocation when compared with other feasible alternatives? To answer this question one has to introduce *value judgements*, because different people may rank alternatives differently. Looking for consensus on the way of evaluating allocations, we focus on *the Pareto principle*. This principle says that a feasible allocation is better than another one, when it is preferred by *all* consumers; i.e. "better than" means unanimous agreement. A Pareto optimum is a maximal element of this relation: there is no feasible allocation in which all agents can be better off.

Asking for Pareto optimality can be regarded as an expression of John Stuart Mill's value judgement: "the highest welfare for the greatest number". This is something really hard to object. The cost of such a broad consensus is that the Pareto principle is not very informative. In particular: (a) Many alternative allocations are not comparable, according to this principle (those in which some consumers are better off and some others are worse off). (b) The set of Pareto optimal allocations can be very large, and include extremely different welfare distributions (this indicates that the Pareto criterion is devoid of any distributive justice feature).

In spite of these shortcomings, the Pareto principle is a good starting point for the welfare analysis of market economies. First, because it gives us an efficiency property: if an allocation is not Pareto optimal, then all people can be made better off by shifting to another feasible one. Most would think that this is the least we can ask, to find the working of an economy acceptable. Second, because this criterion bites; namely, there are economies in which market outcomes fail to satisfy this minimal test of desirability.

The next definition makes this requirement precise:

Definition 4.4 *A feasible allocation* $[(\mathbf{x}_i^\circ)_{i=1}^m, (\mathbf{y}_j^\circ)_{j=1}^n]$ *is* **Pareto optimal** *when there is no other feasible allocation* $[(\mathbf{x}_i')_{i=1}^n, (\mathbf{y}_j')_{j=1}^n]$ *such that,* $u_i(\mathbf{x}_i^\circ) \geq u_i(\mathbf{x}_i')$ *for all* i, *with* $u_i(\mathbf{x}_k^\circ) > u_i(\mathbf{x}_k')$ *for some* k.

We shall now show two results that are known as the Two Fundamental Theorems of Welfare Economics. The first one says that every competitive equilibrium is an optimum, provided that consumers are not satiated. This result ensures that competitive outcomes are efficient. Then, we consider the converse of this result, under a more demanding set of axioms. The Second Welfare Theorem establishes that every optimum is an equilibrium, provided that we can freely redistribute wealth among consumers. Hence, if we can select an efficient allocation as a socially desirable outcome, there is a redistribution of initial endowments and firms' shares, and a price vector, that yield this particular allocation as a competitive equilibrium. In other words, any efficient allocation can be decentralized as an equilibrium. The message of this theorem is twofold: (1) Equity and efficiency are not incompatible aspirations in a competitive economy; (2) The desired outcome can be obtained by a suitable modification of property rights, without having to impose particular actions on individual agents.

4.5.2 The Two Welfare Theorems

We prove now the two welfare theorems.

Theorem 4.3 (First Welfare Theorem) *Let* E_{pp} *be a private ownership market economy in which every consumer has a locally non-satiated utility function. And let* $\left(\mathbf{p}^*, [(\mathbf{x}_i^*)_{i=1}^m, (\mathbf{y}_j^*)_{j=1}^n]\right)$ *be a competitive equilibrium. Then the allocation* $[(\mathbf{x}_i^*)_{i=1}^m, (\mathbf{y}_j^*)_{j=1}^n]$ *is Pareto efficient.*

Proof. Suppose that this is not true, that is, there exists a feasible allocation $[(\mathbf{x}_i')_{i=1}^m, (\mathbf{y}_j')_{j=1}^n]$ such that $u_i(\mathbf{x}_i') \geq u_i(\mathbf{x}_i^*)$, for all i, with $u_k(\mathbf{x}_k') > u_k(\mathbf{x}_k^*)$, for some k.

Local non-satiation implies that $\mathbf{p}^*\mathbf{x}_i' \geq \mathbf{p}^*\mathbf{x}_i^*$, for all i, with $\mathbf{p}^*\mathbf{x}_k' > \mathbf{p}^*\mathbf{x}_k^*$ for those consumers with $u_k(\mathbf{x}_k') > u_k(\mathbf{x}_k^*)$. Hence, $\mathbf{p}^* \sum_{i=1}^m \mathbf{x}_i' > \mathbf{p}^* \sum_{i=1}^m \mathbf{x}_i^*$.

As $\mathbf{p}^*\mathbf{x}_i^* = \mathbf{p}^*\omega_i + \sum_{j=1}^m \theta_{ij}\mathbf{p}^*\mathbf{y}_j^*$, this in turn implies:

$$\mathbf{p}^* \sum_{i=1}^m \mathbf{x}_i' > \mathbf{p}^* \sum_{i=1}^m \omega_i + \mathbf{p}^* \sum_{j=1}^n \mathbf{y}_j^*$$

Moreover, $\sum_{j=1}^n \mathbf{y}_j' \geq \sum_{i=1}^m \mathbf{x}_i' - \omega$, because $[(\mathbf{x}_i')_{i=1}^m, (\mathbf{y}_j')_{j=1}^n]$ is a feasible allocation. Therefore,

$$\mathbf{p}^* \sum_{j=1}^n \mathbf{y}_j' \geq \mathbf{p}^* (\sum_{i=1}^m \mathbf{x}_i' - \sum_{i=1}^m \omega_i) > \mathbf{p}^* \sum_{j=1}^n \mathbf{y}_j^*$$

that is, the aggregate profits at prices $\mathbf{p}^*$ in the attainable allocation $[(\mathbf{x}_i')_{i=1}^m, (\mathbf{y}_j')_{j=1}^n]$ are higher that those associated with the competitive equilibrium $\left(\mathbf{p}^*, [(\mathbf{x}_i^*)_{i=1}^m, (\mathbf{y}_j^*)_{j=1}^n]\right)$. But this is not possible, because total profits are maximized if and only if each firm maximizes profits individually, and this is what happens at prices $\mathbf{p}^*$ with production plans $(\mathbf{y}_j^*)_{j=1}^n$ (see proposition 3.6). $\boxed{\text{Q.e.d.}}$

We know that in a competitive equilibrium every consumer gets a consumption plan better than or equal to her initial endowments. The final distribution of welfare is therefore heavily conditioned by the initial distribution of resources (initial endowments and firms' property). Competitive markets produce "conservative results" in this respect: if the initial distribution of resources is unequal, the final distribution will be unequal as well. The second welfare theorem, however, gives us a tool with which to achieve a pre-determined efficient allocation, to be interpreted as a social desideratum. It permits us to attain this goal by altering the distribution of property rights, without modifying the market mechanism. Formally:

Theorem 4.4 (Second Welfare Theorem) *Let $E = [(X_i, u_i), (Y_j), \omega]$ be an economy such that: (a) X_i is convex and u_i is continuous, quasi-concave and locally non-satiated, for all i; (b) $Y = \sum_{j=1}^n Y_j$ is closed and convex. Let $[(\mathbf{x}_i^*)_{i=1}^m, (\mathbf{y}_j^*)_{j=1}^n]$ be a Pareto optimal allocation, with $\mathbf{x}_i^* \in intX_i$ for all i. Then, there exists a price vector $\mathbf{p}^* \in \mathbb{R}_+^\ell - \{\mathbf{0}\}$ and a wealth distribution such that $\left(\mathbf{p}^*, [(\mathbf{x}_i^*)_{i=1}^m, (\mathbf{y}_j^*)_{j=1}^n]\right)$ is a competitive equilibrium.*

Proof. Let $Y \equiv \sum_{j=1}^n Y_j$, $X \equiv \sum_{i=1}^m X_i$, $\mathbf{x}^* = \sum_{i=1}^m \mathbf{x}_i^*$, $\mathbf{y}^* = \sum_{j=1}^n \mathbf{y}_j^*$, and define

$$\mathbf{Q} \equiv Y + \{\omega\} ,$$

$$\mathcal{BE}(\mathbf{x}^*) \equiv \{\mathbf{x} \in X \ / \ u_i(\mathbf{x}_i) \geq u_i(\mathbf{x}_i^*), \forall i\},$$

both convex sets. As $[(\mathbf{x}_i^*)_{i=1}^m, (\mathbf{y}_j^*)_{j=1}^n]$ is feasible, $\mathbf{x}^* \leq \mathbf{y}^* + \omega$, it follows that $\mathbf{Q} \cap \mathcal{BE}(\mathbf{x}^*) \neq \emptyset$. Moreover $\mathbf{Q} \cap int\mathcal{BE}(\mathbf{x}^*) = \emptyset$, because $[(\mathbf{x}_i^*)_{i=1}^m, (\mathbf{y}_j^*)_{j=1}^n]$ is a Pareto optimal allocation. Therefore, we can (weakly) separate these two sets $\mathbf{Q}$, $\mathcal{BE}(\mathbf{x}^*)$, that is, we can find a vector $\mathbf{p}^* \neq \mathbf{0}$ such that, for all $\mathbf{q} \in \mathbf{Q}$, all $\mathbf{x} \in \mathcal{BE}(\mathbf{x}^*)$, $\mathbf{p}^*\mathbf{q} \leq \mathbf{p}^*\mathbf{x}$. This implies,

$$\mathbf{p}^*\mathbf{x}^* = \min \mathbf{p}^*\mathbf{x}, \quad \forall \ \mathbf{x} \in \mathcal{BE}(\mathbf{x}^*)$$

$$\mathbf{p}^*(\mathbf{y}^* + \omega) = \max \mathbf{p}^*\mathbf{q}, \quad \forall \ \mathbf{q} \in \mathbf{Q}$$

$$\mathbf{p}^*\mathbf{x}^* = \mathbf{p}^*(\mathbf{y}^* + \omega)$$

Hence, $\mathbf{x}^*$ minimizes aggregate expenditure at prices $\mathbf{p}^*$ on $\mathcal{BE}(\mathbf{x}^*)$. It is easy to see that this implies that $\mathbf{x}_i^*$ is an expenditure minimizing consumption plan at prices $\mathbf{p}^*$ on the set of consumption plans that are better than or equal to $\mathbf{x}_i^*$, for all i. For suppose not, that is, there is a consumer t and a consumption plan $\mathbf{x}_t' \in \mathcal{BE}_t(\mathbf{x}_t^*)$ such that $\mathbf{p}^*\mathbf{x}_t' < \mathbf{p}^*\mathbf{x}_t^*$. Clearly, $\left(\sum_{i \neq t} \mathbf{x}_i^* + \mathbf{x}_t'\right) \in \mathcal{BE}(\mathbf{x}^*)$, and $\mathbf{p}^*\left(\sum_{i \neq t} \mathbf{x}_i^* + \mathbf{x}_t'\right) < \mathbf{p}^*\mathbf{x}^*$, contradicting the fact that $\mathbf{x}^*$ minimizes total expenditure on $\mathcal{BE}(\mathbf{x}^*)$. Moreover, as $\mathbf{x}_i^* \in intX_i$, for all i, this is equivalent to utility maximization on the set of consumption plans that satisfy the budget restriction $\mathbf{p}^*\mathbf{x}_i \leq \mathbf{p}^*\mathbf{x}_i^*$ (see Proposition 2.6). Thus, $\mathbf{x}_i^*$ is the ith consumer's demand at prices $\mathbf{p}^*$.

Observe now that $\mathbf{y}^*$ maximizes total profits relative to $\mathbf{p}^*$, so that $\mathbf{y}_j^*$ is the jth firm's supply for all j (Proposition 3.6).

A particular distribution of the initial endowments and firms' profits that satisfies the consumer's wealth restriction is as follows: Let

$$\omega_i = \mathbf{x}_i^* - \frac{1}{m}\sum_{j=1}^h \mathbf{y}_j^* \quad i = 1, 2, ..., m$$

$$\theta_{ij} = \frac{1}{m} \quad i = 1, 2, ..., m: \quad j = 1, 2, ..., n$$

It follows that $\sum_{i=1}^m \theta_{ij} = 1$, for all j, and $\sum_{i=1}^m \omega_i = \mathbf{x}^* - \mathbf{y}^*$. Then,

$$\mathbf{p}^*\omega_i + \sum_{i=1}^m \theta_{ij}\mathbf{p}^*\mathbf{y}_j^* = \mathbf{p}^*\mathbf{x}_i^* - \frac{1}{m}\sum_{j=1}^n \mathbf{p}^*\mathbf{y}_j^* + \sum_{j=1}^n \frac{1}{m}\mathbf{p}^*\mathbf{y}_j^* = \mathbf{p}^*\mathbf{x}_i^*$$

for all i, so that $[\mathbf{p}^*, (\mathbf{x}_i^*)_{i=1}^m, (\mathbf{y}_j^*)_{j=1}^n]$ is a competitive equilibrium for this private ownership economy. $\boxed{\text{Q.e.d.}}$

4.5.3 Optimum and equilibrium: a differential approach

Let us now consider the marginal properties of efficient allocations, and their relation to the marginal properties of equilibrium outcomes. To make things simpler, we restrict the model as follows:

(i) For all $i = 1, 2, ..., m$, take $X_i = \mathbb{R}_+^{\ell}$, and suppose that utilities are strictly quasi-concave and differentiable.

(ii) Each firm produces a single net output (*single production*); moreover, the jth firm's technology is described by a differentiable **production function** f_j which we assume to be strictly concave (decreasing returns to scale).

The expression $q_{jk} = f_j(\mathbf{r}_j)$ describes the jth firm efficient production of $q_{jk} \geq 0$ units of output k, obtained by means of a vector $\mathbf{r}_j \in \mathbb{R}_+^{\ell-1}$ of inputs. This corresponds to a production set defined by:

$$Y_j = \{(q_{jk}, -\mathbf{r}_j) \in \mathbb{R}^{\ell} \mid q_{jk} \leq f_j(\mathbf{r}_j)\}$$

Consider one of these simplified economies with m consumers, n firms, and ℓ commodities, and let ω denote the vector of initial endowments. Under such circumstances, an allocation $[(\mathbf{x}_i)_{i=1}^n, (q_{jk}, -\mathbf{r}_j)_{j=1}^n]$ is attainable when it satisfies the following restrictions:

(i) $\mathbf{x}_i \geq 0, \forall i$.

(ii) $q_{jk} \leq f_j(\mathbf{r}_j), \forall j$.

(iii) For all $k = 1, 2, \ldots, \ell$, $\sum_{i=1}^m x_{ik} \leq \sum_{j=1}^n q_{jk} - \sum_{j=1}^n r_{jk} + \sum_{i=1}^m \omega_{ik}$.

The characterization of efficient allocations

One way of selecting an efficient allocation is to maximize the function $\sum_{i=1}^m \alpha_i u_i(\mathbf{x}_i)$, on the set of attainable allocations, for some positive scalars $\alpha_1, \alpha_2, ..., \alpha_m$. Namely,

$$
\left.
\begin{aligned}
& Max \ \sum_{i=1}^m \alpha_i u_i(\mathbf{x}_i) \\
& \text{s.t.} \\
& \qquad \sum_{i=1}^m x_{ik} \leq \sum_{j=1}^n q_{jk} - \sum_{j=1}^n r_{jk} + \omega_k, \quad k = 1, 2, ..., \ell \\
& \qquad q_{jk} \leq f_j(\mathbf{r}_j), \qquad\qquad j = 1, 2, ..., n \\
& \qquad \mathbf{x}_i \geq 0 \qquad\qquad\qquad\quad i = 1, 2, ..., m
\end{aligned}
\right\}
$$

where the relevant variables are the consumption plans $\mathbf{x}_i$, and the production levels $(q_{jk}, \mathbf{r}_j)$. The associated Lagrangian function is given by:

$$
L(\cdot) = \sum_{i=1}^m \alpha_i u_i(\mathbf{x}_i) - \sum_{k=1}^{\ell} \lambda_k \left(\sum_{i=1}^m \mathbf{x}_i - \sum_{j=1}^n q_{jk} + \sum_{j=1}^n r_{jk} - \sum_{i=1}^m \omega_{ik} \right) -
$$

$$-\sum_{j=1}^{n} \mu_j \left[q_{jk} - f_j \left(\mathbf{r}_j \right) \right]$$

Assuming interior solutions, the first order conditions can be expressed as:

$$\frac{\partial L}{\partial x_{ik}} = 0 = \alpha_i \frac{\partial u_i}{\partial x_{ik}} - \lambda_k \qquad \begin{array}{l} i = 1, 2, ..., m \\ k = 1, 2, ..., \ell \end{array}$$

$$\frac{\partial L}{\partial r_{jt}} = 0 = -\lambda_t - \mu_j \frac{\partial f_j}{\partial r_{jt}} \qquad \begin{array}{l} j = 1, 2, ..., n \\ t = 1, 2, ..., \ell \end{array}$$

$$\frac{\partial L}{\partial q_{jk}} = 0 = \lambda_k - \mu_j \qquad \begin{array}{l} j = 1, 2, ..., n \\ k = 1, 2, ..., \ell \end{array}$$

For a given consumer and two commodities the above conditions imply:

$$\alpha_i = \frac{\lambda_k}{\partial u_i \ / \ \partial x_{ik}} = \frac{\lambda_t}{\partial u_i \ / \ \partial x_{it}}, \qquad k, t = 1, 2, ..., \ell$$

so that

$$\frac{\partial u_i \ / \ \partial x_{it}}{\partial u_i \ / \ \partial x_{ik}} = \frac{\lambda_t}{\lambda_k} = MRS_{kt}^i, \qquad k, t = 1, 2, ..., \ell$$

that is, the marginal rates of substitution of any pair of commodities must be equal to the quotient of the corresponding multipliers (that obviously correspond to shadow prices).

As the multipliers are associated with the commodities, and not to the consumers, this relation will hold for all consumers simultaneously. Hence, taking two consumers i, h, and two commodities k, t, we have:

$$\frac{\partial u_i \ / \ \partial x_{it}}{\partial u_i \ / \ \partial x_{ik}} = \frac{\lambda_t}{\lambda_k} = \frac{\partial u_h \ / \ \partial x_{ht}}{\partial u_h \ / \ \partial x_{hk}} \qquad \begin{array}{l} k, t = 1, 2, ..., \ell \\ i, h = 1, 2, ..., m \end{array}$$

Namely, *a necessary condition for optimality is that the marginal rates of substitution of every pair of commodities must be equal for all consumers.* More briefly,

$$MRS_{k,t}^i = MRS_{k,t}^h \qquad \begin{array}{l} k, t = 1, 2, ..., \ell \\ i, h = 1, 2, ..., m \end{array}$$

Taking now a firm j and two commodities k, t, the first order conditions entail:

$$\mu_j = \frac{-\lambda_t}{\partial f_j \ / \partial r_{jt}} = \frac{-\lambda_k}{\partial f_j \ / \partial r_{jk}} \qquad t, k = 1, 2, ..., \ell$$

so that,

$$\frac{\partial f_j / \partial r_{jk}}{\partial f_j / \partial r_{jt}} = \frac{\lambda_k}{\lambda_t} = MRT_{t,k}^j \qquad t, k = 1, 2, ..., \ell$$

which states that the marginal rate of transformation must coincide with the quotient of the corresponding multipliers (the input shadow prices).

As before, taking two different firms j, s, it follows:

$$\frac{\partial f_j / \partial r_{jk}}{\partial f_j / \partial r_{jt}} = \frac{\lambda_k}{\lambda_t} = \frac{\partial f_s / \partial r_{sk}}{\partial f_s / \partial r_{st}} \qquad \begin{array}{l} t, k = 1, 2, ..., \ell \\ j, s = 1, 2, ..., n \end{array}$$

In words: *a necessary condition for optimality is that the marginal rates of transformation must be equal for all firms.* In short:

$$MRT_{t,k}^j = MRT_{t,k}^s \qquad t, k = 1, 2, ..., \ell \quad j, s = 1, 2, ..., n$$

Applying this to a consumer i and a firm j, with respect to a pair of commodities k, t, it follows that:

$$\frac{\partial u_i / \partial x_{it}}{\partial u_i / \partial x_{ik}} = \frac{\lambda_t}{\lambda_k} = \frac{\partial f_j / \partial r_{jt}}{\partial f_j / \partial r_{jk}} \qquad \begin{array}{l} k, t = 1, 2, ..., \ell \\ i = 1, 2, ..., m \\ j = 1, 2, ..., n \end{array}$$

That is, *for any pair of commodities, every consumer's marginal rate of substitution is equal to every firm' marginal rate of transformation.*

Finally, note that the last of the first order conditions implies that $\lambda_k = \mu_j$ (where j is a firm that produces commodity k as a net output). That means that the corresponding shadow price for the kth commodity, considered as a production factor, must be equal to the corresponding shadow price of this commodity considered as an output. Namely, *a necessary condition for an optimum is that the marginal worth of a commodity must be equal, whether it is an input or an output.*

In summary: The necessary conditions for the optimality of an allocation require all commodities to have the same marginal value in all possible uses and for all agents. This is a rather intuitive property; if this were not the case, there would be potential improvements by shifting resources to those uses with higher value (or to those agents with higher marginal values in their payoff functions).

Note that these conditions do not depend on the quasi-concavity of utility functions or the concavity of production functions. Yet, when these properties hold, these necessary conditions turn out to be sufficient as well. Hence, they characterize efficient allocations.

The equilibrium marginal conditions

Let us check now the marginal properties of an equilibrium allocation, and compare this with the characterization of an optimum that we have just presented.

Let $\mathbf{p}^*$ be an equilibrium price vector and suppose that $\mathbf{p}^* \gg 0$, with $r_i(\mathbf{p}^*) > 0$. The ith consumer's demand is obtained as a solution to the problem

$$\left. \begin{array}{c} Max\ u_i(\mathbf{x}_i) \\ \text{s.t.}\ \mathbf{p}^*\mathbf{x}_i \leq r_i(\mathbf{p}^*) \end{array} \right\}$$

The Lagrangian function of this problem is:

$$L(.) = u_i(\mathbf{x}_i) - \lambda(\mathbf{p}^*\mathbf{x}_i - r_i(\mathbf{p}^*))$$

and the first order conditions, assuming again interior solutions, are given by:

$$\frac{\partial L}{\partial x_{ik}} = 0 = \frac{\partial u_i}{\partial x_{ik}} - \lambda p_k^* \qquad k = 1, 2, ..., \ell$$

Therefore, for all $k, t = 1, 2, \ldots, \ell$, in equilibrium we have:

$$\frac{\partial u_i / \partial x_{ik}}{\partial u_i / \partial x_{it}} = \frac{p_k^*}{p_t^*} \left(= MRS_{t,k}^i\right)$$

As all consumers confront the same market prices, this relation holds for all consumers simultaneously. That is,

$$\frac{\partial u_1 / x_{1k}}{\partial u_1 / \partial x_{1t}} = \frac{\partial u_2 / x_{2k}}{\partial u_2 / \partial x_{2t}} = \ldots = \frac{\partial u_m / \partial x_{mk}}{\partial u_m / \partial x_{mt}} = \frac{p_k^*}{p_t^*}$$

(in equilibrium, all consumers marginal rates of substitution are equal and coincide with the quotient of the corresponding prices).

The jth firm, on the other hand, solves the problem:

$$\left. \begin{array}{c} Max\ p_k^* q_{jk} - \sum_{t=1}^{\ell} p_t^* r_{jt} \\ \text{s.t.}\ \ q_{jk} \leq f_j(\mathbf{r}_j) \end{array} \right\}$$

whose Lagrangian function is:

$$L(\cdot) = p_k^* q_{jk} - \sum_{t=1}^{\ell} p_t^* r_{jt} - \mu\left[q_{jk} - f_j(\mathbf{r}_j)\right]$$

With interior solutions the first order conditions establish that:

$$\frac{\partial L}{\partial r_{jt}} = 0 = -p_t^* + \mu \frac{\partial f_j}{\partial r_{jt}}, \qquad t = 1, 2, ..., \ell$$

so that, for any pair of commodities z, t, we have:

$$\frac{\partial f_j / \partial r_{jz}}{\partial f_j / \partial r_{jt}} = \frac{p_z^*}{p_t^*} \quad \left(= MRT_{t,z}^j\right)$$

Because all firms face the same prices, it follows that:

$$\frac{\partial f_1 / \partial r_{1z}}{\partial f_1 / \partial r_{1t}} = \frac{\partial f_2 / \partial r_{2z}}{\partial f_2 / \partial r_{2t}} = ... = \frac{\partial f_n / \partial r_{nz}}{\partial f_n / \partial r_{nt}} = \frac{p_z^*}{p_t^*}$$

(in equilibrium the marginal rates of transformation of any pair of commodities is equal for all firms, and coincides with the quotient of their market prices).

Finally, as prices are common for consumers and firms, we get:

$$\frac{p_z^*}{p_t^*} = MRS_{t,z}^i = MRT_{t,z}^j$$

for all $t, z = 1, 2, \ldots, \ell$, all $i = 1, 2, \ldots, m$, and all $j = 1, 2, \ldots, n$.

A competitive equilibrium therefore satisfies the necessary conditions for optimality, which under the standard assumptions are also sufficient.

On the equivalence between optimum and equilibrium

We can identify four basic elements that explain the identity between optimum and equilibrium: Complete markets, convexity, parametric prices and no spill-over..

Complete markets says that all commodities have associated a price. This implies that each agent faces as many relative prices as necessary, to solve her individual optimization problem.

The assumption of *convexity* has many implications. It amounts to saying that agents maximize quasi-concave functions over convex sets. As a consequence, the behaviour of economic agents can be described in terms of upper hemicontinuous correspondences, with non-empty, closed and convex values. This permits us to apply a fixed-point argument in order to prove the existence of equilibrium. Moreover, local maxima are global maxima, so that marginal conditions are sufficient to characterize the behaviour of individual agents.

It follows from the assumption of *parametric prices* that individual maximization implies the equalization of marginal rates with the corresponding prices. As a consequence, under complete markets, all commodities have the same marginal value in all possible uses and for all agents. The assumptions of complete markets, convexity and parametric prices, together, imply that the maximization of individual objective functions turns out to be equivalent to the maximization of aggregate objective functions (utilities and profits). The properties of existence and efficiency of equilibria therefore do not depend on the number of agents (provided this number is finite).

The implicit assumption of *no spill-overs* says that all non-price variables affecting individual agents' decision problems belong to their individual choice sets. Therefore, efficiency only requires the equalization of *private* marginal rates to relative prices.[3] Complete markets, convexity, parametric prices and no spill-overs, together, imply that the local properties that characterize the maximization of individual objective functions imply, global maximization. Marginal conditions are therefore sufficient to ensure the efficiency of equilibrium allocations.

In summary: Complete markets, convexity, parametric prices and no spill-overs imply that the set of competitive equilibria of a given economy coincides with the set of efficient allocations (the two welfare theorems). Observe that these four assumptions also give us a guideline about the environments in which we can expect *market failures* (typically the lack of efficiency of market allocations): Incomplete markets, monopolistic competition, increasing returns to scale or other forms of non-convexities, and economies with externalities and public goods.

4.6 Abstract economies

By an **abstract economy** we mean a society made of h agents, each of which has to choose, within her choice set, an action that maximizes her objective function, subject to some environmental restrictions. An *equilibrium* is a situation in which all the actions chosen by individual agents are compatible. We shall show here that this extension of the competitive equilibrium model has a solution, and that this model is applicable to different settings (particularly those involving externalities).

---

[3]To illustrate this, think of a pure exchange economy (X_i, u_i, ω) where agents utilities depend on the whole allocation of the endowments, that is, $u_i : \mathbb{R}^{\ell m} \to \mathbb{R}$. In this case the necessary conditions for optimality are given by $\sum_{i=1}^{m} \alpha_t \frac{\partial u_t}{\partial x_{ik}} = \lambda_k$, $k = 1, 2, ..., \ell$, that are clearly different from the equilibrium conditions.

An abstract economy can be summarized by

$$AE = (A_i, v_i, \gamma_i)_{i=1}^h$$

where:

(a) $A_i \subset \mathbb{R}^\ell$ stands for the ith agent's *choice set*, whose elements are denoted by $\mathbf{a}_i$.

(b) v_i is her *objective function* (a real-valued function that expresses the way in which this agent ranks the different alternatives).

(c) γ_i is a mapping that describes the *restrictions* faced by the agent.

To give this problem a general treatment, agents' objective functions and restrictions are allowed to depend on other agents' choices. Hence, let $\mathbb{A} = \prod_{i=1}^h A_i$ and call $\mathbf{a} = (\mathbf{a}_1, ..., \mathbf{a}_h)$ an element of $\mathbb{A}$, with $\mathbf{a}_i \in A_i$ for all i). Without loss of generality, let describe the ith agent's restrictions as a mapping: $\gamma_i : \mathbb{A} \rightarrow A_i$, which tells us the actions of A_i that are available for the ith agent when all other agents choose the actions

$$\mathbf{a}_{-i} = (\mathbf{a}_1, ..., \mathbf{a}_{i-1}, \mathbf{a}_{i+1}, ..., \mathbf{a}_h)$$

Therefore, for all $\mathbf{a} \in \mathbb{A}$, $\gamma_i(\mathbf{a})$ is the feasible set for the ith agent; note that γ_i is actually independent on its ith coordinate vector (that is, $\gamma_i(\mathbf{a}_{-i}, \mathbf{a}_i) = \gamma_i(\mathbf{a}_{-i}, \mathbf{a}_i')$, for all $\mathbf{a}_i, \mathbf{a}_i'$ in A_i, all $\mathbf{a}_{-i} \in \prod_{t \neq i} A_t$).[4]

Similarly, in order to permit the ith agent's objective function to depend on other agents' choices, we let $v_i : \mathbb{A} \rightarrow \mathbb{R}$. Some times we shall write $v_i(\mathbf{a}) = v_i(\mathbf{a}_i, \mathbf{a}_{-i})$, to emphasize that the value of the ith agent's objective function, when she chooses $\mathbf{a}_i$, depends on the actions taken by other agents, $\mathbf{a}_{-i} \in \prod_{t \neq i} A_t$.

The ith agent's rational behaviour can be described by a correspondence $\mu_i : \mathbb{A} \rightarrow A_i$ given by:

$$\mu_i(\mathbf{a}) = \{\mathbf{a}_i' \in \gamma_i(\mathbf{a}) \ / \ v_i(\mathbf{a}_i', \mathbf{a}_{-i}) \geq v_i(\overline{\mathbf{a}}_i, \mathbf{a}_{-i}) \ \forall \ \overline{\mathbf{a}}_i \in \gamma_i(\mathbf{a})\}$$

That is, the ith agent maximizes her objective function on her feasible set, which is determined by others' decisions.[5]

---

[4]A more intuitive way of describing these restrictions would be by letting $\widehat{\gamma}_k$: $\prod_{t \neq k} A_t \rightarrow A_k$, where $\widehat{\gamma}_k(\mathbf{a}_{-k})$ is the feasibel set. Note that we can always transform this mapping into that used in our formulation by simply making $\gamma_k(\mathbf{a}) = \widehat{\gamma}_k(\mathbf{a}_{-k})$, for all $\mathbf{a} \in \mathbb{A}$.

[5]Note that the kth agent takes other agents' actions as given, assuming that these actions will not change in response to her own decision. Hence, the associated equilibrium notion corresponds to the Nash equilibrium of a non-cooperative game.

Definition 4.5 *An **equilibrium for an abstract economy** $[A_i, v_i, \gamma_i]_{i=1}^{h}$ is a point $\mathbf{a}^* \in \mathbb{A}$ such that, for all $i = 1, 2, ..., h$, we have:*

$$v_i(\mathbf{a}_i^*, \mathbf{a}_{-i}^*) \geq v_i(\mathbf{a}_i, \mathbf{a}_{-i}^*), \quad \forall \, \mathbf{a}_i \in \gamma_i(\mathbf{a}^*)$$

An equilibrium is a situation in which every agent maximizes her objective function subject to her restrictions, and all actions are compatible. More formally, $\mathbf{a}^*$ is an equilibrium if and only if $\mathbf{a}_i^* \in \mu_i(\mathbf{a}^*)$ for all i. This can be re-stated as follows: Let $\mu : \mathbb{A} \to \mathbb{A}$ be a mapping defined by $\mu(\mathbf{a}) = \prod_{i=1}^{h} \mu_i(\mathbf{a})$; then, $\mathbf{a}^*$ is an equilibrium if and only if $\mathbf{a}^* \in \mu(\mathbf{a}^*)$, that is, if and only if $\mathbf{a}^*$ is a fixed point of the correspondence μ.

The next theorem [Debreu (1952)] establishes conditions under which an equilibrium for an abstract economy exists:

Theorem 4.5 *Let $[A_i, v_i, \gamma_i]_{i=1}^{h}$ be an abstract economy. An equilibrium exists if, for all $i = 1, 2, ..., h$, the following conditions hold: (a) $A_i \subset \mathbb{R}^\ell$ is non-empty, compact and convex; (b) $v_i : \mathbb{A} \to \mathbb{R}$ is a continuous function, quasi-concave in $\mathbf{a}_i$; and (c) $\gamma_i : \mathbb{A} \to A_i$ is a continuous correspondence, with non-empty, compact and convex values.*

    Proof. Under the assumptions established, the Maximum Theorem is applicable. Hence, μ_i is an upper hemicontinuous correspondence for all i. Moreover, it is immediate to check that $\mu_i(\mathbf{a})$ is non-empty (Weierstrass' theorem), compact and convex. Therefore, μ is an upper hemicontinuous correspondence, with non-empty, compact and convex values. Finally, note that $\mathbb{A}$ is a non-empty, compact and convex subset of $\mathbb{R}^{\ell h}$. Thus, Kakutani's fixed point theorem ensures the existence of some point $\mathbf{a}^*$ in $\mathbb{A}$ such that $\mathbf{a}^* \in \mu(\mathbf{a}^*)$. $\boxed{\textbf{Q.e.d.}}$

It is now easy to show that a competitive equilibrium is a special case of an equilibrium for an abstract economy. Take $h = m + n + 1$, with:
(a) For all $i = 1, 2, ..., m$, $A_i = X_i$, $\gamma_i(\mathbf{a}) = \beta_i(\mathbf{p})$, $v_i(\mathbf{a}) = u_i(\mathbf{x}_i)$.
(b) For all $i = m + 1, ..., m + n$, $A_i = \gamma_i(\mathbf{a}) = Y_i$, $v_i(\mathbf{a}) = \mathbf{p}\mathbf{y}_i$.
(c) For $i = h$, $A_h = \gamma_h(\mathbf{a}) = \mathbb{P}$, for all $\mathbf{a} \in \mathbb{A}$, and:

$$v_h(\mathbf{a}) = \mathbf{p} \left[\sum_{i=1}^{m} (\mathbf{x}_i - \omega_i) - \sum_{j=1}^{n} \mathbf{y}_j \right].$$

An equilibrium for this economy is therefore a competitive one. Note that the last "agent" can be understood as an expression of the functioning of competitive markets (usually identified with *the auctioneer*). Her choice set is the price simplex, and her choice criterion consists of maximizing the worth of the excess demand (in such a way prices go up when demand exceeds supply and viceversa). Yet, the interest of this framework lies in the fact that it permits us to extend the equilibrium model of former sections, to analyze situations in which there can be externalities in both, the agents' feasible sets and the utility functions. Hence, aspects such as contamination, public goods, resources of common property or money illusion can be dealt with as an abstract economy problem.

Note that the presence of externalities breaks the equivalence between equilibrium and efficiency which was discussed in the former section.

4.7   References to the literature

The classic works of Arrow & Debreu (1954) and McKenzie (1959) are still exciting readings. Debreu (1959), (1982), Arrow & Hahn (1971), Cornwall (1984), Mas-Colell, Whinston & Green (1995) or Starr (1996), among many others, discuss this problem more thoroughly. Debreu (1962) offers a number of interesting extensions to the model presented here.

There are three classical topics in the analysis of equilibrium that we have omitted: the uniqueness, stability and core properties of competitive equilibria. Mas-Colell et al (1995) provide a suitable introduction to the analysis of these topics. Hildenbrand & Kirman (1988) and Cornwall (1984) contain detailed analysis of the core and its connection with competitive equilibria. Further references can be found there.

Chapter 5

EQUILIBRIUM WITH NON-CONVEX FIRMS

5.1 Introduction

General equilibrium models face serious difficulties in the presence of non-convex technologies, when there are finitely many firms and non-convexities are not negligible. Such difficulties are both analytical and theoretical and are mainly concerned with the fact that the supply correspondence may not be convex-valued or even defined, so that the existence of competitive equilibrium will typically fail. This implies that, if we want to analyze a general equilibrium model allowing for non-convex technologies, *we must permit the firms to follow more general rules of behaviour*, and suitably *re-define the equilibrium notion*. This will imply, however, that the *identification between equilibrium and optimum will no longer hold* (the Invisible Hand Theorem now splits into two halves). Thus, the existence of equilibria under nonconvex technologies, and the analysis of their properties of optimality now become two very different questions.

The modern approach to these problems consists of building up a general equilibrium model that constitutes a genuine extension of the standard one. To do so, an equilibrium for the economy is understood as a price vector, a list of consumption allocations, and a list of production plans such that: (a) consumers maximize their preferences subject to their budget constraints; (b) each individual firm is in "equilibrium" at those prices and production plans; and (c) the markets for all goods clear. It is the nature of the equilibrium condition (b) which establishes the difference with respect to the Walrasian model. The central question now becomes *how to consistently model the behaviour of non-convex firms,* according to relevant positive or normative criteria.

A very general and powerful way of dealing with this question consists of associating the equilibrium of firms with the notion of a *pricing rule*, rather than to that of a supply correspondence. A pricing rule is a mapping from each firm's set of efficient production plans to the price space. The graph of such a mapping describes the prices-production pairs that a firm finds "acceptable" (a pricing rule may be thought of as the inverse mapping of a generalized "supply correspondence"). The advantage of formulating the problem in this way is twofold: (1) The notion of a pricing rule is an abstract construction which permits one to model different types of behaviour, and thus, to analyze situations where profit maximization is not applicable. (2) These mappings may be upper hemicontinuous and convex-valued, even when the supply correspondence is not, making it possible to use a fixed point argument (on the "inverse supply" mapping), in order to get the existence of an equilibrium.

As for the ways of modelling the behaviour of non-convex firms in terms of pricing rules, both positive and normative approaches are possible. *Positive models* are meant to describe plausible behaviour patterns of firms in the context of unregulated markets, while *normative models* typically associate non-convex firms with public utilities (which may be privately owned but regulated). Models within the first category include constrained profit maximization (i.e., situations where firms maximize profits in the presence of some type of quantity constraint), and average cost (or more generally, mark-up) pricing. Normative models concentrate on two main pricing rules: marginal (cost) pricing, and regulation under break-even constraints (including the case of two-part tariffs, which may satisfy both criteria).

The main theme here is the analysis of the existence of equilibrium when the firms' behaviour is described in terms of *abstract* pricing rules. The goal is to provide a "blanket model" that could encompass most of the relevant specific models that can be discussed within this setting.

The abstract pricing rule approach has to cope with a number of problems when we come to analyze the existence of equilibrium. These problems, which concern technique and substance, do not exist in the standard competitive world, and happen to be interdependent and appear simultaneously. Let us comment briefly on three of these, in order to clarify the nature of the assumptions that we shall meet later on:

1) Pricing rules cannot be completely arbitrary. An equilibrium can only be obtained if these pricing rules satisfy some continuity property and exhibit some sensitivity with respect to its variables. Continuity is required in order to allow for the use of a fixed point argument (on the "inverse supply" map-

pings) to prove the existence of equilibrium. Sensitivity is needed in order to induce an agreement between firms on the prices they find acceptable.

2) When firms do not behave as profit maximizers at given prices, they may suffer losses in equilibrium. This is the case of marginal pricing, which yields negative profits under increasing returns to scale. Hence, some restriction must be imposed on the distribution of wealth in order to avoid difficulties for the survival of consumers (and the upper hemicontinuity of the demand mapping).

3) There are pricing policies (particularly relevant when production sets are not convex), that induce discontinuous wealth functions. The best known example is that of two-part tariffs, applied regularly by Telephone and Electricity companies. But this is also the case when firms offer discounts or pay salaries that include productivity bonuses, etc. If we want to cover these cases as well we must permit wealth functions to be discontinuous.

5.2 Pricing rules

5.2.1 The concept

Let $\mathbb{F}_j$ denote the jth firm's set of weakly efficient production plans, that is,

$$\mathbb{F}_j \equiv \{\mathbf{y}_j \in Y_j \mid \mathbf{y}'_j >> \mathbf{y}_j \Rightarrow \mathbf{y}'_j \notin Y_j\},$$

and call $\mathbb{F}$ the Cartesian product of the n sets of weakly efficient production plans, i.e. $\mathbb{F} \equiv \Pi_{j=1}^n \mathbb{F}_j$. Observe that when production sets are closed and comprehensive (axioms 3.1 and 3.2), $\mathbb{F}_j$ corresponds precisely to the boundary of Y_j (Proposition 3.2). Thus, in this case we can use $\mathbb{F}_j$ and ∂Y_j equivalently.

The firms' behaviour will now be defined in terms of a *pricing rule*. A pricing rule for the jth firm is usually defined as a mapping Φ_j applying the set of efficient production plans $\mathbb{F}_j$ to the price simplex $\mathbb{P}$. For a point $\mathbf{y}_j$ in $\mathbb{F}_j$, $\Phi_j(\mathbf{y}_j)$ has to be interpreted as the set of price vectors that are "acceptable" to the jth firm when producing $\mathbf{y}_j$. In other words, the jth firm is in equilibrium at the pair $(\mathbf{p}, \mathbf{y}_j)$, if $\mathbf{p} \in \Phi_j(\mathbf{y}_j)$. Even though, in most cases, the jth firm's pricing rule depends only on $\mathbf{y}_j$, we shall adopt here a more general notion of firms' behaviour, by allowing each firm's pricing rule to depend on other firms' actions and "market prices". To do so, let $\widetilde{\mathbf{y}} = (\mathbf{y}_1, \mathbf{y}_2, \ldots, \mathbf{y}_n)$ denote a point in $\mathbb{F}$. Therefore,

Definition 5.1 *A* ***pricing rule*** *for the jth firm is a correspondence,*

$$\phi_j : \mathbb{P} \times \mathbb{F} \rightarrow \mathbb{P}$$

A pricing rule is thus a mapping which describes the jth firm's set of admissible prices as a function of "market conditions". That is, $\mathbf{y}_j$ is an equilibrium production plan for the jth firm at prices $\mathbf{p}$, if and only if, $\mathbf{p} \in \phi_j(\mathbf{p}, \widetilde{\mathbf{y}})$ (where $\mathbf{y}_j$ is precisely the jth firm's production plan in $\widetilde{\mathbf{y}}$). For the purpose of interpretation, we may think of a market mechanism in which there is an auctioneer who proposes a vector of market prices $\mathbf{p}$, and a collection of efficient production plans $\widetilde{\mathbf{y}}$. Then, the jth firm checks whether the pair $(\mathbf{p}, \widetilde{\mathbf{y}})$ agrees with its objectives (formally, $[(\mathbf{p}, \widetilde{\mathbf{y}}), \mathbf{p}]$ belongs to the graph of ϕ_j).

Three points are worth stressing here:

(i) Since consumers' choices depend on market prices and the firms' production, we may think of each ϕ_j as also being dependent on the consumers' decisions. That is, $\phi_j(\mathbf{p}, \widetilde{\mathbf{y}}) = \Theta_j[\mathbf{p}, \widetilde{\mathbf{y}}, \xi(\mathbf{p}, \widetilde{\mathbf{y}})]$. This provides enough flexibility to deal with market situations in which the firms' target payoffs may depend on demand conditions (e.g. monopolistic competition, Boiteaux-Ramsey prices).

(ii) The pricing rule "may be either endogenous or exogenous to the model, and ...allows both price-taking and price-setting behaviors" [Cf. Cornet (1988, p. 106)]. Also, note that different firms may follow different pricing rules.

(iii) Pricing rules may refer to both normative and positive models. Normative models are intended to formalize regulation policies for non-convex firms, mainly in terms of pricing policies that satisfy some desirable properties (they typically aim at first or second best efficiency). Positive models try to describe plausible scenarios of market economies in which firms may exhibit increasing returns to scale, and profit maximization at given prices is not applicable.

A situation in which all firms find the proposed combination between prices and production plans acceptable is called a *production equilibrium*. Formally:

Definition 5.2 *A pair* $(\mathbf{p}, \widetilde{\mathbf{y}}) \in \mathbb{P} \times \mathbb{F}$ *is a* **production equilibrium***, relative to the pricing rules* $\phi = (\phi_1, \phi_2, \ldots, \phi_n)$*, if:*

$$\mathbf{p} \in \bigcap_{j=1}^{n} \phi_j(\mathbf{p}, \widetilde{\mathbf{y}}).$$

We shall denote the set of production equilibria by **PE***.*

The set of production equilibria describes the combination of prices and firms' production plans that are *candidates* for an equilibrium. Obviously, an equilibrium also requires that consumers maximize their preferences and that all markets clear. We shall be more precise on this in the next section. For the time being, note that the non-emptiness of the set **PE** is a necessary condition for the existence of equilibrium.

5.2.2 Admissible pricing rules

In order to analyze the existence of equilibrium in an economy with non-convex production sets, we have to introduce some restrictions on the admissible pricing rules. There will be two such restrictions. The first one refers to the continuity and convex-valuedness of the mapping ϕ_j. The second one regards the sensitivity of this mapping with respect to changes in $\mathbf{y}_j$.

Consider the following definition:

Definition 5.3 $\phi_j : \mathbb{P} \times \mathbb{F} \to \mathbb{P}$ *is a* **regular** *pricing rule, if* ϕ_j *is an upper hemicontinuous correspondence with non-empty, closed and convex values.*

A pricing rule is called *regular* when it satisfies some convenient analytical properties: The graph of the mapping is closed, and its values are non-empty, compact and convex.[1] This is the standard extension of continuous functions to set-valued mappings, which ensures that the graph of the pricing rule is closed and connected. The role of this restriction is to facilitate the use of a fixed-point argument.

It is worth advancing that the most relevant pricing rules do satisfy this requirement, under the standard assumptions on production sets. In particular, the following pricing rules will be shown to be regular:

(1) Profit maximization at given prices (when production sets are assumed to be convex, or when non-convexities are due to external economies).

(2) Average cost pricing (i.e. firms choose prices so that they just break-even).

(3) Marginal pricing (firms are instructed to sell their outputs at prices that satisfy the necessary conditions for optimality).

(4) Constrained Profit Maximization (a situation in which firms maximize profits at given prices, subject to quantity constraints).

---

[1]Let us recall here that a correspondence $\Gamma : D \subset \mathbb{R}^\ell \to \mathbb{R}^\ell$ is **closed** when its graph is closed [that is, if for all sequences $\{\mathbf{z}^\nu\} \subset D, \{\mathbf{f}^\nu\} \subset \mathbb{R}^\ell$, such that $\mathbf{f}^\nu \in \Gamma(\mathbf{z}^\nu)$ for all ν, and $\{\mathbf{z}^\nu\} \to \mathbf{z}, \{\mathbf{f}^\nu\} \to \mathbf{f}$, we have: $\mathbf{f} \in \Gamma(\mathbf{z})$]. A correspondence is **closed-valued**, when $\Gamma(\mathbf{z})$ is closed, for each $\mathbf{z} \in D$. If Γ is closed and applies on a compact space, then Γ is upper hemicontinuous.

The regularity of pricing rules is not sufficient for the existence of equilibrium. To understand this, consider an economy with two firms, each of which chooses a different constant price vector for all pairs $(\mathbf{p}, \widetilde{\mathbf{y}})$. That is, $\phi_j(\mathbf{p}, \widetilde{\mathbf{y}}) \equiv \{\overline{\mathbf{q}}_j\}$ (constant) for all $(\mathbf{p}, \widetilde{\mathbf{y}})$ in $\mathbb{P} \times \mathbb{F}$, $j = 1, 2$, with $\overline{\mathbf{q}}_1 \neq \overline{\mathbf{q}}_2$. These are perfectly regular pricing rules. However, the set of production equilibria is empty, so that no equilibrium exists.

To avoid this problem, we have to ensure that the pricing rule exhibits some sensitivity with respect to its variables (production plans and/or market prices). There are different ways of introducing this property. A natural requirement is that the losses a firm finds acceptable are bounded. Formally:

Definition 5.4 $\phi_j : \mathbb{P} \times \mathbb{F} \to \mathbb{P}$ *is a pricing rule with* **bounded losses***, if there is a scalar* $\alpha_j \leq 0$ *such that, for each* $(\mathbf{p}, \widetilde{\mathbf{y}})$ *in* $\mathbb{P} \times \mathbb{F}$,

$$\mathbf{q}\mathbf{y}_j \geq \alpha_j, \forall \, \mathbf{q} \in \phi_j(\mathbf{p}, \widetilde{\mathbf{y}})$$

The jth firm's pricing rule satisfies the *bounded losses* condition if there is a limit to the losses that this firm is prepared to accept, for any given production plan. This is a sensible property that imposes some structure on production sets for particular pricing rules (e.g. marginal pricing, as will be discussed later). When combined with the regularity requirement, the bounded losses property induces a sensitivity feature on the pricing rule; in particular, it prevents the case $\phi_j(\mathbf{p}, \widetilde{\mathbf{y}}) \equiv \{\overline{\mathbf{q}}_j\}$, for all $(\mathbf{p}, \widetilde{\mathbf{y}})$ in $\mathbb{P} \times \mathbb{F}$, to occur.[2]

A particular subfamily of pricing rules with bounded losses is that in which the firms' admissible profits are always non-negative. Formally:

Definition 5.5 $\phi_j : \mathbb{P} \times \mathbb{F} \to \mathbb{P}$ *is a* **loss-free** *pricing rule when, for all* $(\mathbf{p}, \widetilde{\mathbf{y}})$ *in* $\mathbb{P} \times \mathbb{F}$, $\mathbf{q}\mathbf{y}_j \geq 0, \forall \, \mathbf{q} \in \phi_j(\mathbf{p}, \widetilde{\mathbf{y}})$.

This restriction is rather natural in the context of un-regulated firms, when $\mathbf{0} \in Y_j$.

Note that the condition of bounded-losses is actually independent of the proposed market prices $\mathbf{p}$. A different type of restriction, when this is not the case, is associated with the monotonicity of the pricing rule with respect to

---

[2]To see this, let $\mathbf{y}_j < \mathbf{0}$ be a production plan in the boundary of Y_j. As $\overline{\mathbf{q}}_j > 0$, it follows that $\overline{\mathbf{q}}_j \mathbf{y}_j \leq 0$. Take now a sequence of production plans in ∂Y_j, whose components are progressively smaller than $\mathbf{y}_j$ in those components associated with positive prices. Clearly, losses get larger and larger without bound. See also Bonnisseau & Cornet (1988a, Remark 2.6).

p. An example is that in which we require, for every given pair $(\mathbf{p}, \widetilde{\mathbf{y}}) \in \mathbb{P} \times \mathbb{F}$, all $\mathbf{q}_j \in \phi_j(\mathbf{p}, \widetilde{\mathbf{y}})$, the existence of some commodity c for which $y_{jc} \geq 0$ and $q_{jc} \geq p_c$ (this means that the jth firm would never propose a reduction on the prices of all its outputs). A weaker version of this property, which allows us to encompass most of the relevant pricing rules, is presented in Vohra (1988a).

5.3 The model

5.3.1 Description of the economy

Let us briefly summarize the main features of the economy. Consider an economy with ℓ perfectly divisible commodities, m competitive consumers, and n firms. A point $\omega \in \mathbb{R}^\ell$ denotes the vector of initial endowments. We denote the standard price simplex by $\mathbb{P} \subset \mathbb{R}^\ell_+$, that is, $\mathbb{P} = \{\mathbf{p} \in \mathbb{R}^\ell_+ \ / \ \sum_{t=1}^\ell p_t = 1\}$.

For $j = 1, 2, \ldots, n$, $Y_j \subset \mathbb{R}^\ell$ denotes the jth firm's production set, while $\mathbb{F}_j$ stands for the jth firm's set of weakly efficient production plans, and $\mathbb{F}$ the Cartesian product of the n sets of weakly efficient production plans, that is, $\mathbb{F} \equiv \Pi_{j=1}^n \mathbb{F}_j$. We denote the aggregate production set by $Y = \sum_{j=1}^n Y_j$.

The jth firm's behaviour is described by a pricing rule correspondence $\phi_j : \mathbb{P} \times \mathbb{F} \to \mathbb{P}$, that establishes the jth firm's set of admissible prices as a function of "market conditions". A production equilibrium is a situation in which all firms find the proposed combination between market prices and production plans acceptable. That is, a pair $(\mathbf{p}, \widetilde{\mathbf{y}})$ such that $\mathbf{p} \in \bigcap_{j=1}^n \phi_j(\mathbf{p}, \widetilde{\mathbf{y}})$. The set of production equilibria is denoted by **PE**.

The ith consumer is characterized by a triple, $[X_i, u_i, r_i]$, in which X_i, u_i stand for the ith consumer's consumption set and utility function, respectively. The term r_i denotes the ith consumer's wealth. Throughout this chapter, r_i is taken to be a mapping from $\mathbb{P} \times \mathbb{R}^{\ell n}$ into $\mathbb{R}$ so that, for each pair $(\mathbf{p}, \widetilde{\mathbf{y}})$, $r_i(\mathbf{p}, \widetilde{\mathbf{y}})$ gives us the ith consumer's wealth. For a given $\mathbf{p} \in \mathbb{P}$, $\min \mathbf{p} X_i$ denotes the minimum of $\mathbf{p} \mathbf{x}_i$ over X_i. Under the usual assumptions this is a continuous function, by virtue of the Maximum Theorem.

Let $(\mathbf{p}, \widetilde{\mathbf{y}}) \in \mathbb{P} \times \mathbb{F}$ be given. Then, the ith consumer solves the problem:

$$\left. \begin{array}{c} Max \ \ u_i(\mathbf{x}_i) \\ s.t. : \ \ \mathbf{p}\mathbf{x}_i \leq r_i(\mathbf{p}, \widetilde{\mathbf{y}}) \\ \mathbf{x}_i \in X_i \end{array} \right\}$$

Let ξ_i stand for the ith consumer's demand correspondence, that is, $\xi_i(\mathbf{p}, \widetilde{\mathbf{y}})$ is the set of solutions to the program above. The consumers' behaviour can therefore be summarized by an aggregate demand correspondence $\xi : \mathbb{P} \times \mathbb{F} \to \sum_{i=1}^{m} X_i$, given by $\xi(\mathbf{p}, \widetilde{\mathbf{y}}) \equiv \sum_{i=1}^{m} \xi_i(\mathbf{p}, \widetilde{\mathbf{y}})$.

An **economy** can be summarized as:

$$E = \left[(X_i, u_i, r_i)_{i=1}^{m}, (Y_j, \phi_j)_{j=1}^{n}, \omega \right]$$

An allocation of this economy is a point $\left[(\mathbf{x}_i)_{i=1}^{m}, (\mathbf{y}_j)_{j=1}^{n} \right]$ in $\Pi_{i=1}^{m} X_i \times \Pi_{j=1}^{n} Y_j$. The set of **attainable allocations** is given by:

$$\Omega \equiv \{ [(\mathbf{x}_i)_{i=1}^{m}, (\mathbf{y}_j)_{j=1}^{n}] \in \prod_{i=1}^{m} X_i \times \prod_{j=1}^{n} Y_j \ / \ \sum_{i=1}^{m} \mathbf{x}_i - \omega \leq \sum_{j=1}^{n} \mathbf{y}_j \}$$

The projections of Ω on the spaces containing X_i, Y_j give us the ith *consumer's set of attainable consumptions*, X_i^A, and the jth *firm's set of attainable production plans*, Y_j^A, respectively.

5.3.2 Assumptions

Consider now the following assumptions:

Axiom 5.1 *For each $i = 1, 2, \ldots, m$:*
   (i) X_i is a non-empty, closed and convex subset of $\mathbb{R}^\ell$, bounded from below.
   (ii) $u_i : X_i \to \mathbb{R}$ is a continuous, quasi-concave$^+$ and non-satiable utility function.

Axiom 5.2 *For each firm $j = 1, 2, \ldots, n$:*
   (i) Y_j is a closed subset of $\mathbb{R}^\ell$.
   (ii) $Y_j - \mathbb{R}_+^\ell \subset Y_j$.
   (iii) ϕ_j is a regular pricing rule with bounded losses.

Axiom 5.3 *Ω is compact.*

Axiom 5.4 *Let **PE** stand for the set of production equilibria. The restriction of r_i over **PE** is continuous, with $r_i(\mathbf{p}, \widetilde{\mathbf{y}}) > \min \mathbf{p} X_i$, and $\sum_{i=1}^{m} r_i(\mathbf{p}, \widetilde{\mathbf{y}}) = \mathbf{p}(\omega + \sum_{j=1}^{n} \mathbf{y}_j)$.*

Axiom 5.1 is standard. It assumes that consumers have complete, continuous, convex and non-satiable preferences, defined on convex choice sets bounded from below.

Axiom 5.2 refers to individual firms. Besides closedness, it is assumed that Y_j is comprehensive. Observe that parts (i) and (ii) of axiom 2 imply that the set of weakly efficient production plans $\mathbb{F}_j$, consists exactly of those points in the boundary of Y_j. Note that we have not assumed here that $\mathbf{0} \in Y_j$. Part (iii) establishes that each firm's pricing rule is an upper hemicontinuous correspondence with non-empty, compact and convex values, and that the losses that the firm finds acceptable are bounded.

Axiom 5.3 says that the set of attainable allocations is compact. In particular, it is not possible to obtain unlimited amounts of production from a finite amount of endowments. As shown later in chapter 12, this axiom can be derived from more primitive assumptions.

Axiom 5.4 refers to production equilibria. First, it assumes the continuity of wealth functions, when restricted to the set of production equilibria (a much weaker requirement than assuming that r_i is continuous over $\mathbb{P} \times \mathbb{F}$). Then, it introduces the "cheaper point" requirement: in a production equilibrium the ith consumer's demand does not minimize $\mathbf{px}_i$ on X_i. This implies of course a survival condition (every consumer will survive in equilibrium). Finally, it also says that total wealth equals the value of the aggregate initial endowments plus total profits.

Notice that even though Ω is compact, we do not know whether it is empty or not (that will follow from the existence theorem).

5.3.3   Equilibrium

The following definition makes the equilibrium notion precise:

Definition 5.6 *An **equilibrium** is a price vector* $\mathbf{p}^* \in \mathbb{P}$ *and an allocation* $[(\mathbf{x}_i^*), \widetilde{\mathbf{y}}^*]$, *such that:*

(α) $\mathbf{x}_i^* \in \xi_i(\mathbf{p}^*, \widetilde{\mathbf{y}}^*)$, *for all* $i = 1, 2, \ldots, m$.

(β) $\mathbf{p}^* \in \bigcap_{j=1}^{n} \phi_j(\mathbf{p}^*, \widetilde{\mathbf{y}}^*)$.

(γ) $\sum_{i=1}^{m} \mathbf{x}_i^* - \sum_{j=1}^{n} \mathbf{y}_j^* \leq \omega$, *and* $\sum_{i=1}^{m} x_{it}^* - \sum_{j=1}^{n} y_{jt}^* < \omega_t \Rightarrow p_t^* = 0$.

That is, an equilibrium is a situation in which: (a) Consumers maximize their preferences subject to their budget constraints; (b) Every firm is in equilibrium; and (c) All markets clear (meaning that net production is greater or equal than net demand on all markets, and that only free goods can be produced in excess).

The main result of this chapter is as follows:

Theorem 5.1 *Let E stand for an economy satisfying axioms 5.1 to 5.4. Then an equilibrium exists.*

(The proof of this theorem is given in the next section)

This theorem says that, under rather general conditions, an equilibrium exists when consumers behave competitively and the firms' pricing rules are regular and have bounded losses. It is worth stressing that:

1) In an equilibrium, different firms may follow different rules of behaviour (e.g. there may be convex firms that behave competitively, non-convex firms that use mark-up pricing to set their prices, and regulated monopolies that sell their outputs according to the marginal pricing principle).

2) The existence result presented here allows for discontinuous wealth functions (continuity is only assumed on the set of production equilibria). This is important because it allows us to deal with income schedules which are relevant but usually difficult to handle in a general equilibrium framework (e.g. two-part tariffs, salaries that include productivity bonuses, etc.).

3) The structure of the model (and the proof of the existence theorem) allows us to interpret the functioning of this economy as follows: (a) There is an auctioneer who calls both a price vector (to be seen as proposed market prices), and a vector of efficient production plans. (b) Given these prices and production plans, the ith consumer chooses the consumption bundle that maximizes her utility, subject to her wealth constraint. (c) Firms check whether the proposed prices-production pair agrees with their objectives. When this is so, the price vector is a candidate for market equilibrium. (d) When not all firms agree on the proposed prices-production combination, or markets do not clear, the auctioneer tries a new proposal. For that, she chooses those prices and production plans that maximize the value of the "excess demand", and minimize the distance between each pricing rule and the proposed prices.

Remark 5.1 *Even though in this abstract framework the existence result allows for pricing rules that may depend on $\mathbb{P} \times \mathbb{F}$, in the case of particular pricing rules we shall restrict their domain to the smallest possible one (in particular, pricing rules will appear in most cases as mappings from $\mathbb{F}_j$ into $\mathbb{P}$). It should be clear that this is a particular case of the general setting presented in this chapter.*

5.4 The existence of equilibrium

The strategy of the proof of Theorem 5.1 goes along the lines of the standard one for convex economies, presented in chapter 4. Namely, we shall apply a fixed-point argument over an artificial economy (which satisfies all the required properties for that), and show that this actually corresponds to an equilibrium in the original one. In order to understand the construction of this artificial economy we shall begin by pointing out two difficulties and providing the means to handling them.

5.4.1   Two difficulties

The reader should notice two different complications that have to be considered in order to apply the scheme of proof mentioned above. The first one refers to axiom 5.4, which establishes conditions on the set of production equilibria *only*. The second one refers to axiom 5.2. Let us present these difficulties:

(i) Axiom 5.4 ensures the continuity of wealth functions, the minimum wealth requirement $r_i(\mathbf{p},\widetilde{\mathbf{y}}) > \min \mathbf{p} X_i$, and the Walras Law, on the set of production equilibria only, and not on the relevant domain $\mathbb{P} \times \mathbb{F}$. Hence the demand correspondence may fail to be upper hemicontinuous and the Walras Law may not hold.

(ii) According to (iii) of axiom 5.2, we are describing the behaviour of firms in terms of upper hemicontinuous and convex-valued correspondences (the regular pricing rules). Yet these correspondences are defined over non-convex sets, so that we are not able to apply Kakutani's Fixed-point Theorem directly.

These two complications will be "remedied" in the way of constructing the artificial economy, where we shall show that an equilibrium exists.

Handling the first difficulty

The following lemma is required to prove the next proposition, which aims at solving the first complication mentioned above:[3]

Lemma 5.1 *Let E be a metric space, A a closed subset of E, f a continuous bounded mapping of A into $\mathbb{R}$. Then, there exists a continuous mapping g of E into $\mathbb{R}$ which coincides with f in A and is such that*

$$\sup_{x \in E} g(\mathbf{x}) = \sup_{y \in A} f(\mathbf{y}) \quad , \qquad \inf_{x \in E} g(\mathbf{x}) = \inf_{y \in A} f(\mathbf{y})$$

Proof.   Suppose that $\inf_{y \in A} f(y) = 1$, $\sup_{y \in A} f(y) = 2$, without loss of generality (in case f is constant the result is trivial). Now call $h(x)$ the following mapping: $h(x) = \inf_{y \in A}[f(y) \cdot d(x,y)]$ (where d stands for distance). Define $g(x)$ as equal to $f(x)$ for $x \in A$, and equal to $h(x)/d(x,A)$ for $x \in$

---

[3]This result is known as the Tietze-Urysohn Extenstion Theorem. The proof presented here is borrowed from Dieudonné (1969), pp.89-90.

$E - A$. It follows that $1 \leq g(x) \leq 2$ for $x \in E - A$. We need to prove that g is continuous on E. If $x \in A$, g is continuous by assumption. Thus, we simply have to prove that h is continuous in the open set $E - A$ (because $d(x, A)$ is continuous and different from zero).

Let $R = d(x, A)$; for $d(x, x') \leq \varepsilon < R$, we have $d(x, y) \leq d(x', y) + \varepsilon$, hence $h(x) \leq h(x') + 2\varepsilon$ (since $f(y) \leq 2$), and similarly $h(x') \leq h(x) + 2\varepsilon$, which proves the continuity of h in this case.

Suppose now that $x \in \partial A$. Given $\varepsilon > 0$, let $R > 0$ be such that for $y \in A \cap B(x; R)$ (a ball of centre x and radius R), $\mid f(y) - f(x) \mid \leq \varepsilon$. Let $C = A \cap B(x; R)$, $D = A - C$; if $x' \in E - A$ and $d(x, x') \leq R/4$, we have, for each y in D, $d(x', y) \geq d(x, y) - d(x, x') \geq 3R/4$, hence

$$\inf_{y \in D} [f(y) \cdot d(x', y)] \geq 3R/4$$

On the other hand, $f(x)d(x', x) \leq 2d(x', x) \leq R/2$, and therefore

$$\inf_{y \in A} [f(y) \cdot d(x', y)] = \inf_{y \in C} [f(y) \cdot d(x', y)]$$

But, as $f(x) - \varepsilon \leq f(y) \leq f(x) + \varepsilon$ for $y \in C$, and $\inf_{y \in C} d(x', y) = d(x', A)$, we have

$$[f(x) - \varepsilon]d(x', A) \leq \inf_{y \in A}[f(y) \cdot d(x', y)] \leq [f(x) + \varepsilon]d(x', A)$$

which proves that $\mid g(x') - f(x) \mid \leq \varepsilon$ for $x' \in E - A$ and $d(x, x') \leq R/4$. On the other hand, if $x' \in A$ and $d(x, x') \leq R/4$, we have

$$\mid g(x') - f(x) \mid = \mid f(x') - f(x) \mid \leq \varepsilon$$

The proof is in this way complete. $\boxed{\textbf{Q.e.d.}}$

Proposition 5.1 *Under axioms 5.1 to 5.4, for every $i = 1, 2, ..., m$, there exists a continuous function $R_i : \mathbb{P} \times \mathbb{F} \to \mathbb{R}$ such that $R_i(\mathbf{p}, \widetilde{\mathbf{y}}) > \min \mathbf{p} X_i$, for all $(\mathbf{p}, \widetilde{\mathbf{y}})$, with $R_i(\mathbf{p}, \widetilde{\mathbf{y}}) = r_i(\mathbf{p}, \widetilde{\mathbf{y}})$ whenever $(\mathbf{p}, \widetilde{\mathbf{y}})$ is a production equilibrium.*

     Proof.   Under axioms 5.1 and 5.3, the set of production equilibria is a closed (possibly empty) set. By axiom 5.4, r_i is continuous over the set of production equilibria. Lemma 5.1 ensures the existence of a continuous function $R_i : \mathbb{P} \times \mathbb{F} \to \mathbb{R}$ such that $R_i(\mathbf{p}, \widetilde{\mathbf{y}})$ coincides with $r_i(\mathbf{p}, \widetilde{\mathbf{y}})$ over the set of production equilibria, and $R_i(\mathbf{p}, \widetilde{\mathbf{y}}) > \min \mathbf{p} X_i$ for all $(\mathbf{p}, \widetilde{\mathbf{y}}) \in$

$\mathbb{P} \times \mathbb{F}$ (because $\min \mathbf{p} X_i < r_i(\mathbf{p}, \widetilde{\mathbf{y}})$ over the set of production equilibria, by assumption, and $\min \mathbf{p} X_i$ is continuous and bounded from below). $\boxed{\text{Q.e.d.}}$

Proposition 5.1 permits the substitution of the consumers' original wealth functions by continuous mappings that satisfy the cheapest point requirement, and coincide with the original ones in the set of production equilibria.

But there still remains the problem of the Walras Law. In order to deal with this complication, let $\overline{R}$ stand for a scalar such that $\overline{R} > R_i(\mathbf{p}, \widetilde{\mathbf{y}})$, for all i, all $(\mathbf{p}, \widetilde{\mathbf{y}}) \in \mathbb{P} \times \mathbb{F}^A$, where $\mathbb{F}^A = \Pi_{j=1}^n \mathbb{F}_j^A$, and $\mathbb{F}_j^A$ stands for the set of attainable and weakly efficient production plans for the jth firm (a compact set under axiom 5.3). Now define a mapping $g : \mathbb{P} \times \mathbb{F} \to \mathbb{R}^{\ell n}$, such that it associates with every $(\mathbf{p}, \widetilde{\mathbf{y}})$ in $\mathbb{P} \times \mathbb{F}$, the set of points $\widetilde{\mathbf{t}} = (\mathbf{t}_1, ..., \mathbf{t}_n)$ in $\mathbb{R}^{\ell n}$, with $\mathbf{t}_j = g_j(\mathbf{p}, \widetilde{\mathbf{y}})$, which solve the following program:

$$\left. \begin{array}{c} Min \ \ dist \left[\widetilde{\mathbf{t}}, \ \widetilde{\mathbf{y}} \right] \\ s.t. : \mathbf{p} \left(\omega + \sum_{j=1}^n \mathbf{t}_j \right) = \sum_{i=1}^m \min\{R_i(\mathbf{p}, \widetilde{\mathbf{y}}), \overline{R}\} \\ \mathbf{p} \mathbf{t}_j \geq \alpha_j, \quad j = 1, 2, ..., n \end{array} \right\}$$

Observe that the feasible set is non-empty and convex, and the objective function is strictly convex. Therefore, for each $(\mathbf{p}, \widetilde{\mathbf{y}})$ in $\mathbb{P} \times \mathbb{F}$, there is a unique solution to this program, which varies continuously with $(\mathbf{p}, \widetilde{\mathbf{y}})$ over any compact subset of $\mathbb{P} \times \mathbb{F}$ (by virtue of the maximum theorem). Note that we have incorporated the bounded losses assumption within mapping g.

Define now:

$$\mathbb{F}' = \{\widetilde{\mathbf{y}} \in \mathbb{F} \ / \ \sum_{j=1}^n g_j(\mathbf{p}, \widetilde{\mathbf{y}}) + \omega \in \sum_{i=1}^m X_i + \mathbb{R}_+^\ell, \ \ \mathbf{p} \in \mathbb{P}\}$$

This set plays the role of the set of attainable allocations in an economy in which we substitute the original attainable production plans $\widetilde{\mathbf{y}}$, by those $\widetilde{\mathbf{t}}$ that satisfy the two restrictions included in the program above (they yield an aggregate income equal to the worth of aggregate resources plus total profits, and, for each $j = 1, 2, ..., n$, and all $\mathbf{p} \in \mathbb{P}$, the associated profits are above the maximum losses admissible, α_j).

We claim that, under the assumptions established, this set is bounded. To see this, note that, on the one hand, $\sum_{j=1}^n g_j(\mathbf{p}, \widetilde{\mathbf{y}}) \leq (\overline{R}m - \alpha n)\mathbf{e}$, where $\mathbf{e}$ stands for the unit vector in $\mathbb{R}^\ell$ and $\alpha = \min_j\{\alpha_j\}$. On the other hand, we require $\sum_{j=1}^n g_j(\mathbf{p}, \widetilde{\mathbf{y}}) \geq \sum_{j=1}^n \mathbf{b}_i$, where $\mathbf{b}_i$ is a lower bound of X_i, $i = 1, 2, ..., m$. The construction of function g implies the boundedness of $\mathbb{F}'$.

Now let $k > 0$ be a large enough scalar so that every attainable consumption set belongs *to the interior* of $[-k\mathbf{e}, k\mathbf{e}]$, and $\mathbb{F}^* = \mathbb{F} \bigcap [-k\mathbf{e}, k\mathbf{e}]^n$

contains the set $\mathbb{F}'$ *in its relative interior.* Under the axioms established this number k can always be found. We call $\mathbb{F}^*_j$, $\mathbb{F}'_j$ the projections of $\mathbb{F}^*$, $\mathbb{F}'$ on Y_j, respectively.

Handling the second difficulty

The next proposition deals with the second complication mentioned above:

Proposition 5.2 *Under axioms 5.2 and 5.3, $\mathbb{F}^*_j$ can be made homeomorphic to a simplex $S_j = \{s_j \in \mathbb{R}^\ell_+ \ / \ \sum_{i=1}^\ell s_{ij} = 1\}$, so that the points in $\mathbb{F}'_j$ are mapped into the interior of S_j.*

Proof.   Under axioms 5.2 and 5.3, $\mathbb{F}'_j$ is in the (relative) interior of $\mathbb{F}^*_j$, for all j. Moreover, the way of constructing $\mathbb{F}^*_j$ implies that the set $\mathbb{F}^*_j + \{ke\}$ will be in $\mathbb{R}^\ell_+$, and the set $\mathbb{F}'_j + \{ke\}$ will be in the interior of $\mathbb{R}^\ell_+$ (where e stands for the unit vector in $\mathbb{R}^\ell_+$). Now define a mapping $H_j : \mathbb{F}^*_j \to S_j$ as follows (see figure 5.1 below):

$$H_j(\mathbf{y}_j) = \{s_j \in S_j \ / \ \exists \ \lambda \geq 0 \ : \ \lambda s_j = \mathbf{y}_j + ke\}$$

Axiom 5.2 implies that this mapping is well defined, continuous, onto and that for each $\mathbf{y}_j \in \mathbb{F}^*_j$ there exists a unique point $s_j \in S_j$ such that $s_j = H_j(\mathbf{y}_j)$ (if there were two one would be strictly smaller than the other, contradicting the fact that both are points in S_j).

Let now h_j denote the inverse mapping of H (that is, $h_j : S_j \to \mathbb{F}^*_j$ with $h_j(s_j) = \lambda s_j - ke = \mathbf{y}_j$). This is an onto, continuous function which maps the interior of S_j into the interior of $\mathbb{F}^*_j$, so that no point in ∂S_j has associated with it a point in $\mathbb{F}'_j$. This mapping gives us the postulated homeomorphism between S_j and $\mathbb{F}^*_j$. **Q.e.d.**

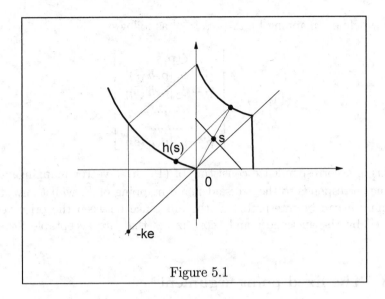

Figure 5.1

5.4.2 The artificial economy

For each $j = 1, 2, \ldots, n$, let h_j denote the continuous mapping that associates a unique $\mathbf{y}_j$ in $\mathbb{F}_j^*$ with every $\mathbf{s}_j$ in S_j. Let $\mathbb{S} \equiv \Pi_{j=1}^n S_j$, and define $\Delta \equiv \mathbb{P} \times \mathbb{S}$. A vector $\widetilde{\mathbf{s}} = (\mathbf{s}_1, \ldots, \mathbf{s}_n)$ denotes a point in $\mathbb{S}$. We shall write:

$$h(\widetilde{\mathbf{s}}) \equiv [h_1(\mathbf{s}_1), h_2(\mathbf{s}_2), \ldots, h_n(\mathbf{s}_n)]$$

$$\widehat{g}(\mathbf{p}, \widetilde{\mathbf{s}}) \equiv g[\mathbf{p}, h(\widetilde{\mathbf{s}})]$$

$$\widehat{R}_i(\mathbf{p}, \widetilde{\mathbf{s}}) \equiv R_i[\mathbf{p}, h(\widetilde{\mathbf{s}})]$$

which are obviously continuous functions on $\mathbb{S}$ and Δ, respectively.

Let $\widehat{X}_i = X_i \bigcap [-k\mathbf{e}, k\mathbf{e}]$, and let $\widehat{\xi}_i(\mathbf{p}, \mathbf{s})$ stand for the set of solutions to the program:

$$\left. \begin{array}{l} Max \quad u_i(\mathbf{x}_i) \\ s.t. : \mathbf{x}_i \in \widehat{X}_i \\ \mathbf{px}_i \leq \min\{\widehat{R}_i(\mathbf{p}, \widetilde{\mathbf{s}}), \overline{R}\} \end{array} \right\}$$

Call $\widehat{E}$ the economy constructed in that way, and let $\widehat{\zeta}$ be the corresponding excess demand mapping, that is,

$$\widehat{\zeta}(\mathbf{p}, \widetilde{\mathbf{s}}) \equiv \sum_{i=1}^m \widehat{\xi}_i(\mathbf{p}, \widetilde{\mathbf{s}}) - \sum_{j=1}^n \widehat{g}_j(\mathbf{p}, \widetilde{\mathbf{s}}) - \{\omega\}$$

Now define a mapping $\Gamma : \Delta \to \mathbb{R}^{\ell(1+n)}$ as follows:

$$\Gamma(\mathbf{p}, \mathbf{s}) \equiv \begin{bmatrix} \widehat{\zeta}(\mathbf{p}, \widetilde{\mathbf{s}}) \\ \mathbf{p} - \phi_1 [\mathbf{p}, h(\widetilde{\mathbf{s}})] \\ \mathbf{p} - \phi_2 [\mathbf{p}, h(\widetilde{\mathbf{s}})] \\ \cdots\cdots\cdots \\ \cdots\cdots\cdots \\ \mathbf{p} - \phi_n [\mathbf{p}, h(\widetilde{\mathbf{s}})] \end{bmatrix}$$

This is a correspondence consisting of $(1+n)$ ℓ-vector mappings. The first one corresponds to the excess demand mapping of $\widehat{E}$, whilst any of the remaining n can be interpreted as the difference between the price vector proposed by the auctioneer and those prices that are acceptable for each firm.

5.4.3   The fixed point argument

The following result, which is a variant of the classical Gale-Nikaido-Debreu Lemma, embodies the fixed-point argument required for the proof of the theorem:

Proposition 5.3 *Let D be a compact and convex subset of $\mathbb{R}^\ell$, and $\Gamma : D \to \mathbb{R}^\ell$ an upper hemicontinuous correspondence, with non-empty, compact and convex values. Then points $\mathbf{x}^* \in D$, $\mathbf{y}^* \in \Gamma(\mathbf{x}^*)$ exist such that $(\mathbf{x} - \mathbf{x}^*)\mathbf{y}^* \leq 0$, for all $\mathbf{x} \in D$.*

Proof.   Let $T = \Gamma(D)$. Since D is compact, T will be a compact set [see for instance Border (1985,11.16)]. Let $Co(T)$ denote the convex hull of T. By construction $Co(T)$ is a compact and convex set. Now define a correspondence $\rho : Co(T) \to D$ as follows:

$$\rho(\mathbf{y}) = \{\mathbf{x} \in D \ / \ \mathbf{x}\mathbf{y} \geq \mathbf{z}\mathbf{y}, \ \forall \, \mathbf{z} \in D\}$$

Clearly ρ is a non-empty, convex-valued correspondence. Furthermore, ρ is upper hemicontinuous in view of the Maximum Theorem (we are maximizing a continuous function over a fixed set, which can be regarded as a continuous correspondence). Now define a new correspondence, ϕ from $D \times Co(T)$ into itself as follows:

$$\phi(\mathbf{x}, \mathbf{y}) = \rho(\mathbf{y}) \times \Gamma(\mathbf{x})$$

By construction, ϕ is an upper hemicontinuous correspondence with non-empty, compact and convex values, mapping a compact and convex set into itself. Thus, Kakutani's fixed point theorem applies and there exists $(\mathbf{x}^*, \mathbf{y}^*) \in \phi(\mathbf{x}^*, \mathbf{y}^*)$, that is,

$$\mathbf{x}^* \in \rho(\mathbf{y}^*), \quad \mathbf{y}^* \in \Gamma(\mathbf{x}^*)$$

By definition of ρ we have:

$$\mathbf{x}^* \mathbf{y}^* = \max \, \mathbf{z} \mathbf{y}^*, \, \mathbf{z} \in D$$

Hence, the result follows. $\boxed{\text{Q.e.d.}}$

5.4.4 Proof of the existence theorem

We are now ready to prove:

Theorem 5.1 *Let E stand for an economy satisfying axioms 5.1 to 5.4. Then an equilibrium exists.*

Proof. Let $\widehat{E}$ stand for the economy defined above. Under the assumptions of the theorem, for every $i = 1, 2, \ldots, m$, the mapping $\widehat{\beta}_i : \Delta \to \widehat{X}_i$ given by:

$$\widehat{\beta}_i(\mathbf{p}, \widetilde{\mathbf{s}}) = \{\mathbf{x}_i \in \widehat{X}_i \, / \, \mathbf{p}\mathbf{x}_i \leq \min\{\widehat{R}_i(\mathbf{p}, \widetilde{\mathbf{s}}), \overline{R}\}\}$$

is continuous in $(\mathbf{p}, \widetilde{\mathbf{s}})$ (Theorem 2.2), with non-empty, compact and convex values. Therefore, since preferences are assumed to be continuous and convex, for each pair $(\mathbf{p}, \widetilde{\mathbf{s}}) \in \Delta$, every $\widehat{\xi}_i$ will be an upper-hemicontinuous correspondence, with non-empty, compact and convex values (Theorem 2.4). The way of constructing the $\widehat{g}$ mapping implies that $\widehat{\zeta}$ inherits these properties. Since we have assumed that pricing rules are regular, this also applies to Γ.

Thus, Γ is an upper-hemicontinuous correspondence, with non-empty, compact and convex values, applying a compact and convex set, $\Delta \subset \mathbb{R}_+^{\ell(1+n)}$ into $\mathbb{R}^{\ell(1+n)}$. Then, Proposition 5.3 ensures the existence of points $(\mathbf{p}^*, \widetilde{\mathbf{s}}^*)$ in Δ, $(\mathbf{z}^*, \widetilde{\mathbf{v}}^*)$ in $\Gamma(\mathbf{p}^*, \widetilde{\mathbf{s}}^*)$ such that,

$$(\mathbf{p}^*, \widetilde{\mathbf{s}}^*)(\mathbf{z}^*, \widetilde{\mathbf{v}}^*) \geq (\mathbf{p}, \widetilde{\mathbf{s}})(\mathbf{z}^*, \widetilde{\mathbf{v}}^*)$$

for every pair $(\mathbf{p}, \widetilde{\mathbf{s}})$ in Δ. In particular,

$$(\mathbf{p}^*, \widetilde{\mathbf{s}}^*)(\mathbf{z}^*, \widetilde{\mathbf{v}}^*) \geq (\mathbf{p}, \widetilde{\mathbf{s}}^*)(\mathbf{z}^*, \widetilde{\mathbf{v}}^*), \quad \forall \, \mathbf{p} \in \mathbb{P} \qquad [1]$$

$$(\mathbf{p}^*, \widetilde{\mathbf{s}}^*)(\mathbf{z}^*, \widetilde{\mathbf{v}}^*) \geq (\mathbf{p}^*, \widetilde{\mathbf{s}})(\mathbf{z}^*, \widetilde{\mathbf{v}}^*), \quad \forall \, \widetilde{\mathbf{s}} \in \mathbb{S} \qquad [2]$$

From [1] it follows that $\mathbf{p}^*\mathbf{z}^* \geq \mathbf{p}\mathbf{z}^*$, for all $\mathbf{p} \in \mathbb{P}$, which implies:

$$\mathbf{p}^*\mathbf{z}^* = \max_j \; z_j^*$$

By construction,

$$\mathbf{p}^*\mathbf{z}^* = \sum_{i=1}^{m} \min\{\widehat{R}_i(\mathbf{p}^*,\widetilde{\mathbf{s}}^*), \overline{R}\} - \mathbf{p}^* \left[\omega + \sum_{j=1}^{n} \widehat{g}_j(\mathbf{p}^*,\widetilde{\mathbf{s}}^*) \right] = 0$$

so that $\max_j z_j^* = 0$, and hence, $\mathbf{z}^* \leq \mathbf{0}$, with $p_k^* = 0$ whenever $z_k^* < 0$.

Note that $\mathbf{z}^* \leq \mathbf{0}$ means that $\sum_{i=1}^{m} \mathbf{x}_i^* \leq \sum_{j=1}^{n} \widehat{g}_j(\mathbf{p}^*,\mathbf{s}_j^*) - \{\omega\}$, and consequently, $[h_1(\widetilde{\mathbf{s}}^*), \; ..., \; h_n(\widetilde{\mathbf{s}}^*)] \in \mathbb{F}' \subset int\mathbb{F}^*$. Moreover, as $\mathbb{F}'_j$ is mapped by function H_j into the interior of S_j, it follows that $\mathbf{s}_j^* \in intS_j$, for all j.

Now from [2] we deduce that $\widetilde{\mathbf{s}}^*\widetilde{\mathbf{v}}^* \geq \widetilde{\mathbf{s}}\widetilde{\mathbf{v}}^*$, for all $\widetilde{\mathbf{s}}$ in $\mathbb{S}$, and hence for each $j = 1, 2, \ldots, n$ we have:

$$\mathbf{s}_j^*\mathbf{v}_j^* = \max_i \; v_{ij}^*$$

This implies that either $v_{kj}^* = \{\max_i v_{ij}^*\}$, or else $s_{kj}^* = 0$, for all k. As $\mathbf{s}_j^* >> \mathbf{0}$ for all j, $p_k^* - q_{jk}^* = \gamma_j$ (constant for each j), for all k. But $\mathbf{v}_j^* \equiv \mathbf{p}^* - \mathbf{q}_j^*$ consists of the difference between two points in $\mathbb{P}$ (for some $\mathbf{q}_j^* \in \phi_j[\mathbf{p}_j^*, h(\widetilde{\mathbf{s}}^*)]$), so that $\mathbf{v}_j^* = \mathbf{0}$, for all j. This in turn means that $\mathbf{p}^* \in \cap_{j=1}^{n} \phi_j[\mathbf{p}^*, h(\widetilde{\mathbf{s}}^*)]$, that is, $[\mathbf{p}^*, h(\widetilde{\mathbf{s}}^*)]$ is a production equilibrium of the original economy.

Axiom 5.4 ensures that

$$\mathbf{p}^* \left[\omega + \sum_{j=1}^{m} h_j(\widetilde{\mathbf{s}}^*) \right] = \sum_{i=1}^{m} \widehat{R}_i(\mathbf{p}^*,\widetilde{\mathbf{s}}^*) = \sum_{i=1}^{m} r_i[\mathbf{p}^*, h(\widetilde{\mathbf{s}}^*)]$$

Moreover, the bounded-losses assumption implies that $\mathbf{p}^*h_j(\widetilde{\mathbf{s}}^*) \geq \alpha_j$ for all j. Hence $\widehat{g}_j(\mathbf{p}^*,\widetilde{\mathbf{s}}^*) = h_j(\widetilde{\mathbf{s}}^*) = \mathbf{y}_j^*$, and consequently,

$$0 \geq \mathbf{z}^* \in \sum_{i=1}^{m} \widehat{\xi}_i(\mathbf{p}^*,\widetilde{\mathbf{s}}^*) - \sum_{j=1}^{n} \mathbf{y}_j^* - \{\omega\}$$

Finally, it remains to show that, for all i, $\mathbf{x}_i^*$ maximizes u_i on the set

$$\beta_i(\mathbf{p}^*,\widetilde{\mathbf{y}}^*) \equiv \{\mathbf{x}_i \in X_i \; / \; \mathbf{p}^*\mathbf{x}_i \leq r_i(\mathbf{p}^*,\widetilde{\mathbf{y}}^*)\}$$

i.e. that $\beta_i(\mathbf{p}^*,\widetilde{\mathbf{y}}^*) = \widehat{\beta}_i(\mathbf{p}^*,\widetilde{\mathbf{s}}^*)$. We know that $\mathbf{x}_i^*$ maximizes u_i on the set of points $\mathbf{x}_i \in \widehat{X}_i$ such that $\mathbf{p}^*\mathbf{x}_i \leq r_i(\mathbf{p}^*,\widetilde{\mathbf{y}}^*)$. Suppose that there exists some $\mathbf{x}_i'$ in $\beta_i(\mathbf{p}^*,\widetilde{\mathbf{y}}^*)$ with $u_i(\mathbf{x}_i') > u_i(\mathbf{x}_i^*)$. Because $\mathbf{x}_i^*$ is feasible, it must be a point in the interior of $\widehat{X}_i$. Hence, there will be some $\mathbf{x}_i''$ in the segment $[\mathbf{x}_i^*, \mathbf{x}_i']$, different from $\mathbf{x}_i^*$ but close enough to be in $\widehat{X}_i$ (a convex set). The convexity and non-satiability of preferences imply that $u_i(\mathbf{x}_i'') > u_i(\mathbf{x}_i^*)$, whereas $\mathbf{p}^*\mathbf{x}_i'' \leq r_i(\mathbf{p}^*, \widetilde{\mathbf{y}}^*)$, by construction. But this contradicts the fact that $\mathbf{x}_i^*$ maximizes u_i in $\widehat{X}_i$.

In this way the proof is completed. $\boxed{\textbf{Q.e.d.}}$

5.5 References to the literature

There is a number of existence results that refer to abstract pricing rules, that can be particularized so as to encompass most of the pricing rules to be considered in next chapters.

The papers by MacKinnon (1979) and Dierker, Guesnerie & Neuefeind (1985) are pioneering contributions in this area. Bonnisseau & Cornet (1988a) provide an extremely general existence result, for the case in which firms' losses are bounded (this paper may be thought of as a benchmark in the literature on the existence of equilibria with non-convex technologies). Vohra (1988a) presents an alternative existence result, using slightly different assumptions and an easier proof. A degree theoretic existence result can be found in Kamiya (1988) (where the question of uniqueness is also analyzed). Simplified versions of Bonnisseau & Cornet's model appear in Villar (1991),(1994b) where relatively easy existence proofs are provided. See also Bonnisseau (1988), (1991) for a discussion on some interconnections. All of these models, however, assume the continuity of wealth functions on the entire domain.

The reader is encouraged to go through Brown's (1991) survey and Bonnisseau & Cornet's (1988a) paper to get a deeper insight into the existence results. An extension to abstract market games is provided in Villar (1999c).

Chapter 6

MARGINAL PRICING

6.1 Introduction

When production sets are convex, profit maximization at given prices implies the choice of production plans for which marginal rates of transformation coincide with market prices. This is precisely a necessary condition for the efficiency of market allocations (if this were not the case, it would be possible to reallocate commodities more productively). When the behaviour of competitive firms is modelled in terms of inverse supply mappings, profit maximization amounts to selecting those prices that support efficient production plans. These supporting vectors are "marginal prices", because they correspond to the marginal rates of transformation.

We know that profit maximization at given prices is not well defined when production sets are not convex. Yet, the notion of marginal prices can be defined without assuming convex production sets (which correspond to the cone of normals to the boundary of the production set at a given point). Moreover, the necessary conditions for optimality do not depend on the convexity assumption either. The equalization between prices and marginal rates (for both consumers and firms) is a general principle for achieving Pareto optimality, irrespective of convexity. It is therefore natural to explore the extension of the marginal pricing principle to more general production sets, since it represents a pricing policy that satisfies the necessary conditions for optimality and coincides with profit maximization when production sets are convex.

When production sets have a smooth (i.e. differentiable) boundary, marginal rates of transformation are well defined, and marginal prices are associated with the vector of partial derivatives at every efficient production plan. When production sets are convex but do not have a smooth boundary, one has to take a generalized view of what marginal rates of transformation are. In particular, marginal prices can be associated with the cone of normals which is defined as follows: Let A be a closed and convex subset of $\mathbb{R}^\ell$, and $\mathbf{s} \in A$; the **normal cone** of A at $\mathbf{s}$, $\mathbb{N}_A(\mathbf{s})$, is given by:

$$\mathbb{N}_A(\mathbf{s}) \equiv \{\mathbf{p} \in \mathbb{R}^\ell \mid \mathbf{p}(\mathbf{y} - \mathbf{s}) \leq 0, \ \forall \ \mathbf{y} \in A\}$$

Thus, when production sets are convex, marginal pricing implies profit maximization at given prices.

When production sets are neither convex nor smooth, we need some way of extending the notion of "marginal rates of transformation" even further. There are several alternatives for doing so; yet, nowadays the standard definition is based on *Clarke normal cones*. In order to define marginal prices properly in this general context, we shall first present the auxiliary notions of *limsup of a correspondence*, and the *cone of perpendicular vectors*, after which, the concept and main properties of Clarke cones will be analyzed. We shall then be ready to define the notion of marginal pricing, and analyze the most useful properties of this pricing rule.

Remark 6.1 *The expression "marginal pricing" is used, instead of the usual "marginal cost pricing", in order to remind us that, in the absence of convexity, this pricing rule does not imply cost minimization. See the discussion in Guesnerie (1990, Section 5.2).*

Does marginal pricing achieve its goal? We shall see that, under very general assumptions, any Pareto optimal allocation can be decentralized as a marginal pricing equilibrium. This is good news, because marginal pricing defines a regulation policy such that, when combined with arbitrary lump-sum transfers, permits to achieve any predetermined efficient allocation. It also tells us that marginal pricing, defined in this general context, continues to be a necessary condition for optimality. Yet, marginal pricing equilibria do not induce efficient allocations, as will be illustrated by a number of examples. Roughly speaking, the essence of the problem is that local conditions do not translate to global properties in the absence of convexity. Hence, this chapter also tells the story of an impossibility result: Under general conditions, there is no way of efficiently allocating the resources through a price mechanism, in the presence of increasing returns to scale (unless we can freely arrange the income distribution).

A more general question then arises: the analysis of the non-emptiness of the core in an economy with increasing returns. It is well known that the core of a standard convex competitive economy is non-empty (indeed, every competitive equilibrium is in the core). One might think that the presence of increasing returns may facilitate the non-emptiness of the core: bigger coalitions are more likely to be more productive in organizing the economic activity. This intuition, however, is rather inaccurate: Scarf (1986) shows that if all commodities can be consumed, the core of an economy may be empty unless the aggregate production set is a convex cone.

These negative aspects can be summarized in the following *warning*: When production sets are not convex, the necessary conditions for optimality (which lead to marginal pricing) are not sufficient. Furthermore, when there are increasing returns to scale, marginal pricing implies losses, so that it requires the simultaneous design of a system of taxes and transfers, in order to cover the resulting losses. This all implies that marginal pricing is a regulation policy that requires lots of information and control, and may very well not achieve its goal.

6.2 Preliminaries

This is a purely mathematical section, which is nevertheless quite instructive. It refers to the notions of limsup of a correspondence, and the Clarke cone. The main properties of marginal pricing rely on the analysis presented here.[1]

Definition 6.1 *Let* $Y \subset \mathbb{R}^\ell$, $\Gamma : Y \to \mathbb{R}^\ell$ *a set valued mapping, and* $\mathbf{y}^*$ *a point in* Y. *The **limsup** of* Γ *at* $\mathbf{y}^*$ *is given by:*

$$LS[\Gamma(\mathbf{y}^*)] \equiv \{\mathbf{p} = \lim \mathbf{p}^\nu \ / \ \exists \{\mathbf{y}^\nu\} \subset Y, \{\mathbf{y}^\nu\} \to \mathbf{y}^* \text{ and } \mathbf{p}^\nu \in \Gamma(\mathbf{y}^\nu) \ \forall\nu\}$$

In words: By Limsup of Γ at $\mathbf{y}^*$ we denote the set of all points that are limits of sequences of points $\mathbf{p}^\nu \in \Gamma(\mathbf{y}^\nu)$, when $\mathbf{y}^\nu \to \mathbf{y}^*$. Observe that when Γ has a closed graph, $LS[\Gamma(\mathbf{y}^*)] = \Gamma(\mathbf{y}^*)$, for each $\mathbf{y}^* \in Y$. When this is not so, the Limsup may be thought of as an operator that "closes the graph" of Γ. Yet, this does not mean that it coincides with $\Gamma(\mathbf{y}^*)$ when Γ is closed-valued.

Remark 6.2 *If* $\Gamma(\mathbf{y})$ *is a cone, then* $LS[\Gamma(\mathbf{y}^*)]$ *is also a cone (which follows trivially from the definition).*

Lemma 6.1 *Let* $Y \subset \mathbb{R}^\ell$, $\Gamma:Y \to \mathbb{R}^\ell$ *be a set valued mapping. The correspondence* $\varphi : Y \to \mathbb{R}^\ell$ *given by* $\varphi(\mathbf{y}) = LS[\Gamma(\mathbf{y}^*)]$ *has a closed graph.*

Proof. Let two sequences

$$\{\mathbf{y}^r\} \subset Y \text{ with } \{\mathbf{y}^r\} \to \mathbf{y}^*$$

---

[1]This section corresponds to Alós & Villar (1995).

$$\{\mathbf{p}^r\} \subset \mathbb{R}^\ell \text{ with } \{\mathbf{p}^r\} \to \mathbf{p}^*$$

be such that $\mathbf{p}^r \in LS[\Gamma(\mathbf{y}^r)]$. We have to show that $\mathbf{p}^* \in LS[\Gamma(\mathbf{y}^*)]$. Now, for each r let $\{\mathbf{p}^r_\nu\}, \{\mathbf{y}^r_\nu\}$ be such that:

$$\{\mathbf{p}^r_\nu\} \to \mathbf{p}^r, \{\mathbf{y}^r_\nu\} \to \mathbf{y}^r, \mathbf{p}^r_\nu \in \Gamma(\mathbf{y}^r_\nu) \quad \forall \nu$$

Let $r \geq 1$. For each r there exists ν' such that:

$$\| \mathbf{p}^r_{\nu'} - \mathbf{p}^r \| < 1/r, \text{ and } \| \mathbf{y}^r_{\nu'} - \mathbf{y}^r \| < 1/r$$

Clearly $\{\mathbf{p}^r_{\nu'}\} \to \mathbf{p}^*, \{\mathbf{y}^r_{\nu'}\} \to \mathbf{y}^*$, and $\mathbf{p}^r_{\nu'} \in \Gamma(\mathbf{y}^r_{\nu'})$ so that, according to the definition above, $\mathbf{p}^* \in LS[\Gamma(\mathbf{y}^*)]$. $\boxed{\text{Q.e.d.}}$

The next proposition contains the key result for the upper hemicontinuity of the marginal pricing rule:

Proposition 6.1 *Let $Y \subset \mathbb{R}^\ell$ be a closed set, and $\Gamma : Y \to \mathbb{R}^\ell_+$ a correspondence such that $\Gamma(\mathbf{y})$ is a cone, for each $\mathbf{y} \in Y$. Define a new correspondence $\psi : Y \to \mathbb{R}^\ell_+$ that associates the convex hull of $LS[\Gamma(\mathbf{y}^*)]$ to each $\mathbf{y}^* \in Y$. That is, $\psi(\mathbf{y}^*) = coLS[\Gamma(\mathbf{y}^*)]$. Then ψ has a closed graph (and, in particular, $\psi(\mathbf{y}^*)$ is closed for every $\mathbf{y}^* \in Y$).*

Proof. Let $\{\mathbf{y}^\nu\} \to \mathbf{y}^*$ be a sequence in Y, and let $\{\mathbf{p}^\nu\} \to \mathbf{p}^*$ be a sequence in $\mathbb{R}^\ell_+$ such that $\mathbf{p}^\nu \in \psi(\mathbf{y}^\nu) \ \forall \nu$. We need to show that $\mathbf{p}^* \in \psi(\mathbf{y}^*)$. Making use of Carathéodory's Theorem,[2] we can write:

$$\mathbf{p}^\nu = \sum_{i=1}^{\ell+1} \lambda^\nu_i \mathbf{p}^\nu_i, \text{ with } \mathbf{p}^\nu_i \in LS[\Gamma(\mathbf{y}^\nu)], \ \lambda^\nu_i \geq 0 \ \forall \nu, i, \ \sum_{i=1}^{\ell+1} \lambda^\nu_i = 1, \ \forall \nu$$

Now observe that $\Gamma(\mathbf{y}) \subset \mathbb{R}^\ell_+, \forall \ \mathbf{y} \in Y$, and $\{\mathbf{p}^\nu\} \to \mathbf{p}^*$ implies that $\mathbf{p}^*$ is also in $\mathbb{R}^\ell_+$. Trivially, $\mathbf{0} \in \psi(\mathbf{y}^*)$ (because $\Gamma(\mathbf{y})$ is a cone for all $\mathbf{y} \in Y$). Then, if $\mathbf{p}^* = \mathbf{0}$ the proof is done. Suppose that $\mathbf{p}^* > \mathbf{0}$, and let $\mathbf{e}$ stand for the unit vector, $\mathbf{e} \equiv (1, 1, \ldots, 1)$. It follows that $\mathbf{p}^*\mathbf{e} > 0$, and that $\mathbf{p}^\nu\mathbf{e} > 0$ for ν big enough (for every $\nu > \nu'$, say).
Therefore, for $\nu > \nu'$ we have:

$$\mathbf{p}^\nu = \mathbf{p}^\nu\mathbf{e} \sum_{i=1}^{\ell+1} \pi^\nu_i, \text{ with } \pi^\nu_i = \frac{\lambda^\nu_i}{\mathbf{p}^\nu\mathbf{e}} \mathbf{p}^\nu_i \in \mathbb{R}^\ell_+$$

---

[2] Carathéodory's Theorem: Let $S \subset \mathbb{R}^\ell$ and $\mathbf{x} \in coS$ (the convex hull of S). Then, there exist $(\ell + 1)$ points $\mathbf{x}^i \in S$ and $(\ell + 1)$ non-negative scalars λ_i $(i = 1, 2, \ldots, \ell+1)$, such that $\mathbf{x} = \sum_{i=1}^{\ell+1} \lambda_i \mathbf{x}^i$, with $\sum_{i=1}^{\ell+1} \lambda_i = 1$.

and

$$\pi_i^{\nu} \mathbf{e} = \frac{\lambda_i^{\nu}}{\mathbf{p}^{\nu} \mathbf{e}} \mathbf{p}_i^{\nu} \mathbf{e} \leq 1$$

that is, for every i, $\pi_i^{\nu} \in K \equiv \{\mathbf{p} \in \mathbb{R}_+^{\ell} \ / \ \mathbf{pe} \leq 1\}$, which is a compact set. This in turn implies that we can choose a convergent subsequence $\{\pi_i^{\nu}\} \to \pi_i \in K$.

We know from Lemma 6.1 that the mapping LS has a closed graph. Since $LS[\Gamma(\mathbf{y})]$ is a cone for each $\mathbf{y} \in Y$ (see Remark 6.1), then $\pi_i^{\nu} \in LS[\Gamma(\mathbf{y}^{\nu})]$. Hence: $\{\mathbf{y}^{\nu}\} \to \mathbf{y}^*, \{\pi_i^{\nu}\} \to \pi_i$ and $\pi_i^{\nu} \in LS[\Gamma(\mathbf{y}^{\nu})]$ imply that π_i must be a point in $LS[\Gamma(\mathbf{y}^*)]$. Taking limits when $\nu \to \infty$, we have:

$$\mathbf{p}^* = \mathbf{p}^* \mathbf{e} \sum_{i=1}^{\ell+1} \pi_i$$

that is, $\mathbf{p}^* \in coLS[\Gamma(\mathbf{y}^*)] \equiv \psi(\mathbf{y}^*)$. $\boxed{\textbf{Q.e.d.}}$

Let $Y \subset \mathbb{R}^{\ell}$ be non-empty, and let $\mathbf{z}$ be a point in $\mathbb{R}^{\ell}$. The **distance** between $\mathbf{z}$ and Y is a real-valued function d_Y given by:

$$d_Y(\mathbf{z}) = \inf\{\|\mathbf{z} - \mathbf{y}\| \ / \ \mathbf{y} \in Y\}$$

We shall assume that $\|.\|$ stands for the Euclidean norm, that is,

$$\|\mathbf{z} - \mathbf{y}\| = [\sum_{i=1}^{\ell}(z_i - y_i)^2]^{1/2}$$

A vector $\mathbf{p} \in \mathbb{R}^{\ell}$ is **perpendicular** to a closed set Y at $\mathbf{y}$, if $\mathbf{y}$ is the point in Y at the minimum distance of $\mathbf{p}$, that is, if $d_Y(\mathbf{p} + \mathbf{y}) = \| \mathbf{p} \|$ (i.e. if the distance between $(\mathbf{p} + \mathbf{y})$ and Y is precisely the norm of $\mathbf{p}$). Obviously, if $\mathbf{p}$ is perpendicular to Y at $\mathbf{y}$, so is $\lambda\mathbf{p}$, for all $\lambda > 0$. Hence, we can define the cone of perpendicular vectors as follows:

Definition 6.2 *Let $Y \subset \mathbb{R}^{\ell}$ be closed, and let $\mathbf{y} \in Y$. The **cone of vectors which are perpendicular** to Y at $\mathbf{y}$, denoted by $\perp_Y(\mathbf{y})$, is given by:*

$$\perp_Y(\mathbf{y}) = \{\mathbf{p} = \lambda(\mathbf{y}' - \mathbf{y}), \lambda \geq 0, \mathbf{y}' \in \mathbb{R}^{\ell} \text{ and } d_Y(\mathbf{y}') = \| \mathbf{y}' - \mathbf{y} \|\}$$

Observe that if Y is not a convex set, there may be points $\mathbf{y}^* \in Y$ for which no perpendicular vector exists. One way of avoiding this problem is by making use of the limsup operator. Figure 6.1 illustrates the set $LS[\perp_Y(\mathbf{y}^*)]$.

This correspondence associates two different vectors $\mathbf{p}, \mathbf{p}' \in \mathbb{R}^\ell$ as limits of sequences approaching $\mathbf{y}^*$ from the left and right hand side, respectively.

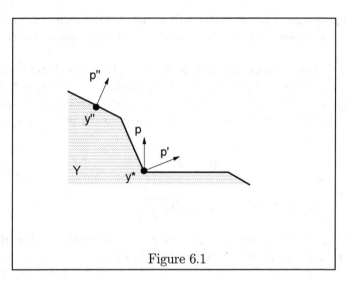

Figure 6.1

The following Proposition gives us a useful characterization of the sets of perpendicular vectors:

Proposition 6.2 *Let $Y \subset \mathbb{R}^\ell$ be closed. Then, the set $\perp_Y(\mathbf{y})$ can equivalently be defined as:*

$$\{\mathbf{p} \in \mathbb{R}^\ell \;/\; \mathbf{p}\mathbf{y} \geq \mathbf{p}\mathbf{y}' - (\lambda/2) \parallel \mathbf{y}-\mathbf{y}' \parallel^2, \; \forall \mathbf{y}' \in Y, \text{ some } \lambda \geq 0\}$$

Proof. ($\Longrightarrow$) Let $\mathbf{p} = \lambda(\mathbf{y}'' - \mathbf{y}) \in \perp_Y(\mathbf{y})$. By definition, $d_Y(\mathbf{y}'') = \parallel \mathbf{y}'' - \mathbf{y} \parallel$ and $\lambda \geq 0$. Let us call $\mathbf{x}^2$ the scalar product $\mathbf{x}\mathbf{x}$, for any $\mathbf{x}$ in $\mathbb{R}^\ell$, and let $\mathbf{y}' \in Y$ be such that $\parallel \mathbf{y}'' - \mathbf{y}' \parallel \geq \parallel \mathbf{y}'' - \mathbf{y} \parallel$. Then,

$\parallel \mathbf{p} \parallel^2 = [\lambda(\mathbf{y}'' - \mathbf{y})]^2 \leq [\lambda(\mathbf{y}'' - \mathbf{y}')]^2 = [\lambda(\mathbf{y}'' - \mathbf{y}) + \lambda(\mathbf{y} - \mathbf{y}')]^2$
$= \lambda^2(\mathbf{y}'' - \mathbf{y})^2 + \lambda^2(\mathbf{y} - \mathbf{y}')^2 + 2\lambda^2(\mathbf{y}'' - \mathbf{y})(\mathbf{y} - \mathbf{y}')$
$= \parallel \mathbf{p} \parallel^2 + \lambda^2 \parallel \mathbf{y} - \mathbf{y}' \parallel^2 + 2\lambda\mathbf{p}(\mathbf{y} - \mathbf{y}')$

Then, $2\lambda\mathbf{p}(\mathbf{y} - \mathbf{y}') \geq -\lambda^2 \parallel \mathbf{y} - \mathbf{y}' \parallel^2$. Trivially, $\lambda = 0$ implies $\mathbf{p} = \mathbf{0}$ and the result follows. For $\lambda > 0$ we have:

$$\mathbf{p}\mathbf{y} \geq \mathbf{p}\mathbf{y}' - (\lambda/2) \parallel \mathbf{y} - \mathbf{y}' \parallel^2, \forall \mathbf{y}' \in Y$$

($\Longleftarrow$) Let $\mathbf{p} \in \mathbb{R}^\ell$, $\lambda \geq 0$, and suppose that $\mathbf{p}(\mathbf{y}-\mathbf{y}') \geq -(\lambda/2) \parallel \mathbf{y}-\mathbf{y}' \parallel^2$ for each $\mathbf{y}' \in Y$. If $\lambda = 0$, $\mathbf{p}(\mathbf{y} - \mathbf{y}') \geq 0 \; \forall \mathbf{y}' \in Y$ and therefore, for $\lambda' > 0$

we have: $\mathbf{p}(\mathbf{y} - \mathbf{y}') \geq -\lambda' \parallel \mathbf{y} - \mathbf{y}' \parallel^2$. Hence we can let $\lambda > 0$ without loss of generality.

Then let $\mathbf{y}'' = \mathbf{y} + (1/\lambda)\mathbf{p}$. It follows that:

(i) $\parallel \mathbf{y}'' - \mathbf{y} \parallel = (1/\lambda) \parallel \mathbf{p} \parallel$

(ii) $\forall \mathbf{y}' \in Y, \parallel \mathbf{y}'' - \mathbf{y}' \parallel^2 = \parallel \mathbf{y} - \mathbf{y}' + (1/\lambda)\mathbf{p} \parallel^2$

$= [\mathbf{y} - \mathbf{y}' + (1/\lambda)\mathbf{p}]^2 = \parallel \mathbf{y} - \mathbf{y}' \parallel^2 + (1/\lambda^2) \parallel \mathbf{p} \parallel^2 + (2/\lambda)\mathbf{p}(\mathbf{y} - \mathbf{y}')$

$\geq \parallel \mathbf{y} - \mathbf{y}' \parallel^2 + [(1/\lambda) \parallel \mathbf{p} \parallel]^2 - (2/\lambda)(\lambda/2) \parallel \mathbf{y} - \mathbf{y}' \parallel^2$

and therefore,

$$\parallel \mathbf{y} - \mathbf{y}' \parallel \geq (1/\lambda) \parallel \mathbf{p} \parallel = \parallel \mathbf{y}'' - \mathbf{y} \parallel$$

We conclude then that $d_Y(\mathbf{y}) = \parallel \mathbf{y}'' - \mathbf{y} \parallel$ implies that

$$\mathbf{p} = \lambda(\mathbf{y}'' - \mathbf{y}) \in \perp_Y (\mathbf{y})$$

Q.e.d.

The notion of Clarke cone is now easy to understand: it consists of the convex hull of this set $LS[\perp_Y (\mathbf{y}^*)]$. Formally:

Definition 6.3 *Let Y be a closed subset of $\mathbb{R}^\ell$ and $\mathbf{y}^* \in Y$. Then, the* **Clarke normal cone** $\mathbb{N}_Y(\mathbf{y}^*)$ *to Y at $\mathbf{y}^*$ is given by* [3]

$$\mathbb{N}_Y(\mathbf{y}^*) \equiv coLS[\perp_y (\mathbf{y}^*)]$$

By this definition the Clarke Normal Cone at a point $\mathbf{y}^*$ is the convex cone generated by the vectors perpendicular to Y at $\mathbf{y}^*$, and the limits of vectors which are perpendicular to Y in a neighbourhood of $\mathbf{y}^*$ [Cf. Quinzii (1992, p. 19)]. Next figure provides an illustration.

---

[3]Clarke (1975) defines this cone as the closed and convex hull of $LS[\perp_Y (\mathbf{y}^*)]$. Closedness is not required, since it is a derived property, as will be shown below.

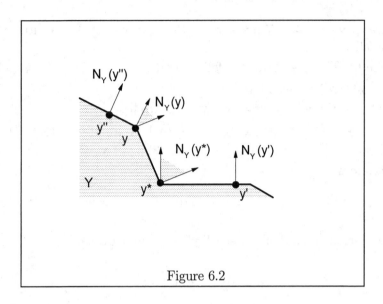

Figure 6.2

The following results give us the main properties of Clarke normal cones:

Proposition 6.3 *Let Y be a closed subset of $\mathbb{R}^\ell$, and $\mathbf{y} \in Y$. Then:*
(i) If $\mathbf{py} \geq \mathbf{py}'$ for all $\mathbf{y}' \in Y$, then $\mathbf{p} \in \mathbb{N}_Y(\mathbf{y})$.
(ii) If Y is also convex, then,

$$\mathbb{N}_Y(y) = \perp_Y (y) = \{\mathbf{p} \in \mathbb{R}^\ell \ / \ \mathbf{p}(\mathbf{y}' - \mathbf{y}) \leq 0 \ \forall \ \mathbf{y}' \in Y\}$$

Proof. (i) Follows directly from Proposition 6.2, by letting $\lambda = 0$.

(ii) Let $\nabla_Y(\mathbf{y}) = \{\mathbf{p} \in \mathbb{R}^\ell \ / \ \mathbf{p}(\mathbf{y}' - \mathbf{y}) \leq 0, \ \forall \ \mathbf{y}' \in Y\}$. We shall first show that $\perp_Y (\mathbf{y}) = \nabla_Y(\mathbf{y})$.

It follows again from Proposition 6.2 that $\nabla_Y(\mathbf{y}) \subseteq \perp_Y (\mathbf{y})$. To see that the other inclusion holds, note that $\forall \mathbf{y}' \in Y$ we have:
$\mathbf{py} \geq \mathbf{py}' - (\lambda/2) \parallel \mathbf{y} - \mathbf{y}' \parallel^2$
Since Y is assumed to be convex, for each $t \in [0, 1], \mathbf{y} + t(\mathbf{y}' - \mathbf{y}) \in Y$. Thus,

$$\mathbf{py} \geq \mathbf{p}[\mathbf{y} + t(\mathbf{y}' - \mathbf{y})] - (\lambda/2) \parallel t(\mathbf{y}' - \mathbf{y}) \parallel^2$$

which implies: $0 \geq t\mathbf{p}(\mathbf{y}' - \mathbf{y}) - (\lambda/2)t^2 \parallel \mathbf{y}' - \mathbf{y} \parallel^2$. Hence,

$$t\mathbf{p}(\mathbf{y}' - \mathbf{y})] \leq (\lambda/2)t^2 \parallel \mathbf{y}' - \mathbf{y} \parallel^2$$

which, when $t > 0$ the result is

$$\mathbf{p}(\mathbf{y}' - \mathbf{y})] \leq (\lambda/2)t \parallel \mathbf{y}' - \mathbf{y} \parallel^2$$

Taking limits, when $t \to 0$, we get $\mathbf{p}(\mathbf{y}' - \mathbf{y}) \leq 0$, which is the desired result.

Let us now show that $\mathbb{N}_Y(\mathbf{y}) = \perp_Y(\mathbf{y})$. It follows from the definition that $\perp_Y(\mathbf{y}) \subset \mathbb{N}_Y(\mathbf{y})$. We shall prove then that the other inclusion also holds. Let $\{\mathbf{y}^\nu\} \to \mathbf{y}$ be a sequence in Y, and $\{\mathbf{p}^\nu\} \to \mathbf{p}$ a sequence in $\mathbb{R}^\ell$, such that $\mathbf{p}^\nu \in \perp_Y(\mathbf{y}^\nu) \; \forall \nu$. It follows from the previous inclusion that $\forall \nu, \forall \mathbf{y}' \in Y$, $\mathbf{p}^\nu(\mathbf{y}' - \mathbf{y}^\nu) \leq 0$. Taking limits we conclude:

$$\mathbf{p}(\mathbf{y}' - \mathbf{y}) \leq 0, \forall \mathbf{y}' \in Y$$

Since $\nabla_Y(\mathbf{y})$ is a closed and convex set, the inclusion follows. $\boxed{\textbf{Q.e.d.}}$

Here comes the main result of this section:

Theorem 6.1 *Let Y be a non-empty and closed subset in $\mathbb{R}^\ell$, and suppose that $Y - \mathbb{R}_+^\ell \subset Y$. Then:*

(i) $\mathbb{N}_Y(\mathbf{y})$ is a cone in $\mathbb{R}_+^\ell$ with vertex zero, $\forall \mathbf{y} \in Y$.

(ii) The correspondence $\mathbb{N}_Y : Y \to \mathbb{R}^\ell$ that associates $\mathbb{N}_Y(\mathbf{y})$ to each $\mathbf{y} \in Y$ is closed.

(iii) $\mathbb{N}_Y(\mathbf{y}) = \{\mathbf{0}\}$ if and only if $\mathbf{y} \in \text{int} Y$.

Proof. (i) Let $\mathbf{p} \in \perp_Y(\mathbf{y})$. Proposition 6.2 implies that there is $\lambda \geq 0$ such that

$$\mathbf{p}\mathbf{y} \geq \mathbf{p}\mathbf{y}' - (\lambda/2) \| \mathbf{y} - \mathbf{y}' \|^2, \forall \mathbf{y}' \in Y$$

Take an arbitrary point $\mathbf{v} \in \mathbb{R}_+^\ell$, and let $t > 0$. We can pick a point $\mathbf{y}'$ in Y which is given by: $\mathbf{y}' = \mathbf{y} - t\mathbf{v}$ (this is possible, since $Y - \mathbb{R}_+^\ell \subset Y$, by assumption). Then, $\mathbf{p}\mathbf{y} \geq \mathbf{p}(\mathbf{y} - t\mathbf{v}) - (\lambda/2) \| t\mathbf{v} \|^2$, and hence:

$$0 \geq -t\mathbf{p}\mathbf{v} - (\lambda/2)t^2 \| \mathbf{v} \|^2$$

that is, $\mathbf{p}\mathbf{v} \geq -(\lambda/2)t \| \mathbf{v} \|^2$. Taking limits when t goes to zero, we conclude: $\mathbf{p}\mathbf{v} \geq 0$ for every $\mathbf{v} \in \mathbb{R}_+^\ell$ which is true if and only if $\mathbf{p} \in \mathbb{R}_+^\ell$.

(ii) It follows directly from Proposition 6.1 and definition 6.3.

(iii $\Longrightarrow$) Let $\{\mathbf{y}^\nu\} \to \mathbf{y} \in \text{int} Y$. Then, for ν big enough ($\nu > \nu'$,say), $\mathbf{y}^\nu \in \text{int} Y$, so that $\perp_Y(\mathbf{y}^\nu) = \{\mathbf{0}\}$ by definition. Therefore, $\{\mathbf{p}^\nu\}$ converges to $\mathbf{p}$ and $\mathbf{p}^\nu \in \perp_Y(\mathbf{y}^\nu)$ imply that $\mathbf{p} = \mathbf{0}$.

(iii $\Longleftarrow$) Let $\mathbb{N}_Y(\mathbf{y}) = \{\mathbf{0}\}$, and suppose $\mathbf{y} \in \partial Y$. Then there exists a sequence $\{\mathbf{z}^\nu\} \to \mathbf{y}$, such that $\mathbf{z}^\nu \notin Y$ for all ν. As Y is closed, choose $\mathbf{y}^\nu \in Y$ such that $0 < d_Y(\mathbf{z}^\nu) = \text{dist}[\mathbf{y}^\nu, \mathbf{z}^\nu]$ (i.e., we choose $\mathbf{y}^\nu$ so that for each $\mathbf{z}^\nu$ is a point in Y at minimum distance). Then,

$$\mathbf{p}^\nu \equiv \mathbf{z}^\nu - \mathbf{y}^\nu \in \perp_Y(\mathbf{y}^\nu)$$

with $\mathbf{p}^\nu \in \mathbb{R}^\ell_+$ [as shown in part (i) above], and $\mathbf{p}^\nu \neq \mathbf{0}$. Being $\perp_Y (.)$ a cone, it follows that $\hat{\mathbf{p}}^\nu = \mathbf{p}^\nu/\mathbf{p}^\nu \mathbf{e} \in \perp_Y (\mathbf{y}^\nu) \bigcap \mathbb{P}$ (where $\mathbb{P}$ stands for the unit simplex). Thus $\{\hat{\mathbf{p}}^\nu\}$ is a sequence in a compact set. There is a convergent subsequence such that $\{\hat{\mathbf{p}}^\nu\} \to \mathbf{p}$ (a point in $\mathbb{P}$). Since, by construction, $\{\mathbf{y}^\nu\} \to \mathbf{y}$, and the graph of $\mathbb{N}_Y(.)$ is closed [see (ii) above], it follows that $\mathbf{p} \notin \mathbb{N}_Y(\mathbf{y}) = \{\mathbf{0}\}$. $\boxed{\text{Q.e.d.}}$

6.3   Marginal pricing

6.3.1   The marginal pricing rule and the existence of equilibrium

It is now time to present the definition and main properties of the marginal pricing rule. To do so, let us recall that $\mathbb{P}$ denotes the unit simplex in $\mathbb{R}^\ell_+$.

Definition 6.4 *Let Y_j be a production set, and $\mathbf{y}_j$ a boundary point. The* **marginal pricing rule** *for the jth firm is a correspondence $\phi_j^{MP} : \partial Y_j \to \mathbb{P}$ given by:*

$$\phi_j^{MP}(\mathbf{y}_j) \equiv \mathbb{N}_{Y_j}(\mathbf{y}_j) \bigcap \mathbb{P}$$

The marginal pricing rule associates, to each point $\mathbf{y}_j$ in the boundary of Y_j (to be interpreted as an efficient production plan), the convex hull of the set of vectors that are perpendicular to $\mathbf{y}_j$, and the limits of vectors which are perpendicular to Y_j in a neighbourhood of $\mathbf{y}_j$, normalized to unity. Such a convex hull corresponds to the marginal rates of transformation of the jth firm at $\mathbf{y}_j$. Normalizing these vectors to unity permits one to treat them as normalized prices.

The following result is obtained:

Proposition 6.4 *Let Y_j be a closed subset of $\mathbb{R}^\ell$, such that $Y_j - \mathbb{R}^\ell_+ \subset Y_j$, and let $\phi_j^{MP} : \partial Y_j \to \mathbb{P}$ be the Marginal Pricing correspondence. Then, ϕ_j^{MP} is a regular mapping.*

Proof. According to part (ii) of Theorem 6.1, $\mathbb{N}_{Y_j}$ has a closed graph. Being ϕ_j^{MP} the intersection of $\mathbb{N}_{Y_j}$ with $\mathbb{P}$, its values are compact, and hence ϕ_j^{MP} is upper hemicontinuous. Part (i) of the theorem tells us that $\mathbb{N}_{Y_j}$ is a convex cone, so that $\mathbb{N}_{Y_j}(\mathbf{y}_j) \bigcap \mathbb{P}$ is also convex. Finally, part (iii) of Theorem 6.1 establishes that $\mathbb{N}_{Y_j}(\mathbf{y}_j)$ is a non-degenerate cone if $\mathbf{y} \in \partial Y_j$, so that $\mathbb{N}_{Y_j}(\mathbf{y}_j) \bigcap \mathbb{P}$ is non-empty.. $\boxed{\text{Q.e.d.}}$

Now consider the following definition, that identifies a family of production sets which is slightly less general than those in chapter 5, but still compatible with the presence of increasing returns or other forms of non-convexities in production:

Definition 6.5 *A production set $Y_j \subset \mathbb{R}^\ell$ is called **star-shaped**, if there is a scalar $\alpha_j \leq 0$ such that, for every $\mathbf{y}_j \in \partial Y_j$, the segment $[\alpha_j \mathbf{e}, \mathbf{y}_j]$ is contained in Y_j.*

A production set Y_j is star-shaped if there is point in the diagonal of the negative orthant, $\alpha_j \mathbf{e} \in Y_j$, such that all segments connecting this point to the boundary of Y_j are contained in Y_j. Clearly, when Y_j is convex and comprehensive this point always exists. Yet, there are non-convex comprehensive sets that satisfy this property, as illustrated in the next figure.

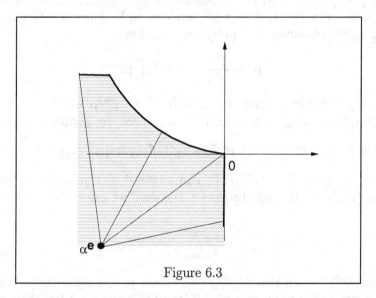

Figure 6.3

The next result shows that when production sets are star-shaped, marginal pricing implies bounded losses. Formally:

Proposition 6.5 *Let Y_j be a non-empty and closed subset of $\mathbb{R}^\ell$. If Y_j is star-shaped, then marginal pricing is a pricing rule with bounded losses (in particular, for each $\mathbf{p} \in \mathbb{N}_{Y_j}(\mathbf{y}_j) \bigcap \mathbb{P}$, every $\mathbf{y}_j \in \partial Y_j$ we have: $\mathbf{p}\mathbf{y}_j \geq \alpha_j$).*

*   **Proof.**   We shall divide the proof into three steps, and omit subscripts to simplify notation.

(Step 1: : $[\mathbf{y} \in \partial Y \ \& \ \mathbf{p} \in \perp_Y (\mathbf{y})] \Rightarrow \mathbf{py} \geq \alpha]$)

Let $\{t^\nu\} \to 0$ be a sequence in $(0, 1]$. Then, $\mathbf{y} + t^\nu(\alpha\mathbf{e} - \mathbf{y})$ is a point in the segment $[\alpha\mathbf{e}, \mathbf{y}] \subset Y$. It follows from proposition 6.2 that

$$\mathbf{py} \geq \mathbf{p}[\mathbf{y} + t^\nu(\alpha\mathbf{e} - \mathbf{y})] - (\lambda/2) \parallel \mathbf{y} + t^\nu(\alpha\mathbf{e} - \mathbf{y}) - \mathbf{y} \parallel^2$$

and hence,

$$t^\nu\mathbf{p}(\alpha\mathbf{e} - \mathbf{y}) \leq (\lambda/2)(t^\nu)^2 \parallel \alpha\mathbf{e} - \mathbf{y} \parallel^2$$

and, since $t^\nu > 0$, $\mathbf{p}(\alpha\mathbf{e} - \mathbf{y}) \leq (\lambda/2)t^\nu \parallel \alpha\mathbf{e} - \mathbf{y} \parallel^2$. Taking limits when t goes to zero, it follows that: $\mathbf{p}(\alpha\mathbf{e} - \mathbf{y}) \leq 0$ so that $\mathbf{py} \geq \alpha\mathbf{pe} = \alpha$ (since $\mathbf{p} \in \mathbb{P}$).

(Step 2: $[y \in \partial Y \ \& \ \mathbf{p} \in [LS[\perp_y (\mathbf{y'})]] \bigcap \mathbb{P} \Rightarrow \mathbf{py} \geq \alpha$)

Let $\mathbf{p} \in [LS[\perp_Y (\mathbf{y})] \bigcap \mathbb{P}$. By definition, $\mathbf{p} = \lim_{\nu \to \infty} \mathbf{p}^\nu$, where $\mathbf{p}^\nu$ is a point in $\perp_Y (\mathbf{y}^\nu)$, and $\{\mathbf{y}^\nu\} \to \mathbf{y}$ is a sequence in Y. Since $\mathbf{p} \neq \mathbf{0}$, $\mathbf{y}$ must be a point in the boundary of Y (Theorem 6.1). Let

$$\hat{\mathbf{p}}^\nu = \frac{\mathbf{p}^\nu}{\mathbf{p}^\nu\mathbf{e}} \in \perp_Y (\mathbf{y}^\nu) \bigcap \mathbb{P}$$

From Step 1 it follows that, for all $\nu, \hat{\mathbf{p}}^\nu\mathbf{y}^\nu = (\mathbf{p}^\nu/\mathbf{p}^\nu\mathbf{e})\mathbf{y}^\nu \geq \alpha$, that is, $\mathbf{p}^\nu\mathbf{y}^\nu \geq \alpha\mathbf{p}^\nu\mathbf{e}$. Taking limits when $\nu \to \infty$, we get: $\mathbf{py} \geq \alpha\mathbf{pe} = \alpha$.

(Step 3: $[y \in \partial Y \& \mathbf{p} \in Co[LS[\perp_Y (\mathbf{y'})]] \bigcap \mathbb{P}] \Rightarrow \mathbf{py} \geq \alpha$)

Let $\mathbf{p} \in Co[LS[\perp_Y (\mathbf{y'})]] \bigcap \mathbb{P}$, and suppose that $\mathbf{p}$ is not a point in $[LS[\perp_Y (\mathbf{y'})]] \bigcap \mathbb{P}$. By Caratheodory's Theorem, we can write:

$$\mathbf{p} = \sum_{i=1}^{\ell+1} \lambda_i\mathbf{p}_i$$

for some $\lambda_i \geq 0$ such that $\sum_{i=1}^{\ell+1} \lambda_i = 1$, some $\mathbf{p}_i \in LS[\perp_Y (\mathbf{y'})]$. Without loss of generality, suppose that $\mathbf{p}_i \neq \mathbf{0}$ for all i (otherwise delete those points $\mathbf{p}_i = \mathbf{0}$). Define then

$$\hat{\mathbf{p}}_i = \frac{\mathbf{p}_i}{\mathbf{p}_i\mathbf{e}} \in \perp_Y (\mathbf{y}^\nu) \bigcap \mathbb{P}$$

From Step 2 it follows that: $\hat{\mathbf{p}}_i\mathbf{y} = (\mathbf{p}_i/\mathbf{p}_i\mathbf{e})\mathbf{y} \geq \alpha$, that is, $\mathbf{p}_i\mathbf{y} \geq \alpha\mathbf{p}_i\mathbf{e}$ for all i. Then,

$$\mathbf{py} = \left(\sum_{i=1}^{\ell+1} \lambda_i\mathbf{p}_i \right) y \geq \alpha \left(\sum_{i=1}^{\ell+1} \lambda_i\mathbf{p}_i \right) \mathbf{e} = \alpha\mathbf{pe} = \alpha \qquad \boxed{\text{Q.e.d.}}$$

Remark 6.3 *Bonnisseau & Cornet (1988a, Lemma 4.2)], prove that, if one also assumes that $Y - \mathbb{R}^{\ell}_+ \subset Y$, then the converse is also true. Furthermore they show that these conditions are satisfied if there exists a non-empty, compact subset K_j of $\mathbb{R}^{\ell}$, if*

$$\alpha_j = \inf_h \{y_{jh} \ / \ y_j = (y_{jh}) \in K_j\}$$

and if one of the following conditions holds: either (C.1) $Y_j = K_j - \mathbb{R}^{\ell}_+$; or (C.2) $Y_j \backslash K_j$ is convex.

Consider now the following axioms:

Axiom 6.1 *For all $i = 1, 2, \ldots, m$: (a) X_i is a non-empty, closed and convex subset of $\mathbb{R}^{\ell}$, bounded from below; (b) $u_i : X_i \to \mathbb{R}$ is a continuous, quasi-concave$^+$ and non-satiable utility function.*

Axiom 6.2 *For all $j = 1, 2, \ldots, n$, Y_j is a closed, comprehensive and star-shaped subset of $\mathbb{R}^{\ell}$.*

Axiom 6.3 *Let **PE** denote the set of production equilibria. The restriction of r_i on **PE** is continuous, with $r_i(\mathbf{p}, \widetilde{\mathbf{y}}) > \min \mathbf{p} X_i$, and $\sum_{i=1}^{m} r_i(\mathbf{p}, \widetilde{\mathbf{y}}) = \mathbf{p}(\omega + \sum_{j=1}^{n} \mathbf{y}_j)$.*

Axiom 6.4 *The set of attainable allocation Ω is compact.*

Axioms 6.1, 6.3 and 6.4 correspond to axioms 5.1, 5.3 and 5.4. Axiom 6.2 is a strengthening of axiom 5.2, because it postulates star-shapedness as well.

Definition 6.6 *A **marginal pricing equilibrium** is a price vector $\mathbf{p}^* \in \mathbb{P}$ and an allocation $[(\mathbf{x}_i^*), \widetilde{\mathbf{y}}^*]$, such that:*
(a) $\mathbf{x}_i^*$ maximizes u_i over the budget set $\{\mathbf{x}_i \in X_i \ / \ \mathbf{p}^* \mathbf{x}_i^* \leq r_i(\mathbf{p}^*, \widetilde{\mathbf{y}}^*)\}$, for all $i = 1, 2, \ldots, m$.
(b) $\mathbf{p}^* \in \bigcap_{j=1}^{n} \phi_j^{MP}(\mathbf{y}_j^*)$.
(c) $\sum_{i=1}^{m} \mathbf{x}_i^* \leq \sum_{j=1}^{n} \mathbf{y}_j^* + \omega$, with $p_k^* = 0$ when the corresponding inequality is strict.

A marginal pricing equilibrium is an equilibrium in which all firms follow the marginal pricing rule.

We can now present the existence result for marginal pricing:

Proposition 6.6 *Under axioms 6.1 to 6.4 a marginal pricing equilibrium exists.*

    Proof. Propositions 6.4 and 6.5 imply that ϕ_j^{MP} is a regular pricing rule with bounded losses, for all j. Then, the result follows from Theorem 5.1. Q.e.d.

    There are two properties of marginal pricing worth noting:

    (i) This pricing rule satisfies the necessary conditions for optimality, and it coincides with profit maximization when production sets are convex (Proposition 6.3). Yet, when production sets are not convex, these necessary conditions may well not be sufficient (we elaborate on this later on).

    (ii) When there are increasing returns to scale, marginal pricing entails losses ("marginal costs" are smaller than "average costs"). This implies that this pricing rule requires the designing of a system of transfers (embodied in consumers' wealth functions, for example), so that these firms can cover their losses. Apart from the informational problem [see Calsamiglia (1977)], this can be seen as an additional complication of the regulation policy, which requires making decisions about its distributional impact.

6.3.2 Competitive equilibrium revisited

Here we consider the existence of competitive equilibrium in the standard convex model discussed in chapter 4, and show that this can be achieved as an application of theorem 5.1.

    Consider now the following axioms that correspond precisely to those in chapter 4:

Axiom 6.1' *For all* $i = 1, 2, ..., m$: *(i)* $X_i \subset \mathbb{R}^\ell$ *is a non-empty, closed convex set, bounded from below;* *(ii)* $u_i : X_i \to \mathbb{R}$ *is continuous, quasi-concave$^+$ and non-satiable utility function;* *(iii)* $\omega_i \in X_i$, *and there exists* $\mathbf{x}_i^0 \in X_i$ *with* $\mathbf{x}_i^0 << \omega_i$.

Axiom 6.2' *For all* $j = 1, 2, ..., n$: *(i)* Y_j *is a closed subset of* $\mathbb{R}^\ell$; *(ii)* $Y_j - \mathbb{R}_+^\ell \subset Y_j$; *(iii)* $\mathbf{0} \in Y_j$; *(iv)* Y_j *is convex.*

    The behaviour of competitive firms is characterized by the choice of production plans that maximize profits, relative to the price vector. This can be described in terms of the following pricing rule:

Definition 6.7 *The **profit maximization** pricing rule is a mapping* $\phi_j^{PM} : \mathbb{F}_j \to \mathbb{P}$, *given by:*

$$\phi_j^{PM}(\mathbf{y}_j) \equiv \{\mathbf{q} \in \mathbb{P} \mid \mathbf{q}\mathbf{y}_j \geq \mathbf{q}\mathbf{y}_j', \forall \; \mathbf{y}_j' \in Y_j\}$$

This pricing rule associates the set of prices which *support* it as the most profitable one with every efficient production plan; that is, ϕ_j^{PM} is precisely the *inverse supply mapping* (see section 3.5.3). The following figure provides an illustration of this:

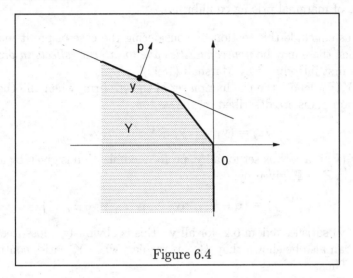

Figure 6.4

The following result explains the main properties of this pricing rule:

Proposition 6.7 *Under axiom 6.2', ϕ_j^{PM} is a regular and loss-free pricing rule.*

Proof. It follows from Proposition 6.3 that, when Y_j is closed, convex and comprehensive, $\phi_j^{PM}(\mathbf{y}_j) = \mathbb{N}_Y(\mathbf{y}_j) \bigcap \mathbb{P}$ (where $\mathbb{N}_Y(\mathbf{y}_j)$ is the normal cone to Y_j at $\mathbf{y}_j$). Therefore, Theorem 6.1 ensures that ϕ_j^{PM} is a regular pricing rule. Moreover, if $\mathbf{0} \in Y_j$, it cannot be the case that, for some $\mathbf{y}_j \in \mathbb{F}_j$, one has $\mathbf{q} \in \phi_j^{PM}(\mathbf{y}_j)$ and $\mathbf{qy}_j < 0$. $\boxed{\text{Q.e.d.}}$

In a private ownership economy, the ith consumer's wealth mapping is given by $r_i(\mathbf{p}, \widetilde{\mathbf{y}}) = \mathbf{p}\omega_i + \sum_{j=1}^n \theta_{ij} \mathbf{py}_j$. Note that when $\mathbf{p} \in \phi^{PM}(\mathbf{y}_j)$, $\mathbf{py}_j \geq 0$, so that axiom 6.3 follows from axiom 6.1'. That is, if $(\mathbf{p}, \widetilde{\mathbf{y}})$ is a production equilibrium and axiom 6.1' holds, then $r_i(\mathbf{p}, \widetilde{\mathbf{y}}) > \min \mathbf{p} X_i$, for all i.

A **competitive equilibrium** is an equilibrium for a private ownership market economy in which firms follow the profit maximization pricing rule. The following result is obtained as an immediate consequence of those presented above:

Corollary 6.1 *Let E be a private ownership economy satisfying axioms 6.1', 6.2' and 6.4. Then, a competitive equilibrium exists.*

This result is relevant because it ensures that the model developed in chapter 5, actually encompasses the standard general equilibrium model of a competitive economy, and also, that competitive equilibrium is a particular instance of marginal pricing equilibrium.

Let us conclude this section by considering the case of profit maximization, when there may be *non-convexities due to external effects in production* [an idea first introduced by Marshall (1890)].

Let $Y_j(\widetilde{\mathbf{y}})$ denote the production set of the jth firm, when all other firms' production plans are described by the vector

$$\widetilde{\mathbf{y}}_{-j} = (\mathbf{y}_1, \ldots, \mathbf{y}_{j-1}, \mathbf{y}_{j+1}, \ldots, \mathbf{y}_n)$$

When $Y_j(\widetilde{\mathbf{y}})$ is a convex set for all $\widetilde{\mathbf{y}}$, profit maximization is given by a pricing rule $\psi_j^{PM} : \mathbb{F} \to \mathbb{P}$, given by:

$$\psi_j^{PM}(\widetilde{\mathbf{y}}) \equiv \{\mathbf{q} \in \mathbb{P} \ / \ \mathbf{q}\mathbf{y}_j \geq \mathbf{q}\mathbf{y}_j', \ \forall \mathbf{y}_j' \in Y_j(\widetilde{\mathbf{y}})\}$$

If $Y_j(\widetilde{\mathbf{y}})$ satisfies axiom 6.2' for all $\widetilde{\mathbf{y}}$, this is obviously a loss-free pricing rule. It can also be shown that ψ_j^{PM} is regular, when Y_j varies continuously with $\widetilde{\mathbf{y}}$. Thus,

Corollary 6.2 *Let E be an economy satisfying axioms 6.1' and 6.4, and suppose that, for each $\widetilde{\mathbf{y}} \in \mathbb{F}$, all j, $Y_j(\widetilde{\mathbf{y}})$ is a continuous correspondence, with closed and convex values, and such that $\mathbf{0} \in Y_j(\widetilde{\mathbf{y}})$ and $-\mathbb{R}_+^\ell \subset Y_j(\widetilde{\mathbf{y}})$. Then a competitive equilibrium does exist.*

The reader should understand that the efficiency of competitive equilibria no longer holds in this context: individual maximization is no longer equivalent to global maximization.

6.4   The efficiency problem

Marginal pricing is an abstract principle that derives from the necessary conditions for optimality. This follows from the observation that when prices do not coincide with the associated marginal rates of transformation, improvements are possible. Hence, equating prices to such marginal rates ensures that the necessary conditions for efficiency are satisfied. From this perspective, marginal pricing can be understood as a regulation policy that is applicable to firms with increasing returns to scale (natural monopolies). If

Pareto efficiency is a social goal, those firms with increasing returns should be instructed to set prices equal to marginal costs. Interestingly enough, when production sets are convex, this pricing principle corresponds to profit maximization at given prices. Therefore, an equilibrium in which firms follow the marginal pricing rule corresponds in this case to a competitive equilibrium.

Let us now analyze the efficiency of marginal pricing equilibrium allocations when firms follow the marginal pricing rule. We shall first show that the second welfare theorem holds (that is, every efficient allocation can be decentralized as a marginal pricing equilibrium), but also that the first welfare theorem fails (marginal pricing does not ensure efficiency).

6.4.1 The Second Welfare Theorem

We consider here the extension of the second welfare theorem to economies with non-convex production sets. In order to do so, let $E = \{(X_i, u_i)_{i=1}^m,$ $(Y_j)_{j=1}^n, \omega\}$ describe our economy of reference. That is, an economy with ℓ commodities, m consumers (characterized by their consumption sets and utility functions), n firms (characterized by their production sets), and a vector of initial endowments $\omega \in \mathbb{R}^\ell$. It will be shown here that, under the standard axioms of chapter 5, every efficient allocation can be decentralized as a marginal pricing equilibrium, provided we are free to make arbitrary transfers.

The following lemma (which is stated without proof), gives us a key instrumental result for the extension of the second welfare theorem:[4]

Lemma 6.2 [Clarke (1983, Th. 2.4.5)] *Let Y be a closed subset of $\mathbb{R}^\ell$, and let $\mathbb{T}_Y(\mathbf{y})$ denote the polar cone of $\mathbb{N}_Y(\mathbf{y})$ (also called Tangent Cone). A point $\mathbf{v}$ belongs to $\mathbb{T}_Y(\mathbf{y})$ if and only if, for every sequence $\{\mathbf{y}^\nu\} \to \mathbf{y}$ in Y, $\{t^\nu\} \to 0$ in $(0, +\infty)$, there is a sequence $\{\mathbf{v}^\nu\} \to \mathbf{v}$ in $\mathbb{R}^\ell$ such that $(\mathbf{y}^\nu + t^\nu \mathbf{v}^\nu) \in Y$, for all ν.*

The following result [first presented by Guesnerie (1975)], is an extension of the Second Welfare Theorem to economies with nonconvex production sets [see also Vohra (1991, th.1), Quinzii (1992, th.2.6)]:

Theorem 6.2 *Let $E = \{(X_i, u_i)_{i=1}^m, (Y_j)_{j=1}^n, \omega\}$ be an economy such that:*
(i) For every $j = 1, 2, \ldots, n, Y_j$ is a closed subset of $\mathbb{R}^\ell$, with $Y_j - \mathbb{R}_+^\ell \subset Y_j$.

---

[4]Proving this result is not particularly difficult, but it takes a rather long excursion through Clarke's "Generalized Gradients" (chapter 2 of his book).

(ii) For every $i = 1, 2, \ldots, m$, $X_i \subset \mathbb{R}^\ell$ is non-empty, closed and convex, and $u_i : X_i \to \mathbb{R}$ is a continuous, quasi-concave$^+$ and non-satiable utility function. Let $[(\mathbf{x}_i^*), \widetilde{\mathbf{y}}^*]$ be a Pareto Optimal allocation. Then, there exists $\mathbf{p} \in \mathbb{P}$, such that:

(a) For all i, $u_i(\mathbf{x}_i) \geq u_i(\mathbf{x}_i^*) \Longrightarrow \mathbf{p}\mathbf{x}_i \geq \mathbf{p}\mathbf{x}_i^*$.

(b) $\mathbf{p} \in \phi_j^{MP}(\mathbf{p}, \widetilde{\mathbf{y}}^*)$, for all j.

Proof.   Let us define the following sets:

$$\mathcal{BE}_i(\mathbf{x}_i^*) \equiv \{\mathbf{x}_i \in X_i \ / \ u_i(\mathbf{x}_i) \geq u_i(\mathbf{x}_i^*)\}$$

$$\mathcal{B}_i(\mathbf{x}_i^*) \equiv \{\mathbf{x}_i \in X_i \ / \ u_i(\mathbf{x}_i) > u_i(\mathbf{x}_i^*)\}$$

and, by letting $\mathbf{x}^* \equiv \sum_{i=1}^m \mathbf{x}_i^*$, write: $\mathcal{BE}(\mathbf{x}^*) \equiv \sum_{i=1}^m \mathcal{BE}_i(\mathbf{x}_i^*)$. Now define:

$$G \equiv \sum_{j=1}^n [\mathbb{T}_{Y_j}(\mathbf{y}_j^*) + \{\mathbf{y}_j^*\}] + \{\omega\}$$

Under the assumptions established, the sets G and $\mathcal{BE}(\mathbf{x}^*)$ are convex. Moreover, since $\mathbf{0} \in \mathbb{T}_{Y_j}(\mathbf{y}_j^*)$ and $\omega = \sum_{i=1}^m \mathbf{x}_i^* - \sum_{j=1}^n \mathbf{y}_j^*$ (because $[(\mathbf{x}_i^*), (\mathbf{y}_j^*)]$ is a feasible allocation), we deduce that $G \bigcap \mathcal{BE}(\mathbf{x}^*) \neq \emptyset$.

Let us now show that $G \bigcap int\mathcal{BE}(\mathbf{x}^*) = \emptyset$ (where $int\mathcal{BE}(\mathbf{x}^*)$ denotes the interior of $\mathcal{BE}(\mathbf{x}^*)$, i.e. the set of points that can be expressed as the sum of points $\mathbf{x}_i$ such that $\mathbf{x}_i \in \mathcal{BE}_i(\mathbf{x}_i^*) \forall i$, and $\mathbf{x}_h \in \mathcal{B}_h(\mathbf{x}_h^*)$ for some h). To do so, suppose that there exists $\mathbf{x}_i \in \mathcal{BE}_i(\mathbf{x}_i^*), i = 1, 2, \ldots, m$, with $\mathbf{x}_h \in \mathcal{B}_h(\mathbf{x}_h^*)$, for some h, and $\mathbf{z}_j \in \mathbb{T}_{Y_j}(\mathbf{y}_j^*)$, $j = 1, 2, \ldots, n$, such that:

$$\sum_{i=1}^m \mathbf{x}_i - \sum_{j=1}^n (\mathbf{z}_j + \mathbf{y}_j^*) = \omega$$

Since $\omega = \sum_{i=1}^m \mathbf{x}_i^* - \sum_{j=1}^n \mathbf{y}_j^*$, we have:

$$\sum_{i=1}^m \mathbf{x}_i - \sum_{j=1}^n (\mathbf{z}_j + \mathbf{y}_j^*) = \sum_{i=1}^m \mathbf{x}_i^* - \sum_{j=1}^n \mathbf{y}_j^*$$

and hence

$$\sum_{j=1}^n \mathbf{z}_j = \sum_{i=1}^m (\mathbf{x}_i - \mathbf{x}_i^*) \qquad [1]$$

The convexity of consumption sets and the quasi-concavity$^+$ of preferences imply that, for every $t \in (0, 1)$, we have:

$$t\mathbf{x}_i + (1-t)\mathbf{x}_i^* = \mathbf{x}_i^* + t(\mathbf{x}_i - \mathbf{x}_i^*) \in \mathcal{BE}_i(\mathbf{x}_i^*), \forall i$$

$$t\mathbf{x}_h + (1-t)\mathbf{x}_h^* = \mathbf{x}_h^* + t(\mathbf{x}_h - \mathbf{x}_h^*) \in \mathcal{B}_h(\mathbf{x}_h^*), \text{ some } h$$

Then, from [1] we have:

$$\sum_{i=1}^{m} \mathbf{x}_i^* + t \sum_{j=1}^{n} \mathbf{z}_j \in int\mathcal{BE}(\mathbf{x}^*), \forall t \in (0,1) \qquad [2]$$

As $\mathbf{z}_j \in \mathbb{T}_{Y_j}(\mathbf{y}_j^*)$ for all j, it follows from Lemma 6.2 that, for any sequence of positive real numbers $\{t^q\} \to 0$, there exists a sequence $\{\mathbf{z}_j^q\} \to \mathbf{z}_j$, for each j, such that $y_j^* + t^q \mathbf{z}_j^q \in Y_j$. For a large enough q, $\sum_{j=1}^{n} \mathbf{z}_j^q$ becomes arbitrarily close to $\sum_{j=1}^{n} \mathbf{z}_j$. By the continuity of utilities and [2], there exists a large enough q such that:

$$\sum_{i=1}^{m} \mathbf{x}_i^* + t^q \sum_{j=1}^{n} \mathbf{z}_j^q \in int\mathcal{BE}(\mathbf{x}^*) \qquad [3]$$

Because $\omega = \sum_{i=1}^{m} \mathbf{x}_i^* - \sum_{j=1}^{n} \mathbf{y}_j^*$, we can write:

$$\sum_{i=1}^{m} \mathbf{x}_i^* + t^q \sum_{j=1}^{n} \mathbf{z}_j^q - \sum_{j=1}^{n} (t^q \mathbf{z}_j^q + \mathbf{y}_j^*) = \omega$$

with $\sum_{j=1}^{n} (t^q \mathbf{z}_j^q + \mathbf{y}_j^*) \in \sum_{j=1}^{n} Y_j$. But this along with [3] contradicts the Pareto optimality of $[(\mathbf{x}_i^*), (\mathbf{y}_j^*)]$. Therefore, $G \bigcap int\mathcal{BE}(\mathbf{x}^*) = \emptyset$.

Thus, we can now apply the separating hyperplane theorem to assert that $\mathbf{p} \in \mathbb{R}^\ell$, $\mathbf{p} \neq \mathbf{0}$ exists, such that for each $\mathbf{x} \in \mathcal{BE}(\mathbf{x}^*)$, and every $\mathbf{q}$ in G,

$$\mathbf{px} \geq \mathbf{pq} \qquad [4]$$

In particular, since $\omega = \sum_{i=1}^{m} \mathbf{x}_i^* - \sum_{j=1}^{n} \mathbf{y}_j^*$, and $\{\omega\} + \sum_{j=1}^{n} \mathbf{y}_j^* \in G$, we get: $\mathbf{px}^* = \mathbf{p}\omega + \mathbf{p} \sum_{j=1}^{n} \mathbf{y}_j^* \leq \mathbf{px}, \forall \mathbf{x} \in \mathcal{BE}(\mathbf{x}^*)$, that is, $\mathbf{px} \geq \mathbf{px}^*$ for all points in $\mathcal{BE}(\mathbf{x}^*)$. It is easy to deduce that this happens if and only if $\mathbf{px}_i^*$ minimizes $\mathbf{px}_i$ over $\mathcal{BE}_i(\mathbf{x}_i^*)$ for every i.

Applying the same reasoning, we deduce that for every $\mathbf{q}$ in G, we have: $\mathbf{pq} \leq \mathbf{p}\omega + \mathbf{p} \sum_{j=1}^{n} \mathbf{y}_j^*$, i.e., $\mathbf{p}\omega + \mathbf{p} \sum_{j=1}^{n} \mathbf{y}_j^*$ maximizes the value of points $\sum_{j=1}^{n} \mathbf{z}_j + \sum_{j=1}^{n} \mathbf{y}_j^* + \{\omega\}$ over G, which happens to be true if and only if it maximizes $\mathbf{z}_j + \mathbf{y}_j^*$ over $\{\mathbb{T}_{Y_j}(\mathbf{y}_j^*) + \{\mathbf{y}_j^*\}\}$ for each j. Now, since $\mathbf{y}_j^* \in \mathbb{T}_{Y_j}(\mathbf{y}_j^*) + \{\mathbf{y}_j^*\}$ for every j, it follows that $\mathbf{py}_j^* \geq \mathbf{p}(\mathbf{z}_j + \mathbf{y}_j^*)$, for every $\mathbf{z}_j \in \mathbb{T}_{Y_j}(\mathbf{y}_j^*)$. That is, $\mathbf{pz}_j \leq 0$, $\forall \mathbf{z}_j \in \mathbb{T}_{Y_j}(\mathbf{y}_j^*)$, and hence $\mathbf{p}$ is in $\mathbb{N}_{Y_j}(\mathbf{y}_j^*)$, for all j.

Finally, since $Y_j - \mathbb{R}_+^\ell \subset Y_j$ by assumption, Theorem 6.1 ensures that $\mathbb{N}_{Y_j}(\mathbf{y}_j^*) \subset \mathbb{R}_+^\ell$ for all j, and hence, $\mathbf{p} > 0$. $\boxed{\text{Q.e.d.}}$

The next figure illustrates this situation:

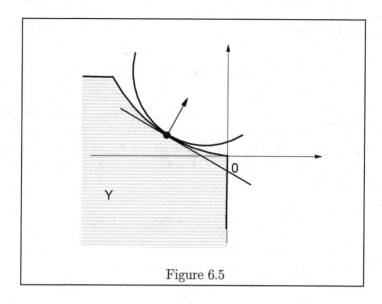

Figure 6.5

Remark 6.4 *Let* $[(\mathbf{x}_i^*), \widetilde{\mathbf{y}}]$ *be a Pareto Optimal allocation, and suppose that for some consumer* u_i *is differentiable at* $\mathbf{x}_i^* \in int X_i$. *Then, for this consumer, the (normalized) vector of marginal rates of substitution is unique. Thus, the price vector supporting that allocation turns out to be unique. Let us also recall here that, according to proposition 2.4, cost minimization implies utility maximization if* $\mathbf{p}^* \mathbf{x}_i^* > \min \mathbf{p}^* X_i$.

Theorem 6.2 provides an extension of the second welfare theorem allowing for nonconvex production sets. It tells us that any efficient allocation can be decentralized as a marginal pricing equilibrium, provided we are free to carry out any feasible lump-sum transfer that may be required. This shows that interpreting marginal rates of transformation as Clarke normal cones is appropriate. The above remark reinforces such an idea: it says that (under very mild regularity conditions) *marginal pricing is a necessary condition for achieving Pareto optimality through a price mechanism.*

Thus, in the context of a regulated economy in which arbitrary lump-sum transfers are possible, efficiency can be achieved by instructing firms to follow marginal pricing. Note that when production sets are convex, marginal pricing corresponds to profit maximization. We can therefore interpret this result in terms of a mixed economy with a competitive sector (convex firms) and a regulated one, in which all firms follow marginal pricing, and efficiency is achieved by suitably redistributing wealth.

6.4.2   The First Welfare Theorem

We have already seen that a marginal pricing equilibrium exists, and that
every efficient allocation can be decentralized as a marginal pricing equilibrium. Yet, those allocations induced by a marginal pricing equilibrium need
not be efficient (marginal pricing is a necessary but not a sufficient condition for optimality, a general problem in nonconvex programming). To see
this we shall briefly report on some key examples. First, we shall show that
production efficiency may fail in a marginal pricing equilibrium, due to the
fact that there is an inadequate number of active firms (example 1). In order
to avoid this type of complication, we shall concentrate on economies with
a single firm. The second example shows a single-firm economy in which no
marginal pricing equilibrium is Pareto efficient. The third example presents
a situation of a single-firm economy in which marginal pricing is Pareto dom-
inated by average cost pricing (and thus is not even second best efficient).
Each of these examples illustrates a different aspect of the problem.[5]

Example 6.1

Let us begin by considering a constant returns to scale economy, with two
identical firms, two identical consumers and two goods (good 1 is an input
whereas good 2 is an output). Each firm's efficient production plan takes the
form $\lambda(-1, 1)$. At equilibrium prices $\mathbf{p}' = (0.5, 0.5)$, each consumer supplies
one unit of input and demands one unit of output. Consumer 1 trades with
firm 1, and consumer 2 trades with firm 2, say. Suppose now that firm 1's
technology changes, so that the slope of the boundary becomes steeper for
those production plans involving more than 1.5 units of input (i.e. firm 1 becomes more productive for higher levels of output). It is clear that efficiency
requires closing down firm 2, and operating only the more efficient firm. Yet
$\mathbf{p}'$ still gives us a marginal pricing equilibrium in which each consumer trades
one unit of input against one unit of output in each firm. This implies that
marginal pricing equilibria do not ensure production efficiency when there
are several firms [see Beato & Mas-Colell (1983), (1985) for a more detailed
example].

---

[5]We shall address the efficiency problem en the context of two-part tariffs in the next
chapter.

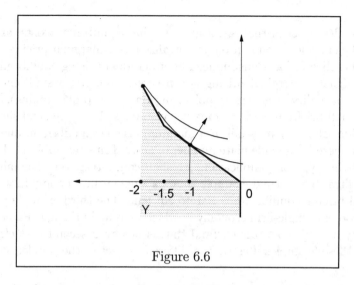

Figure 6.6

The simple economy described above illustrates an extremely serious problem: when there are increasing returns to scale, the necessary conditions for optimality may yield equilibrium allocations in which aggregate production belongs to the interior of the aggregate production set. Is this the only source of concern? The answer is no. The following examples consider economies with a single firm in which marginal pricing still fails to achieve Pareto optimality.

Example 6.2

Consider an economy with two goods, a single non-convex firm and two consumers.[6] The production set, which presents an extreme form of indivisibility, is given by:

$$Y \equiv \left(\mathbf{y} \in \mathbb{R}^2 \text{ with } \left\{ \begin{array}{l} y_1 > -7, y_2 \leq 0 \\ y_1 \leq -7, y_2 \leq 7 \end{array} \right. \right)$$

that is, no output can be produced with less than 7 units of input and seven units of output can be produced with 7 or more units of input. The only efficient production plans are thus $\mathbf{y}^o = (0,0)$, and $\mathbf{y}' = (-7,7)$. Moreover, $\mathbb{N}_Y(\mathbf{y}^o) = \mathbb{N}_Y(\mathbf{y}') = \mathbb{R}_+^2$ (that is, marginal pricing imposes no restriction on equilibrium prices). Consumers' preferences are described by the following

---

[6]This example is developed in Brown & Heal (1979), after Guesnerie's (1975) previous one. See also Quinzii (1992,Ch.4)

utilities:

$$u_1(\mathbf{x}_1) = \begin{cases} x_{12} + \frac{4}{3}x_{11} & \text{if } x_{12} \geq x_{11} \\ \frac{700}{312}\left(x_{12} + \frac{4}{100}x_{11}\right) & \text{if } x_{12} \leq x_{11} \end{cases}$$

$$u_2(\mathbf{x}_2) = \begin{cases} \frac{3x_{22}+5x_{21}}{18} & \text{if } x_{22} \geq \frac{1}{3}x_{21} \\ x_{22} & \text{if } x_{22} \leq \frac{1}{3}x_{21} \end{cases}$$

Initial endowments and shares are given by:

$$\omega_1 = (0,5), \quad \omega_2 = (15,0), \quad \theta_1 = 1, \quad \theta_2 = 0$$

In this economy there are two equilibria that are candidates to efficient marginal pricing equilibria. The structure of the model implies that both of them may well be regarded as pure exchange equilibria, the first one because it does not involve production, and the second one because it can be viewed as an equilibrium of an economy with no production and initial endowments given by:

$$\omega_1' = (-7, 12), \quad \omega_2' = (15, 0)$$

The first equilibrium is given by:

$$\mathbf{p}^o = (4, 100), \quad \mathbf{y}^o = (0,0), \quad \mathbf{x}_1^o = (13.393, 4.464), \quad \mathbf{x}_2^o = (1.607, 0.536)$$

with utilities

$$u_1(\mathbf{x}_1^o) = 11.216, \quad u_2(\mathbf{x}_2^o) = 0.536$$

The second equilibrium is given by:

$$\mathbf{p}' = (5, 3), \quad \mathbf{y}' = (-7, 7), \quad \mathbf{x}_1' = (0, 1/3), \quad \mathbf{x}_2' = (8, 35/3)$$

with utilities

$$u_1(\mathbf{x}_1') = 1/3, \quad u_2(\mathbf{x}_2') = 4.166$$

Now consider the allocation $\mathbf{x}_1 = (1.5, 0.5)$, $\mathbf{x}_2 = (13.5, 4.5)$ which is feasible for the economy when no production takes place. The utilities associated with this allocation are:

$$u_1(\mathbf{x}_1) = 1.256, \quad u_2(\mathbf{x}_2) = 4.5$$

which are strictly greater than those associated with the equilibrium involving production. Now take the allocation $\mathbf{x}_1'' = (1.2, 9.8)$, $\mathbf{x}_2'' = (6.8, 2.2)$, which is feasible for the economy producing $\mathbf{y}' = (-7, 7)$. The utilities associated with this allocation are:

$$u_1(\mathbf{x}_1'') = 11.4, \quad u_2(\mathbf{x}_2'') = 2.2$$

which Pareto dominate the first equilibrium allocation. Therefore, no marginal pricing equilibrium is Pareto optimal.

Example 6.3

Consider a private ownership economy with two goods, two consumers and a single non-convex firm, whose data are summarized as follows:[7]

$$X_1 = \mathbb{R}^2_+, \quad u_1(x_1) = x_{12},$$
$$\omega_1 = (0, 10), \quad \theta_1 = 1$$

$$X_2 = \mathbb{R}^2_+, \quad u_2(x_2) = 4\log x_{21} + x_{22},$$
$$\omega_2 = (20, 0), \quad \theta_2 = 0$$

$$Y = \{\mathbf{y} \in \mathbb{R}^2 \mid y_1 \leq 0; \ y_1 + y_2 \leq 0 \text{ if } y_1 \geq -16$$
$$\text{and } 10y_1 + y_2 + 144 \leq 0 \text{ if } y_1 \leq -16\}$$

In view of u_1 we can take $p_2 = 1$. It can be shown that the only marginal pricing equilibrium of this economy corresponds to:

$$\mathbf{p}^* = (1, 1), \quad \mathbf{y}^* = (-16, 16), \quad \mathbf{x}_1^* = (0, 10), \quad \mathbf{x}_2^* = (4, 16)$$

Now let us think of the situation that corresponds to an average cost pricing equilibrium. That is, a situation in which firms find those prices-production combinations that yield zero profits acceptable. It can be checked that

$$\mathbf{p}' = (2, 1), \quad \mathbf{y}' = (-18, 36), \quad \mathbf{x}_1' = (0, 10), \quad \mathbf{x}_2' = (2, 36)$$

is an average cost pricing equilibrium. Notice that the first consumer's utility is the same as in the marginal pricing equilibrium ($u_1' = 10$), while the second consumer is now better-off (since $u_2' = 4\log .2 + 36$ is greater than $u_2^* = 4\log .4 + 16$).

The analysis developed so far points out that there are two factors that can be considered "responsible" of this asymmetry between the validity of the second welfare theorem and the failure of the first one:

(i) There may be a wrong number of active firms in a marginal pricing equilibrium: decentralization with increasing returns may result in production inefficiency.

(ii) There are single-firm economies for which the rules of income distribution are inherently incompatible with efficiency. The reason for this is that, contrary to the convex case, the mapping that associates efficient allocations with income distributions is *not onto*. Thus, for fixed income distribution

---

[7]Vohra (1988b)

schemes, we can find non-convex economies in which the agents' characteristics (technology and preferences) are such that marginal pricing generates
an income distribution that has an empty intersection with the subset of efficient income distributions. Examples 2 and 3 show this feature. The third
example also indicates that there may be better alternatives than marginal
pricing, in specific contexts in which Pareto optimality fails.

6.4.3 The core

The underlying idea is that of social stability: if an allocation is in the core
of an economy, there is no group of agents who can do better on their own.
Let us present this notion more formally.

Let $E = \{(X_i, u_i)_{i=1}^m, Y, \omega\}$ be an economy, where $Y = \sum_{j=1}^n Y_j$ denotes
the aggregate production set. Let $\mathcal{M}$ denote the set of indices identifying
the m consumers, that is, $\mathcal{M} = \{1, 2, \ldots, m\}$. Any non-empty subset of $\mathcal{M}$
is called a **coalition**. Let $[(x_i'), y'] \in \Pi_{i=1}^m X_i \times Y$ be a given allocation, and
denote an allocation relative to a coalition $S \subset \mathcal{M}$ by $[(x_i), y]^S \in \Pi_{i \in S} X_i \times Y$.
We say that a coalition S can *improve upon* the allocation $[(x_i'), y']$, if there
exists an allocation $[(x_i), y]^S$ relative to the coalition S, such that:

a) $\sum_{i \in S} x_i \leq \sum_{i \in S} \omega_i + y$.

b) $u_i(x_i) \geq u_i(x_i')$ for all $i \in S$, and $u_h(x_h) > u_h(x_h')$ for some $h \in S$.

That is, a coalition can improve upon an allocation if there is another
allocation that is feasible for that coalition [condition a)], and its members
are better-off [condition b)].

Definition 6.8 *The **core** of an economy $E = \{(X_i, u_i)_{i=1}^m, Y, \omega\}$ is the set
of feasible allocations that cannot be improved upon by any coalition.*

Observe that if an allocation is in the core, then it is Pareto optimal.
Note also that no reference to prices or markets appears in the definition of
the core.

At first glance, one would expect that the presence of increasing returns
may facilitate the non-emptiness of the core: larger coalitions are more likely
to attain higher productivity. This intuition, however, is far from being true.
Scarf (1986) (a paper written in 1963) provides the following result [see the
proof in Quinzii (1992, Th. 6.2)]:

Theorem 6.3 *Let Y be a closed subset of $\mathbb{R}^\ell$ (to be interpreted as the
aggregate production set), such that $0 \in Y$, $Y - \mathbb{R}_+^\ell \subset Y$, and $\{\omega\} + Y$
is bounded from above, for all $\omega \in \mathbb{R}^\ell$. Consider the class of economies
$E(Y) \equiv \{[(X_i, u_i, \omega_i)_{i=1}^m, Y]\}$, where, for each $i = 1, 2, , \ldots, m$: (a) $X_i = \mathbb{R}_+^\ell$;*

(b) $u_i : X_i \to \mathbb{R}$ is a continuous and quasi-concave function, that satisfies local non-satiation; and (c) $\omega_i >> 0$. Then, each economy in $E(Y)$ has a non-empty core if and only if Y is a convex cone.

This result says that, with the degree of generality given by the assumptions of the theorem, we can always construct economies with increasing returns and empty cores. Hence, the difficulties between increasing returns and efficiency are somehow more substantial than the way of pricing commodities.

6.5   References to the literature

6.5.1   Marginal pricing

The idea of regulating nonconvex firms by setting prices equal to marginal costs is an old wisdom (which, in the context of partial analysis, can be associated with the names of Dupuit, Marshall, Pigou, Lange, Lerner, Allais and Hotelling among others). It is based on the observation that a necessary condition for Pareto optimality is that all agents equate prices to their marginal rates of transformation. The distortion introduced by the need to cover the firms' losses was the subject of an interesting discussion which is reviewed in Ruggles (1949),(1950).

From a general equilibrium standpoint, Mantel (1979) and Beato (1982) independently showed the existence of equilibrium in an economy with a single firm whose production set has a smooth boundary, but need not be convex. Cornet (1990) (a paper written in 1982) provides the first existence theorem for marginal pricing in an economy with a single firm but dispensing with the smoothness assumption. To do so he introduces Clarke's normal cones as the proper way of defining marginal pricing in the general case. Brown & Heal (1982) gave an index-theoretic proof of existence for Mantel's model. Beato & Mas-Colell (1985) extend the existence results to the case of several non-convex firms, and Brown, Heal, Khan & Vohra (1986) analyze the case of a private ownership economy with a single non-convex firm and several convex firms. More general results on this specific pricing rule appear in Bonnisseau & Cornet (1990a,b) and Vohra (1992). See also the problem raised in Jouini's (1988) paper and Bonnisseau (1991).

On the properties of normal cones for non-convex sets, see Clarke (1983, ch. 2), Kahn & Vohra (1987, Section 2) and Cornet (1990, Appendix).

6.5.2 Efficiency

In a remarkable paper, Guesnerie (1975) showed that marginal pricing is a necessary condition for optimality. He did so by extending the second welfare theorem to economies with non-convex production sets, and using the Dubovickii-Miljutin cones of interior displacements as the main tool for extending the notion of marginal pricing to non-smooth, non-convex sets. After Cornet's introduction of the Clarke normal cones for this type of analysis, Khan & Vohra (1987) extended this result to economies with public goods, and Bonnisseau & Cornet (1988b) to economies with an infinite dimensional commodity space [see also Cornet (1986)]. Vohra (1991) and Quinzii (1992, Ch. 2) provide elegant and easy proofs of this result.

The failure of marginal pricing equilibria to achieve Pareto optimality was also shown in Guesnerie (1975) (who gave the first example of an economy in which *all* marginal pricing equilibria were inefficient). Additional examples of this phenomenon appeared in Brown & Heal (1979). Beato & Mas-Colell (1983) provided a first example in which marginal pricing equilibria were not in the set of efficient aggregate productions. Vohra (1988b), (1990) develops a systematic analysis of the inefficiency of marginal pricing for fixed rules of income distribution, and of the inefficiency of two-part tariffs, respectively. An excellent exposition of the efficiency problems in this context appears in Vohra (1991).

Some positive results are available for the case of a single non-convex firm. Brown & Heal (1983) showed that assuming homothetic preferences (which implies that Scitovsky's community indifference curves do not intersect), there exists at least one Pareto optimal marginal pricing equilibrium. Sufficient conditions for the optimality of marginal pricing in a more general context are analyzed in Dierker (1986) and Quinzii (1991). These conditions refer to the relative curvature of the production frontier and of the community indifference curves, so that when the social indifference curve is tangent to the feasible set, it never cuts across it. See also the special cases analyzed in Vohra (1991) and Quinzii (1992).

On the validity of the two welfare theorems in economies with nonconvex production sets, see the enlightening discussions in Guesnerie (1990), Vohra (1991) and Quinzii (1992 Chs. 1 - 4).

An excellent and very detailed discussion on the non-emptiness of the core of an economy with nonconvex technologies can be found in Quinzii (1992, Ch.6). Sharkey's (1989) survey is also highly recommended. Assuming that there are some inputs that are not consumed, Scarf (1986) identifies a particular family of economies with increasing returns to scale and non-empty cores. Other contributions on this line are Sharkey (1979) (for the case of a single input), Quinzii (1982), Ichiischi & Quinzii (1983) (dispensing with the requirement of "inputs that are not consumed"), and Reichert (1986) (who uses a nonlinear single-production input-output model, to allow for the presence of many nonconvex firms).

Chapter 7

INCREASING RETURNS AND MONOPOLIES

7.1 Introduction

The presence of increasing returns in market economies may lead to the creation of natural monopolies. When productivity increases with size, efficiency calls for a single firm to serve the market. This is a fact already pointed out by John Stuart Mill: "It is obvious, for example, how great economy of labour would be obtained if London were supplied by a single gas or water company instead of the existing plurality. While there are even as many as two, this implies double establishments of all sorts, when one only, with a small increase, could probably perform the whole operation equally well. Were there only one establishment, it could make lower charges, consistent with making the rate of profit now realized. But would it do so? Even if it did not, the community in the aggregate would still be a gainer." [Mill (1848), quoted in Quinzii (1992)].

Mill's observation already shows the tension between the benefit of a single firm in those markets with increasing returns, and the pricing policy that one can expect from monopolies. Indeed, it is well established that monopolies generate inefficiencies in the allocation of resources, irrespective of the increasing returns feature, because they sell their output at prices that make marginal revenues equal to marginal costs, rather than using marginal pricing, as efficiency requires.

From this it follows that natural monopolies can be considered as public utilities, hence regulated. The analysis in the previous chapter suggests that regulation can be associated to the use of marginal pricing, because it satisfies the necessary conditions for optimality, and coincides with profit maximization when production sets are convex. Therefore, this pricing rule describes competitive behaviour in the convex case, and defines a specific regulation policy that satisfies the necessary conditions for optimality.

When there are increasing returns to scale, however, this regulation policy has two main shortcomings. First, it does not ensure the achievement of efficient allocations. Secondly, marginal pricing implies losses, so it requires the simultaneous designing of a system of taxes and transfers to ensure a balanced budget. This can be seen as an additional complication which requires making decisions about its distributional impact. In particular, a marginal pricing equilibrium may not be individually rational, and even if it were individually rational, some consumers might feel that they were paying "too much", so there is little hope for social stability (high income consumers might be subsidizing those with lower incomes who consume goods produced by non-convex firms).

These distributional problems induced the consideration of regulation policies that satisfy a break-even constraint. *Two-part marginal pricing* is a case in point, already proposed by Coase in 1946. The main idea is that those consumers who buy positive amounts of the goods produced by non-convex firms, are charged an entrance fee plus a proportional one (which corresponds to marginal pricing). Therefore, by using a system of non-linear prices, one can meet both the necessary conditions for optimality and a break-even constraint. Two-part tariffs can be regarded as the simplest of these non-linear pricing schemes (even though it involves discontinuous wealth functions, because wealth jumps when the consumption of those goods produced by non-convex firms falls to zero).

As in the case of marginal pricing, the optimality of two-part marginal pricing is not guaranteed. Yet, one can think of a number of reasons to argue in favour of this regulation policy. In particular, because:

(i) It always offers the consumer the possibility of not paying the hook-up by abstaining from buying the monopoly good. Therefore, the fees collected reflect the surplus that society derives from the availability of these goods.

(ii) It does not require the designing of an explicit redistribution policy, since it establishes limits on the agents' liability (no one is taxed while someone else is subsidized). In contrast to lump-sum taxation, the fixed part of the tariff only taxes the benefit that the consumer derives from the commodity.

(iii) It may provide more flexibility than the fixed rules of income distribution, as it allows for personalized charges.

Clearly, these advantages are obviously not independent of the way in which fixed charges are determined. In particular, uniform charges will be typically inefficient because different consumers may have different tastes and incomes leading to different willingness to pay. A uniform tariff will exclude some agents from consuming the monopoly goods, whereas it would be beneficial for all of them to increase production by allowing for a personalized system of fixed charges.

Partial equilibrium analysis also suggests a different avenue to conciliate monopolies and efficiency: *perfect price discrimination*. Indeed, some authors, such as Demsetz (1968), argue that publicly owned or regulated firms waste resources, and so monopoly rights should be auctioned. Price discrimination appears to be an alternative way of reaching the social goal of maximizing the sum of producer and consumer surplus in the monopoly market. Note that, even though the efficiency of perfect price discrimination is considered well-established, the existing proofs typically use partial equilibrium arguments that often depend upon convexity and that do not account for interactions with other markets or for the circular flow of income. [Cf. Edlin, Epelbaum & Heller (1998)].

This chapter is devoted to the analysis of market economies in which firms with increasing returns to scale are considered natural monopolies. First we discuss the regulation policy based on the use of two-part tariffs. We shall pay attention to the case in which increasing returns derive from the presence of fixed costs, because in this environment two-part marginal pricing yields efficient allocations. We shall then consider the case of a perfectly discriminating monopoly. Here, we closely follow the contributions of Brown, Heller & Starr (1992), Moriguchi (1996) and Edlin, Epelbaum & Heller (1998).

7.2 The reference model

Consider a private ownership market economy with ℓ commodities, m consumers and n firms. As usual, $\omega \in \mathbb{R}^\ell$ denotes the vector of initial endowments. We can distinguish two sectors in the economy, the competitive sector and the monopoly sector. The competitive sector consists of the m consumers and a subset $C \subset N = \{1, 2, ..., n\}$ of firms; firms in C are standard convex firms. The monopoly sector consists of a subset $M \subset N$ of possibly nonconvex firms. Each monopoly $j \in M$ is the exclusive producer of a subset of commodities L_j. This induces a partition of the set of commodity indices $\mathcal{L} = \{1, 2, ..., \ell\}$, into two different subsets: $\mathcal{L}^C = \{1, 2, ..., c\}$ that corresponds to the set of *competitive commodities*, and $\mathcal{L}^M = \{c+1, c+2, ..., \ell\}$ that corresponds to the set of *monopoly goods*. By definition, $\mathcal{L}^C \cup \mathcal{L}^M = \mathcal{L}$, $\mathcal{L}^C \cap \mathcal{L}^M = \emptyset$, $\mathcal{L}^M = \bigcup_{j \in M} L_j$, and $L_j \cap L_t = \emptyset$, for all $j, t \in M$.

In order to make things simpler, we shall assume that monopoly goods are pure consumption goods, that the initial endowment of monopoly goods is zero, and also that monopoly goods cannot be resold (otherwise the non-linear pricing scheme is not well defined).

Consider now the following axioms:

Axiom 7.1 For all $i = 1, 2, \ldots, m$: (i) X_i is a closed convex subset of $\mathbb{R}^\ell$, bounded from below; (ii) $u_i : X_i \to \mathbb{R}$ is a continuous and quasi-concave$^+$ utility function that satisfies non-satiation; (iii) $\omega_i \in X_i$ and $\omega_{ik} = 0$ for $k \in \mathcal{L}^M$ (i.e. when k is a monopoly good).

Axiom 7.2 For all $j \in C$, $Y_j = Y_j^C \times \{0\}$, where $0 \in \mathbb{R}^{\ell-c}$, and Y_j^C is a convex and closed subset of $\mathbb{R}^c$, such that $0 \in Y_j^C$, and $Y_j^C - \mathbb{R}_+^c \subset Y_j^C$.

Axiom 7.3 For all $j \in M$: (i) Y_j is a closed, comprehensive and star-shaped subset of $\mathbb{R}^\ell$, with $0 \in Y_j$; (ii) The jth firm is the only producer of a subset L_j of monopoly goods.

Axiom 7.1 is standard, except that we assume there are no initial endowments of monopoly goods. The wealth mapping will be specified later, depending on the particular model discussed.

Axiom 7.2 says that competitive firms are standard convex firms in the subspace of competitive commodities. They neither use nor produce monopoly goods. We have chosen to describe production sets as the Cartesian product of $Y_j^C \subset \mathbb{R}^c$ and $0 \in \mathbb{R}^{\ell-c}$, to simplify the notation of scalar products.

Axiom 7.3 describes the monopoly sector. Each monopoly has a closed, comprehensive and star shaped production set, and is the exclusive producer of a subset of monopoly goods. Note that joint production is permitted but no monopoly good can be produced by more than one firm as a net output.

Competitive consumers maximize utility at given prices, under their wealth restrictions. Even though these wealth mappings will depend on the model considered, in a private ownership market economy they can be given the general form of:

$$r_i(\mathbf{p}, \widetilde{\mathbf{y}}) = \mathbf{p}\omega_i + \sum_{j=1}^{n} \theta_{ij} \pi_j(\mathbf{p}) - \sum_{k \in \mathcal{L}^M} t_{ik}$$

where θ_{ij} stands for the ith consumer's share in the jth firm's profits (with $\sum_{i=1}^{m} \theta_{ij} = 1$, for all j), and each $t_{ik} \geq 0$ represents the non-linear part of the price system associated with the consumption of the kth monopoly good.

Convex firms maximize profits at given prices. That is, the jth firm's supply is given by a mapping $\eta_j : \mathbb{P} \to Y_j$ such that $\mathbf{y}_j \in \eta_j(\mathbf{p})$ means that

$\mathbf{py}_j \geq \mathbf{py}'_j$ for all $\mathbf{y}'_j \in Y_j$. The corresponding profit function is defined by $\pi_j : \mathbb{P} \to \mathbb{R}$, with $\pi_j(\mathbf{p}) = \mathbf{py}_j$, for $\mathbf{y}_j \in \eta_j(\mathbf{p})$.

The behaviour of monopolies is analyzed below under two alternative scenarios. The first one is that in which monopolies are regulated in terms of two-part tariffs. The second one is that in which monopolies realize a perfect price discrimination policy.

7.3 Two-part marginal pricing

7.3.1 Generalities

We consider here a private ownership market economy in which monopolies are privately owned but regulated. Regulation takes the form of marginal pricing with personalized "hook-up" fees, charged for the right to consume the monopoly goods. The hook-up fees are intended to recover the losses incurred by the monopolies when using marginal pricing. Hence in equilibrium monopolies make non-negative profits.

Consider the following definitions,

Definition 7.1 *A **hook-up system** is a family of $m(\ell - c)$ functions h_{ik} from $\mathbb{P} \times \mathbb{F}$ into $\mathbb{R}$ such that, for each $j \in M$:*

(i) $h_{ik}(\mathbf{p}, \widetilde{\mathbf{y}}) = 0$, if $x^*_{ik} = 0$, $i = 1, 2, \ldots, m$, (where x^*_{ik} stands for the ith consumer's demand of the kth commodity).

(ii) $\sum_{k \in L_j} \sum_{i=1}^{m} h_{ik}(\mathbf{p}, \widetilde{\mathbf{y}}) = \max\{0, -\mathbf{py}_j\}$, for all $j \in M$.

(iii) $h_{ik}(\mathbf{p}, \widetilde{\mathbf{y}}) \geq 0$, for all $i = 1, 2, ..., m$, all $k \in \mathcal{L}^M$.

A hook-up system is thus a collection of $m(\ell - c)$ mappings such that: (a) Every h_{ik} takes on the value zero if the ith consumer does not consume the kth monopoly good; (b) The aggregate hook-up fees offset the losses derived from the production of the monopoly goods; and (c) All hook-ups are non-negative. From this it follows that hook-ups can only be used to recover the losses of the monopoly. In particular, $h_{ik}(\mathbf{p}, \widetilde{\mathbf{y}}) = 0$ if the kth monopoly good is produced by a firm with positive profits at $(\mathbf{p}, \widetilde{\mathbf{y}})$.

Remark 7.1 *Note that this is not the only way of defining a hook-up system, even though it seems the most natural. One can also define the fixed part of the tariff as depending not on the commodity consumed but on the firm (that is, the ith consumer pays a fixed part to the jth firm, whenever it consumes a positive amount of some commodity produced by this firm). Going still further, one can also define the hook-ups as relative to the consumption of some commodity produced by the monopoly sector.*

Definition 7.2 *A **production equilibrium** PE relative to a hook-up system (h_{ik}) is a pair $(\mathbf{p}^*, \widetilde{\mathbf{y}}^*) \in \mathbb{P} \times \mathbb{F}$ such that $\mathbf{p}^* \in \phi_j^{MP}(\mathbf{y}_j^*)$ for all j.*

The notion of a production equilibrium is standard, once the pricing rules and the hook-ups have been specified. Note that by asking all firms to follow the marginal pricing rule we are modelling competitive firms as profit maximizers at given prices. Moreover, according to the definition of a hook-up system, in a production equilibrium non-convex firms recover their losses with the hook-ups set on consumers.

Therefore, the profits of the jth monopoly associated to a production $\mathbf{y}_j$ and a price $\mathbf{p} \in \phi_j^{MP}(\mathbf{y}_j)$ are given by:

$$\pi_j(\mathbf{p}, \mathbf{y}_j) = \max\{0, \ \mathbf{p}\mathbf{y}_j\}$$

That is, the monopoly has zero profits when marginal pricing implies losses (as will be the case with increasing returns to scale), and distributes profits, if any, according to property rights, otherwise.

This pricing policy implies that the ith consumer's budget constraint will exhibit the following structure:

$$r_i(\mathbf{p}, \widetilde{\mathbf{y}}) = \mathbf{p}\omega_i + \sum_{j=1}^{n} \theta_{ij}\pi_j(\mathbf{p}) - \sum_{k \in \mathcal{L}^M} h_{ik}(\mathbf{p}, \widetilde{\mathbf{y}})$$

where θ_{ij} stands for the ith consumer's share in the jth firm's profits (with $\sum_{i=1}^{m} \theta_{ij} = 1$, for all j), and $h_{ik}(.) \geq 0$ represents the ith consumer's kth hook-up fee, which she only pays when she consumes positive amounts of the kth monopoly good, $k \in \mathcal{L}^M$.

Definition 7.3 *A **two-part marginal pricing equilibrium** relative to a hook-up system (h_{ik}) is a price vector $\mathbf{p}^* \in \mathbb{P}$ and an allocation $[(\mathbf{x}_i^*), \widetilde{\mathbf{y}}^*]$ such that:*
(α) For all $i = 1, 2, \ldots, m$, $u_i(\mathbf{x}_i^*) \geq u_i(\mathbf{x}_i)$, for every $\mathbf{x}_i$ such that $\mathbf{p}^*\mathbf{x}_i \leq \mathbf{p}^*\omega_i + \sum_{j=1}^{n} \theta_{ij}\pi_j(\mathbf{p}^*) - \sum_{k \in \mathcal{L}^M} h_{ik}(\mathbf{p}^*, \widetilde{\mathbf{y}}^*).$
(β) $\mathbf{p}^* \in \bigcap_{j=1}^{n} \phi_j^{MP}(\mathbf{y}_j^*)$
(γ) $\sum_{i=1}^{m} \mathbf{x}_i^* - \sum_{j=1}^{n} \mathbf{y}_j^* - \omega \leq \mathbf{0}$, and $p_k^* = 0$ if the kth inequality is strict.

A Two-Part Marginal Pricing Equilibrium relative to (h_{ik}) is thus a price vector and an allocation such that: (i) Every consumer maximizes utility at given prices within her budget set (which includes the hook-up fees conditional upon consumption of the monopoly goods); (ii) $(\mathbf{p}^*, \widetilde{\mathbf{y}}^*)$ is a production equilibrium, relative to (h_{ik}); and (iii) All markets clear.

Now consider the following axioms:

Axiom 7.4 *The set of attainable allocations is compact.*

Axiom 7.5 *Let* **PE** *stand for the set of production equilibria relative to the hook-up system* (h_{ik}). *Then, the restriction of* r_i *over* **PE** *is continuous, with* $r_i(\mathbf{p}, \widetilde{\mathbf{y}}) > \min \mathbf{p} X_i$.

Axioms 7.4 and 7.5 are already familiar. Note that the continuity part in axiom 7.5 is satisfied whenever all h_{ik} are continuous mappings on **PE**. Also observe that the structure of wealth mappings implies that $\sum_{i=1}^{m} r_i(\mathbf{p}, \widetilde{\mathbf{y}}) = \mathbf{p}(\omega + \sum_{j=1}^{n} \mathbf{y}_j)$.
The next result follows:

Proposition 7.1 *Let E be an economy satisfying axioms 7.1 to 7.5. Then there exists a two-part marginal pricing equilibrium relative to* (h_{ik}).

Proof. First note that all firms follow the marginal pricing rule (which corresponds to profit maximization when Y_j is a convex set). We know from Proposition 6.4 that marginal pricing is a regular pricing rule. Therefore, the assumptions of the theorem clearly imply all axioms in Theorem 5.1, and the result follows. $\boxed{\textbf{Q.e.d.}}$

Proposition 7.1 gives us a rather general existence result on two-part marginal pricing equilibria. Note that there might well be that some consumer who decides not to demand any monopoly goods, given the hook-up fee associated, and yet she would be better off consuming monopoly goods at marginal prices. This is a potential source of inefficiency on which we shall elaborate later on.

The properties of these equilibria will clearly depend on the hook-up system under consideration. We now illustrate this point by considering two different hook-up systems in a particular example. First, we define these hook-up systems assuming single production in the monopoly sector (that is, each monopoly is assumed to be the exclusive producer of exactly one monopoly good). Without loss of generality we can identify the jth monopoly with the producer of the jth monopoly good.

The **uniform hook-up system** (h_{ij}^U) is defined as follows: (a) $h_{ij}^U(\mathbf{p}, \widetilde{\mathbf{y}})$ is equal to zero, if the ith consumer does not consume the jth monopoly good; and (b) $h_{ij}^U(\mathbf{p}, \widetilde{\mathbf{y}}) = \max\{0, \frac{-\mathbf{p}\mathbf{y}_j}{m^j}\}$ otherwise, where m^j is the number of consumers with positive demand at $(\mathbf{p}, \widetilde{\mathbf{y}})$. This is the simplest hook-up system: the losses incurred by the monopoly are equally shared among all the consumers of the monopoly good. Observe that when $\mathbf{p}\omega_i + \sum_{j=1}^{n} \theta_{ij}\pi_j(\mathbf{p}) -$

$\sum_{j=1}^{n} \frac{-\mathbf{py}_j}{m^j} > \min \mathbf{p}X_i$ over the set of production equilibria, for all i, the existence result applies.

The **proportional hook-up system** (h_{ij}^P) is defined as follows: For each $j = 1, 2, \ldots, h$: (a) $h_{ij}^P(\mathbf{p}, \widetilde{\mathbf{y}}) = 0$, if the ith consumer does not consume the jth monopoly good; and (b) Otherwise we have:

$$h_{ij}^P(\mathbf{p}, \widetilde{\mathbf{y}}) = \frac{\mathbf{p}\omega_i + \sum_{s=1}^{n} \theta_{is}\pi_j(\mathbf{p}, \mathbf{y}_s)}{\mathbf{p}\omega + \sum_{s=1}^{n} \pi_s(\mathbf{p}, \mathbf{y}_s)} \max\{0, -\mathbf{py}_j\}$$

This hook-up system corresponds to the case in which the fixed part of the tariff is proportional to agents' wealth. If we assume that $\mathbf{p}\omega + \sum_{j=h+1}^{n} \mathbf{py}_j > 0$ over the set of production equilibria, then h_{ij}^P turns out to be continuous on **PE**, and the existence result applies. Note that in this case the restriction $r_i(\mathbf{p}, \widetilde{\mathbf{y}}) > \min \mathbf{p}X_i$ puts a limit on the losses that are admissible for monopolies.

Example 7.1

Consider now an economy with two goods, two consumers and a single firm with increasing returns to scale.[1] The description of the economy is given by:

$$u_1(\mathbf{x}_1) = x_{11} + 3x_{12}, \quad \omega_1 = (2, \ 0)$$
$$u_2(\mathbf{x}_2) = 2x_{21} + 3x_{22}, \quad \omega_2 = (1, \ 0)$$

The firm uses good 1 as an input and produces good 2 as an output, with a technology with a fixed cost and constant marginal rate of transformation. In particular, $Y = A \bigcup B$, where:

$$A = \{(y_1, y_2) \in \mathbb{R}^2 \ / \ -1 \leq y_1 \leq 0, \ y_2 \leq 0\}$$
$$B = \{(y_1, y_2) \in \mathbb{R}^2 \ / \ y_1 \leq -1, \ y_2 \leq -(y_1 + 1)\}$$

---

[1]The example is due to Alós & Ania (1997).

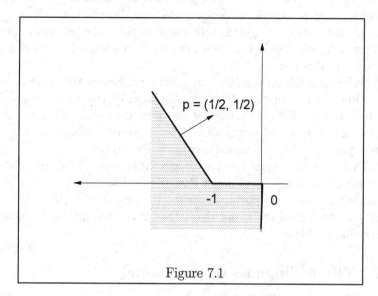

Figure 7.1

Note that, for any positive production, marginal prices are given by $\mathbf{p} = (\frac{1}{2}, \frac{1}{2})$.

A two-part marginal pricing equilibrium with a *uniform hook-up system* is given by $\mathbf{p} = (\frac{1}{2}, \frac{1}{2})$, $\mathbf{x}_1^* = (0, 1)$, $\mathbf{x}_2^* = (1, 0)$, $\mathbf{y}^* = (-2, 1)$, with $h_1^U(.) = 0.5$, $h_2^U(.) = 0$. This means that the first consumer is the only demander of the monopoly good, and covers the fixed cost alone. The resulting utility distribution is $u_1(\mathbf{x}_1^*) = 3 > u_1(\omega_1) = 2$, $u_2(\mathbf{x}_2^*) = 2$.

The use of a *proportional hook-up system* induces two different equilibria. The first one is given by $\mathbf{p}^* = (\frac{1}{2}, \frac{1}{2})$, $\mathbf{x}_1^* = (0, \frac{8}{6})$, $\mathbf{x}_2^* = (0, \frac{4}{6})$, $\mathbf{y}^* = (-3, 2)$, $h_1^P(.) = \frac{2}{6}$, $h_2^P(.) = \frac{1}{6}$. The corresponding utilities are $u_1(\mathbf{x}_1^*) = 4$, $u_2(\mathbf{x}_2^*) = 2$. This allocation weakly dominates what corresponds to the uniform hook-up system. As consumer 2 is indifferent between $\mathbf{x}_2' = (1, 0)$ and $\mathbf{x}_2^* = (0, \frac{4}{6})$, we can also consider the equilibrium associated with this alternative. Namely, $\mathbf{x}_1' = (0, 1)$, $\mathbf{x}_2' = (1, 0)$ $\mathbf{y}' = (-2, 1)$, $h_1^P(.) = 0.5$, $h_2^P(.) = 0$, that is precisely the equilibrium corresponding to the uniform hook-up system.

This example illustrates some relevant aspects of two-part tariffs. We stress the following:

(1) A two-part marginal pricing equilibrium, relative to the uniform hook-up system, may easily exclude some agents from the consumption of the monopoly good, due to the relative size of the hook-up. This is clearly a source of inefficiencies, because we are excluding some agents from consumption, who are willing to consume the monopoly good and contributing for

that (although not as much as is required for the uniform tariff). This invites considering personalized hook-up systems, in which the fixed part is divided proportionally to agents' willingness to pay. The proportional hook-up system is a first step in this direction; later on we shall consider a richer formulation of this idea.

(2) Different hook-up systems may yield equilibrium allocations that are Pareto ranked. The first equilibrium allocation of the proportional hook-up system Pareto dominates that of the uniform tariff. Observe that in this allocation the use of personalized tariffs avoids inefficiency due to the exclusion problem. Indeed, this allocation is Pareto optimal.

(3) There can be several two-part marginal pricing equilibria, relative to a given hook-up system, and some Pareto dominate others. This is what happens in the case of proportional tariffs: the first equilibrium allocation is efficient but the second one is not. Note that in the second one we again find the exclusion problem.

7.3.2   The willingness to pay model

Brown, Heller & Starr (1992) develop a two-part marginal pricing model with a specific hook-up system, based on consumers' willingness to pay. Let us present here this model.

Consider now the following assumptions:

Axiom 7.1'   *For all $i = 1, 2, \ldots, m$: (i) $X_i = \mathbb{R}_+^\ell$; (ii) $u_i : X_i \to \mathbb{R}$ is a continuous and strictly quasi-concave utility function that satisfies non-satiation; (iii) $\omega_i \in X_i$ and $\omega_{ik} = 0$ for all $k \in \mathcal{L}^M$.*

Axiom 7.3'   *There is a single monopoly, firm n, that is the exclusive producer of a unique monopoly good, that we take to be good ℓ (that is, $\mathcal{L}^M = L_n = \{\ell\}$). Moreover, Y_n is a closed, comprehensive and star-shaped subset of $\mathbb{R}^\ell$, with $\mathbf{0} \in Y_j$.*

Axiom 7.1' modifies former axiom 7.1 in that it takes the non-negative orthant as the consumption set, and assumes that utilities are strictly quasi-concave. Axiom 7.3' introduces the simplification of a single nonconvex firm, indexed as firm n, that produces a single output (the only monopoly good), which we take to be good ℓ.[2]

Let $\widehat{X}_i$ denote a convex compact subset of $\mathbb{R}^\ell$ containing in its (relative) interior the ith consumer's set of attainable consumptions. As utilities are strictly quasi-concave, we can calculate each household's "reservation level of

---

[2]This case is generalized in Edlin & Epelbaum (1993).

utility", i.e. the maximum utility level $v_i(\mathbf{p})$ she could obtain if the monopoly good were not available, as the solution to the following program:

$$\left.\begin{array}{c} Max \ \ u_i(\mathbf{x}_i) \\ s.t. : \mathbf{px}_i \leq \mathbf{p}\omega_i + \sum_{j=1}^n \theta_{ij}\pi_j(\mathbf{p}) \\ x_{i\ell} = 0, \ \text{and} \ \mathbf{x}_i \in \widehat{X}_i \end{array}\right\}$$

The expenditure function can be used to calculate the income necessary to reach the reservation utility level, when the monopoly good is available. This income, $e_i[\mathbf{p}, v_i(\mathbf{p})]$, is given by the solution to:

$$\left.\begin{array}{c} Min \ \ \mathbf{px}_i \\ s.t. : u_i(\mathbf{x}_i) \geq v_i(\mathbf{p}) \\ \mathbf{x}_i \in \widehat{X}_i \end{array}\right\}$$

Then, each consumer's willingness to pay for the monopolist's output, at $\mathbf{p}$ is given by:

$$s_i(\mathbf{p}) = \mathbf{p}\omega_i + \sum_{j=1}^n \theta_{ij}\pi_j(\mathbf{p}) - e_i[\mathbf{p}, v_i(\mathbf{p})]$$

that is to say, "it is the amount at current prices that must be subtracted from current income to reduce utility to what it was when the monopoly good was unavailable... Of course, s_i is an ordinal concept, i.e., it is independent of the utility representation" [Cf. Brown, Heller & Starr (1992, p. 62)].

In order to define the **Brown-Heller-Starr** (BHS, for short) **hook-up system**, let $s(\mathbf{p}) = \sum_{i=1}^m s_i(\mathbf{p})$, and

$$g(\mathbf{p}, \mathbf{y}_n) = \frac{\max\{0, -\mathbf{py}_n\}}{s(\mathbf{p})}$$

Observe that, when $s(\mathbf{p}) > -\mathbf{py}_n > 0$, g is well defined over the set of production equilibria. This condition says that the aggregate willingness to pay exceeds the monopoly losses. The *BHS hook-up system* is given by:

$$h_i^{BHS}(\mathbf{p}, \mathbf{y}_n) \equiv g(\mathbf{p}, \mathbf{y}_n)s_i(\mathbf{p})$$

that is, the proportional hook-up charge for the ith consumer is a fraction of her willingness to pay.

When utilities are strictly quasi-concave and $s(\mathbf{p}) > -\mathbf{py}_n$, besides the standard axioms, h_i^{BHS} is a continuous function of $(\mathbf{p}, \mathbf{y}_n)$ over the set of production equilibria, such that: a) It is always non-negative and smaller than $s_i(\mathbf{p})$ when this is a positive number; and b) It is equal to zero if $s_i = 0$.

The next corollary immediately follows from the former proposition:

Corollary 7.1 *Let E an economy satisfying axioms 7.1', 7.2, 7.3', 7.4 and 7.5. Suppose furthermore that $\sum_{i=1}^{m} s_i(\mathbf{p}) > -\mathbf{p}y_n$ over the set* **PE**. *Then, there exists a Two-Part Marginal Pricing Equilibrium relative to* $\left(h_i^{BHS}\right)$.

Let us solve the equilibrium relative to the *Brown-Heller-Starr hook-up system*, in example 7.1. It is easy to see that the agents' willingness to pay is $s_1(.) = \frac{4}{3}$, $s_2(.) = \frac{1}{3}$, which gives an aggregate willingness to pay of $s(.) = \frac{5}{3} > 1$. There is a two-part marginal pricing equilibrium given by $\mathbf{p}^* = (\frac{1}{2}, \frac{1}{2})$, $\mathbf{x}_1^* = (0, \frac{6}{5})$, $\mathbf{x}_2^* = (0, \frac{4}{5})$, $\mathbf{y}^* = (-3, 2)$, $h_1^{BHS}(.) = \frac{4}{10}$, $h_2^{BHS}(.) = \frac{1}{10}$. Here both consumers demand positive quantities of the monopoly good. Moreover, $u_1(\mathbf{x}_1^*) = \frac{18}{5} > 3$, $u_2(\mathbf{x}_2^*) = \frac{12}{5} > 2$, which means that this equilibrium (strictly) Pareto dominates that with a uniform hook-up system. Thus the application of the BHS hook-up system gives us a new efficient allocation, different from that which corresponds to the proportional one.

Can efficient allocations be decentralized as two-part marginal pricing equilibrium? It seems rather intuitive that a necessary condition for this to happen is that the aggregate willingness to pay exceed the losses associated with the production of the monopoly good. Yet this condition may not be met, if price taking consumers find it profitable not to consume the monopoly good, and use the income derived from not paying the hook-ups to buy other commodities. The following example, due to Brown, Heller & Starr (1992, # V) illustrates this:[3]

Example 7.2

Consider an economy with one input commodity (labour), denoted by L, and two consumption goods, denoted by 1, 2. Good 2 is the monopoly good. There is a single consumer in the economy, whose endowment vector is $\omega = (0, 0, \pi/2)$, and whose utility function is $u(L, x_1, x_2) = x_1 + x_2$. There are two firms in this economy. Firm 1, the competitive firm, produces commodity y_1, and firm 2, the monopoly, produces the monopoly good y_2. The technology of the economy is described by the following production functions:

$$y_1 = F_1(L_1) = \begin{cases} L_1 \text{ for } L_1 \leq \frac{1}{3} \\ \frac{1}{3} + \sin(L_1 - \frac{1}{3}) \text{ for } \frac{\pi}{2} \geq L_1 \geq \frac{1}{3} \end{cases}$$

and

$$y_2 = F_2(L_2) = \begin{cases} 0, \text{ for } L_2 \leq \frac{1}{10} \\ L_2 - \frac{1}{10} \text{ for } \frac{\pi}{2} - \frac{1}{10} \geq L_2 \geq \frac{1}{10} \\ \frac{\pi}{2} - \frac{2}{10} + \sin(L_2 - [\frac{\pi}{2} - \frac{1}{10}]) \text{ for } \frac{\pi}{2} \geq L_2 \geq \frac{\pi}{2} - \frac{1}{10} \end{cases}$$

---

[3]For another example see Quinzii (1992, pp. 36–39).

Efficient allocations are characterized by:

$$\begin{cases} x_1 = y_1 = L_1 \in [\frac{1}{10}, \frac{1}{3}] \\ x_2 = y_2 = L_2 - \frac{1}{10} = \frac{\pi}{2} - L_1 - \frac{1}{10} \end{cases}$$

This allocation can only be sustained by a price system with $p_1 = p_2 = p_3$. The required hook-up is $h = \frac{1}{10} p_3$. Yet, whenever h is positive the competitive consumer will choose not to consume the monopoly good, because her surplus is nil. Therefore, no equilibrium exists at these prices and there is no way of decentralizing this allocation as a two-part marginal pricing.

This example illustrates that there are efficient allocations that cannot be decentralized as two-part marginal equilibria, because they involve a production of the monopoly good whose cost is larger than the willingness to pay. The reason why this happens is that marginal pricing is associated with the local structure of production sets, whereas price taking consumers are guided by linear extrapolations. This also tells us that two-part marginal pricing equilibria and marginal pricing equilibria yield different allocations; in particular, that two part marginal pricing equilibria may not be flexible enough to decentralize all efficient allocations.

Can we decentralize efficient allocations when there is sufficient willingness to pay? The answer is yes, provided this willingness to pay is evaluated at the marginal prices associated with efficient allocations. This is illustrated in the following proposition:

Proposition 7.2 Let $[(\mathbf{x}_i^*)_{i=1}^m, (\mathbf{y}_j^*)_{j=1}^n]$ be a Pareto optimal allocation where $\mathbf{x}_i^* \in int X_i$ for all i. Suppose furthermore that axioms 7.1', 7.2 and 7.3' hold, and choose an associated marginal price vector $\mathbf{p}^* \in \bigcap_{j=1}^m \phi_j^{MP}(\mathbf{y}_j^*)$. If $\sum_{i=1}^m s_i(\mathbf{p}^*) > -\mathbf{p}^* \mathbf{y}_n^*$, then $[\mathbf{p}^*, (\mathbf{x}_i^*)_{i=1}^m, (\mathbf{y}_j^*)_{j=1}^n]$ is a two-part marginal pricing equilibrium relative to the (h^{BHS}) hook-up system, after suitable redistribution of income.

Proof. We know from the previous chapter that every efficient allocation can be decentralized as a marginal pricing equilibrium. Let $\mathbf{p}^*$ denote the price system associated with this equilibrium. Now we must find hook-up charges and incomes such that conditions (α), (β) and (γ) of definition 7.3 hold.

Bearing in mind that $\sum_{i=1}^m s_i(\mathbf{p}^*) > 0$, define:

$$\lambda^* = \frac{\max\{0, -\mathbf{p}^* \mathbf{y}_n^*\}}{\sum_{i=1}^m s_i(\mathbf{p}^*)}$$

By letting $h_i(\mathbf{p}^*, \widetilde{\mathbf{y}}^*) = \lambda^* s_i(\mathbf{p}^*)$, it follows that $\sum_{i=1}^m h_i(\mathbf{p}^*, \widetilde{\mathbf{y}}^*) = -\mathbf{p}^* \mathbf{y}_n^*$, so that, in view of the definition of s_i, (h_i) is a hook-up system. Specifically, it is the BHS hook-up system.

Now define $r_i^*(.) = \mathbf{p}^* \mathbf{x}_i^* + h_i(\mathbf{p}^*, \widetilde{\mathbf{y}}^*)$. The feasibility of Pareto efficient allocations implies that $\sum_{i=1}^m \mathbf{x}_i^* = \sum_{j=1}^m \mathbf{y}_j^* + \omega$. Moreover, we deduce from the strict convexity and non-satiation hypothesis that $\mathbf{p}^* \sum_{i=1}^m \mathbf{x}_i^* = \mathbf{p}^*(\sum_{j=1}^m \mathbf{y}_j^* + \omega)$. Therefore,

$$\sum_{i=1}^m [r_i^*(.) - h_i(\mathbf{p}^*, \widetilde{\mathbf{y}}^*)] = \mathbf{p}^* \sum_{i=1}^m \mathbf{x}_i^* = \mathbf{p}^*(\sum_{j=1}^m \mathbf{y}_j^* + \omega)$$

so the Walras Law holds, and (r_i^*) is a feasible income distribution associated with the marginal pricing equilibrium $[\mathbf{p}^*, (\mathbf{x}_i^*)_{i=1}^m, (\mathbf{y}_j^*)_{j=1}^n]$, in which two-part tariffs cover the monopoly losses. $\boxed{\text{Q.e.d.}}$

This result shows that, in this model, the "willingness to pay condition" is necessary and sufficient for the decentralization of efficient allocations.

7.4   The efficiency of two-part tariffs

7.4.1   Bad news

It was pointed out in the Introduction that two-part marginal pricing may avoid some of the inefficiencies associated with marginal pricing because it provides more flexibility than fixed rules of income distribution. Example 7.1 shows that, for a given economy, there may be some hook-up systems that yield efficient allocations while others don't. It is then natural to explore the problem in a more general context. Namely, whether there is some possibility of obtaining efficiency in the case of fixed distribution rules that are supplemented by some limited transfers.

Vohra's (1990), (1991) papers address this point. He considers the case in which transfers can only be used to finance the possible losses of nonconvex firms, and not for redistribution purposes. Hence, these transfers will be taxes if nonconvex firms have losses, and subsidies otherwise (so that "no consumer is subsidized if some other consumer is taxed"). This idea corresponds to the notion of two-part tariffs. The question can be formulated as follows: Can we find some (generalized) hook-up system whose associated two-part marginal pricing equilibrium is efficient? The following example, tells us the bad news: The answer is no in general.

Example 7.3

Consider a private ownership economy with 3 commodities, 2 consumers and 2 firms, whose data are summarized as follows:[4]

$$X_1 = X_2 = \mathbb{R}^3_+; \quad \omega_1 = \omega_2 = (20, 0, 0); \quad \theta_{11} = 0, \quad \theta_{21} = 1$$

$$u_1(\mathbf{x}_1) = \begin{cases} 0.5x_{11} + x_{12} + x_{13} & \text{if } x_{12} + x_{13} \leq 12 \\ 0.5x_{11} + 12 & \text{otherwise} \end{cases}$$

$$u_2(\mathbf{x}_2) = \begin{cases} 3x_{21} + x_{22} + x_{23} & \text{if } x_{21} \leq 19.5 \\ 57.5 + x_{22} + x_{23} & \text{otherwise} \end{cases}$$

$$Y_1 = \begin{cases} \{\mathbf{y}_1 \in \mathbb{R}^3 \ / \ y_{11} \leq 0; \ 1.5y_{13} + y_{12} \leq 0\} & \text{if } y_{11} \geq -4 \\ \{\mathbf{y}_1 \in \mathbb{R}^3 \ / \ y_{11} \leq 0; \ y_{13} + y_{12} - 2 \leq 0\} & \text{otherwise} \end{cases}$$

$$Y_2 = \begin{cases} \{\mathbf{y}_2 \in \mathbb{R}^3 \ / \ y_{21} \leq 0, \ y_{22} \leq 0, y_{23} \leq 0\} & \text{if } y_{21} \geq -5 \\ \{\mathbf{y}_2 \in \mathbb{R}^3 \ / \ y_{21} \leq 0, \ y_{22} \leq 0, \ 2y_{23} + 10 \leq 0\} & \text{otherwise} \end{cases}$$

Since commodities 2 and 3 are perfect substitutes in consumption, efficiency requires that only firm 1 be active when low levels of aggregate output are produced, and only firm 2 be used for producing high levels. In particular, efficiency demands that either

(a) $y_{23} = 0$ and $y_{12} \leq 14$; or

(b) $y_{12} = 0$ and $y_{23} \geq 14$.

Take first case (a). We can let $p_2 = 1$ (in view of consumer's 2 preferences). From technology, it follows that marginal pricing implies that $p_1 \geq 1$ for firm 1. Since firm 2 is not active, there are no losses, and hence consumer 1's income is greater than or equal to 20. As $y_{23} = 0$, it follows that consumer 1 will consume at least 12 units of commodity 2. Thus in equilibrium, $y_{12} \geq 12$. Given the technology of firm 1, this implies that in equilibrium, $p_1 = 1$ and $y_{12} = 12$. Since $y_{12} > 6$, the profit of firm 1 is 2 and consumer 2's income is 22. This implies that $x_{22} = 2.5$. Thus $y_{12} = 14.5 > 14$ which is a contradiction.

Take now case (b). We can let $p_3 = 1$. Since $y_{23} > 0$ the marginal pricing rule implies that $p_1 = 2$. The total loss of the firm is 10 and $q_1 + q_2 = 10$. We know that $x_{13} \leq 12$. Consumer 2 will consume 19.5 units of commodity 1, since $(20, 0, 0)$ is feasible. Any remaining income is spent on commodity 3. Since income cannot be greater than 40, and 19.5 units of commodity 1 cost 39, $x_{23} \leq 1$. Thus, $x_{13} + x_{23} \leq 13$, and $y_{23} \leq 13$, a contradiction.

---

[4]Vohra (1990, Example 4.1). Helpful drawings of the situation involved can be found in Vohra's paper.

This example shows that the partial equilibrium intuition about the efficiency of two-part marginal pricing equilibrium fails. Note that we have not imposed any specific structure on the hook-up system. That is, for the economy in the example, there is no way of achieving efficient outcomes by means of two-part marginal pricing equilibrium. We find the same negative conclusion here as in the case of marginal pricing: There is no general way of ensuring Pareto optimality by instructing non-convex firms to follow marginal pricing, if we are not ready to perform an explicit redistribution policy.

7.4.2   And good news

In example 7.1 we have seen that two-part marginal pricing is inefficient when some consumer is excluded from the consumption of the monopoly goods, due to the operation of the hook-up system. Another source of inefficiency appears in example 7.3: there efficiency requires the operation of a single firm, whereas there is no two-part marginal pricing equilibrium with this property. Can we ensure the efficiency of two-part marginal pricing by avoiding these two problems? The answer to this question is partially positive. The analysis developed in Moriguchi (1996) shows that when non-convexities are due to the presence of fixed costs, all non-convex firms are active, and the hook-up system avoids the exclusion problem, two-part tariffs yield efficient outcomes.

Let us analyze here the case of **pure fixed cost economies**. The key feature of these economies is that non-convexities are due to the presence of fixed costs. Even though this is probably the simplest form of non-convexity in production, it is an interesting case widely used in the literature [see for instance the classical papers by Dixit & Stiglitz (1979) or Romer (1980)].

Consider again the type of economy presented in section 7.2. That is, an economy with a set C of competitive firms and a set M of monopolies, each of which is the exclusive producer of a fixed subset of consumption goods (the set L_j of the monopoly goods produced by the firm $j \in M$).

The next definitions provide the conceptual framework for the ensuing analysis:

Definition 7.4 *An economy is said to be **pure fixed cost** if, for all $j \in M$, the set $Y_j^+ = \{\mathbf{y}_j \in Y_j$ with $y_{jk} > 0$, for some $k \in L_j\}$ is convex.*

By this definition we identify those economies in which non-convexities are due solely to the presence of fixed costs. That is to say, once a monopoly starts producing a positive amount of monopoly goods, its technology exhibits constant or decreasing returns to scale.

Definition 7.5 *A two-part marginal pricing equilibrium $[\mathbf{p}^*, (\mathbf{x}_i^*)_{i=1}^m, (\mathbf{y}_j^*)_{j=1}^m]$ relative to a hook-up system (h_{ik}) is said to be with **active monopolies** if for all $j \in M$ there exists some $k \in L_j$ with $y_{jk}^* > 0$.*

Definition 7.6 *A two-part marginal pricing equilibrium $[\mathbf{p}^*, (\mathbf{x}_i^*)_{i=1}^m, (\mathbf{y}_j^*)_{j=1}^m]$ relative to a hook-up system (h_{ik}) is said to be with **no-exclusion** if for all $i = 1, 2, ..., m$, all $k \in \mathcal{L}^M$, $h_{ik}^* > 0 \Longrightarrow x_{ik}^* > 0$.*

An equilibrium with active monopolies is one in which all monopolies are producing positive amounts of some monopoly good. An equilibrium with no-exclusion is one in which all consumers who are assigned a positive hook-up for the consumption of a monopoly good, find it beneficial to consume a positive amount of this good and pay for it its marginal price plus the corresponding fixed part.

The following result, due to Moriguchi (1996, Th.1), is obtained:

Proposition 7.4 *Let E be a pure fixed cost economy satisfying axioms 7.1, 7.2 and 7.3. Then, a two-part marginal pricing equilibrium $[\mathbf{p}^*, (\mathbf{x}_i^*)_{i=1}^m, (\mathbf{y}_j^*)_{j=1}^n, (h_{ik}^*)]$ with active monopolies and no exclusion is Pareto optimal.*

Proof. Suppose that there is an allocation $[(\mathbf{x}_i)_{i=1}^m, (\mathbf{y}_j)_{j=1}^n]$ that is Pareto superior. Relative to this allocation, let us now define the set of indices of active monopolies, that of monopoly goods consumed, and of monopoly goods consumed by the ith agent:

$J = \{j \in M \text{ with } y_{jk} > 0, \text{ for some } k \in L_j\}$

$H = \{k \in \mathcal{L}^M \ / \ y_{jk} > 0, \text{ for some } j \in M\}$

$H(i) = \{k \in \mathcal{L}^M \text{ with } x_{ik} > 0\}$

Under the assumptions of the model, feasibility implies that if $y_{jk} = 0$ then $x_{ik} = 0$, for all i, so that $H(i) \subset H$ for all i. From non-satiation it follows that

$$\sum_{i=1}^m \mathbf{p}^* \mathbf{x}_i > \sum_{i=1}^m \left[\mathbf{p}^* \omega_i + \sum_{j=1}^n \theta_{ij} \pi_j(\mathbf{p}^*) - \sum_{k \in \mathcal{L}^M} h_{ik}^* \right]$$

Using the fact that $\mathbf{p}^* \mathbf{y}_j^* \geq \mathbf{p}^* \mathbf{y}_j$, for all $j \in C$, we can deduce that $\sum_{i=1}^m \mathbf{p}^* \mathbf{x}_i$ is actually greater than

$$\sum_{i=1}^m \mathbf{p}^* \omega_i + \sum_{j \in C} \mathbf{p}^* \mathbf{y}_j + \sum_{j \in M} \max\{0, \mathbf{p}^* \mathbf{y}_j^*\} - \sum_{i=1}^m \sum_{k \in H(i)} h_{ik}^*$$

As $h_{ik}^* \geq 0$ for all i, k, $H(i) \subset H$ for all i, and $J \subset M$, it follows that

$$\mathbf{p}^* \left[\sum_{i=1}^m (\mathbf{x}_i - \omega_i) - \sum_{j \in C} \mathbf{y}_j \right] > \sum_{j \in J} \max\{0, \mathbf{p}^* \mathbf{y}_j^*\} - \sum_{i=1}^m \sum_{k \in H} h_{ik}^*$$

By (ii) of definition 7.1 and the no-exclusion condition, for all $j \in M$, we have

$$\sum_{i=1}^{m}\sum_{k \in L_j} h_{ik}^* = \max\{0, -\mathbf{p}^*\mathbf{y}_j^*\}$$

so that, $\sum_{i=1}^{m}\sum_{k \in H} h_{ik}^* \leq \sum_{j \in J}\max\{0, -\mathbf{p}^*\mathbf{y}_j^*\}$. Therefore,

$$\mathbf{p}^*\left[\sum_{i=1}^{m}\mathbf{x}_i - \omega - \sum_{j \in C}\mathbf{y}_j\right] > \sum_{j \in J}\max\{0, \mathbf{p}^*\mathbf{y}_j^*\} - \sum_{j \in J}\max\{0, -\mathbf{p}^*\mathbf{y}_j^*\} = \sum_{j \in J}\mathbf{p}^*\mathbf{y}_j^*$$

As $\sum_{j \in J}\mathbf{y}_j \geq \sum_{j \in M}\mathbf{y}_j$, it follows that

$$\mathbf{p}^*\left[\sum_{i=1}^{m}(\mathbf{x}_i - \omega_i) - \sum_{j \in C}\mathbf{y}_j\right] \leq \mathbf{p}^*\sum_{j \in M}\mathbf{y}_j \leq \mathbf{p}^*\sum_{j \in J}\mathbf{y}_j$$

Consequently we have

$$\mathbf{p}^*\sum_{j \in J}\mathbf{y}_j > \mathbf{p}^*\sum_{j \in J}\mathbf{y}_j^*$$

Now observe that $J = \emptyset$ is not possible due to the last inequality. Suppose $J \neq \emptyset$. Since all monopolies are active in equilibrium, $\mathbf{y}_j^* \in \partial Y_j^+$ for all $j \in J$. By the definition of J, $\mathbf{y}_j \in Y_j^+$ for all $j \in J$. Note that $\mathbf{p}^* \in \phi_j^{MP}(\mathbf{y}_j^*)$ implies that $\mathbf{p}^*$ is a normal vector at $\mathbf{y}_j^* \in \partial Y_j^+$, that is, $\mathbf{p}^*(\mathbf{y}_j^* - \mathbf{y}_j) \geq 0$, for all $j \in J$, contradicting the above inequality. $\boxed{\textbf{Q.e.d.}}$

This proposition shows that two-part tariff equilibria are efficient, provided the following three conditions are met: (i) The economy is a pure fixed cost economy; (ii) All monopolies are active; and (iii) No consumer is excluded by the hook-up system.

7.5   Perfect price discrimination

We now take up the case in which monopolies are not regulated, by presenting a version of the model developed by Edlin, Epelbaum & Heller (1998) of a perfectly discriminating monopoly.

We consider an economy with ℓ commodities, m consumers and n firms. There are $n-1$ standard competitive firms and one monopoly (the nth firm). The monopoly is the only producer of a subset of commodities $\mathcal{L}^M$, the monopoly goods, that are assumed to be pure consumption goods. Again we assume that commodities $1, 2, ..., c$ are competitive commodities, and commodities $c+1, c+2, ..., \ell$, are monopoly goods. For a vector $\mathbf{z} \in \mathbb{R}^\ell$, we write $\mathbf{z} = (\mathbf{z}^C, \mathbf{z}^M)$, where $\mathbf{z}^C \in \mathbb{R}^c$, is a vector consisting of competitive commodities, and $\mathbf{z}^M \in \mathbb{R}^{\ell-c}$ a vector of monopoly goods. For reasons that will be apparent, a price vector is a point $\mathbf{p} \in \mathbb{R}^c_+$ (i.e. a price vector only includes prices for competitive commodities).

To make things simpler, we assume again that, for all $i = 1, 2, ..., m$, the ith consumer consumption set is $X_i = \mathbb{R}^\ell_+$, and that the ith consumer's utility function $u_i : X_i \to \mathbb{R}$ is continuous, strictly quasi-concave and monotone. The ith consumer initial endowments are given by a vector $w_i^C \in \mathbb{R}^c_+$ (that is, there are no initial endowments of monopoly goods); her income function is given by: $r_i(.) = \mathbf{p}w_i^C + \sum_{j=1}^n \theta_{ij}\pi_j(.)$, where $\pi_j(.)$ describes the jth firm's profits (to be specified later).

We assume that axiom 7.2 holds. That is, $Y_j = Y_j^C \times \{\mathbf{0}\}$, with $Y_j^C \subset \mathbb{R}^c$, as monopoly goods are pure consumption goods that can only be produced by the nth firm. For $j = 1, 2, ..., n-1$, the jth firm's behaviour is characterized by the choice of production plans that maximize profits at given prices. Namely, for a given $\mathbf{p} \in \mathbb{R}^c_+$, the jth firm chooses a production plan $\mathbf{y}_j^C \in Y_j^C$ such that $\mathbf{p}\mathbf{y}_j^C \geq \mathbf{p}\hat{\mathbf{y}}_j^C$, for all $\hat{\mathbf{y}}_j^C \in Y_j^C$. Note that we are making implicit use of axiom 7.2 in the description of competitive production sets. Thus, for $j \neq n$, $\pi_j(\mathbf{p}) = \sup_{\mathbf{y}_j \in Y_j} \mathbf{p}\mathbf{y}_j$.

Given a price vector $\mathbf{p} >> \mathbf{0}$, a vector of monopoly goods for the ith consumer $\mathbf{x}_i^M \in \mathbb{R}^{\ell-c}_+$, and an income r_i, we define:

$$V_i(\mathbf{x}_i^M, r_i, \mathbf{p}) = \max_{\mathbf{x}_i^c} u_i(\mathbf{x}_i^C, \mathbf{x}_i^M) \text{ subject to } \mathbf{p}\mathbf{x}_i^C \leq r_i$$

For a given price vector, $\mathbf{p} \in \mathbb{R}^c_+$, the behaviour of the monopoly consists of choosing a production plan $\mathbf{y}_n = (\mathbf{y}_n^C, \mathbf{y}_n^M) \in Y_n \subset \mathbb{R}^\ell$, an allocation of the monopoly goods among consumers $(\mathbf{x}_i^M)_{i=1}^m$, with $\sum_{i=1}^m \mathbf{x}_i^M = \mathbf{y}_n^M$, and a vector $(t_i)_{i=1}^m$ in $\mathbb{R}^m_+$ of charges to consumers for the right to consume $(\mathbf{x}_i^M)_{i=1}^m$, such that $[\mathbf{y}_n, (\mathbf{x}_i^M, t_i)_{i=1}^m]$ solves the following program:

$$\left. \begin{array}{c} \max \ \mathbf{p}\mathbf{y}_n^C + \sum_{i=1}^m t_i \\ s.t. \ V_i(\mathbf{x}_i^M, r_i - t_i, \mathbf{p}) \geq V_i(\mathbf{0}^M, r_i, \mathbf{p}) \\ (\mathbf{y}_n^C, \sum_{i=1}^m \mathbf{x}_i^M) \in Y_n \end{array} \right\} \qquad [M]$$

That is, the monopoly chooses a production plan $\mathbf{y}_n$ in Y_n, a distribution of the monopoly goods $\mathbf{y}_n^M$ among consumers, and a corresponding vector of personalized charges, so that total profits are maximized under the restriction that all consumers find the offer $(\mathbf{x}_i^M, t_i)_{i=1}^m$ acceptable. The monopoly's profits $\pi_n(.)$ are given by the value function of this program.

Now consider the following:

Definition 7.7 *A **perfectly discriminating monopoly equilibrium** is a point $[\mathbf{p}^*, (\mathbf{x}_i^*, t_i^*)_{i=1}^m, (\mathbf{y}_j^*)_{j=1}^n]$ in $\mathbb{R}^c_+ \times \Pi_{i=1}^m X_i \times \mathbb{R}^m_+ \times \Pi_{j=1}^n Y_j$, such that:*

(a) $u_i(\mathbf{x}_i^*) = V_i(\mathbf{x}_i^{M*}, r_i^* - t_i^*, \mathbf{p}^*) \geq V_i(\mathbf{0}^M, r_i^*, \mathbf{p}^*)$, for all i, where $r_i^* = \mathbf{p}^*\omega_i^C + \sum_{j=1}^{n-1} \theta_{ij}\mathbf{p}^*\mathbf{y}_j^* + \theta_{in}(\mathbf{p}^*\mathbf{y}_n^{C*} + \sum_{i=1}^m t_i^*)$.
(b) For all $j \neq n$, $\mathbf{p}^*\mathbf{y}_j^{C*} \geq \mathbf{p}^*\mathbf{y}_j^C$, $\forall \, \mathbf{y}_j^C \in Y_j^C$.
(c) $[\mathbf{y}_n^*, (\mathbf{x}_i^{M*}, t_i^*)_{i=1}^m]$ solves program $[M]$.
(d) $\sum_{i=1}^m \mathbf{x}_i^* = (\omega^C, 0) + \sum_{j=1}^{n-1}(\mathbf{y}_j^{C*}, 0) + \mathbf{y}_n^*$.

Consider now the following assumptions:

Axiom 7.3" *There is a single monopoly, firm n, that is the exclusive producer of monopoly goods (that is, $\mathcal{L}^M = L_n = \{c+1, c+2, ..., \ell\}$). Moreover, Y_n is a closed, comprehensive and star-shaped subset of $\mathbb{R}^\ell$.*

Axiom 7.6 For all $\mathbf{y}_n \in Y_n$ where $\mathbf{y}_n^M > \mathbf{0}^M$, and for all $\mathbf{z}^M$ such that $\mathbf{0}^M \leq \mathbf{y}_n^M - \mathbf{z}^M < \mathbf{y}_n^M$, there exists $\mathbf{z}^C > \mathbf{0}^C$ such that $\mathbf{y}_n + (\mathbf{z}^C, -\mathbf{z}^M) \in Y_n$.

Axiom 7.3" lies between axiom 7.3 and axiom 7.3'. It keeps the assumption of a single monopoly, as in 7.3', but allows for the presence of several monopoly goods that are jointly produced by the monopoly, as in 7.3.

Axiom 7.6 says that the monopoly goods are costly in that discrete reductions in output imply discrete reductions in costs.

The following result is obtained [Edlin, Epelbaum & Heller (1998, Th. 3.1)]:

Proposition 7.3 *Under axioms 7.1', 7.3" and 7.6, perfect discriminating monopoly equilibria are Pareto optimal.*

Proof. We first show that if there exists a feasible allocation $[(\widehat{\mathbf{x}}_i)_{i=1}^m, (\widehat{\mathbf{y}}_j)_{j=1}^n]$ that is Pareto superior to the equilibrium allocation, then $[(\widehat{\mathbf{x}}_i^M, \widehat{t}_i)_{i=1}^m, \widehat{\mathbf{y}}_n^M]$ is a profitable strategy for the monopoly, with $\widehat{t}_i = t_i^* + \mathbf{p}^*(\mathbf{x}_i^{c*} - \widehat{\mathbf{x}}_i^c)$, for all i.

To see this note that $(\widehat{\mathbf{x}}_i^M, \widehat{t}_i)$ is acceptable to the ith consumer, because $\widehat{\mathbf{x}}_i$ costs no more than $\mathbf{x}_i^*$, and yields a greater or equal utility, which in turn yield at leas the reservation utility.[5] Moreover, monopoly profits are now $\widehat{\pi}_n = \mathbf{p}^*\widehat{\mathbf{y}}_n^c + \sum_{i=1}^m [t_i^* + \mathbf{p}^*(\mathbf{x}_i^c - \widehat{\mathbf{x}}_i^c)]$, whereas equilibrium profits are $\pi_n^* = \mathbf{p}^*\mathbf{y}_n^{c*} + \sum_{i=1}^n t_i^*$. Therefore,

$\widehat{\pi}_n - \pi_n^* = \mathbf{p}^*\widehat{\mathbf{y}}_n^c + \sum_{i=1}^n [t_i^* + \mathbf{p}^*(\mathbf{x}_i^c - \widehat{\mathbf{x}}_i^c)] - [\mathbf{p}^*\mathbf{y}_n^{c*} + \sum_{i=1}^m t_i^*]$

$= \mathbf{p}^*[(\sum_{i=1}^m \mathbf{x}_i^{c*} - \mathbf{y}_n^{c*}) - (\sum_{i=1}^m \widehat{\mathbf{x}}_i^c - \widehat{\mathbf{y}}_n^c)]$

$= \mathbf{p}^*[\sum_{i=1}^m \omega_i - (\sum_{i=1}^n \widehat{\mathbf{x}}_i^c - \widehat{\mathbf{y}}_n^c)]$

Hence, feasibility implies $\widehat{\pi}_n - \pi_n^* \geq 0$.

---

[5] $\mathbf{p}^*\widehat{\mathbf{x}}_i^c + \widehat{t}_i = \mathbf{p}^*\widehat{\mathbf{x}}_i^c + t_i^* + \mathbf{p}^*(\mathbf{x}_i^{c*} - \widehat{\mathbf{x}}_i^c) = \mathbf{p}^*\mathbf{x}_i^{c*} + t_i^*$

We shall now show that the monopoly can do better than that. To see this, let h denote a consumer that is strictly better off in $[(\widehat{\mathbf{x}}_i)_{i=1}^m, (\widehat{\mathbf{y}}_j)_{j=1}^n]$ than in the equilibrium allocation. There are two cases to be considered.

Case A: $\widehat{\mathbf{x}}_h^c > \mathbf{0}^c$. Then, for a small $\varepsilon > 0$ the monopoly would gain by charging $\widehat{t}_h + \varepsilon$, without altering other decisions.

Case B: $\widehat{\mathbf{x}}_h^c = \mathbf{0}^c$. Then. $\widehat{\mathbf{x}}_h^M > \mathbf{0}^M$, and we can decrease this vector by a fraction $\boldsymbol{\varepsilon}^M > \mathbf{0}^M$. By axiom F, there exists $\boldsymbol{\varepsilon}^c > \mathbf{0}^c$ such that $\widehat{\mathbf{y}}_n + (\boldsymbol{\varepsilon}^c, -\boldsymbol{\varepsilon}^M) \in Y_n$. For a sufficiently small $\boldsymbol{\varepsilon}^M$, the monopoly can increase profits $\widehat{\pi}_n + \mathbf{p}^*\boldsymbol{\varepsilon}^c > \widehat{\pi}_n$, by offering $(\widehat{\mathbf{x}}_h^M - \boldsymbol{\varepsilon}^M, \widehat{t}_h)$ to this consumer, adapting the competitive goods plan $\widehat{\mathbf{y}}_n^c + \boldsymbol{\varepsilon}^c$, without changing anything else. $\boxed{\text{Q.e.d.}}$

This theorem establishes that perfect price discrimination yields efficient allocations, with one proviso: the monopoly cannot reduce cost by cutting output. This proviso is the subject of axiom 7.6. Indeed, it can be shown that in the absence of axiom 7.6, these equilibria may fail to be efficient [see Edlin, Epelbaum & Heller (1998, # 3.1)].

Remark 7.2 *There are two additional results in the contribution by Edlin, Epelbaum & Heller worth mentioning. The first one refers to the equivalence between the perfectly discriminating monopoly equilibrium and two-part tariffs equilibria, which holds under a variant of axiom 7.6 (Theorem 4.1 of their paper). The second one deals with the existence and decentralizability of these equilibria; they identify two classes of economies in which these results hold (section 5 of their paper). The first one is that in which there is a single competitive commodity; the second one is the already familiar pure fixed cost economy.*

7.6 References to the literature

Two-part marginal pricing may be understood as a regulation policy that satisfies two principles: the necessary conditions for optimality, and budget balance. The compatibility between these principles is obtained by means of a non-linear pricing schedule, which allows for different ways of covering the monopoly losses (i.e. for alternative pricing policies). Yet, as we have already seen, there is no guarantee of success when using this pricing scheme, except in particular cases (e.g. pure fixed cost economies). This suggests the possibility of considering other pricing rules that satisfy the break-even constraint and have some desirable welfare properties. Note that when marginal pricing is abandoned, prices become policy variables; hence, when there are multiple outputs (the case of joint production), the budget balance condition does not determine the relative output prices.

There is extensive literature on the regulation of public enterprises subject to a break-even constraint [mostly in terms of partial equilibrium analysis, as described for instance in Sharkey (1982) or Bös (1987)]. Ramsey (1927) (for a single agent economy) and Boiteaux (1956) first analyzed the necessary conditions for optimality subject to a break-even constraint and linear pricing.

An interesting pricing principle emerges from the axiomatization of cost allocation schemes inspired by the Shapley Value for non-atomic games [first analyzed in Aumann & Shapley (1974), and used in Billera, Heath & Raanan (1978) for telephone billing rates which share the cost of a telephone system]. As in the case of marginal pricing (and unlike Boiteaux-Ramsey pricing), these prices only depend on the cost of production, and benefit from the fact that the Shapley Value can be defined by an explicit formula. Interestingly enough, they can be characterized by a set of axioms on the cost functions and the quantities produced [see for instance Billera & Heath (1982), Mirman & Tauman (1982), Samet & Tauman (1982)].

Many contributions analyze pricing policies in terms of the associated cost-functions. Besides those already mentioned, let us refer to the works of Mirman, Samet & Tauman (1983), Ten Raa (1983), Greenberg & Shitovitz (1984), Mirman, Tauman & Zang (1985),(1986), Reichert (1986 Part I), Dehez & Drèze (1988b), Mas-Colell & Silvestre (1989) and Hart & Mas-Colell (1990) [see also Sharkey (1989, Section 3)]. Moulin's (1988) excellent monograph is highly recommended for those willing to establish links between these models and more general collective decision mechanisms.

Dierker, Guesnerie & Neufeind (1985) provide an existence result for a family of Average Cost Pricing rules which includes Boiteaux-Ramsey and Aumann-Shapley pricing. Indeed, it can be shown that, under reasonable conditions, these pricing rules are regular, so that Theorem 5.1 applies. Edlin & Epelbaum (1993) extend the Brown-Heller-Starr model by allowing for several monopoly goods.

Kamiya (1995) presents a general equilibrium model in which non-convex firms follow non-linear pricing schemes and the resulting allocation is Pareto optimal. Some of these ideas are applied in Moriguchi (1996) to the case of two-part tariffs, when non-convexities arise from the presence of fixed costs.

We take up non-linear prices again in a later chapter, as a way of ensuring Pareto efficiency when non-convexities are associated with externalities or public goods. Additional references on this more abstract literature will be presented there.

Chapter 8

LOSS-FREE PRICING RULES

8.1 Introduction

This chapter provides an application of the pricing rule approach to the analysis of unregulated market economies with non-convex production sets. Loss-free pricing rules provide a natural framework for this analysis, because the equilibrium of firms implies non-negative profits. When inaction is possible and firms are privately owned, production equilibria can be associated with non-negative profits.

Two specific pricing rules will be considered: *mark-up pricing* and *constrained profit maximization*. Mark-up pricing refers to a pricing policy in which firms set prices by adding a profit component to the average costs. Average cost pricing is a particular case of this pricing rule, in which the mark-up is zero. Constrained profit maximization associates, with each efficient production plan, those prices for which no alternative production involving the use of equal or fewer inputs is more profitable. These pricing rules aim to describe a plausible behaviour of firms that does not depend on the convexity assumption. They are applicable to situations in which there may be increasing returns to scale, fixed costs, or S-shaped production functions, or those in which production involves the use of fixed capital (that is, the use of inputs that are functionally indivisible).

To facilitate the discussion, commodities will be divided into two different categories: capital goods and standard commodities. Capital goods are commodities already produced that are inputs to production; they appear as part of the initial endowments. Standard commodities include pure consumption goods that are already produced as well as those commodities that are obtained through the production process.

Let us present here a disclaimer, in order to asses the relevance of these models: There are few positive models with increasing returns that are both general and interesting. One might well consider that monopolistic competition arises as the natural framework to deal with non-convex firms: firms will not be negligible when there are increasing returns to scale so that they will not behave as price-takers. Alas, the possibility of extending partial equilibrium results to a general equilibrium framework faces enormous difficulties in the realm of imperfect competition, irrespective of the convexity of production sets. To make it precise, there is no satisfactory answer yet to the basic positive problem of general equilibrium with increasing returns: how to model the strategic interaction among firms with market power. Therefore, the results in this chapter correspond to a more modest approach. The analysis of pricing rules that represent plausible behaviour of firms in market economies, when production sets are not assumed to be convex.

8.2 The reference model

Consider an unregulated market economy with ℓ commodities, m consumers and n firms. The Government plays no explicit role in the allocation of resources, apart from ensuring the property rights.

Commodities are classified according to the following scheme:

$$\begin{cases} \text{Produced commodities} \begin{cases} \text{Capital goods} \\ \text{Pure consumption goods} \end{cases} \\ \text{New goods} \end{cases}$$

Produced commodities correspond to those goods and services that are available before production takes place (initial endowments). They include natural resources, land, buildings, used machines, intermediate inputs produced and stored, as well as durable consumption goods and stocks of other pure consumption goods. Produced commodities are in turn divided into *capital goods* and *pure consumption goods*. Capital goods are those produced commodities that are inputs to production (even though some of these commodities can also be consumed). The distinction between these two categories of produced commodities matters, because the amounts of capital goods available may limit effective production possibilities. Moreover, we shall assume at some points that these commodities may generate non-convexities in production.

New goods are those commodities that result from production activities. That is, they are output commodities of some firm. They may include both goods devoted to final uses (consumption and investment) and output commodities that are inputs for some other firms. We call **standard commodities** to the union of pure consumption goods already produced and new goods.

The division that matters for our purposes is that between capital goods and standard commodities. The set of commodity indices $\mathcal{L} \equiv \{1, 2, \ldots, \ell\}$ can be partitioned, accordingly, into two disjoint subsets, $\mathcal{L}^K = \{1, 2, \ldots, k\}$ and $\mathcal{L}^S = \{k+1, k+2, \ldots, \ell\}$. Goods in $\mathcal{L}^K$ are capital goods and goods in $\mathcal{L}^S$ are standard commodities.

There are m competitive consumers in the economy. Each consumer i is characterized by a triple $[X_i, u_i, r_i]$, in which X_i, u_i stand for the ith consumer's consumption set and utility function, respectively, and r_i is her wealth mapping.

Let $(\mathbf{p}, \widetilde{\mathbf{y}}) \in \mathbb{R}_+^\ell \times \mathbb{F}$ be given. The ith consumer's *demand* is obtained as a solution to the program:

$$\left. \begin{array}{r} Max \; u_i\left(\mathbf{x}_i\right) \\ \text{s.t.} \quad \mathbf{x}_i \in X_i \\ \mathbf{p}\mathbf{x}_i \leq r_i(\mathbf{p},\widetilde{\mathbf{y}}) \end{array} \right\}$$

The behaviour of the ith consumer is summarized by a demand correspondence $\xi_i : \mathbb{R}_+^\ell \times \mathbb{F} \to X_i$, where $\xi_i(\mathbf{p}, \widetilde{\mathbf{y}})$ is the set of solutions to the program above.

The next axiom makes it explicit the modelization of consumers:

Axiom 8.1 *For each $i = 1, 2, \ldots, m$: (a) X_i is a closed and convex subset of $\mathbb{R}^\ell$, bounded from below. (b) $u_i : X_i \to \mathbb{R}$ is a continuous, quasi-concave$^+$ and non-satiable utility function.*

This axiom is standard and needs no further comment.

There are n firms in the economy. Each firm is characterized by its production set and the pricing rule it applies, (Y_j, ϕ_j). The next axiom formalizes the assumptions established on production sets:

Axiom 8.2 *For each firm $j = 1, 2, \ldots, n$: (i) Y_j is a closed subset of $\mathbb{R}^\ell$. (ii) $Y_j \bigcap \mathbb{R}_+^\ell = \{\mathbf{0}\}$. (iii) $Y_j - \mathbb{R}_+^\ell \subset Y_j$.*

This axiom is also standard. Note that the feasibility of inaction (i.e. $\mathbf{0} \in Y_j$ for all j), enables firms to close down, at no cost, when market conditions get bad. Consequently, non-negative profits can always be guaranteed in equilibrium.

Let us recall here the following:

Definition 8.1 $\phi_j : \mathbb{P} \times \mathbb{F} \to \mathbb{P}$ *is a **loss-free pricing rule** when, for all* $(\mathbf{p}, \widetilde{\mathbf{y}})$ *in* $\mathbb{P} \times \mathbb{F}$, $\mathbf{qy}_j \geq 0$, $\forall \, \mathbf{q} \in \phi_j(\mathbf{p}, \widetilde{\mathbf{y}})$.

A firm follows a loss-free pricing rule when those prices-production combination that yield negative profits are not acceptable.

It is convenient to think of production plans as given by $\mathbf{y}_j = (\mathbf{a}_j, \mathbf{b}_j)$, in which $\mathbf{a}_j \in -\mathbb{R}_+^k$ and $\mathbf{b}_j \in \mathbb{R}^{\ell-k}$. That is, $\mathbf{a}_j$ is a point in subspace of capital goods and $\mathbf{b}_j$ is a vector of standard commodities.

We call *economy* a specification of the m consumers and the n firms (with their choice sets, their restriction mappings and their choice criteria). An economy can thus be described by:

$$E = \{(X_i, \; u_i, \; r_i)_{i=1}^m; (Y_j, \; \phi_j)_{j=1}^n; \; \omega\}$$

in which $\omega \in \mathbb{R}^\ell$ describes the aggregate initial resources. According to the classification of commodities above, we can write $\omega = (\omega^K, \omega^S)$, where $\omega^K \in \mathbb{R}^k$ denotes the vector of capital goods available, and $\omega^S \in \mathbb{R}^{\ell-k}$ that of standard commodities (in which those entries corresponding to new goods are zero).

The set of attainable allocations of an economy is given by:

$$\Omega \equiv \left\{ [(\mathbf{x}_i), (\mathbf{y}_j)] \in \prod_{i=1}^m X_i \times \prod_{j=1}^n Y_j \; / \; \sum_{i=1}^m \mathbf{x}_i - \omega \leq \sum_{j=1}^n \mathbf{y}_j \right\}$$

The projection of Ω on the spaces containing X_i, Y_j gives us the ith consumer's set of attainable consumptions and the jth firm's set of attainable production plans, respectively.

The following axioms state that set of attainable allocations is bounded, and that the wealth mappings are continuous on the set of production equilibria and satisfy the Walras Law.

Axiom 8.3 The set Ω of attainable allocations is compact.

Axiom 8.4 *Let* **PE** *stand for the set of production equilibria. The restriction of* r_i *over* **PE** *is continuous, with* $r_i(\mathbf{p}, \widetilde{\mathbf{y}}) > \min \mathbf{p} X_i$, *and* $\sum_{i=1}^m r_i(\mathbf{p}, \widetilde{\mathbf{y}}) = \mathbf{p}(\omega + \sum_{j=1}^n \mathbf{y}_j)$.

Note that the ith consumer's wealth mapping is given by $r_i(\mathbf{p}, \widetilde{\mathbf{y}}) = \mathbf{p}\omega_i + \sum_{j=1}^n \theta_{ij} \mathbf{p} \mathbf{y}_j$, in a market economy with private ownership. Namely, the ith consumer's wealth, relative to $(\mathbf{p}, \widetilde{\mathbf{y}}) \in \mathbb{P} \times \mathbb{F}$, consists of the value of her initial endowments plus the profits corresponding to her shares in the property of firms. In this case, r_i is continuous in $(\mathbf{p}, \widetilde{\mathbf{y}})$, and total wealth equals the aggregate worth of initial endowments plus total profits.

The following result is obtained:

Proposition 8.1 *Let E stand for an economy that satisfies axioms 8.1 to 8.4. An equilibrium exists when firms follow regular and loss-free pricing rules.*

Proof. It is immediate to see that all the conditions in Theorem 5.1 are satisfied, when firms follow regular and loss-free pricing rules, and axioms 8.1 to 8.4 hold. Hence, the result follows. $\boxed{\textbf{Q.e.d.}}$

8.3 Mark-up pricing

Mark-up pricing can be regarded as a behavioural decision rule according to which firms sell their output at prices that cover their costs, including a profit component (the mark-up). This profit component is usually treated as a parameter, and embodies the notion of "normal profits". It can be related to some environmental variables, such as the elasticity of the demand, risk factors characteristic of different industries, the degree of monopoly of a firm, the presence of entry barriers, etc.

A relevant case is that in which all firms apply the same mark-up. This can be regarded as a competitive feature, as profitability among firms is identical. More specifically, the uniform mark-up can be associated with the reward of "advanced capital" that results from the competition for investment opportunities (we analyze this case in detail in the next chapter).

Average cost pricing is a particular case of this pricing policy, in which firms' mark-up is equal to zero (i.e. firms just break even). This is a pricing rule with a long tradition, in both positive and normative analysis. It is associated with some regulation policies under a break even constraint (e.g. Boiteaux-Ramsey or two-part marginal pricing), and corresponds with profit maximization when production sets are convex cones (constant returns to scale).

Even though taking mark-ups as given parameters leaves unexplained a key element of the model, mark-up pricing is a reasonable description of firms' behaviour worth considering. This approach may be sufficient for some purposes; in particular, these mark-ups can be taken as constant for the analysis and can be estimated empirically, under stable conditions.

8.3.1   The average cost pricing rule

Average cost-pricing is a pricing principle according to which firms set prices so that they just break even. The next definition formalizes this pricing rule:

Definition 8.2 *The **average cost pricing** rule is a mapping $\phi_j^{AC} : \mathbb{F}_j \to \mathbb{P}$ given by:*
(a) $\phi_j^{AC}(\mathbf{y}_j) \equiv \{\mathbf{q} \in \mathbb{P} \ / \ \mathbf{q}\mathbf{y}_j = 0\}$, if $\mathbf{y}_j \neq \mathbf{0}$.
(b) $\phi_j^{AC}(\mathbf{0})$ is the closed convex hull of the set of points $\mathbf{q} \in \mathbb{P}$ for which there exists a sequence $\{\mathbf{q}^\nu, \mathbf{y}_j^\nu\} \subset \mathbb{P} \times [\mathbb{F}_j - \{\mathbf{0}\}]$, such that $\{\mathbf{q}^\nu, \mathbf{y}_j^\nu\} \to (\mathbf{q}, \mathbf{0})$, with $\mathbf{q}^\nu \mathbf{y}_j^\nu = 0$.

Therefore, this rule associates those prices yielding zero profits with efficient production plans. Note that this pricing principle places no restriction at the origin; namely, for $\mathbf{y}_j = \mathbf{0}$, one would have $\phi_j^{AC}(\mathbf{0}) \equiv \mathbb{P}$. Consequently, the definition has to be completed with part (b), in order to make non-vacuous the associated equilibrium concept. Indeed, if one admits $\phi_j^{AC}(\mathbf{0}) \equiv \mathbb{P}$, the fixed-point argument which gives us the existence of equilibrium might simply correspond to the pure exchange equilibrium. In order to prevent this trivial equilibrium, part (b) of the definition requires taking $\phi_j(\mathbf{0})$ as the closed convex hull of the limit points of those prices associated with sequences of points $\mathbf{y}_j \neq \mathbf{0}$ that converge to zero, and yield null profits.

The following figure gives us an illustration of this pricing rule.

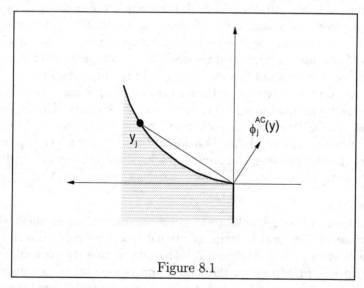

Figure 8.1

An **average cost pricing equilibrium** is an equilibrium in which firms follow the average cost pricing rule. The following result is obtained:[1]

Proposition 8.2 *Let E be an economy that satisfies axioms 8.1 to 8.4. Then an average cost pricing equilibrium exists.*

Proof. First note that, for every $\mathbf{y}'_j \in \mathbb{F}_j$, $\phi_j^{AC}(\mathbf{y}'_j)$ is a non-empty convex set under axiom 8.2. To see that the graph is closed, let $\mathbf{y}_j^o$ be an arbitrary point in $\mathbb{F}_j$, and let $\{\mathbf{y}_j^\nu, \mathbf{p}^\nu\}$ be a sequence in $\mathbb{F}_j \times \mathbb{P}$ such that $\{\mathbf{y}_j^\nu\} \to \mathbf{y}_j^o$, $\{\mathbf{p}^\nu\} \to \mathbf{p}^o$, and $\mathbf{p}^\nu \in \phi_j^{AC}(\mathbf{y}_j^\nu)$, for all ν. As $\mathbf{p}^\nu \mathbf{y}_j^\nu = 0$ for all ν, the continuity of the scalar product implies that $\mathbf{p}^o \mathbf{y}_j^o = 0$, that is to say, $\mathbf{p}^o \in \phi_j^{AC}(\mathbf{y}_j^o)$. Therefore, ϕ_j^{AC} is a regular and loss-free pricing rule, so that Proposition 8.1 ensures the existence of equilibrium. $\boxed{\text{Q.e.d.}}$

Observe that average cost-pricing coincides with profit maximization when the production set is a convex cone. Yet, this is not the case in general.

8.3.2 The mark-up pricing rule

An extension of the average-cost principle is that in which firms sell their output at prices that correspond to average costs, augmented by a mark-up ρ_j, or profit component. To properly formulate this idea, let us write $\mathbf{y}_j = (\mathbf{a}_j, \mathbf{b}_j)$, as indicated above (where $\mathbf{a}_j \in -\mathbb{R}_+^k$ is the vector of capital goods in $\mathbf{y}_j$). Now we can define:

Definition 8.3 *The **mark-up pricing rule**, relative to ρ_j, is a mapping $\phi_j^{\rho_j} : \mathbb{F}_j \to \mathbb{P}$, given by:*

$$\phi_j^{\rho_j}(\mathbf{y}_j) = \phi_j^{AC}[\mathbf{a}_j(1 + \rho_j), \mathbf{b}_j]$$

This simply says that the firm chooses prices so that the net revenue is precisely $-\mathbf{pa}_j \rho_j$. The scalar ρ_j is a parameter that measures the profitability of the jth firm, when it realizes $\mathbf{y}_j$ at prices $\mathbf{p}$. That is, ρ_j is the rate between profits and the cost of capital goods:[2]

$$\rho_j = -\frac{\mathbf{py}_j}{\mathbf{pa}_j}$$

---

[1]This is simply a corollary of Proposition 8.1, once we see that average cost is a regular (and obviously loss-free) pricing rule.

[2]One can also define mark-up pricing differently, applying the mark-up not only on the cost of capital goods but on the cost of all inputs. Yet, we prefer to keep here this formulation because it conveys the idea that profits are the reward of the "advanced capital".

Needless to say that this pricing rule is of little interest, unless we impose some structure on this parameter ρ_j. For instance, if we allow ρ_j to vary freely with $\mathbf{y}_j$, all loss-free pricing rules can be formulated as mark-up pricing rules, by a suitable choice of ρ_j. The model becomes interesting when these mark-ups express some conditions on the environment in which the jth firm operates (e.g. they are related to the elasticity of the jth firm's demand, the existence of fixed costs, the number of firms in the industry, the presence of entry barriers, etc.) A simple but relevant case is that in which all firms apply the same mark-up. This reflects a competitive feature, since profitability among firms is identical (see the analysis in the next chapter).

8.4   Constrained profit maximization

8.4.1   Motivation

Observe that when production sets are not convex cones, average cost pricing does not imply profit maximization. What is worse, we can find firms that would obtain higher profits at the prevailing prices, by changing their input-output configurations without consuming more inputs. This can be regarded as a violation of the "profit principle", that says that an action will be chosen only if there is no feasible alternative yielding higher profits.

This section presents an application of this principle to market economies with non-convex production sets. The distinction between capital goods and standard commodities will be essential here. First, because capital goods will play the role of capacity constraints. Second, because they can be related to the presence of non-convexities in production, when they incorporate a fixed cost or an indivisibility feature.

Constrained profit maximization is a pricing rule that applies the profit principle to this setting. According to this pricing rule, a firm only finds acceptable a prices-production combination when there is no other production plan yielding higher profits and using fewer capital goods. That is to say, firms behave as constrained profit maximizers at given prices. This can be regarded as an incentive requirement. If this property were not satisfied, firms would be willing (and able, given their restrictions) to change their input-output configurations. We call *constrained profit maximization equilibrium* a situation in which the consumers maximize their preferences under their wealth restrictions, the firms behave according to the constrained profit maximization pricing rule, and all markets clear.

This approach enables to deal with short-run situations in which non-convexities are due to the presence of fixed costs, or the use some elements of fixed capital (land, buildings or heavy machinery, say). More specifically, we can think of a two-period economy in which the allocation of fixed capital is decided in period one, taken into account current and future prices (these are "investment decisions" in a complete markets setting). Production and consumption take place in period 2. Now the firms choose those production plans that maximize profits, subject to the investment decisions taken in period 1, and the consumers maximize utility at given prices.

The questions to be analyzed are the following: (i) Is there an equilibrium of this type? (ii) Are these equilibria (unconditionally) efficient? It will be shown that the answer to question (i) is positive under fairly general assumptions. Not surprisingly, the answer to question (ii) is positive only in very specific settings. Yet, this illuminates on the nature of inefficiency in market economies with increasing returns to scale.

8.4.2 The model

There are ℓ commodities in the economy. These commodities include consumption goods, different types of labour and other inputs to production (land, machinery, energy, intermediate inputs, etc.) According to the classification of commodities in section 8.2, we divide the set of commodity indices $\mathcal{L} \equiv \{1, 2, \ldots, \ell\}$ into two disjoint subsets, $\mathcal{L}^K = \{1, 2, \ldots, k\}$ and $\mathcal{L}^S = \{k + 1, k + 2, \ldots, \ell\}$. Goods in $\mathcal{L}^K$ are **capital goods** and goods in $\mathcal{L}^S$ are **standard commodities**. Capital goods refer to a special group of produced commodities, identified *a priori* as inputs to production, that are explicit restrictions on firms' production possibilities, and may give rise to non-convexities in production. We can think of capital goods as elements of fixed capital. Standard commodities include both inputs and outputs.

The set $\mathcal{L}^K$ is defined by $\mathcal{L}^K = \bigcup_{j=1}^n \mathcal{L}_j^K$, where $\mathcal{L}_j^K$ is the set of indices that identifies those capital goods used by the jth firm. By this we mean that each firm may use a particular subset of capital goods. Note that capital goods may or may not be demanded by consumers (e.g. urban land versus machinery). It can be the case that capital goods are firm specific (namely, $\mathcal{L}_j^K \cap \mathcal{L}_h^K = \emptyset$, for any two firms j, h).

Within this framework it is convenient to write production plans in the form $\mathbf{y}_j = (\mathbf{a}_j, \mathbf{b}_j)$, with $\mathbf{a}_j \in -\mathbb{R}_+^k$ (that is, $\mathbf{a}_j$ is a point in subspace of capital goods). Given a price vector $\mathbf{p} \in \mathbb{R}_+^\ell$, the scalar product $\mathbf{p}\mathbf{y}_j$ for $\mathbf{y}_j \in Y_j$ gives us the profits associated with $\mathbf{y}_j$ at prices $\mathbf{p}$.

Now consider the following axiom that applies to all $j = 1, 2, \ldots, n$:

Axiom 8.2'

(i) Y_j is a closed subset of $\mathbb{R}^\ell$.

(ii) $Y_j - \mathbb{R}^\ell_+ \subset Y_j$.

(iii) $Y_j \cap \mathbb{R}^\ell_+ = \{0\}$.

(iv) For all $(\mathbf{a}_j, \mathbf{b}_j), (\mathbf{a}'_j, \mathbf{b}'_j) \in \mathbb{F}_j$, $[\mathbf{a}_j \geq \mathbf{a}'_j \ \& \ \mathbf{b}_j > \mathbf{b}'_j] \Longrightarrow \mathbf{y}_j \leq 0$.

(v) For all $\mathbf{a}'_j \in -\mathbb{R}^k_+$ the set

$$B_j(\mathbf{a}'_j) \equiv \{\mathbf{b}_j \in \mathbb{R}^{\ell-k} \ / \ (\mathbf{a}_j, \mathbf{b}_j) \in Y_j \ \text{for some} \ \mathbf{a}_j \geq \mathbf{a}'_j\}$$

is convex.

Parts (i) to (iii) of axiom 8.2' correspond precisely to those of axiom 8.2 above. They amount to assuming closedness, comprehensiveness, necessity of using some inputs to obtain some outputs, and possibility of inaction.

Part (iv) is a weak monotonicity requirement that discards the presence of "vertical segments", in that part of the boundary of Y_j associated with positive production. It can be interpreted as follows: keeping the use of capital goods constant and increasing all outputs, requires using up more of other inputs. Clearly, when Y_j is convex part (iv) of this axiom is implied by parts (i), (ii) and (iii). This property is closely related to that of "bounded marginal returns" (i.e. the marginal rates of transformation are bounded in all points involving positive production).

Part (v) substitutes the classical assumption of convex production sets by a weaker requirement. It says that the projection on $\mathbb{R}^{\ell-k}$ of those production plans not using more capital goods than those in $\mathbf{a}'_j$ is a convex set, for any given vector of capital goods $\mathbf{a}'_j$. That allows us to interpret these inputs as elements of fixed capital that might give rise to non-convexities. Observe that this assumption is compatible with the presence of firms with constant, decreasing or increasing returns to scale, set-up costs or S-shaped production functions. In particular, the case of pure fixed cost economies analyzed in the previous chapter satisfies this axiom. Clearly, when Y_j is convex, part (v) of axiom 8.2' is automatically satisfied. Moreover, in the one-input—one-output case, this property is implied by the parts (i) to (iii).

Parts (iv) and (v) of axiom 8.2' are needed in order to ensure that constrained profit maximization is well defined. Under these assumptions, the set $B_j(\mathbf{a}'_j)$ is convex and comprehensive, with $b'_j \in \partial B_j(\mathbf{a}'_j)$, for all $\mathbf{y}'_j \in \mathbb{F}_j$. The following figures illustrate the need of these two parts of the axiom. The first figure corresponds to a one-input—one-output production set, that fails to satisfy part (iv). As a consequence, $b'_j \in int B_j(\mathbf{a}'_j)$, and $\mathbf{y}'_j$ cannot be supported as a constrained profit maximizing production plan. Figure 8.3 corresponds to a firm that produces two commodities with a single capital good. The graphic only depicts the set $B_j(a_j)$ for a given amount of the capital good a_j. The lack of convexity of this set implies that there is no price vector $\mathbf{p} \in \mathbb{P}$ for which $\mathbf{y}_j$ maximizes profits under the capital goods constraint.

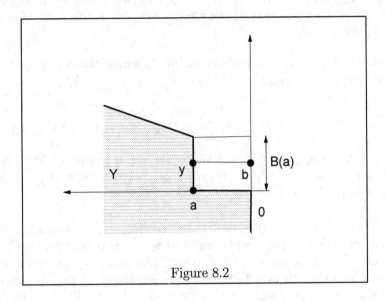

Figure 8.2

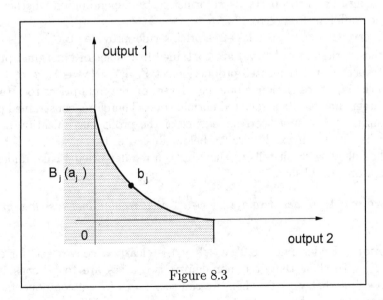

Figure 8.3

8.4.3 The profit principle

The profit principle corresponds to the notion of constrained profit maximization. This can be regarded as an incentive compatibility constraint: for each given $\mathbf{y}_j \in \mathbb{F}_j$, the jth firm chooses prices that maximize profits in the set of production plans that do not use more capital goods than those in $\mathbf{y}_j$. More formally:

Definition 8.4 *The **constrained profit maximization** pricing rule for the jth firm, is a mapping $\phi_j^{CPM} : \mathbb{F}_j \rightarrow \mathbb{R}_+^\ell - \{\mathbf{0}\}$ given by:*
(i) For $\mathbf{y}_j \neq \mathbf{0}$,

$$\phi_j^{CPM}(\mathbf{y}_j) \equiv \{\mathbf{q} \in \mathbb{R}_+^\ell - \{\mathbf{0}\} \ / \ \mathbf{q}\mathbf{y}_j \geq \mathbf{q}\mathbf{y}_j', \forall \mathbf{y}_j' \in Y_j \ with a_j' \geq a_j\}$$

(ii) $\phi_j^{CPM}(\mathbf{0})$ is the closed convex hull of the set of points $\mathbf{q} \in \mathbb{R}_+^\ell - \{\mathbf{0}\}$ for which there exists a sequence $\{\mathbf{q}^\nu, \mathbf{y}_j^\nu\} \subset \mathbb{R}_+^\ell - \{\mathbf{0}\} \times [\mathbb{F}_j - \{\mathbf{0}\}]$, such that $\{\mathbf{q}^\nu, \mathbf{y}_j^\nu\} \rightarrow (\mathbf{q}, \mathbf{0})$, with $\mathbf{q}^\nu \in \phi_j^{CPM}(\mathbf{y}_j^\nu)$.

Thus, ϕ_j^{CPM} pictures the jth firm as selecting prices for which it is not possible to obtain higher profits, within the set of production plans that make use of equal or fewer capital goods. This situation corresponds to a case in which the jth firm faces an input constraint so that it chooses a profit maximizing production within its attainable set. We have to define the pricing rule in two parts, as in former cases, depending on whether $\mathbf{y}_j$ is or is not different from zero.

Observe that ϕ_j^{CPM} is a loss-free pricing rule, provided $\mathbf{0} \in Y_j$. Also note that those prices in $\phi_j^{CPM}(\mathbf{y}_j)$ are contained in the set of "marginal prices" with respect to the truncated production set $Y_j(a_j) = \{\mathbf{y}_j' \in Y_j \ / \ a_j' \geq a_j\}$. When the input restriction is binding, the set of marginal prices to $Y_j(a_j)$ at $\mathbf{y}_j$ is larger than the its associated normal cone. Therefore, constrained profit maximization is a super-correspondence of the profit maximization pricing rule, when Y_j is convex. Figure 8.4 below illustrates this case.

The following result tells us that this is a regular pricing rule, under the assumptions established:

Theorem 8.1 *Under axiom 8.2', ϕ_j^{CPM} is a regular and loss-free pricing rule.*

Proof. Under axiom 8.2', $\phi_j^{CPM}(\mathbf{y}_j')$ is clearly a convex set, for every $\mathbf{y}_j' \in \mathbb{F}_j$. To show that it is non-empty, two cases are to be considered. Suppose first that $\mathbf{y}_j' \leq \mathbf{0}$. Then, we can set $p_k = 0$ for all components with strictly negative values, and $p_k > 0$ whenever $y_{jk} = 0$. This price vector is in

$\phi_j^{CPM}(\mathbf{y}_j')$. Suppose now that $\mathbf{y}_j'$ contains some strictly positive component. It follows from the assumptions that $B_j(\mathbf{a}_j')$ is a convex and comprehensive set, with $\mathbf{b}_j' \in \partial B_j(\mathbf{a}_j')$. Hence, the standard separation argument ensures that there is a point $\mathbf{v} \in \mathbb{R}_+^{\ell-k}$, $\mathbf{v} \neq \mathbf{0}$, which supports $\mathbf{b}_j'$. Call λ to the inverse of $\sum_{h=k+1}^{\ell} v_h$. Then, any vector $\mathbf{q}$ in $\mathbb{P}$ such that $\mathbf{q} = (\mathbf{0}, \lambda\mathbf{v})$ will be in $\phi_j^{CPM}(\mathbf{y}_j')$.

To see that the graph is closed, let $[(\mathbf{a}_j^o, \mathbf{b}_j^o), \mathbf{p}^o]$ be a point in $\mathbb{F}_j \times \mathbb{P}$, and let $\{(\mathbf{a}_j^\nu, \mathbf{b}_j^\nu), \mathbf{p}^\nu\}$ be a sequence converging to $[(\mathbf{a}_j^o, \mathbf{b}_j^o), \mathbf{p}^o]$, such that $[(\mathbf{a}_j^\nu, \mathbf{b}_j^\nu), \mathbf{p}^\nu] \in \mathbb{F}_j \times \mathbb{P}$, and $\mathbf{p}^\nu$ belongs to $\phi_j^{CPM}(\mathbf{a}_j^\nu, \mathbf{b}_j^\nu)$, for all ν. If $\mathbf{p}^o$ is not in $\phi_j^{CPM}(\mathbf{a}_j^o, \mathbf{b}_j^o)$, there exists $(\mathbf{a}_j', \mathbf{b}_j') \in Y_j$, with $\mathbf{a}_j' \geq \mathbf{a}_j^o$, such that $\mathbf{p}^o(\mathbf{a}_j', \mathbf{b}_j') > \mathbf{p}^o(\mathbf{a}_j^o, \mathbf{b}_j^o)$. This implies, for a large enough ν (say $\nu > \nu'$), that we also have:

$$\mathbf{p}^\nu(\mathbf{a}_j', \mathbf{b}_j') > \mathbf{p}^\nu(\mathbf{a}_j^\nu, \mathbf{b}_j^\nu) \qquad [1]$$

If $\mathbf{a}_j' \geq \mathbf{a}_j^\nu$ and $\nu > \nu'$, this contradicts the assumption that $\mathbf{p}^\nu$ belongs to $\phi_j^{CPM}(\mathbf{a}_j^\nu, \mathbf{b}_j^\nu)$. Suppose that this is not the case. There are two possibilities. Suppose first that $\mathbf{a}_j^o < \mathbf{0}$, and construct a new point $(\mathbf{a}_j'', \mathbf{b}_j'')$ in Y_j as follows:

(i) $\mathbf{a}_{jt}'' = \mathbf{a}_{jt}' + \varepsilon$, if $\mathbf{a}_{jt}' < 0$ (where $\varepsilon > 0$ is an arbitrarily small scalar), and $\mathbf{a}_{jt}'' = 0$, otherwise; and

(ii) $\mathbf{b}_{jt}'' = \mathbf{b}_{jt}' - \delta_t$ (where $\delta_t \geq 0$ is a scalar arbitrarily small).

Since Y_j is a closed and comprehensive set, these scalars can always be chosen so that $(\mathbf{a}_j'', \mathbf{b}_j'')$ lies in Y_j, and $\mathbf{p}^o(\mathbf{a}_j'', \mathbf{b}_j'') > \mathbf{p}^o(\mathbf{a}_j^o, \mathbf{b}_j^o)$. Note that, by construction, $\mathbf{a}_j'' > \mathbf{a}_j' \geq \mathbf{a}_j^o$. For a large enough ν, there will be points $(\mathbf{a}_j^\nu, \mathbf{b}_j^\nu)$ close to $(\mathbf{a}_j^o, \mathbf{b}_j^o)$ such that $\mathbf{a}_j'' \geq \mathbf{a}_j^\nu$. For these points we have:

$$\mathbf{p}^\nu(\mathbf{a}_j'', \mathbf{b}_j'') > \mathbf{p}^\nu(\mathbf{a}_j^\nu, \mathbf{b}_j^\nu)$$

while $\mathbf{p}^\nu \in \phi_j^{CPM}(\mathbf{a}_j^\nu, \mathbf{b}_j^\nu)$, contradicting the hypothesis.

Now take the case $\mathbf{a}_j^o = \mathbf{0}$, and consequently $\mathbf{a}_j' = \mathbf{0}$. It follows that either $\mathbf{b}_j' = \mathbf{0}$, and hence the inequality [1] above cannot hold, or $\mathbf{b}_j' \notin \mathbb{R}_+^\ell$ in which case the reasoning above can be repeated by slightly increasing some negative component, and slightly decreasing some positive one in $\mathbf{b}_j'$.

That completes the proof. $\boxed{\textbf{Q.e.d.}}$

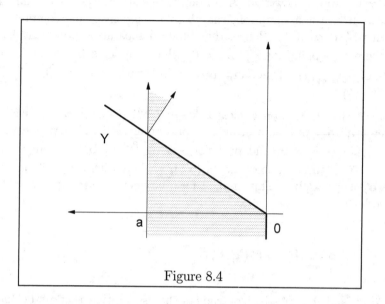

Figure 8.4

8.4.4   Equilibrium

Consider the following definition:

Definition 8.5 *A **constrained profit maximization equilibrium** (CPM equilibrium, for short) is a price vector $\mathbf{p}^* \in \mathbb{P}$, and an allocation $[(\mathbf{x}_i^*), \widetilde{\mathbf{y}}^*]$, such that:*
(α) For all $i = 1, 2, \ldots, m$, $\mathbf{x}_i^* \in \xi_i(\mathbf{p}^*, \widetilde{\mathbf{y}}^*)$.
(β) $\mathbf{p}^* \in \bigcap_{j=1}^{n} \phi_j^{CPM}(\mathbf{y}_j^*)$.
(γ) $\sum_{i=1}^{m} \mathbf{x}_i^* - \sum_{j=1}^{n} \mathbf{y}_j^* \leq \omega$, with $p_k^* = 0$ if the kth inequality is strict.

That is, a *CPM* equilibrium is a situation in which: (a) The consumers maximize their preferences subject to their budget constraints; (b) $(\mathbf{p}^*, \widetilde{\mathbf{y}}^*)$ is a production equilibrium (that is, every firm behaves according to the constrained profit maximization pricing rule); and (c) All markets clear. Hence, an equilibrium consists of a price vector and a feasible allocation in which all agents are maximizing their payoff functions within their feasible sets. These feasible sets correspond to budget sets for the case of consumers, and production sets subject to an input constraint, for the case of firms.

Observe that the equality between "supply" and demand is relevant, because it implies that there are no idle capital goods in equilibrium (except when they are free goods). Therefore, the equilibrium allocation of capital goods cannot be arbitrary. The prices of capital goods cannot be arbitrary either: they generate a cost structure and an income distribution that accommodates the equilibrium between "supply" and demand. Moreover, these prices should coincide with the consumers' "marginal rates of substitution", as usual, when capital goods are consumed.

The following result is an immediate application of Proposition 8.1 and Theorem 8.1:

Proposition 8.3 *Let E be a market economy that satisfies axioms 8.1, 8.2', 8.3 and 8.4. There exists a CPM equilibrium $(\mathbf{p}^*, [(\mathbf{x}_j^*), \widetilde{\mathbf{y}}^*])$.*

Proposition 8.3 tells us that there exists a CPM equilibrium under fairly general assumptions. Given the equilibrium allocation of capital goods, firms behave as profit maximizers at given prices within their attainable sets. No firm finds it profitable to operate with fewer capital goods in equilibrium.

Note that a standard competitive equilibrium is a constrained profit maximization equilibrium when all firms are convex. Yet, the converse is not true. This is so, because the set of constrained supporting prices is larger than those corresponding to (unconstrained) profit maximization, as mentioned before. The following example illustrates this:

Example 8.1 *Consider an economy with two goods, leisure and corn, two consumers, p and r, and one firm. The data of the economy are the following:*
$$X_i = \{\mathbf{x} \in \mathbb{R}_+^2 \ / \ 0 \le x_{i1} \le 1, 0.5 \le x_{i2}\} \quad for\ i = p, r.$$
$$u_p(\mathbf{x}_p) = 0.1x_{p1} + x_{p2}, \qquad \omega_p = (1, 0), \qquad \theta_p = 0$$
$$u_r(\mathbf{x}_2) = 2x_{r1} + x_{r2}, \qquad \omega_r = (1, 1), \qquad \theta_r = 1$$
$$Y = \{\mathbf{y} \in \mathbb{R}^2 \ / \ \mathbf{y} \le \lambda(-1, 1)\}$$
The shape of the consumption sets indicates that no consumer demands labour of the other as a consumption good (so that the maximum leisure they can enjoy is one unit of time), and that they have to consume at least half a unit of corn for survival. Consumer p (the poor), values ten times more consumption than leisure, whereas consumer r (the rich) values her leisure twice as much as her consumption.[3] In a competitive equilibrium we have:
$$\mathbf{p}^* = (1, 1), \quad \mathbf{x}_p^* = (0, 1), \quad \mathbf{x}_r^* = (1, 1), \quad \mathbf{y}^* = (-1, 1).$$
The following situation corresponds to a constrained profit maximization equilibrium:
$$\mathbf{p}' = (\tfrac{1}{2}, 1), \quad \mathbf{x}_p' = (0, \tfrac{1}{2}), \quad \mathbf{x}_r' = (1, 1.5), \quad \mathbf{y}' = (-1, 1).$$

---

[3] We can think that there is a third commodity, a luxury consumption good, that the rich consumer owns and does not trade at any potential equilibrium price.

Note that this is also a Pareto efficient allocation, but now the rich person "exploits" the poor one, via the pricing policy of the firm she owns. Indeed, any allocation of the form $\mathbf{x}_p = (0, 1-\alpha)$, $\mathbf{x}_r = (1, 1+\alpha)$, for $\alpha \in [0, \frac{1}{2}]$, can be supported as a constrained profit maximization equilibrium, with prices $\mathbf{p} = (1-\alpha, 1)$. In this simple case, the parameter α provides us with a measure of the "degree of monopoly".

8.4.5   Efficiency

The welfare analysis developed in chapter 6 showed that marginal pricing is a necessary condition for the efficiency of allocations that can be decentralized by a price system. Therefore, constrained profit maximization may fail to produce efficient allocations when production sets are not convex. This can be easily illustrated when there are increasing returns to scale. In this case the necessary conditions for optimality imply that firms have losses in equilibrium, whereas ϕ_j^{CPM} is a loss-free pricing rule.

Note, however, that equilibrium allocations are efficient *relative to* the allocation of capital goods. Moreover, equilibrium prices belong to the cone of normals to the production sets, truncated by the capital goods involved. This suggest that CPM may yield efficient allocations *when capital goods do not enter the preferences of consumers*. This is so because the necessary conditions for optimality impose no restriction with respect to the prices of capital goods, in such a case. Assuming that capital goods are pure inputs is not an important restriction, as many commodities that are traded in the market are not consumption goods (machinery, minerals and other raw materials, intermediate inputs, etc.)

Scarf (1986) used this approach to ensure the efficiency of equilibrium allocations, in a model with a single firm that exhibits a particular type of non-decreasing returns to scale (see the next chapter for details). Clearly, when the economy consists of several firms, efficiency requires not only that capital goods are not consumed, but also that the equilibrium allocation yields the right truncation of production sets (namely, the "correct" allocation of capital goods). In order to deal with this case, we consider a family of economies in which capital goods are firm specific, and show that this is a sufficient restriction for the efficiency of CPM equilibria.[4]

Even though the results presented are inevitably narrow, there are still worth considering. On the one hand, because they provide particular environments where efficiency can be achieved. On the other hand, because

---

[4]Note the paralelism with the modelling of monopolies in chapter 7. There, each monopoly was the exclusive producer of a subset of monopoly goods. Here, each non-convex firm is the exclusive user of a subset of capital goods.

they enlighten on the causes of market inefficiency in the presence of non-convexities (and hence provide some suggestions on regulation policies).

As capital goods are input commodities already produced, the vector of initial endowments can be written as $\omega = (\omega^K, \omega^S)$, where $\omega^K \in \mathbb{R}^k$ describes the vector of capital goods, and $\omega^S \in \mathbb{R}^{\ell-k}$, the vector of standard commodities available. Consider the following definition:

Definition 8.6 *We say that capital goods are* **idiosyncratic** *if each non-convex firm is the only user of a specific subset of capital goods; namely, $\mathcal{L}_j^K \cap \mathcal{L}_{j'}^K = \emptyset$, for all j, j'. And we say that capital goods are* **idiosyncratic pure inputs** *if they are idiosyncratic and do not enter the preferences of consumers.*

The following result provides an extension of the first welfare theorem to this context:

Proposition 8.4 *Let E be an economy in which consumers are not satiated and capital goods are idiosyncratic pure inputs. If $[\mathbf{p}^*, (\mathbf{x}_i^*), \widetilde{\mathbf{y}}^*]$ is a CPM pricing equilibrium, the allocation $[(\mathbf{x}_i^*), \widetilde{\mathbf{y}}^*]$ is Pareto optimal.*

Proof. The argument is standard. First note that each firm gets the whole amount available of its specific capital-goods in equilibrium, when capital goods are idiosyncratic pure inputs. Moreover, $\sum_{i=1}^m \mathbf{x}_i^* \leq \sum_{i=1}^m \omega_i + \sum_{j=1}^n \mathbf{y}_j^*$, by the feasibility of equilibrium allocations.

Now suppose that there is an allocation $[(\mathbf{x}_i'), (\mathbf{y}_j')]$ such that: (a) $u_i(\mathbf{x}_i') \geq u_i(\mathbf{x}_i^*)$ for every i, with a strict inequality for some consumer; and (b) $\sum_{i=1}^m \mathbf{x}_i' \leq \sum_{i=1}^m \omega_i + \sum_{j=1}^n \mathbf{y}'$. Non-satiation implies that

$$\mathbf{p}^* \sum_{i=1}^m \mathbf{x}_i' > \mathbf{p}^* \sum_{i=1}^m \mathbf{x}_i^* = \mathbf{p}^* \sum_{i=1}^m \omega_i + \sum_{j=1}^n \mathbf{p}^* \mathbf{y}_j^*$$

Therefore substituting we get $\mathbf{p}^* \sum_{j=1}^n \mathbf{y}_j' > \mathbf{p}^* \sum_{j=1}^n \mathbf{y}_j^*$.

But this is not possible, because feasibility and equilibrium imply that $\sum_{j=1}^n \mathbf{a}_j' \geq \omega^K = \sum_{j=1}^n \mathbf{a}_j^*$, whereas $\sum_{j=1}^n \mathbf{y}_j^*$ is precisely a profit maximizing combination of production plans, subject to that restriction. $\boxed{\text{Q.e.d.}}$

This proposition states that the first welfare theorem applies when capital goods are firm-specific and do not enter the preferences of consumers. These two assumptions are crucial for the result. First, because non-convex firms compete neither with other firms nor with consumers for those goods that restrict their production possibilities. This implies that the capital goods constraint is the same for all allocations that satisfy production efficiency. Second, because constrained profit maximization implies that total profits are maximized over the set of attainable allocations.

A particular case of this model, commonly used in the literature, is that in which the economy consists of a single firm. In this case we have:

Corollary 8.1 *Let E be an economy with a single firm in which capital goods are not consumed, and consumers are not satiated. Then CPM equilibria are Pareto optimal.*

This result can also be applied to the case of an economy with $n - 1$ convex competitive firms that do not use capital goods, and a single non-convex firm which is the exclusive user of these special commodities (we can think of this non-convex firm as a monopoly). Then, an equilibrium in which convex firms maximize profits and the non-convex firm follows the constrained profit maximization pricing rule is efficient.

Limited in scope as they are, these results are of some import due to the pervasive negative conclusions on the optimality of market equilibria in nonconvex economies. Other approaches to the problem can be found in Guesnerie (1980), Brown & Heal (1983), Dierker (1986) and Quinzii (1991), for the case of single-firm economies. The model here differs from these contributions in two respects. On the one hand, these models are essentially *normative* (they refer to the efficiency of marginal pricing equilibria and hence involve income redistribution aspects due to the need of financing the associated losses, when there are increasing returns). On the other hand, they usually establish assumptions that are not placed directly on the characteristics of the economy (even though no assumption is made on the existence of some goods that are not consumed).

There is no simple way of extending the argument in Proposition 8.4, when there are several non-convex firms in the economy and the same capital goods can be inputs in more than one of these firms (even if we keep the assumption that capital goods are not consumed). There are two main complications. First and foremost, that the maximization of profits subject to a capital goods constraint by individual firms does not imply that total profits are maximized over the set of attainable allocations.[5] Second, that part (v) of axiom 8.2' does not extend to the aggregate production set.

Concerning the second welfare theorem, the next result tells us that when capital goods are not consumed every efficient allocation can be obtained as a CPM equilibrium (provided wealth can be freely redistributed):

---

[5] A simple example is that in which there are two indentical firms with increasing returns to scale that are active in equilibrium.

Proposition 8.5 *Let E be an economy that satisfies axioms 8.1, 8.2',
8.3 and 8.4, and suppose that capital goods are not consumed. Then, every
efficient allocation $[(\mathbf{x}_i^*), \widetilde{\mathbf{y}}^*]$, with $\mathbf{x}_i^* \in int X_i$ for all i, can be decentralized
as a CPM equilibrium.*

Proof. Define E^S as the economy that results from projecting E on the
space of standard commodities. This is a classical convex economy. Note
that we can always write $\mathbf{x}_i^* = (\mathbf{0}, \mathbf{c}_i^*)$, because capital goods do not enter
the preferences of consumers. Therefore, the standard second welfare the-
orem ensures the existence of a price vector $\mathbf{t}^* \in \mathbb{R}_+^{\ell-k} - \{\mathbf{0}\}$ such that,
$[\mathbf{t}^*, (\mathbf{c}_i^*)_{i=1}^m, (\mathbf{b}_j^*)_{j=1}^n]$ is a competitive equilibrium for the E^S economy. It is
trivial to check that the price vector $\mathbf{p}' = (\mathbf{0}, \mathbf{t}^*)$, belongs to $\phi_j^{CPM}(\mathbf{y}_j^*)$ for all
j. From this construction it follows that $[\mathbf{p}^*, (\mathbf{x}_i^*), \widetilde{\mathbf{y}}^*]$ is a CPM equilibrium.
$\boxed{\text{Q.e.d.}}$

8.5 References to the literature

Existence results for mark-up pricing models abound. Dierker, Guesnerie
& Neuefeind (1985) prove the existence of equilibrium when firms follow
several forms of average cost pricing. Böhm (1986) and Corchón (1988)
develop models in which firms set prices by adding a mark-up over average
costs. Herrero & Villar (1988), and Villar (1991) provide average cost pricing
models in which production is formulated as a nonlinear Leontief (resp. a
nonlinear von Neumann) model. This topic is taken up later in the book.

The idea of using quantity restrictions to analyze market equilibria in
economies with non-convex production sets is by no means new. The contributions by Scarf (1986) and Dehez & Drèze (1988 a,b) are close antecedents
to the material in this chapter. Scarf (1986) presents a single-firm economy
with a *distributive* production set (see the next chapter) that maximizes
profits subject to an input restriction. He shows that an equilibrium exists
and yields a core allocation when the inputs that restrict the firm's production possibilities are not consumed. Dehez & Drèze (1998 a,b) take a dual
approach and develop a model with several nonconvex firms using output
(rather than input) restrictions. See also Dierker, Guesnerie & Neuefeiend
(1985), Böhm (1986), and Dierker & Neuefeind (1988).

It is also interesting to observe that idiosyncratic capital goods can be
regarded as a particular instance of the principle of "non-complementarity",
that is used in Makowski & Ostroy (1995) to analyze the validity of the first
welfare theorem.

Chapter 9

COMPETITION AND INCREASING RETURNS

9.1 Introduction

This chapter provides an application of the loss-free pricing rules presented in chapter 8, to the analysis of competitive markets when there are increasing returns to scale. In order to do so, it will be assumed that non-convex firms exhibit a particular type of increasing returns to scale for which constrained profit maximization and average cost-pricing are compatible (*distributive* production sets).

Two alternative notions of competition will be discussed. The first one, called *competitive pricing equilibrium*, associates competition with a behaviour of firms that is characterized by two principles that are present in the standard competitive markets: the profit principle (constrained profit maximization) and the scarcity principle (firms have to pay for the limiting inputs the maximum worth compatible with their incentives). The second, called *classical equilibrium*, also associates competition with two principles: the profit principle, as in the first case, and the equi-profitability principle (all firms are equally profitable). Therefore, in a classical equilibrium firms are characterized by the use of a uniform mark-up pricing rule, that is the maximum profitability achievable at market prices.

Common to both models is the division of commodities in two separate groups: capital goods (that are inputs to production) and standard commodities (that include both consumption goods and other inputs). As in chapter 8, capital goods impose explicit restrictions on the firms' production possibilities and may generate non-convexities in production.

The two models differ in the way in which the agents' behaviour is modelled. Competitive pricing is a selection of the constrained profit maximization pricing rule that makes expensive the inputs that limit production possibilities. Therefore, we can picture consumers as selling these inputs at the maximum price compatible with the profit principle, taken as given the prices of the standard commodities. As a consequence, the owners of capital goods extract all the surplus that can be derived from production activities. In a classical equilibrium there is an explicit distinction between technology and firms. The technology is freely accessible. Firms are created by those consumers who supply their initial holdings of capital goods. They do so by looking for the highest profitability that can be achieved at given prices. The firms so created maximize profits at given prices within their attainable sets (that are determined by the technology and the inputs supplied by consumers). In the first case, the firms are given *a priori* and the consumers look for the maximum prices for the capital goods they own. In the second case, the consumers become *entrepreneurs* by participating in the creation of firms, guided by the maximum profitability of their investments.

These two equilibrium notions will be discussed in a framework in which non-convex firms are modelled in terms of distributive production sets [an idea originally introduced in Scarf (1986), for the analysis of economies with increasing returns and non-empty cores]. These are sets with a particular form of increasing returns to scale, that extends the properties of convex cones and permits to satisfy the profit principle with zero profits.

9.2   The reference model

We consider a market economy with ℓ commodities, m consumers and n firms. Each consumer i is characterized by a triple $[X_i, u_i, r_i]$, where X_i, u_i stand for the ith consumer's consumption set and utility function, respectively, and r_i is her wealth mapping. The behaviour of the ith consumer is summarized by a demand correspondence $\xi_i : \mathbb{R}^\ell_+ \times \mathbb{F} \to X_i$. The following assumption makes it precise the modelling of consumers:

Axiom 9.1 *For each $i = 1, 2, \ldots, m$: (a) X_i is a closed and convex subset of $\mathbb{R}^\ell$, bounded from below. (b) $u_i : X_i \to \mathbb{R}$ is a continuous, quasi-concave$^+$ and non-satiable utility function.*

This is a standard assumption that needs no further comment.

The set of commodity indices $\mathcal{L} \equiv \{1, 2, \ldots, \ell\}$ can be divided into two disjoint subsets, $\mathcal{L}^K = \{1, 2, ..., k\}$ and $\mathcal{L}^S = \{k+1, k+2, ..., \ell\}$. Goods in

$\mathcal{L}^K$ are **capital goods** (that is, input commodities that are explicit restrictions on firms' production possibilities and may give rise to non-convexities). Goods in $\mathcal{L}^S$ are **standard commodities**, and include both inputs and outputs.

Each of the n firms of the economy is characterized by its production set and the pricing rule it applies, (Y_j, ϕ_j). Here again we describe production plans in the form $\mathbf{y}_j = (\mathbf{a}_j, \mathbf{b}_j)$, where $\mathbf{a}_j \leq \mathbf{0}$ is a vector of capital goods, and $\mathbf{b}_j$ is a vector of standard commodities.

Scarf (1986) introduces the notion of distributive sets, as a class of production sets with non-decreasing returns to scale for which average cost pricing is compatible with input-constrained profit maximization. Let us present formally this idea:

Definition 9.1 *A production set Y_j is **distributive**, if for any collection of points $(\mathbf{y}^t, \lambda^t)$, $t = 1, 2, \ldots, s$, with $\mathbf{y}^t = (\mathbf{a}^t, \mathbf{b}^t) \in Y_j$, $\lambda^t \in \mathbb{R}_+$, the following condition holds:*

$$\sum_{h=1}^{s} \lambda^h \mathbf{a}^h \leq \mathbf{a}^t, \ t = 1, 2, \ldots, s \Rightarrow \sum_{h=1}^{s} \lambda^h \mathbf{y}^h \in Y_j$$

In words: A production set is distributive when any nonnegative weighted sum of feasible production plans is feasible, if it does not use fewer inputs than any of the original plans. From a geometrical standpoint, this amounts to saying that, for any point $\mathbf{y}'_j$ in the boundary of Y_j, $\mathbf{y}'_j$ also belongs to the boundary of the convex cone generated by the set of points $\mathbf{y}_j \in Y_j$ such that $\mathbf{a}_j \geq \mathbf{a}'_j$.

Suppose that Y_j is a closed subset of $\mathbb{R}^\ell$, with $Y_j \bigcap \mathbb{R}^\ell_+ = \{\mathbf{0}\}$ and $Y_j - \mathbb{R}^\ell_+ \subset Y_j$. The following properties of distributive sets are relevant:

Claim 9.1 *A distributive production set exhibits increasing returns to scale. The contrary is not true. Yet, in the one-input—one-output case, both concepts are equivalent.*

Claim 9.2 *Let $(\mathbf{a}_j, \mathbf{b}_j), (\mathbf{a}'_j, \mathbf{b}'_j) \in \mathbb{F}_j$. If Y_j is distributive, then $\mathbf{a}_j \geq \mathbf{a}'_j$ implies $\mathbf{b}_j \not> \mathbf{b}'_j$, unless $\mathbf{b}_j \leq \mathbf{0}$ (therefore part (iv) of axiom 8.2' is automatically satisfied).*

Claim 9.3 *If Y_j is distributive, then it has convex iso-inputs sets, that is, the set $B_j(\mathbf{a}'_j) \equiv \{\mathbf{b}_j \in \mathbb{R}^{\ell - k_j} / (\mathbf{a}_j, \mathbf{b}_j) \in Y_j, \mathbf{a}_j \geq \mathbf{a}'_j\}$ is convex (therefore part (v) of axiom 8.2' is automatically satisfied).*

Claim 9.4 *If Y_j is a convex cone, then it is distributive.*

Distributivity ensures that constrained profit maximization is well defined and compatible with zero profits (indeed this property practically characterizes those production sets for which average cost pricing and constrained profit maximization are compatible).[1] The following result, due to Scarf (1986, Th. 1), shows this property. Its proof illuminates on the nature of the requirements involved in the notion of distributivity.

Theorem 9.1 *Let Y_j be a closed subset of $\mathbb{R}^\ell$, with $Y_j \cap \mathbb{R}^\ell_+ = \{0\}$ and $Y_j - \mathbb{R}^\ell_+ \subset Y_j$. Suppose furthermore that Y_j is distributive. Then, for every $\mathbf{y}'_j \in \mathbb{F}_j$ there exists $\mathbf{p}' \in \mathbb{P}$ such that $0 = \mathbf{p}'\mathbf{y}'_j \geq \mathbf{p}'\mathbf{y}_j$, $\forall\, \mathbf{y} \in Y_j(\mathbf{a}'_j) = \{\mathbf{y}_j \in Y_j \, / \, \mathbf{a}_j \geq \mathbf{a}'_j\}$.*

Proof. Let us drop the firm's subscript, for the sake of simplicity in notation. Three different cases will be considered:

(a) First suppose that $\mathbf{y}' = (\mathbf{a}', \mathbf{b}') \in \mathbb{F}$ is such that $\mathbf{a}' << 0$ (i.e. all capital goods are used at $\mathbf{y}'$). Let $T(\mathbf{y}')$ denote the smallest convex cone with vertex 0 containing $Y(\mathbf{a}')$, that is:

$$T(\mathbf{y}') \equiv \{\mathbf{y} = \sum \alpha^t \mathbf{y}^t \, / \, \alpha^t \geq 0, \ \mathbf{y}^t = (\mathbf{a}^t, \mathbf{b}^t) \in Y, \ \mathbf{a}^t \geq \mathbf{a}'\}$$

$T(\mathbf{y}')$ is comprehensive (since it is a convex cone and Y is itself comprehensive). Now letting $\alpha^1 = 1$, $\alpha^t = 0$, $\forall\, t \neq 1$, it follows that $\mathbf{y}' \in T(\mathbf{y}')$. Furthermore, $\mathbf{y}' \in \partial T(\mathbf{y}')$. To see this, suppose that there exists $\mathbf{y}''$ in $T(\mathbf{y}')$ such that $\mathbf{y}'' >> \mathbf{y}'$. Then, $\mathbf{y}'' = \sum \alpha^t \mathbf{y}^t$ for some $(\alpha^t, \mathbf{y}^t)$ such that for all t, $\mathbf{y}^t \in Y$, $\alpha^t \geq 0$, and $\mathbf{a}^t \geq \mathbf{a}'$. Distributivity implies that $\mathbf{y}'' \in Y$, which is not possible because, under the assumptions established, $\mathbf{y} \in \mathbb{F}$ if and only if it is weakly efficient.

Therefore, since $\mathbf{y}'$ is a point on the boundary of a convex cone with vertex 0, there exists a supporting hyperplane to $T(\mathbf{y}')$ passing through 0 and $\mathbf{y}'$. That is, there exists $\mathbf{p}' \in \mathbb{R}^\ell_+$, $\mathbf{p}' \neq 0$, such that $0 = \mathbf{p}'\mathbf{y}' \geq \mathbf{p}'\mathbf{y}$, for all $\mathbf{y}$ in $T(\mathbf{y}')$ [and hence, in particular, for all $\mathbf{y} \in Y(\mathbf{a}')$].

(b) Now consider the case in which $a'_i < 0$ for some indices, while $a'_j = 0$ for some others. Without loss of generality assume that $y'_1, y'_2, \ldots, y'_h = 0$, while $y'_{h+1}, y'_{h+2}, \ldots, y'_\ell < 0$, for some h. Let Z denote the projection of Y on the space $\mathbb{R}^{\ell-h}$, and call $\mathbf{z}'$ the corresponding projection of $\mathbf{y}'$. It is easy to see that Z is a distributive production set and, applying the reasoning

---

[1]For a more detailed discussion see Scarf (1986), Dehez & Drèze (1988b) and Quinzii (1992, Ch. 6).

in (a), that there exists $\mathbf{q} \in \mathbb{R}_+^{\ell-h}$, $\mathbf{q} \neq \mathbf{0}$, with $0 = \mathbf{qz}' \geq \mathbf{qz}$, for every $\mathbf{z}$ in $Z(\mathbf{z}')$. Choose then $\mathbf{p}' = (\mathbf{0}, \mathbf{q})$ (where $\mathbf{0}$ is the vector all whose components are zero in $\mathbb{R}^h$), and the result follows.

(c) Finally, suppose $\mathbf{a}' = \mathbf{0}$. Then, $Y(\mathbf{a}')$ consists of points of the form $(\mathbf{0}, \mathbf{b})$, and any vector $(\mathbf{q}, \mathbf{0}) \in \mathbb{R}_+^\ell$, with $\mathbf{q} \neq \mathbf{0}$ will do. $\boxed{\textbf{Q.e.d.}}$

The next figure illustrates that assuming increasing returns to scale is not sufficient to obtain this result, even in the case in which we consider that single production prevails and that all inputs are capital goods.

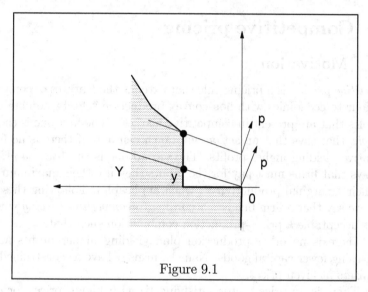

Figure 9.1

Concerning firms it will be assumed:

Axiom 9.2 *For each firm $j = 1, 2, \ldots, n$: (i) Y_j is a closed subset of $\mathbb{R}^\ell$. (ii) $Y_j \cap \mathbb{R}_+^\ell = \{\mathbf{0}\}$. (iii) $Y_j - \mathbb{R}_+^\ell \subset Y_j$. (iv) Y_j is distributive.*

In order to complete the model, let $\omega \in \mathbb{R}^\ell$ stand for the vector of initial endowments. The description of the economy is thus given by:

$$E = \{(X_i,\ u_i,\ r_i)_{i=1}^m; (Y_j,\ \phi_j)_{j=1}^n;\ \omega\}$$

The set of attainable allocations of this economy is:

$$\Omega \equiv \left\{ [(\mathbf{x}_i), (\mathbf{y}_j)] \in \prod_{i=1}^m X_i \times \prod_{j=1}^n Y_j \ / \ \sum_{i=1}^m \mathbf{x}_i - \omega \leq \sum_{j=1}^n \mathbf{y}_j \right\}$$

The following assumptions reproduce those in the reference model of chapter 8, and are thus presented without further comments:

Axiom 9.3 The set Ω of attainable allocations is compact.

Axiom 9.4 *Let* **PE** *stand for the set of production equilibria. The restriction of* r_i *over* **PE** *is continuous, with* $r_i(\mathbf{p}, \widetilde{\mathbf{y}}) > \min \mathbf{p} X_i$, *and* $\sum_{i=1}^{m} r_i(\mathbf{p}, \widetilde{\mathbf{y}}) = \mathbf{p}(\omega + \sum_{j=1}^{n} \mathbf{y}_j)$.

9.3   Competitive pricing

9.3.1   Motivation

Competitive pricing is a pricing rule that extends the features of competitive behaviour to economies with non-convex production sets, by combining two principles that are present in competitive markets. The first one is the *profit principle*, that says that an action will be chosen only if there is no feasible alternative yielding higher profits. The second one is the *scarcity principle*, that says that firms must pay for the inputs they use their maximum worth (i.e. their "marginal productivity", when applicable). Following these principles, we say that a firm behaves according to *competitive pricing* whenever it finds acceptable a prices-production combination such that:

(i) There is no other production plan yielding higher profits at these prices, using fewer capital goods. Namely, firms behave as constrained profit maximizers at given prices.

(ii) There is no price vector satisfying (i) with higher prices for capital goods. In other words, the prices of capital goods are maximal within those satisfying constrained profit maximization.

Part (i) reflects the profit principle and can be regarded as an incentive requirement. Part (ii) expresses the scarcity principle: the use of commodities that restrict production possibilities requires firms to pay the maximum price compatible with constrained profit maximization. This pricing rule describes an environment in which the owners of capital goods sell them to the firms at the maximum price they can afford (i.e. the short-side of the market pays its reservation value). Competitive pricing can also be interpreted as an entry barrier: no potential firm can enter the market in the same conditions by offering a higher price for capital goods, because this would violate the profit principle.[2] Alternatively, it may be regarded as a particularization

---

[2] From this perspective competitive pricing is reminiscent of the notion of *sustainability* [Baumol, Bailey & Willig (1977), Panzar & Willig (1977)].

of the *non-surplus approach* that has been used in the characterization of competitive markets [see for instance Makowski (1980a,b), Ostroy (1980), (1984)].

A situation in which the consumers maximize their preferences under their wealth restrictions, the firms behave according to the competitive pricing rule and all the markets clear will be called a *competitive pricing equilibrium*.

This approach to competition enables to deal with short-run situations in which firms can be thought of as 'being small' but not necessarily convex, due to the presence of fixed costs or the use some elements of fixed capital that generate non-convexities in production (land, buildings or heavy machinery, say). One can think of a two-period economy in which the allocation of fixed capital is decided in period one, taken into account current and future prices. Firms compete in the capital goods market offering the higher prices that are compatible with their incentives. Production and consumption take place in period 2. Now the firms choose those production plans that maximize profits, subject to the investment decisions taken in period 1, and the consumers maximize utility at given prices.

9.3.2   The model

The constrained profit maximization pricing rule, analyzed in section 8.4, summarizes the profit principle. This concept, however, is not very tight. First, because in some cases it imposes few restrictions on the allocation of capital goods (e.g. when capital goods are not consumed). Second, because it may encompass too many market situations (in particular, it does not imply competitive equilibrium when production sets are convex).

We take now a step further, and consider a sub-correspondence of this pricing rule, called competitive pricing, that incorporates another characteristic element of competitive markets: the scarcity principle. The underlying idea is that markets make expensive those commodities that constrain production possibilities. More specifically, competitive pricing requires firms to pay capital goods at the maximum price compatible with constrained profit maximization. That is, for each $\mathbf{y}_j \in \mathbb{F}_j$, the jth firm admits price vectors in ϕ_j^{CPM} that include maximal prices for the capital goods involved.

Definition 9.2 *The **competitive pricing rule** for the jth firm, is a mapping* $\phi_j^* : \mathbb{F}_j \to \mathbb{P}$ *such that, for all* $\mathbf{y}_j \in \mathbb{F}_j$, $\mathbf{p} = (\mathbf{p}^K, \mathbf{p}^S) \in \phi_j^*(\mathbf{y}_j)$ *if and only if the following two conditions hold:*
(i) $\mathbf{p} \in \phi_j^{CPM}(\mathbf{y}_j)$.

(ii) There is no $\overline{\mathbf{p}} = (\overline{\mathbf{p}}^K, \overline{\mathbf{p}}^S) \in \mathbb{P}$ with $\overline{\mathbf{p}}^K > \mathbf{p}^K$, $\overline{\mathbf{p}}^S = \lambda \mathbf{p}^S$, such that $\overline{\mathbf{p}} \in \phi_j^{CPM}(\mathbf{y}_j)$.

The competitive pricing rule is made of those prices that satisfy both constrained profit maximization and maximum prices for capital goods. This idea of maximal prices is formulated keeping constant the relative prices of standard commodities, and adjusting their magnitudes by a scalar $\lambda \in (0, 1)$ so that the new price vector belongs to the price simplex.

Remark 9.1 *The notion of competitive pricing appears in Villar (1999b), where it is analyzed in a more general context. It is shown there that, under axiom 8.2', this is a regular and loss free pricing rule that induces (unconstrained) profit maximization when production sets are convex.*

The following result is obtained:

Theorem 9.2 *Under axioms 9.1 to 9.4 a competitive pricing equilibrium exists.*

Proof. For all $j = 1, 2, ..., n$, all $\mathbf{y}_j \in \mathbb{F}_j$, let

$$\widehat{\phi}_j(\mathbf{y}_j) = \phi_j^{CPM}(\mathbf{y}_j) \bigcap \phi_j^{AC}(\mathbf{y}_j)$$

$\widehat{\phi}_j$ is an upper hemicontinuous correspondence with compact convex values, since constrained profit maximization and average cost are both regular and loss-free pricing rules. Theorem 9.1 shows that $\widehat{\phi}_j$ is also non-empty valued, so that it is a regular and loss-free pricing rule. Therefore, we can apply Proposition 8.1 that ensures the existence of an equilibrium relative to this pricing rule. Moreover, in equilibrium $\mathbf{p}^* \mathbf{y}_j^* = 0$ for all j.

Finally, note that this equilibrium corresponds to a competitive pricing equilibrium, because increasing prices of capital goods will yield negative profits, violating the profit principle. $\boxed{\text{Q.e.d.}}$

It follows immediately from the analysis developed in the previous chapter that, when capital goods are idiosyncratic pure inputs, competitive pricing equilibria yield efficient allocations. Formally:

Corollary 9.1 *Let E be an economy in which consumers are not satiated and capital goods are idiosyncratic pure inputs. If $[\mathbf{p}^*, (\mathbf{x}_i^*), \widetilde{\mathbf{y}}^*]$ is a competitive pricing equilibrium, then the allocation $[(\mathbf{x}_i^*), \widetilde{\mathbf{y}}^*]$ is Pareto optimal.*

Note that, under axiom 9.2, Y_j is convex if and only if it is a convex cone. Hence, competitive pricing coincides with un-constrained profit maximization and the following result is obtained:

Corollary 9.2 *Suppose that axioms 9.1 to 9.4 hold, and that production sets are convex. Then, a competitive pricing equilibrium is a standard competitive equilibrium.*

This corollary says that profit maximization at given prices can be regarded as the outcome of the profit principle and the scarcity principle, when production sets are convex cones. This is so because, under convexity, relaxing the input constraint does not make available more profitable options at given prices: local maximization implies global maximization. Therefore, the standard behaviour of competitive firms, described in chapter 3, may be regarded as a reduced model of a market economy in which firms pay their reservation value for capital goods, due to the competition for those scarce factors that limit production possibilities.

9.4 Classical equilibrium

9.4.1 Motivation

We present here an alternative approach to competition that is also compatible with the presence of increasing returns to scale. The key concept in the analysis will be that of a *classical equilibrium*. A classical equilibrium consists of a price vector and an allocation such that supply equals demand, and all active firms are equally profitable (where the common rate of return is the highest one attainable at these prices).

The idea that competition is a process that implies the equalization of firms' profitability is an old one. It played a central role in the modelling of markets by classical economists, such as Smith, Ricardo or Marx (but also Walras, Wicksell or Hayek). This is an appealing concept which reflects the combination of three key attributes of competitive markets: (1) Technology is freely available (that is, there are no "barriers to entry"); (2) Production and exchange are voluntary (that is, no agent can be forced to participate into production and exchange); and (3) Prices are outside the control of individual agents (which can be identified with price-taking behaviour). As a consequence, no agent will willingly accept a smaller return from her "investment" than the highest one attainable at given prices. Therefore, firms will only become active in those activities which yield such a profitability. Note that these ideas are relatively independent of the nature of technology: irrespective of the kind of returns to scale prevailing, the classical notion of competition can be applied, as long as the aforementioned properties hold. The model presented here will be based on this fact.

Here again commodities are divided into *capital goods* and *standard commodities*. To simplify the discussion, it will be assumed that initial endowments consist of capital goods exclusively. Therefore, capital goods correspond to those factors produced "yesterday" and/or inherited from the past that constitute the initial endowments of today's economy, and hence limit actual production possibilities. They are inputs to production and may or may not be consumed.

The technology is modelled in terms of a finite number of distributive production sets, which now describe different production activities or economic sectors. It is assumed that there is free access to the technology.

The description of consumers is standard. Yet, consumers' decisions also refer to the use of their initial holdings for production purposes (they contribute to the creation of firms by making available their endowments, looking for the highest profitability of their "investment").

Firms are not given a priori, but appear as part of consumers' optimal decisions. A firm is created when a set of consumers coordinate on the use of some of the technological possibilities, by providing the factors that might be required. Firms maximize profits at given prices, subject to their feasible sets (i.e., subject to the amounts of inputs provided by consumers at market prices).

Observe that a key characteristic of the way of modelling the economy is the distinction between *technology* (which belongs to the data of the model) and *firms* (which are dependent on consumers' decisions). The underlying idea is that *factors have to be made available before production takes place*. This implies, on the one hand, that a firm does not exist unless consumers provide some factors. And, on the other hand, that firms will be characterized by both the nature of production activities they carry out, and their feasible sets. Note also that consumers' shares in the firms' profits become now equilibrium variables, rather than parameters.

Here again the model can be interpreted as a two-stage process. In the first stage consumers take investment decisions and firms are created. In the second stage production takes place, consumers get paid and demand is realized. Yet, for the sake of simplicity in exposition, the model refers to a single-period economy. This feature also permits one to discuss the role of profits independently of the "interest rate" (or "discount factor").

9.4.2   The model

Let $1, 2, \ldots, k$ be the indices corresponding to capital goods, and $k + 1, k + 2, \ldots, \ell$ those corresponding to standard commodities. Standard commodities are consumption goods and inputs that can be produced today. Capital goods are produced commodities that are inputs to production (factors), and may also be consumed. By the very definition of commodities, capital goods cannot be produced again, and hence limit today's production possibilities. The aggregate vector of initial endowments takes the form $\omega = (\kappa, 0)$, where $\kappa \in \mathbb{R}^k$ denotes the aggregate endowment of capital goods (that is, commodities which are available before production takes place), and $0 \in \mathbb{R}^{\ell-k}$, describes the availability of standard commodities.

Production possibilities are described by means of n production sets. Each of these sets summarizes the technical knowledge of a specific production activity. Production activities differ in the kind of inputs they use and/or the type of outputs they obtain. One may well interpret these activities as the "industries" or "sectors" of an economy. The *technology* (which encompasses all activities) is publicly known and freely accessible.

As before, a production plan for the jth activity $\mathbf{y}_j \in Y_j$ is described by $\mathbf{y}_j = (\mathbf{a}_j, \mathbf{b}_j)$, where $\mathbf{a}_j \in -\mathbb{R}^k_+$ is a vector in the subspace of capital goods. For a given pair $(\mathbf{p}, \mathbf{y}_j)$ the ratio $\frac{\mathbf{p}\mathbf{y}_j}{\mathbf{p}(-\mathbf{a}_j, 0)}$ gives the profitability that can be obtained in the jth activity when prices are $\mathbf{p}$ and production is $\mathbf{y}_j$. That is, the relation between profits and the "advanced capital" (the cost of capital goods). More formally, let $\rho_j : \mathbb{P} \times \mathbb{F}_j \to \mathbb{R}$ be a mapping given by:

$$\rho_j(\mathbf{p}, \mathbf{y}_j) \equiv \left\{ \begin{array}{ll} \frac{\mathbf{p}\mathbf{y}_j}{\mathbf{p}(-\mathbf{a}_j, 0)}, & \text{if } \mathbf{y}_j \neq 0 \\ 0, & \text{otherwise} \end{array} \right.$$

(ρ_j is left undefined when $\mathbf{p}(-\mathbf{a}_j, 0) = 0$ and $\mathbf{y}_j \neq 0$). Now call $\rho(\mathbf{p}, \widetilde{\mathbf{y}})$ the maximum profitability attainable (whenever defined), that is:

$$\rho(\mathbf{p}, \widetilde{\mathbf{y}}) \equiv \max_j \{\rho_j(\mathbf{p}, \mathbf{y}_j)\}$$

The number $\rho(\mathbf{p}, \widetilde{\mathbf{y}})$ tells us the largest return one can get per dollar invested, when prices are $\mathbf{p}$ and production is evaluated at $\widetilde{\mathbf{y}}$.

There are m consumers, which are supposed to behave *competitively*. Each consumer $i = 1, 2, \ldots, m$, is characterized by a collection $(X_i, u_i, \omega_i,)$, where $X_i \subset \mathbb{R}^\ell$, $u_i : X_i \to \mathbb{R}$, and $\omega_i = (\kappa_i, 0) \in \mathbb{R}^\ell$ stand for the ith consumer's consumption set, utility function and initial endowments, respectively. Note that income mappings are not part of the description of the economy (they are endogenous).

Consumers own the initial endowments and maximize utility at given prices, by suitably choosing consumption bundles under the restriction of their available wealth. Wealth is given by the exchange value of their initial endowments, which depends on prices and the profitability that can be achieved by applying their resources of capital goods to production activities. By construction, consumers are not interested in the nature of production activities they support, but just in the profitability they can obtain. Thus, whenever any two activities yield the highest profitability attainable, they will be indifferent in applying their resources to any of them. Moreover, the supply of inputs will only be directed to those activities yielding a return equal to $\rho(\mathbf{p},\widetilde{\mathbf{y}}) \geq 0$.

This can be formally expressed as follows. Let $\alpha_{ij}(\mathbf{p},\widetilde{\mathbf{y}}) \in \mathbb{R}^k$ denote the ith consumer's investment in the jth sector, and let $\alpha_i(\mathbf{p},\widetilde{\mathbf{y}})$ in $\mathbb{R}^{kn}$ stand for the ith consumer's overall investment distribution. For any given pair $(\mathbf{p},\widetilde{\mathbf{y}})$, the term $\alpha_i(\mathbf{p},\widetilde{\mathbf{y}})$ is chosen as a solution to the program:

$$\left. \begin{array}{c} \max\ \mathbf{p}\left(\sum_{j=1}^{n} \alpha_{ij}[1 + \rho_j(\mathbf{p}, \mathbf{y}_j)],\ \mathbf{0}\right) \\ s.t.:\ \sum_{j=1}^{n} \alpha_{ij} \leq \boldsymbol{\kappa}_i \end{array} \right\}$$

For a given $(\mathbf{p},\widetilde{\mathbf{y}})$, let $I_i(\mathbf{p},\widetilde{\mathbf{y}})$ stand for the ith consumer's aggregate supply of inputs, that is, the set of points $\mathbf{t} \in \mathbb{R}^k$ such that $\mathbf{t} = \sum_{j=1}^{n} \alpha_{ij}(\mathbf{p},\widetilde{\mathbf{y}})$. This supply of inputs is a correspondence I_i from $\mathbb{P} \times \mathbb{F}$ into $\mathbb{R}^k$, that can be expressed as:

$$I_i(\mathbf{p},\widetilde{\mathbf{y}}) = \left\{ \begin{array}{ll} \{\mathbf{0}\}, & \text{if } \rho(\mathbf{p},\widetilde{\mathbf{y}}) < 0 \\ [\mathbf{0},\boldsymbol{\kappa}_i], & \text{if } \rho(\mathbf{p},\widetilde{\mathbf{y}}) = 0 \\ \{\boldsymbol{\kappa}_i\}, & \text{if } \rho(\mathbf{p},\widetilde{\mathbf{y}}) > 0 \end{array} \right.$$

Consumers will not develop production activities if $\rho(\mathbf{p},\widetilde{\mathbf{y}})$ is negative, because no agent can be forced to participate into production. When $\rho(\mathbf{p},\widetilde{\mathbf{y}}) = 0$ the ith consumer's wealth is given by $\mathbf{p}(\boldsymbol{\kappa}_i, \mathbf{0})$, no matter how she allocates her initial endowments; hence the supply of inputs can be taken as the whole interval $[\mathbf{0}, \boldsymbol{\kappa}_i]$. Finally, if $\rho(\mathbf{p},\widetilde{\mathbf{y}}) > 0$ the ith consumer will be willing to devote *all* her resources to the most profitable activities, because this maximizes her wealth (let us recall here that consumers behave competitively, so that they make choices without taking into account any restriction other than wealth).

This allows us to express the ith consumer's wealth function as follows:

$$r_i(\mathbf{p},\widetilde{\mathbf{y}}) \equiv \mathbf{p}\left(\boldsymbol{\kappa}_i[1 + \max\{0, \rho(\mathbf{p},\widetilde{\mathbf{y}})\}],\ \mathbf{0}\right)$$

which may not be defined for some pairs $(\mathbf{p},\widetilde{\mathbf{y}})$.

Remark 9.2.- *Note that this formulation implies that consumers cannot trade with "future yields" before production takes place, when $\rho(\mathbf{p},\widetilde{\mathbf{y}}) > 0$. For interpretative purposes we can think that consumers "invest" capital goods at the beginning of the period, then production takes place, and finally consumers get paid and actually consume at the end of the period.*

The ith consumer's demand is obtained as a solution to the following program:

$$\left.\begin{array}{l} Max \ \ u_i(\mathbf{x}_i) \\ s.t. : \ \mathbf{x}_i \in X_i \\ \mathbf{p}\mathbf{x}_i \leq r_i(\mathbf{p}, \widetilde{\mathbf{y}}) \end{array}\right\}$$

Then, the ith consumer's behaviour can be summarized by a demand correspondence $\xi_i : \mathbb{P} \times \mathbb{F} \to X_i$, such that $\xi_i(\mathbf{p}, \widetilde{\mathbf{y}})$ stands for a solution to the program above.

We have already described the technology and the consumption sector. Let us now refer to firms. A firm results from the application of initial resources to put into work some of the possibilities that the available technology offers. These resources have to be made available "before" production takes place.[3] Thus, a firm can be described by the nature of its production activities and its feasible set (given by the amounts of factors available).

For every pair $(\mathbf{p}', \widetilde{\mathbf{y}}') \in \mathbb{P} \times \mathbb{F}$, consumers will decide to set up firms by choosing the most profitable production activities and making available the inputs they own. In order to make things simpler, let us assume that there can be at most one firm per activity,[4] and consider the following definition:

Definition 9.3 *Given a point* $(\mathbf{p}', \widetilde{\mathbf{y}}') \in \mathbb{P} \times \mathbb{F}$, *an* **input allocation** *relative to* $(\mathbf{p}', \widetilde{\mathbf{y}}')$ *is a point* $\widetilde{\mathbf{a}} \equiv (\mathbf{a}_1, \mathbf{a}_2, \dots, \mathbf{a}_n)$ *in* $-\mathbb{R}_+^{kn}$, *such that, for every* $j = 1, 2, \dots, n$, *one has:* $-\mathbf{a}_j = \sum_{i=1}^m \alpha_{ij}(\mathbf{p}, \widetilde{\mathbf{y}})$.

An input allocation relative to $(\mathbf{p}', \widetilde{\mathbf{y}}')$ is a way of allotting capital goods to firms that is consistent with consumers' decisions. In particular, this implies that no firm will be created in those activities such that $\rho_j(\mathbf{p}', \mathbf{y}'_j)$ is smaller than $\rho(\mathbf{p}', \widetilde{\mathbf{y}}')$ (that is, $\rho_j(\mathbf{p}', \mathbf{y}'_j) < \rho(\mathbf{p}', \widetilde{\mathbf{y}}')$ implies $\mathbf{a}_j = 0$). Also that $\sum_{j=1}^n -\mathbf{a}_j \in \sum_{i=1}^m I_i(\mathbf{p}, \widetilde{\mathbf{y}})$. Needless to say that there are many input allocations relative to a given pair $(\mathbf{p}', \widetilde{\mathbf{y}}')$, and that all of them are equally worthy from consumers' viewpoint.

Thus, given a price vector $\mathbf{p}' \in \mathbb{P}$, a vector of production plans $\widetilde{\mathbf{y}}'$ in $\mathbb{F}$, and an input allocation $\widetilde{\mathbf{a}}$ relative to $(\mathbf{p}', \widetilde{\mathbf{y}}')$, the jth firm's feasible set is given by:

$$Y_j(\mathbf{p}', \widetilde{\mathbf{y}}', \widetilde{\mathbf{a}}) \equiv \{\mathbf{y}''_j \in Y_j \ / \ \mathbf{a}''_j \geq \mathbf{a}_j\}$$

---

[3]This is an intuitive way of saying that produced commodities are essential inputs to production. The assumptions established make this point clear.

[4]It will be seen soon after that this implies no loss of generality, under the assumptions of our model.

The behaviour of firms can now be described as follows: Given a point $(\mathbf{p}', \widetilde{\mathbf{y}}') \in \mathbb{P} \times \mathbb{F}$ and an input allocation $\widetilde{\mathbf{a}}$ relative to $(\mathbf{p}', \widetilde{\mathbf{y}}')$, the jth firm's supply is obtained by solving the program:

$$\left. \begin{array}{c} Max \ \ \mathbf{p}'\mathbf{y}''_j \\ s.t. : \mathbf{y}''_j \in Y_j \left(\mathbf{p}', \widetilde{\mathbf{y}}', \widetilde{\mathbf{a}} \right) \end{array} \right\}$$

that is, the jth firm maximizes profits over its feasible set.

Let $\lambda \in \mathbb{R}_+$ be a scalar, to be interpreted as a parametric rate of profits, and consider the following definitions which will enable to make precise (and non-vacuous) the equilibrium notion:

Definition 9.4   *The pair* $(\mathbf{p}', \mathbf{y}'_j) \in \mathbb{P} \times \mathbb{F}_j$, *is an* **equilibrium relative to** λ *for the jth activity, if:*
  (i) For $\mathbf{y}'_j \neq \mathbf{0}$,

$$\mathbf{p}'(-\mathbf{a}'_j, \mathbf{0})\lambda = \mathbf{p}'\mathbf{y}'_j \geq \mathbf{p}'\mathbf{y}_j, \quad \forall \, \mathbf{y}_j \in Y_j \text{ with } \mathbf{a}_j \geq \mathbf{a}'_j$$

  (ii) For $\mathbf{y}'_j = \mathbf{0}$, $\mathbf{p}'$ *belongs to the closed convex hull of the following set:*

$$\{\mathbf{q} \in \mathbb{P} \ / \ \exists \{\mathbf{q}'', \mathbf{y}''_j\} \subset \mathbb{P} \times [\mathbb{F}_j \backslash \{\mathbf{0}\}]$$

$$\text{with } \{\mathbf{q}'', \mathbf{y}''_j\} \to (\mathbf{q}, \mathbf{0}) \text{ and } \mathbf{q}''\mathbf{y}''_j = \mathbf{q}''(-\mathbf{a}''_j, \mathbf{0})\lambda\}$$

Definition 9.5   *The pair* $(\mathbf{p}', \widetilde{\mathbf{y}}') \in \mathbb{P} \times \mathbb{F}$ *is a* **production equilibrium relative to** λ *if, for all* $j = 1, 2, \ldots, n$, $(\mathbf{p}', \mathbf{y}'_j)$ *is an equilibrium relative to λ for the jth activity.*

The jth activity is in equilibrium relative to λ when $\mathbf{y}'_j = (\mathbf{a}'_j, \mathbf{b}'_j)$ is a profit maximizing production plan at prices $\mathbf{p}'$, subject to the restriction of not using more capital goods than those determined by $\mathbf{a}'_j$, and such that $\mathbf{p}'\mathbf{y}'_j = \mathbf{p}'(-\mathbf{a}'_j, \mathbf{0})\lambda$. Since this places no restriction on prices when $\mathbf{y}'_j = \mathbf{0}$, we require in this case $(\mathbf{p}', \mathbf{0})$ to be a limit point of a sequence of pairs yielding a profitability equal to λ. A production equilibrium is a situation in which all activities are in equilibrium relative to a common λ, for the same price vector.

Consider now the following definition:

Definition 9.6   *A* **classical equilibrium** *is a price vector* $\mathbf{p}^* \in \mathbb{P}$, *a scalar* λ^*, *and an allocation* $[(\mathbf{x}^*_i), \widetilde{\mathbf{y}}^*] \in \Pi_{i=1}^m X_i \times \mathbb{F}$, *such that:*

(α) $\mathbf{x}_i^* \in \xi_i(\mathbf{p}^*, \widetilde{\mathbf{y}}^*)$, for all i.

(β) $\widetilde{\mathbf{a}}^* \equiv (\mathbf{a}_1^*, \mathbf{a}_2^*, \ldots, \mathbf{a}_n^*)$ is an input allocation relative to $(\mathbf{p}^*, \widetilde{\mathbf{y}}^*)$ [in which these $\mathbf{a}_j^*$ are such that $\mathbf{y}_j^* = (\mathbf{a}_j^*, \mathbf{b}_j^*)$].

(γ) $(\mathbf{p}^*, \widetilde{\mathbf{y}}^*)$ is a production equilibrium relative to $\lambda^* = \rho(\mathbf{p}^*, \widetilde{\mathbf{y}}^*)$.

(δ) $\sum_{i=1}^m \mathbf{x}_i^* \leq \sum_{j=1}^n \mathbf{y}_j^* + \omega$, with $p_h^* = 0$ for strict inequalities.

That is, a classical equilibrium is a price vector and an allocation such that: (a) The consumers maximize preferences within their budget sets; (b) The consumers voluntarily provide all inputs that are needed for production purposes; (c,1) All the firms maximize profits at given prices subject to their feasible sets; (c,2) All active firms are equally profitable; (c,3) The common rate of return is the maximum profitability attainable across sectors; and (d) All markets clear. Observe that part (γ) of the definition implies that we are discarding those trivial equilibria obtained by setting $\mathbf{y}_j = \mathbf{0}$ for all j and finding a pure exchange equilibrium.

In order to get a suitable bound for the rate of profits define, for each λ in $\mathbb{R}_+$, the set:

$$\Omega(\lambda) \equiv \{[(\mathbf{x}_i), \widetilde{\mathbf{y}}] \in \prod_{i=1}^m X_i \times \mathbb{F} \ / \ \sum_{i=1}^m \mathbf{x}_i - \omega - \sum_{j=1}^n [\mathbf{a}_j(1 + \lambda), \mathbf{b}_j] \leq \mathbf{0}\}$$

Also define $\Lambda \equiv \{\lambda \in \mathbb{R}_+ \ / \ \Omega(\lambda) \neq \emptyset\}$. That is, the set of profit rates for which $\Omega(\lambda)$ is nonempty. Note that this set is an interval which will be nonempty whenever the set of attainable allocations is nonempty.

The following axiom specifies that production requires using up some capital goods (this translates the idea that inputs have to be made available "before" production takes place):

Axiom 9.5   For all $j = 1, 2, \ldots, n$, $\mathbf{b}_j \leq \mathbf{0}$ whenever $\mathbf{a}_j = \mathbf{0}$.

Let us conclude this section commenting on the simplifying hypothesis of (at most) one active firm per activity. Suppose, for the sake of the argument, that any number of firms can be created in a given sector. Under axiom 9.2, there can only be production activities with non-decreasing returns to scale. For those sectors exhibiting constant returns to scale, the number of firms is actually irrelevant (since production sets are convex cones, and thus satisfy additivity and divisibility). For those sectors with increasing returns to scale there can only be one active firm in each activity in equilibrium. Otherwise $(\mathbf{p}^*, \widetilde{\mathbf{y}}^*)$ would not be a production equilibrium relative to $\lambda = \rho(\mathbf{p}^*, \widetilde{\mathbf{y}}^*)$. Therefore, modelling one firm per activity has only served the purpose of simplifying the writing of the model, without any loss of generality.

9.4.3   The existence of equilibrium

Let us begin presenting the main result of this section:

Proposition 9.3   *Under axioms 9.1 to 9.5, there exists a classical equilibrium with $\rho(\mathbf{p}^*, \widetilde{\mathbf{y}}^*) = 0$. Moreover, no classical equilibrium exists with $\rho(\mathbf{p}^*, \widetilde{\mathbf{y}}^*) > 0$, in which capital goods with positive prices are consumed.*

> *Proof.*
> The first part is obtained as an immediate application of the results in former sections, because a classical equilibrium with null profits is simply a competitive pricing equilibrium (that yields zero profits when production sets are distributive).
> The second part derives from the structure of the model. In a classical equilibrium with positive profits, no consumption of capital goods with positive prices can occur. This is so because in this case consumers devote *all* their initial endowments to production activities (in order to maximize wealth), and hence in equilibrium these commodities are actually *used up* by firms. Unless this condition holds, zero would be the only profit rate compatible with the existence of equilibrium. $\boxed{\textbf{Q.e.d.}}$

This proposition tells us that there exist classical equilibria under fairly general assumptions. These equilibria describe a market situation in which production is carried out in order to exploit the benefits derived from technical knowledge, as part of consumers' rational behaviour. Consumers maximize utility subject to their budget constraints. Firms are created only when they yield the highest profitability attainable at given prices, and maximize profits subject to their feasible sets. Proposition 9.3 ensures that all these actions are compatible for some pair $(\mathbf{p}^*, \widetilde{\mathbf{y}}^*)$. It is easy to see that there is no feasible way of making consumers better-off, preserving the distribution of capital goods between firms.[5]

The case in which equilibrium profits are positive is slightly more complex. First observe that Proposition 9.3 does not ensure that such an equilibrium exists. It only establishes a necessary condition for that to happen. This condition says that the prices of capital goods must be high enough, relative to consumers' willingness to pay, so that no consumer demands these commodities in equilibrium. It is then natural to consider again the case in

---

[5]Note that this model offers an additional justification of *competitive pricing*, as a simplified description of an economy if which the owners of capital goods decide to participate in production activities by looking for the highest profitability of their investment, and the firms so created maximize profits at given prices within their attainable sets. Note that this model provides us with an endogenous way of determining the input restrictions.

which capital goods do not enter the preferences of consumers, and analyze if there are equilibria with positive profit rates in this context.

The following result answers this question:

Proposition 9.4 *Let E be an economy satisfying axioms 9.1 to 9.5 and suppose that capital goods are pure inputs. Then, for any given $\lambda \in \Lambda$, there exists a classical equilibrium with $\rho(\mathbf{p}^*, \widetilde{\mathbf{y}}^*) = \lambda$.*

Proof. (i) Consider an economy $E(\lambda)$, for $\lambda > 0$, which is identical to the original one except in the following:

a) The ith consumer's initial endowments are given by:

$$\omega_i(\lambda) \equiv [\kappa_i(1+\lambda), \; \mathbf{0}]$$

b) The jth production set, is now defined as:

$$Y_j(\lambda) \equiv \{\mathbf{s} \in \mathbb{R}^\ell \; / \; \mathbf{s} = [\mathbf{a}_j(1+\lambda), \mathbf{b}_j], \text{ with } (\mathbf{a}_j, \mathbf{b}_j) \in Y_j\}$$

whose elements will be denoted by $\mathbf{y}_j(\lambda)$.

This economy also satisfies axioms 9.1 to 9.5, so that we can apply proposition 9.3 which ensures the existence of a classical equilibrium for the $E(\lambda)$ economy, $[\mathbf{p}^*, (\mathbf{x}_i^*), \widetilde{\mathbf{y}}^*(\lambda)]$, with $\rho[\mathbf{p}^*, \widetilde{\mathbf{y}}^*(\lambda)] = 0$.

(ii) Let us now show that $[\mathbf{p}^*, (\mathbf{x}_i^*), \widetilde{\mathbf{y}}^*]$ is a classical equilibrium for the original economy, with $\rho(\mathbf{p}^*, \widetilde{\mathbf{y}}^*) = \lambda$. First note that $[(\mathbf{x}_i^*), \widetilde{\mathbf{y}}^*]$ is an attainable allocation. To see this observe that, by assumption,

$$\sum_{i=1}^m \mathbf{x}_i^* - \omega(\lambda) - \sum_{j=1}^n \mathbf{y}_j^*(\lambda) \leq \mathbf{0} \qquad [1]$$

The structure of the model and the assumption of pure inputs allow us to write

$$\sum_{i=1}^m \mathbf{x}_i^* = \begin{bmatrix} \mathbf{0} \\ \mathbf{d} \end{bmatrix}, \quad \omega(\lambda) = \begin{bmatrix} \boldsymbol{\kappa}(1+\lambda) \\ \mathbf{0} \end{bmatrix}, \quad \sum_{j=1}^n \mathbf{y}_j^*(\lambda) = \begin{bmatrix} \mathbf{a}(1+\lambda) \\ \mathbf{b} \end{bmatrix}$$

Then, equation [1] can be rewritten as follows:

$$\begin{bmatrix} \mathbf{0} \\ \mathbf{d} \end{bmatrix} - \begin{bmatrix} \boldsymbol{\kappa}(1+\lambda) \\ \mathbf{0} \end{bmatrix} - \begin{bmatrix} \mathbf{a}(1+\lambda) \\ \mathbf{b} \end{bmatrix} \leq \begin{bmatrix} \mathbf{0} \\ \mathbf{0} \end{bmatrix}$$

which implies that $\mathbf{d} \leq \mathbf{b}$ and $-\boldsymbol{\kappa}(1+\lambda) \leq \mathbf{a}(1+\lambda)$. Consequently, $-\boldsymbol{\kappa} \leq \mathbf{a}$ and:

$$\sum_{i=1}^m \mathbf{x}_i^* - \omega - \sum_{j=1}^n \mathbf{y}_j^* \leq \mathbf{0}$$

It is easy to see that, for each j, $\mathbf{p}^*\mathbf{y}_j^* \geq \mathbf{p}^*\mathbf{y}_j$ for all $\mathbf{y}_j$ such that $\mathbf{a}_j \geq \mathbf{a}_j^*$. For suppose not, that is, suppose that there exists a firm j and a production plan $\mathbf{y}_j'$ such that $\mathbf{p}^*\mathbf{y}_j' > \mathbf{p}^*\mathbf{y}_j^*$, with $\mathbf{a}_j' \geq \mathbf{a}_j^*$. In that case we would also have that $\mathbf{p}^*\mathbf{y}_j'(\lambda) > \mathbf{p}^*\mathbf{y}_j^*(\lambda)$, against the hypothesis that $[\mathbf{p}^*, (\mathbf{x}_i^*), \widetilde{\mathbf{y}}^*(\lambda)]$ is a classical equilibrium for the $E(\lambda)$ economy.

It remains to show that $\mathbf{x}_i^*$ is the ith consumer's demand in the original economy. But this follows immediately from the way in which the $E(\lambda)$ economy has been constructed. $\boxed{\textbf{Q.e.d.}}$

Proposition 9.4 says that there exists an equilibrium with a rate of profits $\rho(\mathbf{p}^*, \widetilde{\mathbf{y}}^*) = \lambda$, for any pre-established $\lambda \in \Lambda$. This points out a strong indeterminacy of the model: there may be many possible equilibria with different profit rates and, consequently, different income distributions, employment levels, etc. Profits are to be interpreted as the rents of those scarce factors which are required in order to carry out production activities. The profit rate may be seen as a parameter of the way in which the total surplus is distributed among the agents.[6]

This result also tells us that competitive pricing and classical equilibrium may differ in this context (even though both are equilibrium concepts that satisfy constrained profit maximization). In a classical equilibrium with positive profits the *scarcity principle* is violated. Hence, looking for the highest prices for capital goods and looking for the highest profitability are two different behavioural rules, that yield different outcomes. These differences are illustrated in example 8.1 of the previous chapter.

It was already pointed out that one may interpret the model as including a *sequence* of transactions within the period. Investment decisions are taken first, then the firms are created and production occurs, and finally income is realized and consumption takes place. This sequential feature is relevant again for the analysis of equilibria with positive profits. For suppose that consumers can spend, before production takes place, the profits that will result from production activities. Then, whenever $\rho(\mathbf{p}, \widetilde{\mathbf{y}}) > 0$, consumers will use their profits $\mathbf{p}[\kappa\rho(\mathbf{p}, \widetilde{\mathbf{y}}), \mathbf{0}]$ to buy additional endowments, and spend the additional future yields to buy even more endowments, and will repeat this process again and again before deciding their consumption. But this income cannot be realized as an equilibrium, so that the only possible equilibria would be those with $\rho(.) = 0$.

---

[6]Note, however, that the informative content of this parameter is rather ambiguous, except in very specific models, as in Sraffa (1960). We refer to this question again at the end of chapter 11.

9.5 References to the literature

Scarf (1986) uses the concept of distributive production sets to identify a family of single-firm economies with increasing returns to scale in which equilibrium allocations are in the core. Dehez & Drèze (1988 b) apply this concept to the case of output-constrained profit maximization. They also analyze an alternative competitive scenario in which firms sell the constrained output at the minimum prices that are compatible with output-constrained profit maximization.

The notion of competitive pricing is analyzed in a more general context in Villar (1999b), based on the ideas mentioned above. It is worth noting the connection between the ideas underlying the competitive pricing model and the analysis of competitive markets developed in the works of Ostroy (1979), (1980), (1984), Makowski (1980a, b), Makowski & Ostroy (1995). Competitive pricing shares the spirit of the non-surplus condition, both in terms of the restrictions imposed and in terms of the general approach (price taking behaviour is not the essence of competitive markets, but a reduced form that results from more primary considerations).

The classical equilibrium model presented here is related to the literature on coalition production economies, originated in Debreu & Scarf (1963) and Hildenbrand (1968). The interested reader is referred to Ishiischi (1993) for a discussion of these economies.

Reichert (1986) addresses some of these issues by means of a non-linear input-output model with single production.

Chapter 10

NON-CONVEXITIES AS PUBLIC GOODS

10.1 Introduction

The inefficiency of marginal pricing equilibrium allocations, in economies with non-convex firms, conveys the message that production decisions affect the allocation of resources in a way that is not fully captured by the price system. Therefore, the presence of increasing returns to scale, fixed costs, or other forms of non-convexities, can be interpreted as an instance of externalities or as a public good feature.

Classical writers like Say (1826), Dupuit (1844), or Hotelling (1938) discussed large projects such as those involving roads, bridges, canals, or railways. Whether or not the constructor and/or the operator is privately owned, such projects inevitably have many of the features of a public good. In part, this is because they create pecuniary externalities in the form of modifications to the price system as a whole, specially in the geographical vicinity of any such project. For this reason, a major issue of public policy is to create guidelines for determining the criteria under which each such potential project is to be accepted or rejected, and how the project is to be financed if it is accepted. In fact, whether a private firm should incur significant set-up costs is virtually always a public policy issue, even if it is usually not recognized as such. This is because it shares the key features of a decision affecting public goods or the public environment in some more conventional sense.

This chapter exploits this approach. The basic idea is to embed non-convexities within a category of external effects on agents' choices, and apply non-linear pricing schemes in order to characterize the efficient allocations.[1]

10.1.1   Non-Convexities and the Public Environment

A modern mixed economy can be regarded as combining a private market sector with a public non-market sector. In the private market sector, individual economic agents make decisions within their private feasible sets. These private agents take as given certain important variables which are determined outside the market mechanism, often as a result of deliberate public policy decisions. Examples of such non-market variables include prevailing social rules like the legal system and especially the assignment of property rights. They also include private goods provided by the public sector, such as many transport, health and education services. Often, what matters here is the quality rather than the quantity of these services. Other non-market variables can be used to describe the regulation of private economic activity through quotas, quality standards, legislation affecting health and safety at work, etc. The working of the tax and benefit system in the economy is yet another kind of non-market variable. Finally, many externalities and environmental concerns involve non-market variables, even if the rights or duties to create externalities are allocated through the price mechanism —e.g. through a market for pollution licences, or allocating the contract for providing an unprofitable but socially desirable bus or rail service to whichever private firm demands the lowest subsidy

All such non-market variables constitute what we choose to call the *public environment*, or simply the environment. This is a very broad concept allowing many different economic problems to be treated within one unified framework. The environment in this sense will be treated as a public good, that is as a collection of variables which are common to all agents. Needless to say, the environment may in turn affect agents' feasible sets and objectives. Devising a good procedure which determines each aspect of the public environment, together with the taxes needed to finance that environment, is obviously one of the key tasks of economic policy makers.

In order to encompass many different situations, our mathematical framework follows Mas-Colell (1980) in allowing the vector $\mathbf{z}$ of variables describing the environment to range over an abstract set $\mathbf{Z}$ with no special structure. In particular, $\mathbf{Z}$ need not be convex. This framework allows us to discuss, in principle, not only non-convexities in public sector decisions, but also issues such as whether to allow production by private firms with fixed set-up costs.

With this background in mind, the main concern of this chapter is to char-

---

[1]This chapter reproduces some of the results in Hammond & Villar (1998), (1999).

acterize Pareto efficient allocations in such a mixed economy, when for each given public environment, including variables describing non-convexities, agents trade private goods competitively. In order to do so we shall look for equilibrium concepts for which both the efficiency theorems of welfare economics are true —that is, any equilibrium allocation should be Pareto efficient, and conversely (under suitable assumptions). In this respect, we learnt in chapter 6 that the marginal pricing rule fails because, without suitable lump-sum redistribution of initial wealth, marginal pricing equilibria need not be Pareto efficient. Our characterization will involve suitably revised versions of both the Wicksell (1896) and the Lindahl (1919) approaches to the efficient provision of public goods. More specifically, we shall consider appropriate revisions of the equilibrium notions which more modern economic theorists have created in order to capture their ideas. These notions may be regarded as further extensions of the "Scandinavian consensus" —to use the evocative term due to Bergstrom (1970), who analyzed consumption externalities using a development of Lindahl's approach.

10.1.2 Two kinds of consensus

In fact, the literature on public goods presents us with two main approaches to the problem of achieving a Pareto efficient allocation. The first harks back to Wicksell (1896), but was originally formalized in modern mathematical terms by Foley (1967). This approach tends to regard the choice of public goods z as an essentially political matter, about which the economist has little to say. This is the kind of allocation which Foley called "publicly competitive". The Wicksell-Foley idea is to have either the community of agents, or its representatives in government, draw up proposals for both public good production and taxes to finance this production. These are "public sector proposals". Then any public sector proposal can be amended if and only if each consumer in the economy, and each producer, favours the amendment. A consumer will favour the amendment if, taking present prices for private goods as given, the change in the public goods which are provided gives a net benefit exceeding the net cost of any extra taxes that have to be paid. A firm will favour the amendment if the change in the public goods which are provided, including those which it might be called on to produce, allows it to cover the (net) cost of any extra taxes it has to pay from the extra net profit it makes at fixed prices. An equilibrium results from *a negative consensus*, in which agents are unable lo agree unanimously on how to change the public environment.

The second main approach to the problem of achieving Pareto efficiency with public goods is named after Lindahl (1919). It requires all consumers and private producers to pay a "Lindahl price" for each public good according to the marginal benefits which they receive from it. Each public good is produced so that the total marginal benefit to all private consumers and producers is equal to the marginal cost of providing it. In equilibrium the Lindahl prices must be chosen so as to reach *a positive consensus*, in which all agents agree that the same public environment is optimal, given their budget constraints or profit functions.

When non-convexities are involved, however, setting prices equal to marginal benefits is clearly going to be insufficient, in general. So we adapt an idea due to Mas-Colell (1980) and allow a valuation scheme with non-linear Lindahl pricing —see also Vega-Redondo (1987), as well as Diamantaras and Gilles (1996), Diamantaras, Gilles and Scotchmer (1996). This leads us to consider what Mas-Colell calls a **valuation equilibrium**, which is defined as a price vector, a tax system, a feasible allocation, and a public environment such that: (a) each consumer's equilibrium combination of a private net trade vector together with the public environment is weakly preferred to any other such combination which is affordable, given the non-linear tax system; (b) each firm's combination of a net output vector for private goods together with the public environment is chosen to maximize profit over its production set, given the non-linear tax ; and (c) aggregate net tax payments (i.e. taxes less subsidies) are zero.

10.1.3   Scope and outline of the chapter

The purpose of this chapter is to discuss the efficiency and decentralizability of suitable extensions of the notions of public competitive and valuation equilibria. Note that allowing several private goods offers a choice of how to extend these notions. One possibility is to assume that agents evaluate alternative actions taking the equilibrium prices as given. The alternative is to assume that they compute the new prices that would emerge in different environments. In the first case, agents compare alternatives disregarding the effect on prices that results from a change in the environment. Here private agents are implicitly assumed to be "myopic" (as in the standard competitive or Lindahl equilibrium model). In the second case, they are highly sophisticated and able to calculate the set of conditional equilibria associated with an alternative public environment (and to coordinate on which one if there are several). Of course, when there is only one private good this is not an issue. Also, in the absence of non-convexities, one can usually disregard the effect of any marginal change in the public environment on the equilibrium prices of private goods.

We focus in this chapter on the case in which prices of private commodities are treated as fixed, when agents compare alternative environments (i.e. myopic agents). The interest of this approach is twofold. On the one hand, it allows us to analyze the efficiency of equilibrium allocations with fewer informational requirements. On the other hand, it remains closer to the notion of competitive and Lindahl equilibria and also permits several models to be encompassed within one common framework, as will be illustrated later on.[2]

The rest of the chapter proceeds as follows. Section 10.2 presents the model of a conditionally convex economy. We consider an economy with an abstract set Z of public environments lacking any formal structure. Agents' choice sets and payoff functions are defined conditional on the public environment in such a way that, for each given z in Z, there is a standard convex economy in the subspace of private commodities. Agents' choices are also affected by a *tax system* that modifies net profits and budget sets depending on the public environment. In order to make the model less abstract, we assume that consumers' wealth mappings correspond to that of a private ownership economy (the worth of their initial endowments plus the profits from their shares in firms), modified by the tax system.

Section 10.3 analyzes the welfare properties of public competitive equilibria, using an extension of Foley's definition. We show that every public competitive equilibrium is Pareto optimal, provided consumers are not satiated and aggregate taxes offset aggregate subsidies. We also show that every efficient allocation can be decentralized as a public competitive equilibrium, provided the conditional economy resulting from fixing a public environment is convex.

Section 10.4 turns towards the Lindahl approach, and looks for a simple generalization to economies with many private goods of those results due to Mas-Colell (1980) which characterize Pareto efficient allocations as valuation equilibria. Our main results are: (i) A valuation equilibrium is Pareto optimal (provided the tax system is balanced); (ii) Every Pareto optimal allocation can be decentralized as a valuation equilibrium; and (iii) Every valuation equilibrium yields a core allocation, provided the tax system does not allow for intercoalitional transfers.

Finally, section 10.5 illustrates these equilibrium notions by means of some examples.

---

[2]This does not mean that the case of sophisticated consumers is uninteresting. On the contrary, if there are significant nonconvexities in the provision of public goods, changes in the public environment may induce substantial changes in the prices of private goods that should not be neglected. This analysis has been developed in Hammond & Villar (1998).

10.2   The model

Consider an economy with ℓ private commodities. The vector $\omega \in \mathbb{R}^\ell$ represents the aggregate initial endowments of private goods. There is an abstract set $\mathbf{Z}$ whose members are vectors of those variables defining the *public environment*. Each agent's feasible set and payoff function may be affected by the values taken by these vectors $\mathbf{z} \in \mathbf{Z}$. No particular structure will be postulated on the set $\mathbf{Z}$. We assume that there is some kind of public agency or *public sector* that can determine these variables and/or affect consumers' budget sets and firms' profit functions via taxes and subsidies. Even though the tax system itself can be thought of as part of the public environment, we find it more convenient to treat these variables separately. For the sake of generality, agents' feasible sets will be defined as subsets of $\mathbb{R}^\ell \times \mathbf{Z}$ (where $\mathbb{R}^\ell$ stands for the commodity space and $\mathbf{Z}$ for the public environment space), even though they may actually be independent of many of the variables in $\mathbf{Z}$. A point $\mathbf{p} \in \mathbb{R}^\ell_+$ is a *price vector* relative to private commodities.

There are n firms in the economy. Let $Y_j \subset \mathbb{R}^\ell \times \mathbf{Z}$ be the jth firm's production set, and denote by $Y_j(\mathbf{z})$ the jth firm's **conditional production set** when the environment variables take the value $\mathbf{z} \in \mathbf{Z}$. That is,

$$Y_j(\mathbf{z}) = \{\mathbf{y}_j \in \mathbb{R}^\ell \ / \ (\mathbf{y}_j, \mathbf{z}) \in Y_j\}$$

For each firm $j = 1, 2, ..., n$, the mapping $\sigma_j : \mathbb{R}^\ell_+ \times \mathbf{Z} \to \mathbb{R}$ is assumed to represent the net subsidy this firm receives (or, if negative, pays as taxes), as a function of prevailing prices and the value of the environment variables. Thus for each given $(\mathbf{p}, \mathbf{z})$ in $\mathbb{R}^\ell_+ \times \mathbf{Z}$, the jth firm's conditional profits are given by $\pi_j(\mathbf{p}, \mathbf{z}) = \sup\{\mathbf{p}\mathbf{y}_j + \sigma_j(\mathbf{p}, \mathbf{z}) \ / \ \mathbf{y}_j \in Y_j(\mathbf{z})\}$. In equilibrium this supremum should be attained. This implies that, for each given $(\mathbf{p}, \mathbf{z})$ in $\mathbb{R}^\ell_+ \times \mathbf{Z}$, the jth firm selects a production plan $\mathbf{y}_j(\mathbf{p}, \mathbf{z})$ that maximizes (conditional) profits.

There are m consumers. The ith consumer is characterized by the collection $[X_i, u_i, \omega_i, (\theta_{ij})]$, where $X_i \subset \mathbb{R}^\ell \times \mathbf{Z}$, $u_i : X_i \to \mathbb{R}$, $\omega_i \in \mathbb{R}^\ell$ denote the consumption set, utility function and initial endowments, respectively, and θ_{ij} stands for the ith consumer's share in the jth firm's profits. By definition, $0 \leq \theta_{ij} \leq 1$, and $\sum_{j=1}^n \theta_{ij} = 1$, for all i, j. For a given point $\mathbf{z} \in \mathbf{Z}$ the ith consumer's **conditional consumption set** is given by:

$$X_i(\mathbf{z}) = \{\mathbf{x}_i \in \mathbb{R}^\ell \ / \ (\mathbf{x}_i, \mathbf{z}) \in X_i\}.$$

Evidently, a preference ordering is induced on each of these conditional sets, which can be described by a conditional utility function $u_i^z : X_i(\mathbf{z}) \to \mathbb{R}$ given by $u_i^z(\mathbf{x}_i) = u_i(\mathbf{x}_i, \mathbf{z})$.

A mapping $\tau_i : \mathbb{R}^\ell_+ \times \mathbf{Z} \to \mathbb{R}$, for $i = 1, 2, ..., m$, describes the ith consumer's (net) tax mapping. Given a pair $(\mathbf{p}, \mathbf{z}) \in \mathbb{R}^\ell_+ \times \mathbf{Z}$, the ith consumer's behaviour $\mathbf{x}_i(\mathbf{p}, \mathbf{z})$ is obtained by solving the following program:

$$\left. \begin{array}{rl} Max & u_i^z \\ s.t. & \mathbf{x}_i \in X_i(\mathbf{z}) \\ & \mathbf{p}\mathbf{x}_i \leq \mathbf{p}\omega_i + \sum_{j=1}^n \theta_{ij}\pi_j(\mathbf{p}, \mathbf{z}) + \tau_i(\mathbf{p}, \mathbf{z}) \end{array} \right\}$$

Consider now the following definitions. The first makes precise the notion of a tax system, whereas the second specifies a relevant restriction:

Definition 10.1 *A **tax system** is a collection of mappings $T = [(\sigma_j)_{j=1}^n, (\tau_i)_{i=1}^m]$, where each σ_j and τ_i is a function from $\mathbb{R}^\ell_+ \times \mathbf{Z}$ into $\mathbb{R}$, and such that for every pair $(\mathbf{p}, \mathbf{z}) \in \mathbb{R}^\ell_+ \times \mathbf{Z}$ one has $\sum_{j=1}^n \sigma_j(\mathbf{p}, \mathbf{z}) + \sum_{i=1}^m \tau_i(\mathbf{p}, \mathbf{z}) \leq 0$.*

Definition 10.2 *A tax system T is **balanced** if for any pair $(\mathbf{p}, \mathbf{z}) \in \mathbb{R}^\ell_+ \times \mathbf{Z}$ one has $\sum_{j=1}^n \sigma_j(\mathbf{p}, \mathbf{z}) + \sum_{i=1}^m \tau_i(\mathbf{p}, \mathbf{z}) = 0$.*

A tax system is a collection of functions from $\mathbb{R}^\ell_+ \times \mathbf{Z}$ into $\mathbb{R}$ such that aggregate subsidies do not exceed aggregate taxes. This amounts to saying that the economy is *financially viable* in the sense that the tax system cannot rely on resources from outside. Note that this definition is very general as it can depend on many variables apart from private income and gross profits. A tax system is balanced whenever aggregate taxes equal aggregate subsidies (e.g. a cost-share system). Note that balancedness ensures that Walras Law $\mathbf{p}[\sum_{i=1}^m \mathbf{x}_i(\mathbf{p}, \mathbf{z}) - \sum_{i=1}^m \omega_i - \sum_{j=1}^n \mathbf{y}_j(\mathbf{p}, \mathbf{z})] = 0$ holds, provided consumers are not satiated.

We shall denote by T^0 the degenerate balanced tax system given by $\sigma_j(\mathbf{p}, \mathbf{z}) = \tau_i(\mathbf{p}, \mathbf{z}) = 0$, for all i, j, every $(\mathbf{p}, \mathbf{z})$ in $\mathbb{R}^\ell_+ \times \mathbf{Z}$.

In some cases (in particular when dealing with public competitive equilibria), the tax system can be given a simpler representation. Namely, a pair of vectors $(\mathbf{s}, \mathbf{t})$, where $\mathbf{s} = (s_j)_{j=1}^n$ is a vector of subsidies for producers, and $\mathbf{t} = (t_i)_{i=1}^m$ a vector of taxes on consumers.

Consider now the following definition:

Definition 10.3 *A **private competitive equilibrium**, relative to an environment $\mathbf{z}$ and a tax system $[(\sigma_j)_{j=1}^n, (\tau_i)_{i=1}^m]$, is a price vector $\mathbf{p}^*$ in $\mathbb{R}^\ell_+$, and an allocation $[(\mathbf{x}_i^*), (\mathbf{y}_j^*)]$ in $\prod_{i=1}^m X_i(\mathbf{z}) \times \prod_{j=1}^n Y_j(\mathbf{z})$ such that:*
(i) For all $i = 1, 2, ..., m$, $\mathbf{x}_i^*$ maximizes u_i over the set of points $\mathbf{x}_i \in X_i(\mathbf{z})$ that satisfy $\mathbf{p}^*\mathbf{x}_i \leq \mathbf{p}^*\omega_i + \sum_{j=1}^n \theta_{ij}\pi_j(\mathbf{p}^*, \mathbf{z}) + \tau_i(\mathbf{p}^*, \mathbf{z})$.
(ii) For all $j = 1, 2, ..., n$, $\mathbf{p}^*\mathbf{y}_j^* + \sigma_j(\mathbf{p}^*, \mathbf{z}) \geq \mathbf{p}^*\mathbf{y}_j + \sigma_j(\mathbf{p}^*, \mathbf{z})$ for all $\mathbf{y}_j \in Y_j(\mathbf{z})$.

(iii) $\sum_{i=1}^{m} \mathbf{x}_i^* - \sum_{i=1}^{m} \omega_i = \sum_{j=1}^{n} \mathbf{y}_j^*.$
(iv) $\sum_{j=1}^{n} \sigma_j(\mathbf{p}^*, \mathbf{z}) + \sum_{i=1}^{m} \tau_i(\mathbf{p}^*, \mathbf{z}) = 0.$

That is, a private competitive equilibrium relative to $\{\mathbf{z}, [(\sigma_j)_{j=1}^{n}, (\tau_i)_{i=1}^{m}]\}$, is a competitive equilibrium of the conditional economy resulting from the environment $\mathbf{z}$, with the transfers induced by the tax system.[3]

Consider now the following axioms:

Axiom 10.1 *For every $i = 1, 2, ..., m$ and every $\mathbf{z} \in \mathbf{Z}$:*
(i) $X_i(\mathbf{z})$ is a non-empty, closed and convex subset of $\mathbb{R}^{\ell}$, bounded from below.
(ii) $u_i^z : X_i(\mathbf{z}) \rightarrow \mathbb{R}$ is continuous, quasi-concave$^+$, and satisfies non-satiation.

Axiom 10.2 *For every $j = 1, 2, ..., m$ and each $\mathbf{z} \in \mathbf{Z}$, the set $Y_j(\mathbf{z})$ is closed and convex in $\mathbb{R}^{\ell}$, with $Y_j(\mathbf{z}) \cap \mathbb{R}_+^{\ell} = \{0\}$, and $Y_j(\mathbf{z}) - \mathbb{R}_+^{\ell} \subset Y_j(\mathbf{z})$.*

Axioms 10.1 and 10.2 essentially say that, for any given value of the public environment, the resulting conditional economy is standard. Note that this is compatible with the presence of non-convexities and that we allow public goods to affect both production and consumption possibilities.

Observe that these assumptions involve no restriction on the set $\mathbf{Z}$ whose members may therefore contain all kind of variables.

The preceding analysis on the existence of equilibrium, developed in chapter 4, permits us to establish:

Claim 10.1 *Under axioms 10.1 and 10.2, let $\mathbf{z} \in \mathbf{Z}$ be given. Suppose furthermore that $T = [(\sigma_j)_{j=1}^{n}, (\tau_i)_{i=1}^{m}]$ is a balanced tax system, with all σ_j, all τ_i being continuous functions of $\mathbf{p}$, and that consumers' wealth mappings (including the taxes on consumers and firms) verify the cheaper point requirement. Then, there exists a private competitive equilibrium relative to $(\mathbf{z}, T)$. Moreover, the resulting allocation is efficient relative to the environment $\mathbf{z}$, that is, there is no allocation $[(\mathbf{x}_i')_{i=1}^{m}, (\mathbf{y}_j')_{j=1}^{n}, \mathbf{z}]$, with $\mathbf{z}$ fixed, which is both feasible and Pareto superior. Yet this does not ensure unconditional Pareto optimality.*

10.3   Public competitive equilibrium

Let us apply to this context the Wicksell-Foley approach to the provision of public goods. First, we define a **public sector proposal** $[\hat{\mathbf{z}}, (\hat{\mathbf{s}}, \hat{\mathbf{t}})]$ as a

---

[3]Note that $\mathbf{p}^* \mathbf{y}_j^* + \sigma_j(\mathbf{p}^*, \mathbf{z}) \geq \mathbf{p}^* \mathbf{y}_j + \sigma_j(\mathbf{p}^*, \mathbf{z})$ if and only if $\mathbf{p}^* \mathbf{y}_j^* \geq \mathbf{p}^* \mathbf{y}_j$.

collection consisting of a public environment $\widehat{\mathbf{z}} \in \mathbf{Z}$, together with a vector of taxes $\widehat{\mathbf{t}} = (\widehat{t}_i)_{i=1}^m$ on consumers and a vector of subsidies $\widehat{\mathbf{s}} = (\widehat{s}_j)_{j=1}^n$ for producers, such that $\sum_{i=1}^m \widehat{t}_i + \sum_{j=1}^n \widehat{s}_j = 0$. This simply means that the public sector proposal must be balanced.

Definition 10.4 *A public competitive equilibrium is a price vector* $\mathbf{p}^*$ *in* $\mathbb{R}_+^\ell$, *an environment* $\mathbf{z}^* \in \mathbf{Z}$, *a vector of taxes* $\mathbf{t}^*$ *on consumers, a vector of subsidies* $\mathbf{s}^*$ *for producers, and an allocation* $[(\mathbf{x}_i^*)_{i=1}^m, (\mathbf{y}_j^*)_{j=1}^n]$ *in* $\prod_{i=1}^m X_i(\mathbf{z}^*) \times \prod_{j=1}^n Y_j(\mathbf{z}^*)$, *such that:*

(i) $[\mathbf{p}^*, (\mathbf{x}_i^*)_{i=1}^m, (\mathbf{y}_j^*)_{j=1}^n]$ *is private competitive equilibrium relative to* $[\mathbf{z}^*, (\mathbf{s}^*, \mathbf{t}^*)]$.

(ii) There is no alternative public sector proposal $(\widehat{\mathbf{z}}, \widehat{T})$ *such that:*

(a) For all $i = 1, 2, ..., m$, *there exists* $\mathbf{x}_i \in X_i(\widehat{\mathbf{z}})$ *with* $u_i(\mathbf{x}_i, \widehat{\mathbf{z}}) \geq u_i(\mathbf{x}_i^*, \mathbf{z}^*)$ *for all* i, *with a strict inequality for some agent, satisfying the budget restriction* $\mathbf{p}^* \mathbf{x}_i \leq \mathbf{p}^* \omega_i + \sum_{j=1}^n \theta_{ij} \pi_j(\mathbf{p}^*, \widehat{\mathbf{z}}) + \widehat{t}_i$.

(b) For all $j = 1, 2, ..., n$, *there exists* $\mathbf{y}_j \in Y_j(\widehat{\mathbf{z}})$, *with* $\mathbf{p}^* \mathbf{y}_j + \widehat{s}_j \geq \mathbf{p}^* \mathbf{y}_j^* + s_j^*$.

According to (ii), therefore, there can be no alternative public sector proposal, including the taxes needed to finance the altered production of public goods, which allows all consumers to reach preferred allocations within their respective budget sets, while also allowing each private firm to make no less profit after adjusting the net subsidy. Hence, the public sector proposal cannot be amended in a way which is unanimously approved by all consumers and producers. As Foley admits, this definition leaves open the question of the precise political process which underlies the choice among the many public sector proposals which are feasible and not subject to amendment. The only assumption about the process is that amendments will be made repeatedly until no further amendment which everybody favours can be found.

The following results are obtained:

Theorem 10.1 *Let* $[\mathbf{p}^*, (\mathbf{x}_i^*)_{i=1}^m, (\mathbf{y}_j^*)_{j=1}^n, \mathbf{z}^*, (\mathbf{s}^*, \mathbf{t}^*)]$ *be a public competitive equilibrium, and suppose that consumers are locally non-satiated. Then, the resulting allocation is Pareto optimal.*

Proof. Suppose that there exists an alternative environment $\widehat{\mathbf{z}}$ and an associated feasible allocation $[(\mathbf{x}_i')_{i=1}^m, (\mathbf{y}_j')_{j=1}^n] \in \prod_{i=1}^m X_i(\widehat{\mathbf{z}}) \times \prod_{j=1}^n Y_j(\widehat{\mathbf{z}})$, such that $u_i(\mathbf{x}_i', \widehat{\mathbf{z}}) \geq u_i(\mathbf{x}_i^*, \mathbf{z}^*)$ for all i, with a strict inequality for some agent. Let now $\widehat{t}_i = t_i^* - \mathbf{p}^*(\mathbf{x}_i^* - \mathbf{x}_i')$, for all i, and $\widehat{s}_j = s_j^* + \mathbf{p}^*(\mathbf{y}_j^* - \mathbf{y}_j')$, for all j. It follows that:

$$\sum_{i=1}^m \widehat{t}_i + \sum_{j=1}^n \widehat{s}_j = \sum_{i=1}^m [t_i^* - \mathbf{p}^*(\mathbf{x}_i^* - \mathbf{x}_i')] + \sum_{j=1}^n [s_j^* + \mathbf{p}^*(\mathbf{y}_j^* - \mathbf{y}_j')]$$
$$= \left[\sum_{i=1}^m \mathbf{p}^* \mathbf{x}_i' - \sum_{j=1}^n \mathbf{p}^* \mathbf{y}_j' \right] - \sum_{i=1}^m \left[\mathbf{p}^* \mathbf{x}_i^* - \sum_{j=1}^n \mathbf{p}^* \mathbf{y}_j^* \right]$$

$$= \left[\sum_{i=1}^{m} \mathbf{p}^* \mathbf{x}_i' - \sum_{j=1}^{n} \mathbf{p}^* \mathbf{y}_j' \right] - \mathbf{p}^* \omega = 0.$$

The last equality derives from the fact that $[(\mathbf{x}_i'), (\mathbf{y}_j')]$ is a feasible allocation. Therefore, we have found a public sector proposal $[\hat{\mathbf{z}}, (\hat{\mathbf{s}}, \hat{\mathbf{t}})]$ that makes all agents better off, contradicting the assumption that $[\mathbf{p}^*, (\mathbf{x}_i^*)_{i=1}^{m}, (\mathbf{y}_j^*)_{j=1}^{n}, \mathbf{z}^*,$ $(\mathbf{s}^*, \mathbf{t}^*)]$ is a public competitive equilibrium. This proves that these equilibria yield efficient allocations. $\boxed{\text{Q.e.d.}}$

Theorem 10.2 *Under axioms 10.1 and 10.2, let* $[(\mathbf{x}_i^*)_{i=1}^{m}, (\mathbf{y}_j^*)_{j=1}^{n}, \mathbf{z}^*]$ *be a Pareto optimal allocation, with* $\mathbf{x}_i^* \in intX_i(\mathbf{z}^*)$ *for all* i. *Then, there exist a price vector* $\mathbf{p}^* \in \mathbb{R}_+^{\ell} - \{\mathbf{0}\}$ *and taxes* $(\mathbf{s}^*, \mathbf{t}^*)$ *such that* $[\mathbf{p}^*, (\mathbf{x}_i^*)_{i=1}^{m}, (\mathbf{y}_j^*)_{j=1}^{n},$ $\mathbf{z}^*, (\mathbf{s}^*, \mathbf{t}^*)]$ *is a public competitive equilibrium.*

   Proof. We know that given $\mathbf{z}^*$, the resulting conditional economy is a standard convex economy. Therefore we can apply the conventional argument to show that there exists $\mathbf{p}^* \in \mathbb{R}_+^{\ell} - \{\mathbf{0}\}$, such that $[\mathbf{p}^*, (\mathbf{x}_i^*)_{i=1}^{m}, (\mathbf{y}_j^*)_{j=1}^{n}, \mathbf{z}^*,$ $(\mathbf{0}, \mathbf{0})]$ is a private competitive equilibrium relative to $[\mathbf{z}^*, (\mathbf{0}, \mathbf{0})]$, where $(\mathbf{0}, \mathbf{0})$ is the degenerate tax system with $s_j^* = t_i^* = 0$, for all j, i.

   As $[(\mathbf{x}_i^*, \mathbf{z}^*)_{i=1}^{m}, (\mathbf{y}_j^*, \mathbf{z}^*)_{j=1}^{n}]$ is a Pareto optimal allocation, we cannot find an alternative feasible allocation in which all consumers are better off. Hence, $[\mathbf{p}^*, (\mathbf{x}_i^*)_{i=1}^{m}, (\mathbf{y}_j^*)_{j=1}^{n}, \mathbf{z}^*, (\mathbf{0}, \mathbf{0})]$ is actually a public competitive equilibrium. $\boxed{\text{Q.e.d.}}$

   These two theorems are the counterparts of the standard welfare theorems in the context of a conditionally convex economy, where the choice of the environment is considered as a public choice problem.

10.4   Valuation equilibrium

We take up next the Lindahlian approach to the provision of public goods, applied to our reference model. Here the tax system is defined in its full generality, for reasons that will be clear along the discussion.

   The following defines the equilibrium notion, which is reminiscent of the modern version of Lindahl's equilibrium:

Definition 10.5 *A **valuation equilibrium** is a price vector* $\mathbf{p}^*$ *in* $\mathbb{R}_+^{\ell}$, *an environment* $\mathbf{z}^* \in \mathbf{Z}$, *a tax system* $T^* = [(\sigma_j)_{j=1}^{n}, (\tau_i)_{i=1}^{m}]$, *and an allocation* $[(\mathbf{x}_i^*)_{i=1}^{m}, (\mathbf{y}_j^*)_{j=1}^{n}]$ *in* $\prod_{i=1}^{m} X_i(\mathbf{z}^*) \times \prod_{j=1}^{n} Y_j(\mathbf{z}^*)$, *such that:*
(i) For all $i = 1, 2, ..., m$, $(\mathbf{x}_i^*, \mathbf{z}^*)$ *maximizes* u_i *over the set of points* $(\mathbf{x}_i, \mathbf{z})$ *in* X_i *that satisfy* $\mathbf{p}^* \mathbf{x}_i \leq \mathbf{p}^* \omega_i + \sum_{j=1}^{n} \theta_{ij} \pi_j(\mathbf{p}^*, \mathbf{z}^*) + \tau_i(\mathbf{p}^*, \mathbf{z})$.

(ii) For all $j = 1, 2, ..., n$, $\mathbf{p}^*\mathbf{y}_j^* + \sigma_j(\mathbf{p}^*, \mathbf{z}^*) \geq \mathbf{p}^*\mathbf{y}_j + \sigma_j(\mathbf{p}^*, \mathbf{z})$ for all $(\mathbf{y}_j, \mathbf{z}) \in Y_j$.

(iii) $\sum_{i=1}^m \mathbf{x}_i^* - \sum_{i=1}^m \omega_i = \sum_{j=1}^n \mathbf{y}_j^*$.

(iv) $\sum_{j=1}^n \sigma_j(\mathbf{p}^*, \mathbf{z}^*) + \sum_{i=1}^m \tau_i(\mathbf{p}^*, \mathbf{z}^*) = 0$.

That is, a valuation equilibrium is a price vector, a tax system and a feasible allocation such that no agent finds it individually beneficial to choose an alternative allocation that is affordable at given prices. Note that we assume that every consumer computes her budget by taking prices of private commodities and firms' profits as given (she only allows for changes in the public environment through the effect on her own taxes).[4] Also observe that, in equilibrium, aggregate taxes equal aggregate subsidies. Indeed, the tax system can often be interpreted as an incentive scheme that sustains the equilibrium environment, so that we can picture the situation as agents choosing the environment and the public sector choosing the incentive scheme.

When utility maximization is relaxed to expenditure minimization one gets the standard notion of *compensated* equilibrium, which will be used in order to discuss the second welfare theorem.

Definition 10.6 *A **compensated valuation equilibrium** is defined like a valuation equilibrium except that condition (i) is replaced by:*

(i') For every $i = 1, 2, ..., m$, $\mathbf{p}^*\mathbf{x}_i^* \leq \mathbf{p}^*\omega_i + \sum_{j=1}^n \theta_{ij}\pi_j(\mathbf{p}^*, \mathbf{z}^*) + \tau_i(\mathbf{p}^*, \mathbf{z}^*)$ and $\mathbf{p}^*\mathbf{x}_i \geq \mathbf{p}^*\omega_i + \sum_{j=1}^n \theta_{ij}\pi_j(\mathbf{p}^*, \mathbf{z}^*) + \tau_i(\mathbf{p}^*, \mathbf{z})$ whenever $(\mathbf{x}_i, \mathbf{z}) \in X_i$ with $u_i(\mathbf{x}_i, \mathbf{z}) \geq u_i(\mathbf{x}_i^*, \mathbf{z}^*)$.

The first result says that a valuation equilibrium is Pareto optimal, provided the tax system is balanced. The second establishes that any Pareto efficient allocation can be decentralized as a compensated valuation equilibrium. Finally, it will be shown that a valuation equilibrium is in the core, provided that inter-coalitional transfers are excluded.

Theorem 10.3 *Let $[\mathbf{p}^*, (\mathbf{x}_i^*)_{i=1}^m, (\mathbf{y}_j^*)_{j=1}^n, \mathbf{z}^*, T^*]$ be a valuation equilibrium, and suppose that consumers are locally non-satiated. If T^* is a balanced tax system the resulting allocation is Pareto optimal.*

Proof. Let $[\mathbf{p}^*, (\mathbf{x}_i^*)_{i=1}^m, (\mathbf{y}_j^*)_{j=1}^n, \mathbf{z}^*, T^*]$ be a valuation equilibrium, and suppose that $[(\mathbf{x}_i)_{i=1}^m, (\mathbf{y}_j)_{j=1}^n, \mathbf{z}]$ together satisfy $\mathbf{x}_i \in X_i(\mathbf{z})$ and $u_i(\mathbf{x}_i, \mathbf{z}) \geq u_i(\mathbf{x}_i^*, \mathbf{z}^*)$ for all i, with strict inequality for at least one agent, and $\mathbf{y}_j \in Y_j(\mathbf{z})$.

---

[4]It can be easily shown that the results in this section remain valid if we consider that consumers are more sophisticated, and can also compute the effect on their budget constraint of changes in firm's profits due to the tax system.

Then local non-satiation and the definition of valuation equilibrium imply that:

$$\sum_{i=1}^{m} \mathbf{p}^* \mathbf{x}_i > \mathbf{p}^* \omega + \sum_{j=1}^{n} \left[\mathbf{p}^* \mathbf{y}_j^* + \sigma_j(\mathbf{p}^*, \mathbf{z}^*) \right] + \sum_{i=1}^{m} \tau_i(\mathbf{p}^*, \mathbf{z})$$

and also that $\sum_{j=1}^{n} \mathbf{p}^* \mathbf{y}_j^* + \sum_{j=1}^{n} \sigma_j(\mathbf{p}^*, \mathbf{z}^*) \geq \sum_{j=1}^{n} \mathbf{p}^* \mathbf{y}_j + \sum_{j=1}^{n} \sigma_j(\mathbf{p}^*, \mathbf{z})$. These inequalities imply that

$$\sum_{i=1}^{m} \mathbf{p}^* \mathbf{x}_i > \mathbf{p}^* \omega + \sum_{j=1}^{n} \mathbf{p}^* \mathbf{y}_j + \sum_{j=1}^{n} \sigma_j(\mathbf{p}^*, \mathbf{z}) + \sum_{i=1}^{m} \tau_i(\mathbf{p}^*, \mathbf{z})$$

But T^* is balanced by assumption, so $[\sum_{j=1}^{n} \sigma_j(\mathbf{p}^*, \mathbf{z}) + \sum_{i=1}^{m} \tau_i(\mathbf{p}^*, \mathbf{z})] = 0$. Hence $\sum_{i=1}^{m} \mathbf{p}^* \mathbf{x}_i > \mathbf{p}^* \omega + \sum_{j=1}^{n} \mathbf{p}^* \mathbf{y}_j$, which implies that $[(\mathbf{x}_i), (\mathbf{y}_j), \mathbf{z}]$ cannot be a feasible allocation satisfying $\sum_{i=1}^{m} \mathbf{x}_i \leq \omega + \sum_{j=1}^{n} \mathbf{y}_j$. It follows that no feasible allocation can be Pareto superior. $\boxed{\text{Q.e.d.}}$

Observe that an allocation may fail to be optimal if we drop balancedness. Indeed it is easy to produce a tax system that induces a waste of resources *in* equilibrium and an even greater waste *out* of equilibrium (e.g., the tax system rewards a firm which destroys part of the initial endowments).

Remark 10.1 *It follows from this theorem that, in a valuation equilibrium, the tax system cannot be arbitrary once we put some structure on the set $\mathbf{Z}$. This is because, besides balancedness, the first-order necessary conditions for efficiency must be satisfied in equilibrium. Informally, one can say that consumers' taxes should be equivalent to a non-linear system of Lindahl prices.*

We can prove now:

Theorem 10.4 *Under assumptions 10.1 and 10.2, let $[(\mathbf{x}_i^*)_{i=1}^{m}, (\mathbf{y}_j^*)_{j=1}^{n}, \mathbf{z}^*]$ be a Pareto optimal allocation. Then, there exist a price vector $\mathbf{p}^* \in \mathbb{R}_+^{\ell} - \{\mathbf{0}\}$ and a tax system T^* such that $[\mathbf{p}^*, (\mathbf{x}_i^*)_{i=1}^{m}, (\mathbf{y}_j^*)_{j=1}^{n}, \mathbf{z}^*, T^*]$ is a compensated valuation equilibrium.*

Proof. Take $\mathbf{z}^*$ as given and apply the standard second welfare theorem to the allocation $[(\mathbf{x}_i^*)_{i=1}^{m}, (\mathbf{y}_j^*)_{j=1}^{n}]$ in the resulting convex conditional economy. This theorem ensures the existence of a price vector $\mathbf{p}^* \in \mathbb{R}_+^{\ell} - \{\mathbf{0}\}$ such that $[\mathbf{p}^*, (\mathbf{x}_i^*)_{i=1}^{m}, (\mathbf{y}_j^*)_{j=1}^{n}]$ is a competitive equilibrium relative to the conditional economy resulting from $\mathbf{z}^*$. It will be shown that $[\mathbf{p}^*, (\mathbf{x}_i^*)_{i=1}^{m}, (\mathbf{y}_j^*)_{j=1}^{n}, \mathbf{z}^*, T^*]$ is a valuation equilibrium for a tax system T^*. This requires checking parts (i), (ii) and (iv) of definition 10.5, part (iii) being satisfied by construction.

Define

$$\sigma_j(\mathbf{p}^*, \mathbf{z}) = \inf\{0, \ \mathbf{p}^*\mathbf{y}_j^* - \pi_j(\mathbf{p}^*, \mathbf{z})\}$$

Note that $\sigma_j(\mathbf{p}^*, \mathbf{z}^*) = 0$ because $\pi_j(\mathbf{p}^*, \mathbf{z}^*) = \mathbf{p}^*\mathbf{y}_j^*$. Also, if $(\mathbf{y}_j', \mathbf{z}') \in Y_j$ then:

$$\mathbf{p}^*\mathbf{y}_j' + \sigma_j(\mathbf{p}^*, \mathbf{z}') \le \mathbf{p}^*\mathbf{y}_j' + \mathbf{p}^*\mathbf{y}_j^* - \pi_j(\mathbf{p}^*, \mathbf{z}') \le \mathbf{p}^*\mathbf{y}_j^* = \mathbf{p}^*\mathbf{y}_j^* + \sigma_j(\mathbf{p}^*, \mathbf{z}^*)$$

so that part (ii) of the definition is satisfied.

Taking $\mathbf{p}^*, (\mathbf{x}_i^*, \mathbf{z}^*)$ as given, define the compensation function:

$$E_i(\mathbf{z}) := \inf\{\mathbf{p}^*\mathbf{x}_i \ / \ \mathbf{x}_i \in X_i(\mathbf{z}) \ and \ u_i(\mathbf{x}_i, \mathbf{z}) \ge u_i(\mathbf{x}_i^*, \mathbf{z}^*)\}$$

This is the income that individual i needs to spend on private goods in order to be no worse off than at $(\mathbf{x}_i^*, \mathbf{z}^*)$, when the environment changes to $\mathbf{z}$ and prices are $\mathbf{p}^*$. Now let

$$\tau_i(\mathbf{p}^*, \mathbf{z}) = \min\{0, \ E_i(\mathbf{z}) - \mathbf{p}^*\mathbf{x}_i^*\}$$

By construction, these σ_j, τ_i constitute a tax system, with $\sigma_j(\mathbf{p}^*, \mathbf{z}^*) = \tau_i(\mathbf{p}^*, \mathbf{z}^*) = 0$, for all j, i. In particular, part (iv) of the definition is satisfied.

Finally, take a consumer i and a consumption plan $(\mathbf{x}_i, \mathbf{z}) \in X_i$ such that $u_i(\mathbf{x}_i, \mathbf{z}) \ge u_i(\mathbf{x}_i^*, \mathbf{z}^*)$. Then, $\mathbf{p}^*\mathbf{x}_i - \tau_i(\mathbf{p}^*, \mathbf{z}) \ge \mathbf{p}^*\mathbf{x}_i + \mathbf{p}^*\mathbf{x}_i^* - E_i(\mathbf{z}) \ge \mathbf{p}^*\mathbf{x}_i^*$, which implies that:[5]

$$\mathbf{p}^*\mathbf{x}_i \ge \mathbf{p}^*\omega_i + \sum_{j=1}^{n} \theta_{ij}^*\pi_j(\mathbf{p}^*, \mathbf{z}^*) + \tau_i(\mathbf{p}^*, \mathbf{z})$$

Thus part (i') of the definition of compensated valuation equilibrium is also satisfied and the proof is complete. $\boxed{\textbf{Q.e.d.}}$

Theorem 10.4 tells us that any efficient allocation can be decentralized as a compensated valuation equilibrium. It also tells us that a compensated valuation equilibrium *with transfers* exists, provided that there is at least one Pareto efficient allocation.

Observe that the tax system has been given an explicit form, which has an easy and sensible interpretation. Each $\sigma_j(\mathbf{p}^*, \mathbf{z})$ tells us the tax paid by the jth firm if the environment changes from $\mathbf{z}^*$ to $\mathbf{z}$. It is equal to the firm's change in profits. Similarly, every $\tau_i(\mathbf{p}^*, \mathbf{z})$ specifies the net amount that the ith consumer will have to pay, if the environment is changed from $\mathbf{z}^*$ to $\mathbf{z}$. It

---

[5]The scalars θ_{ij}^* correspond here to a distribution of profits determined by the separation argument.

is equal to the equivalent variation in the sense of Hicks. Moreover, it follows that $\sigma_j(\mathbf{p}^*, \mathbf{z}^*) = \tau_i(\mathbf{p}^*, \mathbf{z}^*) = 0$, for all i, j.

Remark 10.2 *A standard argument shows that the compensated valuation equilibrium of Theorem 10.4 is also a valuation equilibrium provided that, whenever* $(\mathbf{x}_i, \mathbf{z}) \in X_i$ *satisfies* $u_i(\mathbf{x}_i, \mathbf{z}) > u_i(\mathbf{x}_i^*, \mathbf{z}^*)$, *there exists a cheaper point* $\underline{\mathbf{x}}_i \in X_i(\mathbf{z})$ *for which* $\mathbf{p}^* \underline{\mathbf{x}}_i < E_i(\mathbf{z})$. *This can be ensured by means of the "essentiality condition" that appears in Mas-Colell (1980, p. 626), Mas-Colell & Silvestre (1989, p. 250), or Diamantaras & Gilles (1996, p. 855).*

Our last result refers to the core, defined as follows:

Definition 10.7 *A feasible allocation* $[(\mathbf{x}_i), (\mathbf{y}_j), \mathbf{z}]$ *is in the* **core** *if there is no coalition* $S \subset M = \{1, 2, ..., m\}$, *with an allocation* $[(\mathbf{x}_i'), (\mathbf{y}_j'), \mathbf{z}']$, *such that:*
(i) $\sum_{i \in S} \left(\mathbf{x}_i' - \omega_i - \sum_{j=1}^n \theta_{ij} \mathbf{y}_j' \right) = 0$.
(ii) $u_i(\mathbf{x}_i', \mathbf{z}') \geq u_i(\mathbf{x}_i, \mathbf{z}), \forall i \in S$, *with a strict inequality for some agent in* S.

A core allocation is thus one in which no coalition can re-arrange the economy, using its own resources, so that the resulting allocation is preferred by all its members. Observe that profit shares are being interpreted here as production shares (as usual when positive profits are possible).

The following definition helps characterize the tax systems which yield valuation equilibria in the core.

Definition 10.8 *Let* $Q^* = [\mathbf{p}^*, (\mathbf{x}_i^*)_{i=1}^m, (\mathbf{y}_j^*)_{j=1}^n, \mathbf{z}^*, T^*]$ *be a valuation equilibrium. Say that* T^* *satisfies the* **no-transfer condition** *relative to* Q^* *if, for any coalition* $S \subset M$ *and each* $\mathbf{z} \in \mathbf{Z}$, *one has*

$$\sum_{i \in S} \left[\sum_{j=1}^n \theta_{ij} \sigma_j(\mathbf{p}^*, \mathbf{z}) + \tau_i(\mathbf{p}^*, \mathbf{z}) \right] = 0.$$

The no-transfer condition relative to a valuation equilibrium Q^* tells us that the restriction of T^* over any coalition corresponds to a balanced tax system. To understand better the extent of this requirement it is worth thinking of the set $\mathbf{Z}$ as containing all non-empty subsets of M, so that the tax system depends also on the coalition structure. Note that when there are neither taxes nor subsidies this condition is automatically satisfied. Another case in which this requirement holds is when the tax system is given by

$\tau_i(\mathbf{p}, \mathbf{z}) = -\sum_{j=1}^{n} \theta_{ij}\sigma_j(\mathbf{p}, \mathbf{z})$ for all i (each individual i's net tax is equal to i's share of the subsidies paid to the producers whose shares i holds).

The following result is obtained:

Theorem 10.5 *Let* $Q^* = [\mathbf{p}^*, (\mathbf{x}_i^*)_{i=1}^m, (\mathbf{y}_j^*)_{j=1}^n, \mathbf{z}^*, T^*]$ *be a valuation equilibrium. Suppose that consumers are locally non-satiated and that* T^* *satisfies the no-transfer condition relative to* Q^*. *Then, the resulting allocation is in the core.*

    Proof. For any $S \subset M$, consider any alternative allocation $[(\mathbf{x}_i')_{i=1}^m, (\mathbf{y}_j')_{j=1}^n, \mathbf{z}']$ satisfying (i) and (ii) of definition 10.7. From the definition of valuation equilibrium and the fact that preferences are locally non-satiated, it follows that

$$\mathbf{p}^*\mathbf{x}_i' \geq \mathbf{p}^*\omega_i + \sum_{j=1}^{n} \theta_{ij}[\mathbf{p}^*\mathbf{y}_j^* + \sigma_j(\mathbf{p}^*, \mathbf{z}^*)] + \tau_i(\mathbf{p}^*, \mathbf{z}') \qquad [1]$$

for all $i \in S$. Summing over S and making use of the non-transfer condition one gets:

$$\sum_{i \in S} \mathbf{p}^*\mathbf{x}_i' \geq \sum_{i \in S}[\mathbf{p}^*\omega_i + \sum_{j=1}^{n}\theta_{ij}\mathbf{p}^*\mathbf{y}_j^* + \sum_{j=1}^{n}\theta_{ij}\sigma_j(\mathbf{p}^*, \mathbf{z}^*) + \tau_i(\mathbf{p}^*, \mathbf{z}')]$$
$$\geq \sum_{i \in S}[\mathbf{p}^*\omega_i + \sum_{j=1}^{n}\theta_{ij}\mathbf{p}^*\mathbf{y}_j' + \sum_{j=1}^{n}\theta_{ij}\sigma_j(\mathbf{p}', \mathbf{z}') + \tau_i(\mathbf{p}^*, \mathbf{z}')]$$
$$= \sum_{i \in S}[\mathbf{p}^*\omega_i + \sum_{j=1}^{n}\theta_{ij}\mathbf{p}^*\mathbf{y}_j']$$

From (i) above it follows that both weak inequalities are equalities. Hence [1] also holds with equality for all $i \in S$. Because Q^* is a valuation equilibrium, $u_i(\mathbf{x}_i^*, \mathbf{z}^*) \geq u_i(\mathbf{x}_i', \mathbf{z}')$ for all $i \in S$. So S cannot be a blocking coalition. Hence, the resulting allocation is in the core. $\boxed{\text{Q.e.d.}}$

10.5 Examples

We present here some familiar models that can be interpreted as particular cases of public competitive and/or valuation equilibrium. Interestingly enough the existence of equilibrium is also guaranteed in these cases.

    Let us recall that we denote by T^0 the (degenerate) balanced tax system given by $\sigma_j(\mathbf{p}, \mathbf{z}) = \tau_i(\mathbf{p}, \mathbf{z}) = 0$, for all i, j, every $(\mathbf{p}, \mathbf{z})$ in $\mathbb{R}_+^\ell \times \mathbf{Z}$. Consider the following assumption:

Axiom 10.3 *For all* $\mathbf{z} \in \mathbf{Z}$ *one has:*

    (i) $\omega_i \in intX_i(\mathbf{z})$ *(*$i = 1, 2, ..., m$*).*

    (ii) For each $\mathbf{z} \in \mathbf{Z}$*, the set* $\Omega(\mathbf{z})$ *of attainable allocations, relative to* $\mathbf{z}$*, is compact.*

This axiom ensures the cheaper point requirement and the compactness of the set of attainable allocations.

10.5.1   Competitive equilibrium

The simplest instance of a public competitive or a valuation equilibrium is the standard competitive case. To see this, let $E = [(X_i, u_i)_{i=1}^m, (Y_j)_{j=1}^n, \omega]$ stand for a competitive economy, and take $\mathbf{Z} = W \times S$, where W is the set of all possible distributions of initial endowments that satisfy axiom 10.3, and S is the set of all possible distributions of firms' property among consumers. Assume that Y_j, X_i are fixed convex sets for all i, j, and let $T = T^0$. The resulting economy is the standard private ownership model of Arrow and Debreu (1954). It is easy to check that every private competitive equilibrium corresponds to a public competitive equilibrium. And also that a competitive equilibrium is a valuation equilibrium, and viceversa. Hence, under axioms 10.1 to 10.3 these equilibria exist and are in the core, and every Pareto optimal allocation can be decentralized as a competitive equilibrium.

A variant of this model is that in which externalities are allowed. As shown in chapter 4, under standard conditions a competitive equilibrium with externalities exists, though it may fail to be Pareto optimal. Optimality can however be ensured if markets are combined with a suitable tax system (or a system of personalized prices). If one takes $\mathbf{Z}$ as the set of allocations and makes the tax system equivalent to a Lindahl price system, a valuation equilibrium corresponds to an efficient market equilibrium. In this case our equilibrium notion corresponds to what Bergstrom (1970) calls a *distributive Lindahl equilibrium*.

Another case worth mentioning is that of an economy in which commodities can be of different qualities [see for instance Drèze and Hagen (1978)]. Members of the set $\mathbf{Z}$ can be thought of as different *quality standards*. Changes in these standards will typically affect consumers' feasible sets and utilities, as well as firms' production possibilities. For an arbitrary $\mathbf{z} \in \mathbf{Z}$, and $T = T^0$, a private competitive equilibrium is well defined, and exists under assumptions 10.1 to 10.3. Yet it may be inefficient (e.g., some consumers may be willing to pay for higher quality). The results in this section show that any efficient allocation can be decentralized as a valuation equilibrium.[6]

---

[6] See Corchón (1994) for an analysis of the dual case in which prices are taken as the public environment, and qualities take the role of balancing the markets.

10.5.2 Economies with public goods

Consider now an economy with ℓ private commodities and k public goods. To make things simpler, suppose that there are $n - 1$ private firms and a publicly owned technology (the nth firm) that produces the public goods using private goods as inputs. Let $\mathbf{Z} = (Y_n \cap \mathbb{R}^k_+) \times \mathbb{R}^{km}_+$, where Y_n stands for the public firm, $\mathbb{R}^k_+$ for the space of public goods, and $\mathbb{R}^{km}_+$ for the space of personalized prices. Hence, a point $\mathbf{z} = (\mathbf{s}, \mathbf{q}) \in \mathbf{Z}$ describes a vector of public goods $\mathbf{s} \in \mathbb{R}^k_+$ and a vector of personalized prices $\mathbf{q} = (\mathbf{q}^1, ..., \mathbf{q}^m)$, with $\mathbf{q}^i \in \mathbb{R}^k_+$ for all i. There is a mapping $\mathbf{c} : \mathbb{R}^\ell_+ \times \mathbb{R}^k_+ \to \mathbb{R}^\ell$ such that, for each given pair $(\mathbf{p}, \mathbf{s})$ in $\mathbb{R}^\ell_+ \times \mathbb{R}^k_+$ the private goods input vector $\mathbf{c}$ minimizes the cost of producing $\mathbf{s}$. Assume also that this is a well defined single-valued vector mapping, to facilitate the discussion.

The following balanced tax system can now be defined: For $i = 1, 2, ..., m$, let $\tau_i(\mathbf{p}, \mathbf{z}) = -\sum_{r=1}^k q^i_r s_r$, where s_r is the amount of the rth public good supplied, and q^i_r the ith consumer's personalized price for the rth public good. And let $\sigma_n(\mathbf{p}, \mathbf{z}) = -\sum_{i=1}^m \tau_i(\mathbf{p}, \mathbf{z})$ and $\sigma_j(\mathbf{p}, \mathbf{z}) = 0$, for all $j \neq n$. A *Lindahl equilibrium* for this economy (which exists under the assumptions of the model) is a valuation equilibrium $Q^* = [\mathbf{p}^*, (\mathbf{x}^*_i), (\mathbf{y}^*_j), \mathbf{s}^*, \mathbf{q}^*, T^*]$ with $\sum_{i=1}^m \mathbf{x}^*_i = \sum_{i=1}^m \omega_i + \sum_{j=1}^n \mathbf{y}^*_j - \mathbf{c}(\mathbf{p}^*, \mathbf{s}^*)$ and $-\sum_{i=1}^m \tau_i(\mathbf{p}^*, \mathbf{z}^*) = \mathbf{p}^* \mathbf{c}(\mathbf{p}^*, \mathbf{s}^*)$.

10.5.3 Competitive pricing

Some of the models of economies with increasing returns with efficient equilibrium outcomes, analyzed in former chapters, can also be formulated in terms of public competitive or valuation equilibria. In particular, it is trivial to check that a competitive pricing equilibrium in which capital goods are idiosyncratic pure inputs can be regarded either as a public competitive equilibrium or as a valuation equilibrium. For that one can simply identify the set $\mathbf{Z}$ with the set of capital goods allocations that give to each firm all capital goods available that are characteristic of this firm. See remark 9.2.

10.6 References to the literature

The idea of treating non-convexities as externalities appears to be due to Malinvaud (1969, 1972) and to an unpublished Ph. D. thesis due to Beato; see also Dierker (1986) and Laffont (1988).

The Wicksell approach to the allocation of public goods was formalized by Foley (1967), under the name of public competitive equilibrium. Later, Malinvaud (1969, 1972) discusses further this notion, under the name of "politico-economic" equilibrium. In Foley's formulation, as well as in the analysis presented here, private agents are implicitly assumed to be "my-opic" in the sense that they ignore how the equilibrium prices of private goods depend on the choice of public environment. This is an instance of price-taking behaviour in which agents neglect the influence of even collective decisions upon private good prices. By contrast, in Hammond & Villar (1998) it is assumed that all agents see how the change in public environment passes an appropriate cost-benefit test when one considers a suitable new conditional equilibrium price vector. In this sense, agents are assumed to be "far-sighted."

Mas-Colell's (1980) contribution to the pure theory of public goods proposes the notion of valuation equilibrium to address this type of problems. He considers an economy involving a single private good (to be interpreted as a Hicksian composite commodity), and the choice of a single public project from a space where no linear structure is imposed. This equilibrium notion may be regarded as an application to this abstract framework of the Lindahlian approach to the provision of public goods. A valuation equilibrium corresponds to a unanimously agreed choice of public project, the role of the public sector being to design a mechanism that induces such an efficient agreement. In a valuation equilibrium every consumer prefers her consumption plan, consisting of some amount of the private good and a public project, to any other which is affordable given the valuation function (to be interpreted as tax system). Taking the private good as the *numéraire*, Mas-Colell shows that valuation equilibria satisfy the standard properties of competitive equilibria.

Later, Mas-Colell & Silvestre (1989) introduced the concept of *cost-share equilibrium* which extends the work of Kaneko (1977) and Mas-Colell (1980), to allow many public goods. See also Vega-Redondo (1987) and Diamantaras & Wilkie (1994).

Diamantaras & Gilles (1996) and Hammond & Villar (1998) extend Mas-Colell's work by assuming that agents are "far sighted". They present slightly different models with an abstract set of public projects and several private commodities that may be both inputs and outputs. Their notion of valuation equilibria requires agents to maximize their payoff functions taking into account the changes in the prices of private commodities resulting from changes in the public environment. They show that these equilibria satisfy the two fundamental welfare theorems.

Hammond & Villar (1999a) analyze the welfare properties of valuation equilibria, when agents are assumed to be myopic. In a later work, Hammond & Villar (1999b) extend the analysis to economies in which the resulting conditional economies need not be convex, for both myopic and far sighted agents.

Chapter 11

INPUT-OUTPUT ANALYSIS

11.1 Introduction

The input-output analysis, initiated by Wassily Leontief in 1936, can be regarded as a first application of the principles of general equilibrium theory to the empirical analysis. Its goal is the study and quantification of the structural relations between the economic sectors that constitute the economy of a country. The methodological approach consists of representing the structural relations between industries by means of linear equations, whose coefficients are obtained empirically. When these coefficients are stable (e.g. when constant returns to scale prevail), equilibrium relations appear as the solutions to linear equation systems. The key tool for the computation of these coefficients is the input-output table, that is briefly presented below.[1]

Input-output systems provide a modelling device for the analysis of disaggregate economic relations, that has been shown most fruitful. These models usually have an intermediate status between general equilibrium and partial equilibrium analysis. As in general equilibrium, the internal structure of the productive system is taken into account, and the interdependencies among economic sectors are at the center of the picture. As in partial equilibrium, some relevant variables, such as consumers' demand or unitary added values, are treated as parameters whose changes are exogenous to the model. One of the main applications of input-output analysis is, precisely, the study of the impact of such exogenous changes on the inter-industry equilibrium relations.

Input-output is a mathematical tool that can be used as a guide for the implementation of various kinds of economic policies. As such, it requires to ensure the solvability of linear equation systems under non-negativity con-

---

[1] François Quesnay's *tableau économique* is the first antecedent of this approach to the analysis of intersectoral relations. See Meek (1962).

straints (since the variables are typically quantities and prices). This is a topic that has formal interest on its own, and affects the possible extensions of the model to more general environments.

Consider an economy that consists of n industries or economic sectors. In a given time period this economy has produced the amounts $z_1, z_2, ..., z_n$ of n goods (one good per industry). In order to obtain this production, each sector has used some commodities produced by other sectors, that play the role of intermediate inputs, as well as some primary factors (goods that are not producible by the industrial sector, such as labour, raw materials or natural resources). The output of each sector has also two alternative applications: final uses (consumption and investment) and intersectoral exchanges.

We can describe the set of industrial relationships by means of an input-output table, as follows. Call z_{ij} the amount of good i that industry j has used in order to produce the amount z_j of commodity j. And let d_j denote the amount devoted to final uses, that is, $d_j = z_j - \sum_{i=1}^{n} z_{ij}$. Let p_i denote the price of the ith good, and v_i the worth of primary factors used up by the ith industry, when producing z_i (the "added value"). Then, the performance of this economy in the period considered can be described by the following table:

Goods \ Sectors	1	2	...	n	FD	GO
1	$p_1 z_{11}$	$p_1 z_{12}$	...	$p_1 z_{1n}$	$p_1 d_1$	$p_1 z_1$
2	$p_2 z_{21}$	$p_2 z_{22}$	...	$p_2 z_{2n}$	$p_2 d_2$	$p_2 z_2$
...	...	...	...	...	...	...
n	$p_n z_{n1}$	$p_n z_{n2}$	...	$p_n z_{nn}$	$p_n d_n$	$p_n z_n$
v_i	v_1	v_2	...	v_n		
Total revenue	$p_1 z_1$	$p_2 z_2$	...	$p_n z_n$		

The (i, j) entry of this table shows the exchange between productive sectors. The ith row tells us the sales of the ith sector to other sectors, as well as to the final users. The column FD describes the worth of the final demand of different commodities, and the column GO the corresponding worth of the gross output. The jth column describes the purchases of the jth sector plus the added value (including profits). Clearly, the sums of the first n rows and columns coincide, as this table is an accounting device.

Now observe that, letting $a_{ij} = \frac{z_{ij}}{z_j}$, $s_i = \frac{v_i}{z_i}$, we can summarize the information in the above table as follows:

$$\mathbf{Az} + \mathbf{d} := \mathbf{z}$$

$$\mathbf{pA} + \mathbf{s} := \mathbf{p}$$

where $\mathbf{A}$ is an n-square non-negative matrix whose entry (i, j) is a_{ij}, $\mathbf{d}$ is the n-dimensional vector of final demands, $\mathbf{p}$ is the price vector, and $\mathbf{s}$ is the vector of average added values. Note that the symbol $:=$ is meant to stress that these relations are identities, that is, this is simply a compact way of describing the information contained in the input-output table.

When the economy operates under constant returns to scale, the ratios $a_{ij} = \frac{z_{ij}}{z_j}$ do not change with the scale of operations. Therefore, these terms represent the technical coefficients of production, that describe the structural relations between inputs and outputs in different industries. The knowledge of these coefficients permits one to transform the accounting device in a tool for the analysis of equilibrium relations, and to study the performance of the economy. Suppose, for example, that the final demand vector $\mathbf{d}$ changes to a different one, $\mathbf{d}'$ (think of a change in foreign demand, or a change in consumers' tastes). What is the new equilibrium gross output vector? Alternatively, consider a change in the added value (due to a change in salaries, profits or taxes). What are the new equilibrium prices?

The equilibrium in the quantity side of the economy, for a given final demand vector $\mathbf{d} \in \mathbb{R}_+^n$, is given by a solution to the linear equation system:

$$(\mathbf{I} - \mathbf{A})\mathbf{z} = \mathbf{d}$$

This simply means that the aggregate net production matches the final demand.

Similarly, the equilibrium in the price system, for a given vector $\mathbf{s} \in \mathbb{R}_+^n$ of unitary added values, is given by a solution to the linear system:

$$\mathbf{p}(\mathbf{I} - \mathbf{A}) = \mathbf{s}$$

This equation expresses the equality between costs and revenues.

This price system looks as if there were a single primary input in the economy, in which case the prices are technologically determined. Yet, this can be regarded as a simplification device. According to the interpretation of the input-output table, we can take $\mathbf{s}$ the cost of primary inputs, evaluated at prices that are taken parametrically (a composite commodity à la Hicks). Hence, letting $\mathbf{s} = \mathbf{p}^F \mathbf{Q}$, where $\mathbf{Q}$ is the matrix of primary factors consumed per unit of output, and $\mathbf{p}^F$ the vector of prices of these commodities, we can obtain the prices of producible commodities as a function of both the technical coefficients and the prices of primary factors.

Note that the very nature of the equilibrium problems concerning quantities and prices requires the solutions to these systems to be non-negative.

This need not be the case in general: it is well known that a definite linear system, with positive parameters, may have solutions with negative components. Nevertheless, it is easy to see that when the matrix $(\mathbf{I} - \mathbf{A})$ has a non-negative inverse $(\mathbf{I} - \mathbf{A})^{-1} \geq \mathbf{0}$, each of these systems has a unique non-negative solution for any given parameter vector in $\mathbb{R}^n_+$; namely,

$$\mathbf{z}^* = (\mathbf{I} - \mathbf{A})^{-1}\mathbf{d}$$

$$\mathbf{p}^* = \mathbf{s}(\mathbf{I} - \mathbf{A})^{-1}$$

Conditions for the existence and non-negativity of $(\mathbf{I} - \mathbf{A})^{-1}$ are well established in the literature. In particular, as $(\mathbf{I} - \mathbf{A})$ is a Z-matrix,[2] the following results can be applied [see for instance Debreu & Herstein (1953), Berman & Plemmons (1979, ch. 9)]:

Theorem 11.0 *Let* $\mathbf{A} \geq \mathbf{0}$ *be a square n-matrix. The following results are equivalent:*

(i) *There exists a point* $\mathbf{z} \in \mathbb{R}^n_+$ *for which* $(\mathbf{I} - \mathbf{A})\mathbf{z} >> \mathbf{0}$.
(ii) $0 < \lambda(\mathbf{A}) < 1$ *(where $\lambda(\mathbf{A})$ is the Frobenius root of matrix $\mathbf{A}$).[3]*
(iii) *For all* $\mathbf{d} \in \mathbb{R}^n_+$ *there exists* $\mathbf{z} \in \mathbb{R}^n_+$ *such that* $(\mathbf{I} - \mathbf{A})\mathbf{z} = \mathbf{d}$.
(iv) *For all* $\mathbf{s} \in \mathbb{R}^n_+$ *there exists* $\mathbf{p} \in \mathbb{R}^n_+$ *such that* $\mathbf{p}(\mathbf{I} - \mathbf{A}) = \mathbf{s}$.
(v) *The inverse matrix* $(\mathbf{I} - \mathbf{A})^{-1}$ *exists and it is non-negative.*

Therefore, under very weak assumptions [namely, (i) or (ii)], we are able to ensure the solvability of each of these systems, for all non-negative parameter values [namely, (iii), (iv) or (v)].

In summary, under very general conditions, the linear input-output model provides a powerful tool for economic analysis. Its usefulness is enhanced by the extremely good properties that these systems exhibit, from a comparative statics viewpoint.

One can think of a number of extensions that would permit to incorporate some aspects that are disregarded in this simple model, without going to the abstract general equilibrium models analyzed before. There are four such extensions that immediately come to mind (besides the consideration of several primary inputs, already mentioned): the choice of techniques, the presence of joint production, the existence of variable returns to scale, and

---

[2] A Z-matrix (also called N-matrix), is a square matrix all whose off-diagonal components are non-positive.

[3] The Frobenius root is the greatest number λ for which the following relation holds: $\lambda \mathbf{x} = \mathbf{A}\mathbf{x}$, for $\mathbf{x} \in \mathbb{R}^n$. The numbers that solve this system are called eigen-values, and the associated vectors are called eigen-vectors. When $\mathbf{A} \geq \mathbf{0}$ and $\lambda(\mathbf{A}) \in (0, 1)$, $\mathbf{x}$ is non-negative.

the incorporation of the demand sector. All these extensions are taken up in the following sections. Let us briefly comment on their significance and, meanwhile, advance the content of the chapter.

The choice of techniques is one aspect that the model presented above does not take into account. This choice is present whenever production can be developed using alternative input-output combinations. As a consequence, we cannot calculate the equilibrium production levels without first determining the techniques that will be used. We shall see that allowing for many techniques does not change the basic nature of the model. Indeed, the consideration of a single technique can be justified. The non-substitution theorem, presented below, shows that a single technique is a sufficient representation of all technological possibilities in the economy.

The standard model assumes that each industry produces one commodity that is not produced elsewhere. This is a major shortcoming, since it implies, among other things, that durable capital goods cannot be properly treated. Therefore, the extension to the case of joint-production is necessary. This is not a simple step, as solving the resulting equation systems under non-negative constraints is far from trivial. Nevertheless, there are well defined conditions that tell us when can we deal with joint production models and keep the good properties of the single production ones.

The model is based on the idea that technical coefficients are constant, so that changes in production do not affect the input-output relations. When there are variable returns to scale this is no longer the case. Hence, it is interesting to explore the possibility of extending the model allowing for variable coefficients. There are some results that enable to deal with nonlinear input-output models, preserving the good comparative statics properties characteristic of linear models.

Finally, it seems appealing to incorporate the consumption sector into the picture and build a genuine general equilibrium model that exhibits a simple structure and a regular behaviour. This would permit us to go a step further and analyze the global effects of changes in the equilibrium of the economy, taking into account not only the industrial interdependencies, but also the induced effect on the demand side. The construction of applied general equilibrium models, based on input-output tables and estimates of demand functions, is nowadays an important tool for policy makers.

The rest of the chapter is organized as follows. Section 11.2 presents a linear input-output model with joint production, under the assumption that the number of producible commodities equals the number of industries (what is usually called a "square" system). Three themes are discussed: the solvability of the quantity and price systems, the non-substitution theorem, and

the existence of competitive equilibrium. The equilibrium model is interesting because it requires few assumptions on the consumption sector, given
that equilibrium prices are technologically determined.

Section 11.3 provides further extensions of these results. The first one
consists of allowing for positive profits in the linear joint production model
(this is a mark-up pricing model where competition is identified with uniform
profitability among industries). The second one analyzes a non-square linear
joint production model, that is, a model in which the number of producible
commodities may differ from the number of industries. Finally, we present
an abstract non-linear input output model, in which the net production is a
function of gross output.

11.2 The linear model

11.2.1 An input-output model with joint production

Consider an economy with m consumers and n industries that exhibit constant returns to scale. Suppose that there is a single primary input (labour),
and that the number of sectors is equal to the number of producible commodities;[4] that is, $\ell = n + 1$.

The following axioms specify the economy we shall be referring to:

Axiom 11.1 $\ell = n + 1$, and there is a unique primary factor, labour,
that corresponds to the ℓth commodity. Labour is a necessary input for all
production processes.

Axiom 11.2 For all $j = 1, 2, ..., n$, Y_j is a closed convex cone, with $Y_j -
\mathbb{R}^\ell_+ \subset Y_j$ and $Y_j \bigcap \mathbb{R}^\ell_+ = \{0\}$.

It is assumed in axiom 11.1 that there is the same number of productive
sectors than there are producible commodities. And also that labour is the
only primary factor, that is a necessary input for positive production. Axiom
11.2 says that production sets are convex cones (constant returns to scale).

It is useful to think of production plans described as follows:

$$\mathbf{y}_j = [(\mathbf{y}_j^O - \mathbf{y}_j^I), \ y_{j\ell}]$$

where: $\mathbf{y}_j^O \in \mathbb{R}^n_+$ is a gross output vector, $\mathbf{y}_j^I \in \mathbb{R}^n_+$ is a gross input vector
(with signs reversed), and $y_{j\ell} \leq 0$ is the amount of labour required.

---

[4]This is partly a modelling choice. The case in which the number of idustries and the
number of commodities differ is taken up later.

Let $\mathbf{y}_j \neq \mathbf{0}$ be an efficient production plan. Axiom 11.1 implies that $y_{j\ell} < 0$. Moreover, the assumption of constant returns to scale, together with the formulation above, permits to express this production plan as:

$$\mathbf{y}_j = \left[\begin{array}{c} B_j - A_j \\ -1 \end{array} \right] q_j$$

where B_j, $A_j \in \mathbb{R}^n_+$ are column vectors, with $B_{hj} = \frac{y^O_{hj}}{q_j}$, $A_{hj} = \frac{y^I_{jh}}{q_j}$ for $h = 1, 2, ..., n$, and $q_j = -y_{j\ell} > 0$. With this representation we can describe all production plans that are proportional to $\mathbf{y}_j$ as $\left[\begin{array}{c} B_j - A_j \\ -1 \end{array} \right] q_j$, for some q_j. These are the **technical coefficients of production**, and describe a *method of production* available for this sector. They express the production and input requirements per unit of labour. The number q_j can be identified with the jth sector **activity level**, when using this method of production.

Now take one efficient production plan for each sector, $\mathbf{y}_j \in Y_j$ with $j = 1, 2, ..., n$. Making use of the above representation, the corresponding aggregate production plan can be expressed as follows:

$$\sum_{j=1}^{n} \mathbf{y}_j = \left(\begin{array}{c} \mathbf{B} - \mathbf{A} \\ -1 \end{array} \right) \mathbf{q}$$

in which:

(i) $\mathbf{q} \in \mathbb{R}^n_+$ is the vector of activity levels (measured in units of labour).

(i) $\mathbf{B}$ is an $n \times n$ non-negative matrix of gross output per unit of labour (that is, $\mathbf{Bq}$ is the aggregate gross output vector).

(ii) $\mathbf{A}$ is an $n \times n$ non-negative matrix whose entries describe the input coefficients per unit of labour (hence, $\mathbf{Aq}$ is the aggregate gross input vector).

(iv) $\mathbf{1} \in \mathbb{R}^n_+$ is the vector all whose components are equal to 1. Therefore, $\mathbf{1q}$ is the aggregate labour involved in the aggregate production $\mathbf{y}$.

Now we can say that an efficient aggregate production $\mathbf{y} \in Y = \sum_{j=1}^n Y_j$ is possible for the economy, if there is a pair of square matrices $(\mathbf{B}, \mathbf{A})$, and vector of activity levels $\mathbf{q} \in \mathbb{R}^n_+$ such that $\mathbf{y} \leq \left[(\mathbf{B} - \mathbf{A})\mathbf{q}, -\sum_{j=1}^n q_j \right]$.

Note that the availability of alternative production processes translates into the existence of an infinity of matrices $(\mathbf{B}, \mathbf{A})$. This is so because the convexity of Y_j implies that if there are two alternative production processes available for the jth firm, all convex combinations of these two methods will also be available. Each pair of matrices represents a particular combination of production processes, or a *technique* available for the economy.

Consider now the following assumption:

Axiom 11.3 *There exists an efficient production plan* $\mathbf{y}^o \in Y$, *and a pair of matrices* $(\mathbf{B}, \mathbf{A})$ *such that:*

(i) $\mathbf{y}^o = \left[(\mathbf{B} - \mathbf{A})\mathbf{q}^o, \ -\sum_{j=1}^{n} q_j^o \right]$, *with* $\mathbf{q}^o \in \mathbb{R}_+^n$, $(\mathbf{B} - \mathbf{A})\mathbf{q}^o >> \mathbf{0}$.

(ii) $rk(\mathbf{B}) = n$ *(where* $rk(.)$ *stands for rank).*

(iii) For all $\mathbf{z} \in \mathbb{R}^n$, $\mathbf{B}\mathbf{z} \geq \mathbf{0} \Longrightarrow \mathbf{A}\mathbf{z} \geq \mathbf{0}$.

(iv) $[(\mathbf{B} - \mathbf{A})\mathbf{z} \geq \mathbf{0} \ \& \ \mathbf{B}\mathbf{z} \geq \mathbf{0}] \Longrightarrow \mathbf{z} \geq \mathbf{0}$.

Part (i) of axiom 11.3 is a *productivity* condition. It says that there is some technique for which the economy is able to produce positive net amounts of *all* producible commodities.

Part (ii) states that the output matrix of the technique $(\mathbf{B}, \mathbf{A})$ that satisfies (i), is of *full rank*. This is mostly a technical requirement that induces a one to one correspondence between activity levels and gross output vectors.

Part (iii) is a *monotonicity* requirement. It says that in order to increase the gross output vector, more inputs should be used up. Given two vectors of activity levels, $\mathbf{q}, \mathbf{q}' \in \mathbb{R}_+^n$, we can interpret $\mathbf{z} = \mathbf{q} - \mathbf{q}'$; then this axiom establishes that $\mathbf{B}\mathbf{q} \geq \mathbf{B}\mathbf{q}' \Longrightarrow \mathbf{A}\mathbf{q} \geq \mathbf{A}\mathbf{q}'$.

Finally, part (iv) (called *positive inclusion*) is an expression of the following idea: in order to increase the gross and net output vectors we need to increase the vector of activity levels. More precisely, given two vectors of activity levels, $\mathbf{q}, \mathbf{q}' \in \mathbb{R}_+^n$, let $\mathbf{z} = \mathbf{q} - \mathbf{q}'$; then, part (iv) says that if $(\mathbf{B} - \mathbf{A})\mathbf{q} \geq (\mathbf{B} - \mathbf{A})\mathbf{q}'$ and $\mathbf{B}\mathbf{q} \geq \mathbf{B}\mathbf{q}'$, then $\mathbf{q} \geq \mathbf{q}'$. Hence what this condition prevents is the possibility of increasing the gross and net output vectors by increasing some activity levels and decreasing some others.

Remark 11.1 *Note that when* $\mathbf{B} = \mathbf{I}$ *(that is, single production prevails), and matrix* $\mathbf{A}$ *is productive (that is,* $\mathbf{A}\mathbf{q} << \mathbf{q}$ *for some* $\mathbf{q} \in \mathbb{R}_+^n$*), axiom 11.3 is automatically satisfied.*

Let $\mathbf{d} \in \mathbb{R}_+^n$ be a given final demand vector. To find an equilibrium in the quantity side of this economy, relative to this demand and the technique $(\mathbf{B}, \mathbf{A})$, consist of finding a solution to the following linear system:

$$(\mathbf{B} - \mathbf{A})\mathbf{q} = \mathbf{d}$$

When we are able to solve this system for all possible final demand vectors, we can calculate the changes in the corresponding activity levels and input requirements, associated with a change in the final demand.

Let us consider now the price system. We know that, under constant returns to scale, the only price vectors that are compatible with profit maximization are those that imply zero profits. As all firms exhibit constant returns to scale, we can express the equilibrium price system of this economy, relative to a technique $(\mathbf{B}, \mathbf{A})$, as a solution to the following linear equation system:

$$\mathbf{p} \begin{bmatrix} \mathbf{B} - \mathbf{A} \\ -\mathbf{1} \end{bmatrix} = \mathbf{0}$$

where $\mathbf{p} \in \mathbb{R}^{\ell}_{+}$. Letting $\mathbf{p} = (\hat{\mathbf{p}}, p_{\ell})$, with $\hat{\mathbf{p}} \in \mathbb{R}^{n}_{+}$, this equation system can alternatively be written as:

$$\hat{\mathbf{p}}\mathbf{B} = \hat{\mathbf{p}}\mathbf{A} + p_{\ell}\mathbf{1}$$

an expression that says that average revenues equal average costs in all sectors.

The following results are obtained:

Proposition 11.1 *Under axioms 11.1 to 11.3 the linear production system* $(\mathbf{B} - \mathbf{A})\mathbf{q} = \mathbf{d}$ *has a unique non-negative solution for all parameter vectors* $\mathbf{d} \in \mathbb{R}^{n}_{+}$.

Proof. From (ii) of axiom 11.3 it follows that $\mathbf{B}^{-1}$ exists. Then, letting $\mathbf{B}\mathbf{q} = \mathbf{t}$ we can re-write the linear production system as follows:

$$(\mathbf{I} - \mathbf{A}\mathbf{B}^{-1})\mathbf{t} = \mathbf{d}$$

Since $\mathbf{B}\mathbf{q} \geq \mathbf{0}$ implies $\mathbf{A}\mathbf{q} \geq \mathbf{0}$ [(iii) of axiom 11.3], we conclude that $\mathbf{A}\mathbf{B}^{-1}\mathbf{t} \geq \mathbf{0}$ whenever $\mathbf{t} \geq \mathbf{0}$, which is true if and only if $\mathbf{A}\mathbf{B}^{-1} \geq \mathbf{0}$. Therefore, $(\mathbf{I} - \mathbf{A}\mathbf{B}^{-1})$ is a Z-matrix (non-positive off-diagonal elements). Part (i) of axiom 11.3 says that $(\mathbf{I} - \mathbf{A}\mathbf{B}^{-1})\mathbf{t}^{o} >> \mathbf{0}$, for some $\mathbf{t}^{o}$, so that $(\mathbf{I} - \mathbf{A}\mathbf{B}^{-1})$ is *productive* and therefore, $(\mathbf{I} - \mathbf{A}\mathbf{B}^{-1})^{-1}$ exists an is non-negative (Theorem 11.0). Hence,

$$\mathbf{t}^{*} = (\mathbf{I} - \mathbf{A}\mathbf{B}^{-1})^{-1}\mathbf{d}$$

and, consequently,

$$\mathbf{q}^{*} = \mathbf{B}^{-1}(\mathbf{I} - \mathbf{A}\mathbf{B}^{-1})^{-1}\mathbf{d}$$

It follows trivially from part (iv) of axiom 11.4 that $\mathbf{q}^{*} \geq \mathbf{0}$. $\boxed{\text{Q.e.d.}}$

Remark 11.2 *It is shown in Peris & Villar (1993) that, under (ii) and (iii) of axiom 11.3, (i) and (iv) are necessary and sufficient for the solvability of the quantity system, for any given parameter vector in* $\mathbb{R}^{n}_{+}$.

Observe that proving that the system $(\mathbf{B} - \mathbf{A})\mathbf{q} = \mathbf{d}$ has a unique solution $\mathbf{q} \geq \mathbf{0}$, for all $\mathbf{d} \in \mathbb{R}^{n}_{+}$, is equivalent to proving that the inverse matrix $(\mathbf{B} - \mathbf{A})^{-1}$ exists and is non-negative. The elements of matrix $(\mathbf{B} - \mathbf{A})^{-1}$

have an interesting economic interpretation, that can be obtained as follows. Let $\mathbf{e}^j \in \mathbb{R}_+^n$ be a vector with $e_i^j = 0$, for all $i \neq j$, $e_j^j = 1$. This vector can be interpreted as a final demand consisting of exactly one unit of commodity j. Therefore, letting $(\mathbf{B} - \mathbf{A})^{-1}\mathbf{e}^j$ is the vector of activity levels that are required in order to obtain one unit of j as net output. But $(\mathbf{B} - \mathbf{A})^{-1}\mathbf{e}^j$ is, precisely, the jth column of matrix $(\mathbf{B} - \mathbf{A})^{-1}$, so that the (i,j) entry of this matrix tells us the activity level at which sector i is to be activated in order to obtain one unit of commodity j as a net output.

Two immediate consequences can be derived from this proposition (the proofs are trivial, thus omitted):

Corollary 11.1 *Under axioms 11.1 to 11.3, let* $\mathbf{d}, \mathbf{d}' \in \mathbb{R}_{++}^n$ *be such that* $\mathbf{d} \geq \mathbf{d}'$, *and let* $\mathbf{q}, \mathbf{q}' \in \mathbb{R}_+^n$ *be the corresponding equilibrium activity levels. Then,* $\mathbf{q} \geq \mathbf{q}'$.

Corollary 11.2 *Under axioms 11.1 to 11.3, there is a unique vector of relative prices* $\mathbf{p} = (\widehat{\mathbf{p}}, p_\ell)$ *that solves the system* $\widehat{\mathbf{p}}\mathbf{B} = \widehat{\mathbf{p}}\mathbf{A} + p_\ell \mathbf{1}$, *with* $\mathbf{p} \in \mathbb{R}_{++}^\ell$, *and* $\widehat{\mathbf{p}} = p_\ell \mathbf{1}(\mathbf{B} - \mathbf{A})^{-1}$.

Remark 11.3 *If we normalize prices by letting* $p_\ell = 1$, *the equilibrium price vector of producible commodities corresponds to the vector of labour values, that is, competitive prices coincide with the amounts of labour incorporated in the production of producible commodities.*

Remark 11.4 *The assumptions established imply that* $(\mathbf{B} - \mathbf{A})^{-1}$ *exists and is non-negative, requiring neither* $(\mathbf{B} - \mathbf{A})$ *to be a Z-matrix nor* $\mathbf{B}^{-1} \geq \mathbf{0}$. *Indeed, each of these alternatives rules out joint production. In the first case, the very definition of Z-matrix implies that each sector produces a single net output. In the second case, because it is known that a non-negative square matrix has a non-negative inverse only if it is a diagonal matrix, or a permutation of a diagonal one [see Johnson (1983)].*

11.2.2   The non-substitution theorem

One of the most relevant results for this type of economies is that known as the **non-substitution theorem**. It establishes that a single technique $(\mathbf{B}, \mathbf{A})$ can be taken as a sufficient representation of the technology, in spite of the availability of many alternative production processes. This follows from two complementary outcomes. The first one says that all efficient production plans can be obtained by means of a single technique, that is to say, by means of a single pair of matrices $(\mathbf{B}, \mathbf{A})$. The second one shows that, even if there are many techniques that can be used to generate all these efficient production plans, all of them are equivalent from an economic viewpoint, because equilibrium prices are uniquely determined.

Here comes the theorem:

Theorem 11.1 (The Non-Substitution Theorem) *Suppose that axioms 11.1 to 11.3 hold. Then,*

(i) All efficient aggregate production plans $\mathbf{y} = \sum_{j=1}^{n} \mathbf{y}_j$, *with* $\mathbf{y}_j \in Y_j$ *for all* j, *can be obtained by means of a single technique* $(\mathbf{B}, \mathbf{A})$, *that is,* $\mathbf{y} \in \partial Y$ *implies* $\mathbf{y} = \left[(\mathbf{B} - \mathbf{A})\mathbf{q}, -\sum_{j=1}^{n} q_j \right]$, *for some* $\mathbf{q} \in \mathbb{R}_+^n$.

(ii) Let $\mathbf{p} = (\widehat{\mathbf{p}}, p_\ell) \in \mathbb{R}_+^\ell$ *be an equilibrium price vector, associated to* $(\mathbf{B}, \mathbf{A})$, *that is,* $\widehat{\mathbf{p}}(\mathbf{B} - \mathbf{A}) = p_\ell \mathbf{1}$, *and let* $(\mathbf{B}', \mathbf{A}')$ *be another technique of the economy. Then* $\widehat{\mathbf{p}}(\mathbf{B}' - \mathbf{A}') \leq p_\ell \mathbf{1}$.

Proof. (i) Let $\mathbf{y} = (\mathbf{d}, -T)$ be an arbitrary efficient aggregate production plan. As $(\mathbf{B} - \mathbf{A})^{-1}$ exists and is semipositive (Proposition 11.1), there exists a unique $\mathbf{q} \in \mathbb{R}_+^n$ such that $(\mathbf{B} - \mathbf{A})\mathbf{q} = \mathbf{d}$. Let $\mathbf{y}' = [(\mathbf{B} - \mathbf{A})\mathbf{q}, -\sum_{j=1}^{n} q_j]$. By assumption, $\mathbf{y}' \in Y$. Moreover, $T \leq \sum_{j=1}^{n} q_j$ because $\mathbf{y}$ is an efficient aggregate production plan. To prove the result, suppose that $T < \sum_{j=1}^{n} q_j$, for the sake of contradiction. Take a scalar $\alpha < 0$ such that

$$0 < (1 - \alpha)(\mathbf{B} - \mathbf{A})\mathbf{q}^o + \alpha \mathbf{d} = (\mathbf{B} - \mathbf{A})[(1 - \alpha)\mathbf{q}^o + \alpha \mathbf{q}]$$

where $\mathbf{q}^o$ is the vector in part (i) of axiom 11.3. As $(\mathbf{B} - \mathbf{A})^{-1} \geq \mathbf{0}$ it follows that $(1 - \alpha)\mathbf{q}^o + \alpha \mathbf{q} > 0$. Now define $\mathbf{s} = (1 - \alpha)\mathbf{y}^o + \alpha \mathbf{y} = (\mathbf{d}', -T')$, that is,

$$\mathbf{d}' = (\mathbf{B} - \mathbf{A})[(1 - \alpha)\mathbf{q}^o + \alpha \mathbf{q}]$$

$$T' = \mathbf{1}[(1 - \alpha)\mathbf{q}^o + \alpha \mathbf{q}]$$

Clearly, $\mathbf{s} \in Y$. Let $\beta = -\alpha(1 - \alpha)$, $0 < \beta < 1$, and make

$$\mathbf{t} = (1 - \beta)\mathbf{s} + \beta \mathbf{y} = (\mathbf{d}'', -T'')$$

where

$$\mathbf{d}'' = (1 - \beta)\mathbf{d}' + \beta \mathbf{d} = (1 - \beta)(\mathbf{B} - \mathbf{A})[(1 - \alpha)\mathbf{q}^o + \alpha \mathbf{q}] + \beta(\mathbf{B} - \mathbf{A})\mathbf{q}$$

$$= (\mathbf{B} - \mathbf{A})[(1 - \beta)(1 - \alpha)\mathbf{q}^o + (1 - \beta)\alpha \mathbf{q} + \beta \mathbf{q}] = (\mathbf{B} - \mathbf{A})\mathbf{q}^o$$

$$T'' = (1 - \beta)\mathbf{1}[(1 - \alpha)\mathbf{q}^o + \alpha \mathbf{q}] + \beta T = \mathbf{1}\mathbf{q}^o - \beta(\mathbf{1}\mathbf{q} - T)$$

As $T < \sum_{j=1}^{n} q_j$, it follows that $T'' < \mathbf{1}\mathbf{q}^o$. Therefore, $\mathbf{t} > \mathbf{y}^o$. But this cannot be the case, because $\mathbf{y}^o$ is, by construction, an aggregate efficient production plan. Hence, $T = \sum_{j=1}^{n} q_j$ and $\mathbf{y} = [(\mathbf{B} - \mathbf{A})\mathbf{q}, \ -\sum_{j=1}^{n} q_j]$ for all efficient aggregate production plan $\mathbf{y} \in Y$, with $\mathbf{q} \in \mathbb{R}_+^n$.

(ii) Let $\mathbf{p} = (\widehat{\mathbf{p}}, p_\ell) \in \mathbb{R}_+^\ell$ be an equilibrium price vector, that is, $\widehat{\mathbf{p}}(\mathbf{B} - \mathbf{A})$ $= p_\ell \mathbf{1}$. It was shown in Corollary 11.2 that this vector always exists. Suppose that there is a technique $(\mathbf{B}', \mathbf{A}')$ such that $\widehat{\mathbf{p}}(\mathbf{B}' - \mathbf{A}') \not\leq p_\ell \mathbf{1}$. Let $J = \{i \ / \ [\widehat{\mathbf{p}}(\mathbf{B}' - \mathbf{A}')]_i > p_\ell\}$, that is, J is the set of indices for which the corresponding component of vector $\widehat{\mathbf{p}}(\mathbf{B}' - \mathbf{A}')$ is strictly greater than the wage. We know that the set of points $\mathbf{y}^* \in Y$ that maximize the scalar product $\mathbf{p}\mathbf{y}$ yield efficient allocations (see Proposition 3.1). Moreover, $\mathbf{p}\mathbf{y}^* = 0$ under constant returns to scale. Now construct a new technique $(\mathbf{B}'', \mathbf{A}'')$ as follows: Call h_{ij}, h'_{ij}, h''_{ij} the (i, j) entry of the matrices $(\mathbf{B} - \mathbf{A})$, $(\mathbf{B}' - \mathbf{A}')$, $(\mathbf{B}'' - \mathbf{A}'')$, respectively, with

$$h''_{ij} = \begin{cases} h'_{ij} & \text{if } j \in J \\ h_{ij} & \text{if } j \notin J \end{cases}$$

$(\mathbf{B}'', \mathbf{A}'')$ is clearly a technique available for this economy. Then, let $\overline{\mathbf{y}} = (\mathbf{B}'' - \mathbf{A}'')\mathbf{1}$, where $\mathbf{1}$ is an n-vector all whose components are unity. It follows that $\overline{\mathbf{y}} \in Y$, with $\mathbf{p}\overline{\mathbf{y}} > 0$, contradicting the fact that $\max_{\mathbf{y} \in Y} \mathbf{p}\mathbf{y} = 0$. Therefore, $J = \emptyset$. $\boxed{\text{Q.e.d.}}$

The relevance of this theorem is twofold. On the one hand, it enables to determine the competitive equilibrium prices without any reference to the demand side of the economy. This is so because $\mathbf{p}^* = p_\ell \mathbf{1}(\mathbf{B} - \mathbf{A})^{-1}$ is the unique vector of relative prices that is compatible with profit maximization (zero profits for all sectors). On the other hand, it shows that changes in the level or composition of the final demand will affect the activity levels at which the technique $(\mathbf{B}, \mathbf{A})$ operates, but not the technology in use. That is, changes in the demand do not involve the substitution of technological processes (hence the name). As a consequence, empirical analysis it greatly simplified, because the computation of a single technique provides all the information required in order to perform comparative statics analysis.

11.2.3 Equilibrium

Let us consider now the competitive equilibrium of this type of economies, when there are m consumers whose expenditure capacity is given by labour income, exclusively. A consumption plan for the ith consumer is a point

$$\mathbf{x}_i = (\mathbf{d}_i, \ -L_i)$$

where $\mathbf{d}_i \in \mathbb{R}^n_+$ is the demand vector of producible commodities, and L_i is the labour supply. A consumption plan is affordable for the ith consumer whenever $\mathbf{p}(\mathbf{d}_i, -L_i) \leq 0$, that is, if $\widehat{\mathbf{p}}\mathbf{d}_i \leq p_\ell L_i$.

For a given price vector $\mathbf{p} \in \mathbb{R}^\ell_+$, $\xi_i(\mathbf{p})$ stands for the ith consumer's demand, and $\xi(\mathbf{p}) = \sum_{i=1}^m \xi_i(\mathbf{p})$ for the aggregate demand.

Definition 11.1 *A **competitive equilibrium** is a price vector* $\mathbf{p}^* = (\widehat{\mathbf{p}}^*, p_\ell^*)$ *and an allocation* $[(\mathbf{d}_i^*, -L_i^*)_{i=1}^m, (\mathbf{y}_j^*)_{j=1}^n]$ *such that*
(i) $(\mathbf{d}_i^*, -L_i^*) \in \xi_i(\mathbf{p}^*)$, *for all* i.
(iia) $\sum_{j=1}^n \mathbf{y}_j^* = [(\mathbf{B} - \mathbf{A})\mathbf{q}^*, -\sum_{j=1}^n q_j^*]$, *for some* $\mathbf{q}^* \in \mathbb{R}^n_+$, *some technique* $(\mathbf{B}, \mathbf{A})$.
(iib) $\widehat{\mathbf{p}}^* = p_\ell^* \mathbf{1}(\mathbf{B} - \mathbf{A})^{-1}$.
(iii) $\begin{pmatrix} \mathbf{B} - \mathbf{A} \\ -\mathbf{1} \end{pmatrix} \mathbf{q}^* = \begin{pmatrix} \sum_{i=1}^m \mathbf{d}^* \\ -\sum_{i=1}^m L_i^* \end{pmatrix}$

Part (i) says that all consumers choose equilibrium consumption plans at these prices. Parts (iia) and (iib) describe the equilibrium of industries. Part (iii) requires market balance.

Now consider the following assumption:

Axiom 11.4 *For all* $i = 1, 2, ..., m$,
(i) The ith consumer's expenditure capacity is given by labour income.
(ii) For all $\mathbf{p} >> 0$, $\xi_i(\mathbf{p}) \neq \emptyset$, *with* $\mathbf{p}\mathbf{x}_i = 0$, *for all* $\mathbf{x}_i \in \xi_i(\mathbf{p})$.
(iii) $p_\ell = 0 \Longrightarrow L_i < 0$.

Part (i) of this axiom establishes that the consumers' initial endowments consist of their labour capacity, exclusively. Part (ii) says that the ith consumer's demand is non-empty valued, for all positive price vectors, and that the ith consumer expends all her income. Finally, part (iii) states that everybody demands someone else's labour when the wage is zero. That is, labour is a source of disutility, but is a useful good both for production and consumption.

The following result is obtained:

Theorem 11.2 *Under axioms 11.1 to 11.4, there exists a competitive equilibrium for this economy.*

Proof. The non-substitution theorem ensures that all aggregate efficient production plans $\mathbf{y} \in Y$ can be obtained by a single technique $(\mathbf{B}, \mathbf{A})$, with $\mathbf{y} = \left[(\mathbf{B} - \mathbf{A})\mathbf{q}, -\sum_{j=1}^n q_j\right]$ for some $\mathbf{q} \in \mathbb{R}^n_+$.

Note that $p_\ell = 0$ is not compatible with an equilibrium because it implies $\sum_{i=1}^m L_i > 0 \geq -\sum_{j=1}^n q_j, \forall \mathbf{q} \in \mathbb{R}^n_+$. Moreover, if $\mathbf{p}^*$ is a price vector for which all firms maximize profits (i.e. an equilibrium price vector), it satisfies $\widehat{\mathbf{p}}^* = p_\ell^* \mathbf{1}(\mathbf{B} - \mathbf{A})^{-1}$. Therefore, as $p_\ell^* > 0$ the equilibrium prices must be strictly positive.

Let $\mathbf{p}^*$ be the equilibrium price vector. By axiom 11.4, $\xi(\mathbf{p}^*) \neq \emptyset$ for all i. Let $\sum_{i=1}^m (\mathbf{d}_i^*, -L_i^*)$ be a point in $\xi(\mathbf{p}^*)$. The vector of equilibrium activity levels is uniquely obtained as:

$$\mathbf{q}^* = (\mathbf{B} - \mathbf{A})^{-1} \sum_{i=1}^m \mathbf{d}_i^* \qquad [1]$$

Therefore, it only remains to check that $\sum_{j=1}^n q_j^* = \sum_{i=1}^m L_i^*$.

Budget balance implies that $\mathbf{p}^* \mathbf{d}_i^* = p_\ell^* L_i$, for all i, so that $\widehat{\mathbf{p}}^* \sum_{i=1}^m \mathbf{d}_i^* = p_\ell^* \sum_{i=1}^m L_i^*$. Substituting now $\widehat{\mathbf{p}}^*$ by its value we have:

$$p_\ell^* \mathbf{1}(\mathbf{B} - \mathbf{A})^{-1} \sum_{i=1}^m \mathbf{d}_i^* = p_\ell^* \sum_{i=1}^m L_i^*$$

that is, making use of [1] and taking into account that $p_\ell^* > 0$,

$$\mathbf{1}\mathbf{q}^* = \sum_{i=1}^m L_i^*$$

so that the result follows. $\boxed{\textbf{Q.e.d.}}$

This general equilibrium model provides us with a useful representation of the economy of a region or a country, in which economic sectors take the role of firms. The strength of axioms 11.1 to 11.3 permits one to prove the existence of competitive equilibrium, assuming neither the continuity nor the convexity of preferences. It also ensures the uniqueness of the equilibrium prices (a very appealing property of equilibrium outcomes, hard to get on the basis of the fundamentals of the economy). The good comparative statics properties suggests that this might be a suitable framework for some other purposes (e.g. macroeconomic models in which relative prices matter).

11.3　Extensions

We devote this section to present some additional results on input-output modelling. First, we consider a variant of the linear case in which equilibrium prices include a uniform mark-up, or profit rate. Second, we deal with non-square linear systems, that is systems in which the number of firms can be smaller than the number of commodities. Finally, we present an abstract model where the technology is described by a non-linear vector mapping in which the net production is a function of gross output.

11.3.1 Linear models with positive profits

Let us consider again the model in section 11.2, that is, an economy whose production sector satisfies axioms 11.1 to 11.3. We know that for a technique $(\mathbf{B}, \mathbf{A})$ that satisfies axiom 11.3, $\mathbf{AB}^{-1} \geq \mathbf{0}$, with $0 < \lambda(\mathbf{AB}^{-1}) < 1$ (because $(\mathbf{I} - \mathbf{AB}^{-1})^{-1}$ exists and is non-negative, according to Theorem 11.0).

Now suppose that competition is defined by the equi-profitability of industries, rather than by unconditional profit maximization (see the classical equilibrium model in chapter 9 for a discussion). This means that equilibrium prices are given by a solution to the linear equation system:

$$\mathbf{pB} = \mathbf{pA}(1 + \rho) + p_\ell \mathbf{1}$$

where ρ is a parameter that tells us the profitability of the economy. Namely, the jth sector average revenues equal average costs plus a mark-up ρ (that here is supposed to apply only to the "advanced capital" of producible commodities).[5]

Note that $(1 + \rho)\mathbf{AB}^{-1} \geq \mathbf{0}$, so that, according to the analysis in section 11.2, the existence of a non-negative inverse matrix $(\mathbf{B} - (1 + \rho)\mathbf{A})^{-1} \geq \mathbf{0}$, can be ensured whenever $(\mathbf{B} - (1 + \rho)\mathbf{A})\mathbf{q} >> \mathbf{0}$ for some $\mathbf{q} \in \mathbb{R}^\ell_+$. This is in turn equivalent to asking that the Frobenius root of matrix $(1 + \rho)\mathbf{AB}^{-1}$ be positive and smaller than 1. It is easy to see that this happens when

$$0 \leq \rho \leq \frac{1}{\lambda(\mathbf{AB}^{-1})} - 1$$

Therefore we can establish:

Claim 11.1 *For all $\rho \in [0, \frac{1}{\lambda(\mathbf{AB}^{-1})} - 1]$, there is a unique vector of relative prices, $\mathbf{p} \in \mathbb{R}^\ell_+$, that solves the equilibrium price system. This price vector is given by $\widehat{\mathbf{p}} = p_\ell \mathbf{1}[\mathbf{B} - (1 + \rho)\mathbf{A}]^{-1}$.*

With this formulation, the price system has an additional degree of freedom, besides that corresponding to the normalization of absolute prices. This means that equilibrium prices depend on the uniform profit rate ρ, that here is taken as a parameter.

Some would interpret this indeterminacy as a weakness of the model. There is, however, a more positive approach to this matter, since this feature permits one to analyze the relation between the two distributive variables of the model, profits and salaries. Indeed, one can establish an inverse relationship between the profit rate ρ and the wage rate p_ℓ, the *wage-profit frontier*.

---

[5]This corresponds to the idea tha labour is paid at the end of the period. When this is not the case, the price equation is $\mathbf{pB} = (1 + \rho)[\mathbf{pA} + p_\ell \mathbf{1}]$.

To see this let us normalize prices so that $\hat{\mathbf{p}}\mathbf{k} = 1$, for some parameter vector $\mathbf{k} \in \mathbb{R}^n_+$. We can write

$$p_\ell \mathbf{1}[\mathbf{B}-(1+\rho)\mathbf{A}]^{-1}\mathbf{k} = 1$$

that is an implicit function relating profits and wages. As $\mathbf{AB}^{-1} \geq \mathbf{0}$ and we can write

$$[\mathbf{B}-(1+\rho)\mathbf{A}]^{-1} = \mathbf{I}+ \sum_{i=1}^{\infty} \left[(1+\rho)\mathbf{AB}^{-1}\right]^i \qquad [2]$$

it follows that $[\mathbf{B}-(1+\rho)\mathbf{A}]^{-1}$ increases monotonically with ρ, so that there is a continuous function $f : [0, \frac{1}{\lambda(\mathbf{AB}^{-1})}-1] \to \mathbb{R}_+$ that permits one to express the equilibrium wage rate as a decreasing function of the profit rate. Clearly, p_ℓ attains its maximum value for $\rho = 0$ (perfect competition) and becomes zero when $\rho = \rho^* = \frac{1}{\lambda(\mathbf{AB}^{-1})} - 1$. Hence, this model provides us with a theory of value in which the dependence of equilibrium prices on the distribution between different income sources is particularly straightforward.

When we take the wage rate as the *numéraire*, the expression of the inverse matrix given in [2] also tells us that the equilibrium prices of producible commodities $\hat{\mathbf{p}}$, are increasing functions of the rate of profits ρ. This cannot be ensured for other price normalizations, as there is no regular pattern of changes of relative prices when ρ varies.

Remark 11.5 *Note that when positive profits are admitted, the choice of techniques becomes dependent on the parameter ρ (i.e. on the distribution between profits and wages). The complexity of the relationships between prices and the profit rate brings about that one technique can be chosen for different values of ρ, whereas it is abandoned for some others.*[6]

For any given $\rho \in [0, \frac{1}{\lambda(\mathbf{AB}^{-1})} - 1]$, an equilibrium for this type of economy can be obtained by fixing a parametric distribution of profits among consumers (e.g. including the profit shares θ_{ij} as part of the description of the economy). Yet, the profit rate itself remains here unexplained (it can be linked to the growth rate in a dynamic growth model à la von Neumann).

Let $\mathbf{t} \geq \mathbf{0}$ denote the right eigen-vector of matrix $\mathbf{AB}^{-1}$ associated with the Frobenius root, that is,

$$\lambda(\mathbf{AB}^{-1})\mathbf{t} = \mathbf{AB}^{-1}\mathbf{t}$$

---

[6]A phenomenon, known as the *reswitching* of techniques, that generated some literature in the 60's in connection with the possibility of defining an aggregate production function, independently of the distribution.

or, letting $\rho^* = \frac{1}{\lambda(\mathbf{AB}^{-1})} - 1$ (that is, ρ^* is the maximum rate of profits that is attainable, given the technology),

$$\mathbf{t} = (1 + \rho^*)\mathbf{AB}^{-1}\mathbf{t} \qquad [3]$$

Consequently,

$$(\mathbf{I} - \mathbf{AB}^{-1})\mathbf{t} = \rho^*\mathbf{AB}^{-1}\mathbf{t} \qquad [4]$$

Define $\mathbf{d} = \mathbf{t} - \mathbf{AB}^{-1}\mathbf{t}$. Proposition 11.1 ensures the existence of a unique vector $\mathbf{q}^* \in \mathbb{R}^n_+$ such that $(\mathbf{B} - \mathbf{A})\mathbf{q}^* = \mathbf{d}$, with $\mathbf{q}^* = \mathbf{B}^{-1}\mathbf{t}$. Then, we can rewrite equations [3] and [4] as follows:

$$\mathbf{Bq}^* = (1 + \rho^*)\mathbf{Aq}^* \qquad [3']$$

$$(\mathbf{B} - \mathbf{A})\mathbf{q}^* = \rho^*\mathbf{Aq}^* \qquad [4']$$

As these eigen-vectors have a degree of freedom, we can fix the scale by letting: $\mathbf{1B}^{-1}\mathbf{t} = \mathbf{1q}^* = 1$.

Consider now the following normalization rule:

$$\widehat{\mathbf{p}}(\mathbf{B} - \mathbf{A})\mathbf{q}^* = 1$$

That amounts to taking vector $(\mathbf{B} - \mathbf{A})\mathbf{q}^*$ as the standard of value, with $\mathbf{1q}^* = 1$.

Multiplying equation [4'] by $\widehat{\mathbf{p}}$ and using this normalization formula, it follows that:

$$1 = \rho^*\widehat{\mathbf{p}}\mathbf{Aq}^* \qquad [5]$$

and substituting $\mathbf{Aq}^*$ by its value in [3'], we obtain:

$$\widehat{\mathbf{p}}\mathbf{Bq}^* = \frac{1 + \rho^*}{\rho^*}$$

an expression that tells us that the worth of the commodity vector $\mathbf{t} = \mathbf{Bq}^*$ does not change with prices. That is, we have found a basket of commodities whose worth is independent on the relative prices, hence on the distribution.[7] This enables to get a very simple relationship between profits and wages. To see this write

$$\rho = \frac{\widehat{\mathbf{p}}(\mathbf{B} - \mathbf{A})\mathbf{q}^* - p_\ell \mathbf{1q}^*}{\widehat{\mathbf{p}}\mathbf{Aq}^*}$$

---

[7]Note that we can identify this basket of commodities with the Ricardian *standard commodity*, that provides a standard of value independent of the distribution. On this see Sraffa (1960).

Therefore, given the price normalization and equation [5], it follows that

$$\rho = \rho^*(1 - p_\ell)$$

that is a particularly simple expression of the wage-profit frontier, as it is defined through a linear relationship.

Remark 11.6 *Note that the search for a commodity bundle that provides a measure of the worth of commodities independent of the distribution is far from being solved. Indeed, what this analysis suggests is that it has no solution. This is so because changes in the distribution induce changes in the chosen technique and therefore changes in the standard commodity (a circularity problem similar to that of the aggregate capital theory, mentioned before).*

11.3.2 Non-square linear input output models

Consider again a linear input-output model described by a technology $(\mathbf{B}, \mathbf{A}, \mathbf{1})$, where $\mathbf{B}, \mathbf{A}$ are $(\ell-1) \times n$ non-negative matrices, with $\ell - 1 \geq n$, and $\mathbf{1}$ is a row vector with n components. That is, now the number of producible commodities may be larger than the number of productive sectors (this is the interesting case, when we are not considering the selection of techniques).[8]

The equilibrium for quantities and prices results from the solution to the linear systems

$$(\mathbf{B} - \mathbf{A})\mathbf{q} = \mathbf{d}, \quad \mathbf{d} \in \mathbb{R}^{\ell-1}_+, \; \mathbf{q} \in \mathbb{R}^n_+$$
$$\widehat{\mathbf{p}}(\mathbf{B} - \mathbf{A}) = p_\ell \mathbf{1}, \quad \widehat{\mathbf{p}} \in \mathbb{R}^{\ell-1}_+$$

Note that not all vectors in $\mathbb{R}^{\ell-1}_+$ are necessarily in the image of $(\mathbf{B} - \mathbf{A})$ (where the image of $(\mathbf{B} - \mathbf{A})$, denoted by $\mathrm{Im}(\mathbf{B} - \mathbf{A})$, is given by all vectors in $\mathbb{R}^{\ell-1}$ that can be expressed as $(\mathbf{B} - \mathbf{A})\mathbf{z}$, for some $\mathbf{z} \in \mathbb{R}^n$).[9] Therefore, the solvability of the quantity system will be considered restricted to the set of final demand vectors $\mathbf{d} \in \mathrm{Im}(\mathbf{B} - \mathbf{A}) \bigcap \mathbb{R}^{\ell-1}_+$. Similarly, the solvability of the price system can only be considered when $\mathbf{1}^T \in \mathrm{Im}(\mathbf{B} - \mathbf{A})^T$, where superscript T denotes "transpose".

Observe that axioms 11.1 to 11.3 can be applied to this framework, without altering either their statement or their interpretation. Let us point out that assuming $rk(\mathbf{B}) = n$ means that we are discarding those processes that consist of linear combinations of others.

---

[8] We reproduce here the results in section 3 of Peris & Villar (1993).
[9] Mind that no sign restriction on $\mathbf{z}$ is imposed in this definition.

The following result is obtained:

Proposition 11.3 *Suppose that axioms 11.1 to 11.3 hold. Then,*

(i) The equation system $(\mathbf{B} - \mathbf{A})\mathbf{q} = \mathbf{d}$ has a unique non-negative solution $\mathbf{q}^*$ for all $\mathbf{d} \in \mathrm{Im}(\mathbf{B} - \mathbf{A}) \cap \mathbb{R}_+^{\ell-1}$.

(ii) The price system $\widehat{\mathbf{p}}(\mathbf{B} - \mathbf{A}) = p_\ell \mathbf{1}$ has a non-negative solution, provided $\mathbf{1}^T \in \mathrm{Im}(\mathbf{B} - \mathbf{A})^T$.

Proof. (i) Let us write

$$(\mathbf{B} - \mathbf{A}) = \begin{bmatrix} \mathbf{B}_1 - \mathbf{A}_1 \\ \mathbf{B}_2 - \mathbf{A}_2 \end{bmatrix}, \qquad \mathbf{d} = \begin{bmatrix} \mathbf{d}_1 \\ \mathbf{d}_2 \end{bmatrix}$$

where $\mathbf{B}_1$ is an $n \times n$ matrix of full rank, and $\mathbf{d}_1$ has n components. The axioms established ensure that we can always do this (probably after a suitable permutation of rows and columns).

Proposition 11.1 ensures the existence of a unique $\mathbf{q}^* \in \mathbb{R}_+^n$ such that $(\mathbf{B}_1 - \mathbf{A}_1)\mathbf{q}^* = \mathbf{d}_1$, as $(\mathbf{B}_1 - \mathbf{A}_1)^{-1}$ exists and is non-negative. Then, since $\mathbf{d} \in \mathrm{Im}(\mathbf{B} - \mathbf{A})$, it follows that $(\mathbf{B} - \mathbf{A})\mathbf{q}^* = \mathbf{d}$.

(ii) Let $\mathbf{1}^T \in \mathrm{Im}(\mathbf{B} - \mathbf{A})^T$, and suppose that the system:

$$(\mathbf{B} - \mathbf{A})^T \mathbf{v} = p_\ell \mathbf{1}^T, \qquad \mathbf{v} \geq 0$$

has no solution (where $\mathbf{v}$ is an $(\ell - 1)$-column vector, and superscript T denotes "transpose"). Then, Farkas Lemma [see for instance Gale (1960, Th. 2.6)] ensures the existence of some $\mathbf{x}$ such that

$$(\mathbf{B} - \mathbf{A})\mathbf{x} \leq 0, \quad \mathbf{1}\mathbf{x} > 0$$

Let $\mathbf{r} = (\mathbf{B} - \mathbf{A})(-\mathbf{x})$; then $\mathbf{r} \geq 0$, $\mathbf{r} \in \mathrm{Im}(\mathbf{B} - \mathbf{A})$. By (i) above, there exists $\mathbf{q} \geq 0$ such that $(\mathbf{B} - \mathbf{A})\mathbf{q} = \mathbf{r}$. Moreover, as $\mathbf{1}^T \in \mathrm{Im}(\mathbf{B} - \mathbf{A})^T$, there exists $\mathbf{s} \in \mathbb{R}^n$ such that $\mathbf{s}(\mathbf{B} - \mathbf{A}) = \mathbf{1}$. Thus, on the one hand, $\mathbf{s}(\mathbf{B} - \mathbf{A})(-\mathbf{x}) = \mathbf{1}(-\mathbf{x}) < 0$. On the other hand,

$$\mathbf{s}(\mathbf{B} - \mathbf{A})(-\mathbf{x}) = \mathbf{sr} = \mathbf{s}(\mathbf{B} - \mathbf{A})\mathbf{q} = \mathbf{1}\mathbf{q} \geq 0$$

This contradiction shows that there exists $\mathbf{v} \geq 0$ such that $(\mathbf{B} - \mathbf{A})^T \mathbf{v} = p_\ell \mathbf{1}^T$, and $\mathbf{p}^* = (\mathbf{v}^T, p_\ell)$ is an equilibrium price vector. $\boxed{\text{Q.e.d.}}$

Let us now consider a particular family of economies of this type, called *principal product* economies, where the requirements to ensure the solvability of the quantity system and the price system can be weakened.

Definition 11.3 *A linear input-output model* $(\mathbf{B}, \mathbf{A})$ *is said to be a **principal product economy**, when matrix* $(\mathbf{B} - \mathbf{A})$ *can be partitioned (either directly or after a suitable permutation of rows) as follows:*

$$(\mathbf{B} - \mathbf{A}) = \left[\begin{array}{c} \mathbf{I} - \mathbf{A}_1 \\ \mathbf{B}_2 - \mathbf{A}_2 \end{array} \right]$$

where $\mathbf{I}$ *is an n-diagonal matrix,* $\mathbf{A}_1 \geq \mathbf{0}$ *is a square n-matrix, and* $\mathbf{B}_2$, $\mathbf{A}_2$ *are two non-negative* $(\ell - 1 - n) \times n$ *matrices.*

In words, a principal product economy is one in which each sector can be identified as the exclusive producer of a specific commodity, even though it may jointly produce other commodities, which can be associated with used machines and some by-products. Clearly, the standard single production model is a particular case of this one.

From a purely mathematical viewpoint, what is special of principal product economies is that they satisfy automatically parts (iii) and (iv) of axiom 11.3. Hence, the following result is obtained:

Corollary 11.3 Let $(\mathbf{B}, \mathbf{A})$ be a principal product economy, that satisfies (i) and (ii) of axiom 11.3. Then,

(i) For all $\mathbf{d} \in \mathrm{Im}(\mathbf{B} - \mathbf{A}) \bigcap \mathbb{R}_+^{\ell-1}$, the equation system $(\mathbf{B} - \mathbf{A})\mathbf{q} = \mathbf{d}$ has a unique non-negative solution.

(ii) The price system $\widehat{\mathbf{p}}(\mathbf{B} - \mathbf{A}) = p_\ell \mathbf{1}$ has a non-negative solution.

11.3.3 A non-linear input-output model

We address here the case of an input-output economy in which technical coefficients may depend on the vector of activity levels. To do so, we consider an abstract non-linear model in which the inter-industry structure is hidden behind a vector mapping that expresses the net production as a function of gross output (and not directly as a function of individual activity levels). This approach entails the loss of some precision in the description of the economy. In exchange, it permits us to deal with a very general input-output model with variable returns to scale, in which the number of industries may differ from the number of producible commodities.

Let $\mathbf{g} : \mathbb{R}_+^n \rightarrow \mathbb{R}^n$ be a mapping that associates, with each gross output vector $\mathbf{y} \in \mathbb{R}_+^n$, the vector $\mathbf{g}(\mathbf{y})$ of net production that is obtained. As an example, think of $\mathbf{y} = \mathbf{B}(\mathbf{q})\mathbf{q}$, $\mathbf{g}(\mathbf{y}) = [\mathbf{B}(\mathbf{q}) - \mathbf{A}(\mathbf{q})]\mathbf{q}$, where $\mathbf{B}(.)$, $\mathbf{A}(.)$ are matrices whose coefficients may vary with the vector of activity levels $\mathbf{q}$.

Now consider the following axioms:

Axiom 11.5 $\mathbf{g} : \mathbb{R}^n_+ \to \mathbb{R}^n$ *is continuous in* $\mathbf{y}$.

Axiom 11.6 *For all* $\mathbf{d} \in \mathbb{R}^n_+$, *there exists* $\mathbf{y} \in \mathbb{R}^n_+$ *such that* $\mathbf{g}(\mathbf{y}) \geq \mathbf{d}$.

Axiom 11.7 *For all* $\mathbf{y}, \mathbf{y}' \in \mathbb{R}^n_+$ *such that* $\mathbf{y} > \mathbf{y}'$, $y_j = y'_j$ *implies* $g_j(\mathbf{y}) \leq g_j(\mathbf{y}')$.

Axiom 11.5 states that net production varies continuously with the gross-output vector.

Axiom 11.6 is a productivity requirement: for any given final demand vector $\mathbf{d}$ there exists a gross-output vector that yields a net production greater than or equal to $\mathbf{d}$. This axiom excludes some forms of decreasing returns to scale (those in which the aggregate net output is bounded).

Axiom 11.7 is a weak monotonicity property that puts some limits on the increasing returns to scale that are admissible. It says the following. Take a given a gross output vector $\mathbf{y}'$, and increase some of its components, while keeping constant some others. Then, we cannot have an increase in the net output of those commodities whose gross output has not been augmented. This is a weakening of the general principle that says that increasing the production of all commodities requires using up more inputs.[10]

Note that the standard single production linear model satisfies all these requirements.

The following result is obtained:

Proposition 11.4 *Suppose that axioms 11.5, 11.6 and 11.7 hold. Then, for any given* $\mathbf{d} \in \mathbb{R}^n_+$, *there exists a unique efficient vector* $\mathbf{y}^* \in \mathbb{R}^n_+$, *such that* $\mathbf{g}(\mathbf{y}^*) = \mathbf{d}$.

Proof. The proof is divided in two steps. First we show that the system $\mathbf{g}(\mathbf{y}) = \mathbf{d}$ has a non-negative solution $\mathbf{y}^*$. Then, that $\mathbf{y}' > \mathbf{y}^*$ for any other vector $\mathbf{y}'$ that solves this non-linear equation system.

(i) Let $T(\mathbf{d}) = \{\mathbf{y} \in \mathbb{R}^n_+ \ / \ \mathbf{g}(\mathbf{y}) \geq \mathbf{d}\}$, and consider the following program: find a point $\mathbf{y}$ that minimizes $\sum_{j=1}^n y_j$ in $T(\mathbf{d})$. As $T(\mathbf{d})$ is non-empty (axiom 11.6'), closed and bounded from below, and the objective function is continuous, Weierstrass theorem ensures that this problem has a solution $\mathbf{y}^* \geq 0$. Let us show now that $\mathbf{g}(\mathbf{y}^*) = \mathbf{d}$.

Suppose, for the sake of contradiction, that $\mathbf{g}(\mathbf{y}^*) > \mathbf{d}$. Divide the set of indices in two subsets as follows: $N = \{i \ / \ g_i(\mathbf{y}^*) = d_i\}$, $Q = \{i \ / \ g_i(\mathbf{y}^*) > d_i\}$. Let now $\mathbf{z}$ be a point in $\mathbb{R}^n_+$ given by: $z_i = y^*_i$ for $i \in N$, and $z_i < y^*_i$

---

[10]Formally, what axiom 11.7 says is that vector mapping $\mathbf{g}$ is a Z-function. See for instance Moré (1974).

for $i \in Q$, with $g_i(\mathbf{z}) > d_i$ (this is always possible by the continuity of $\mathbf{g}$). As $\mathbf{z} < \mathbf{y}^*$, it follows from axiom 11.7' that $g_i(\mathbf{z}) \geq g_i(\mathbf{y}^*) \geq d_i$ for all $i \in N$. Moreover, $g_i(\mathbf{z}) \geq d_i$ for all $i \in Q$, by construction. Therefore, $\mathbf{z} \in T(\mathbf{d})$ and $\sum_{i=1}^n z_i < \sum_{i=1}^n y_i^*$, a contradiction.

(ii) Let now $\mathbf{y}' \neq \mathbf{y}^*$ be another solution to the system $\mathbf{g}(\mathbf{y}) = \mathbf{d}$, and suppose that $\mathbf{y}' \not> \mathbf{y}^*$. Let $N = \{i \ / \ y_i' < y_i^*\}$, $Q = \{i \ / \ y_i' \geq y_i^*\}$, and let $\mathbf{z} \in \mathbb{R}_+^n$ be given by: $z_i = y_i'$, for $i \in N$, $z_i = y_i^*$, for $i \in Q$. Hence, $\mathbf{z} \leq \mathbf{y}'$ and $\mathbf{z} \leq \mathbf{y}^*$. Making use of axiom 11.7', it follows that:

$g_i(\mathbf{z}) \geq g_i(\mathbf{y}') \geq d_i$, for $i \in N$

$g_i(\mathbf{z}) \geq g_i(\mathbf{y}^*) \geq d_i$, for $i \in Q$

Therefore, $\mathbf{z} \in T(\mathbf{d})$. As $\mathbf{z} \leq \mathbf{y}^*$ this implies that $\mathbf{z} = \mathbf{y}^*$ so that $N = \emptyset$.

$\boxed{\text{Q.e.d.}}$

The next corollaries give us two interesting comparative statics results. The first one says that higher final demands call for higher gross output vectors (with strict inequalities in those commodities for which the final demand is strictly larger). The second one refines this outcome, under an additional assumption, and shows that the greatest relative change in gross output occurs in one of the commodities whose final demand has increased. Formally:

Corollary 11.4 *Suppose that axioms 11.5', 11.6' and 11.7' hold, let* $\mathbf{d}, \mathbf{d}' \in \mathbb{R}_+^n$ *be such that* $\mathbf{d}' \geq \mathbf{d}$, *and let* $\mathbf{y}', \mathbf{y}^*$ *stand for the unique efficient solutions to systems* $\mathbf{g}(\mathbf{y}) = \mathbf{d}$, $\mathbf{g}(\mathbf{y}) = \mathbf{d}'$, *respectively. Then,* $\mathbf{y}' > \mathbf{y}^*$, *with* $y_j' > y_j^*$ *whenever* $d_j' > d_j$.

Proof. Note that $\mathbf{d}' > \mathbf{d}$ implies that $\mathbf{y}' \in T(\mathbf{d})$ so that $\mathbf{y}' > \mathbf{y}^*$, in view of Proposition 11.4. When $y_j' = y_j^*$ axiom 11.7' implies that $g_i(\mathbf{y}^*) = d_i \geq d_i' = g_i(\mathbf{y}')$. Hence, $y_j' > y_j^*$ whenever $d_j' > d_j$. $\boxed{\text{Q.e.d.}}$

Corollary 11.5 *Suppose that axioms 11.5', 11.6' and 11.7' hold, and also that* $\mathbf{g}(\lambda\mathbf{y}) \gg \mathbf{g}(\mathbf{y})$, $\forall \ \lambda > 1$, *whenever* $\mathbf{g}(\mathbf{y}) > 0$. *Let* $\mathbf{d}, \mathbf{d}' \in \mathbb{R}_+^n$ *be such that* $\mathbf{d}' \geq \mathbf{d} \gg 0$, *and let* $\mathbf{y}', \mathbf{y}^*$ *stand for the unique efficient solutions to systems* $\mathbf{g}(\mathbf{y}) = \mathbf{d}$, $\mathbf{g}(\mathbf{y}) = \mathbf{d}'$, *respectively. Let* $S = \{i \ / \ d_i' > d_i\}$, *and* S^C *its complement. Then,*

$$\max_{i \in S} \frac{y_i'}{y_i^*} > \max_{j \in S^C} \frac{y_j'}{y_j^*}$$

Proof. Suppose that there is $t \in S^C$ such that

$$\lambda = \frac{y_t'}{y_t^*} \geq \frac{y_j'}{y_j^*} \quad \text{for all } j$$

Then, $\lambda\mathbf{y}^* > \mathbf{y}'$, with $\lambda y_t^* = y_t'$. Axiom 11.7' implies that $g_t(\mathbf{y}') \geq g_t(\lambda\mathbf{y}^*)$ against the assumption established. Hence, the result follows. $\boxed{\text{Q.e.d.}}$

11.4 References to the literature

Leontief (1966) contains an interesting collection of readings on the nature and applications of input-output analysis. Arrow & Hahn (1971, ch. 2, # 11) and Cornwall (1984, ch. 2), introduce linear input-output models (with single production), as a first step for the analysis of competitive equilibrium. The linear joint-production model and the corresponding non-substitution theorem presented here, appeared formerly in Herrero & Villar (1988a) and Peris & Villar (1993). The non-linear versions of these models extend some to the results in Fujimoto, Herrero & Villar (1985), Herrero & Villar (1985), (1988b). Further references to the literature can be obtained there. See also Villar (1991), (1992, ch. V).

The linear model with positive profits follows the work of Sraffa (1960). For a more detailed discussion see Pasinetti (1975), Bidard (1991). Morishima (1964) is still an interesting reading for a dynamic extension of these models.

An introduction to the use of linear production technologies for the computation of general equilibrium models can be found in Scarf (1982) and Cornwall (1984, ch. 3).

Chapter 12

THE LIMITS OF THE ECONOMY

12.1 Asymptotic cones

12.1.1 Introduction

The existence of equilibrium in production economies has been shown assuming, among other things, that the set of attainable allocations is compact. Even though this is a very reasonable property, it has been introduced as an axiom rather than as a consequence of some primitive assumptions on production and consumption sets. We deal with this point here, analyzing in detail conditions under which the aggregate consumption and production sets are closed, and the set of feasible allocations is compact.

The discussion of these points requires some familiarity with a mathematical object called the *asymptotic cone*. For a given set D in $\mathbb{R}^n$, the associated asymptotic cone is a closed convex cone with vertex zero that contains all unbounded directions of D. We shall see that this is a very useful instrument to discuss the boundedness of a set and the closedness of the sum of a finite collection of sets.

Let D be a subset of $\mathbb{R}^n$. For a given scalar $k \geq 0$ define

$$D^k = \{\mathbf{x} \in D \ / \ \|\mathbf{x}\| \geq k\}$$

that is, D^k is a subset of D containing all points whose norm is greater than k.

Let now $\Gamma(D^k)$ denote the smallest closed convex cone with vertex zero that contains D^k, and consider the following definition:

Definition 12.1   *The **asymptotic cone** of a set $D \subset \mathbb{R}^n$, denoted by $\mathcal{A}(D)$, is given by:*

$$\mathcal{A}(D) = \bigcap_{k \geq 0} \Gamma(D^k).$$

The asymptotic cone of a set $D \subset \mathbb{R}^n$ is given by the intersection of all closed convex cones $\Gamma(D^k)$, for all $k \geq 0$. It follows from this definition that $\mathcal{A}(D)$ selects all unbounded directions within the set D, as illustrated in the next figure.

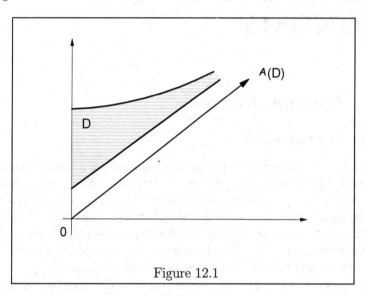

Figure 12.1

12.1.2   Basic properties

The main properties of asymptotic cones are gathered in the following theorem:

Theorem 12.1   *Let $D \subset \mathbb{R}^n$ and $\mathcal{A}(D)$ its asymptotic cone. Then:*
   (i) $\mathcal{A}(D)$ is a closed cone with vertex zero.
   (ii) D is bounded if and only if $\mathcal{A}(D) \subset \{0\}$.
   (iii) When D is closed and convex, with $\mathbf{0} \in D$, $\mathcal{A}(D) \subset D$.
   (iv) Let D_1, $D_2 \subset \mathbb{R}^n$ with $D_1 \subset D_2$. Then, $\mathcal{A}(D_1) \subset \mathcal{A}(D_2)$.
   (v) Let $\mathbf{x}$ be a point in $\mathbb{R}^n$. Then, $\mathcal{A}(D + \{\mathbf{x}\}) = \mathcal{A}(D)$.
   (vi) Let D, T be two non-empty subsets of $\mathbb{R}^n$. Then, $\mathcal{A}(D) \subset \mathcal{A}(D + T)$.
   (vii) Let $D, T \subset \mathbb{R}^n$. Then, $\mathcal{A}(D \bigcup T) = \mathcal{A}(D) \bigcup \mathcal{A}(T)$.

(viii) Let $D \subset \mathbb{R}^{n_1}$ be a bounded set, and $T \subset \mathbb{R}^{n_2}$. Then, $\mathcal{A}(D \times T) = \{0\} \times \mathcal{A}(T)$.

(ix) Let $D \subset \mathbb{R}^{n_1}, T \subset \mathbb{R}^{n_2}$. Then, $\mathcal{A}(D \times T) \subset \mathcal{A}(D) \times \mathcal{A}(T)$.

(x) Let $\{D_i\}_{i \in I}$ denote a family of subsets of $\mathbb{R}^n$. Then, $\bigcap_{i \in I} \mathcal{A}(D_i) = \{0\}$ implies that $\bigcap_{i \in I} D_i$ is bounded.

Proof. (i) This follows trivially from the definition, because $\mathcal{A}(D)$ is the intersection of closed convex cones with vertex zero.

(ii) If D is bounded there exists $\alpha \in \mathbb{R}$ such that $\| \mathbf{x} \| \leq \alpha$, for all $\mathbf{x} \in D$. Hence, for all $k \geq \alpha$, $D^k = \emptyset$ and $\Gamma(D^k) = \{0\}$. Consequently, $\bigcap_{k \geq 0} \Gamma(D^k) = \mathcal{A}(D) \subset \{0\}$.

Now let $\mathcal{A}(D) \subset \{0\}$. By definition, $k \geq k'$ implies $D^k \subset D^{k'}$ and thus $\Gamma(D^k) \subset \Gamma(D^{k'})$. Moreover, as $\mathbf{0} \in \Gamma(D^k)$ for all $k \in \mathbb{R}_+$, there will exist $k \in \mathbb{R}_+$ such that $\Gamma(D^k) = \{0\}$. This implies that either $D^k = \emptyset$ or $D^k = \{0\}$. If $D^k = \emptyset$, then $D^{k'} = \emptyset$ for all $k' \geq k$ and clearly D is bounded because $\| \mathbf{x} \| \leq k$ for all $\mathbf{x} \in D$. If $D^k = \{0\}$, it must be the case that $k = 0$ and $D = \{0\}$ (i.e. D is also bounded in this case).

(iii) When D is bounded the result follows from property (ii) above.

Let D be unbounded and take a point $\mathbf{y} \in \mathcal{A}(D)$. Without loss of generality we can take $\| \mathbf{y} \| = 1$, that is, $\mathbf{y} \in \mathcal{A}(D) \cap \partial B(\mathbf{0}, 1)$ (where $\partial B(\mathbf{0}, 1)$ is the boundary of the unit ball). By compactness, there exists a sequence $\{\mathbf{x}_k\} \subset \mathcal{A}(D) \cap \partial B(\mathbf{0}, 1)$ such that $\lim_{k \to \infty} \mathbf{x}_k = \mathbf{y}$. As $\| \mathbf{x}_k \| = 1$ for all k and $\mathbf{x}_k \in \bigcap_{j \geq 0} \Gamma(D^j)$ (a cone), we can write

$$\mathbf{x}_k = \frac{\mathbf{y}_k}{\| \mathbf{y}_k \|},$$

where $\mathbf{y}_k \in D^k$, for all $k \in \mathbb{N}$, and $\| \mathbf{y}_k \| \geq 1$.[1] Hence,

$$\mathbf{y} = \lim_{k \to \infty} \frac{\mathbf{y}_k}{\| \mathbf{y}_k \|}, \quad \mathbf{y}_k \in D^k$$

Now observe that

$$\frac{\mathbf{y}_k}{\| \mathbf{y}_k \|} = \frac{1}{\| \mathbf{y}_k \|} \mathbf{y}_k + \left[1 - \frac{1}{\| \mathbf{y}_k \|} \right] 0,$$

---

[1] As D is not bounded it contains elements with an arbitrary large norm and $D^k \neq \emptyset$, $\forall k \geq 0$. Therefore, we can always find elements in D^k in the same direction that $\mathbf{x}_k$ and carry out this construction.

with both $\mathbf{y}_k$ and $\mathbf{0}$ in D, that is convex by assumption. Hence

$$\frac{\mathbf{y}_k}{\|\mathbf{y}_k\|} \in D \quad \forall\, k$$

Moreover, as D is closed $\mathbf{y} \in D$.

(iv) Let $D_1, D_2 \subset \mathbb{R}^n$ with $D_1 \subset D_2$. For all $k \in \mathbb{R}_+$ we have $D_1^k \subset D_2^k$, and $\Gamma(D_1^k) \subset \Gamma(D_2^k)$. Hence, $\bigcap_{k\geq 0} \Gamma(D_1^k) \subset \bigcap_{k\geq 0} \Gamma(D_2^k)$, that is, $\mathcal{A}(D_1) \subset \mathcal{A}(D_2)$.

(v) If D is bounded, it follows from (ii). Suppose then that D is not bounded, and let $\mathbf{y} \in \mathcal{A}(D + \{\mathbf{x}\})$, $\mathbf{y} \neq \mathbf{0}$. Without loss of generality take $\|\mathbf{y}\| = 1$. Reasoning as in part (iii) we can find a sequence $\{\mathbf{y}_k + \mathbf{x}\} \in (D + \{\mathbf{x}\})^k$ such that:

$$\lim_{k\to\infty} \frac{\mathbf{y}_k + \mathbf{x}}{\|\mathbf{y}_k + \mathbf{x}\|} = \mathbf{y} \ .$$

Observe that

$$
\begin{aligned}
\mathbf{y} &= \lim_{k\to\infty} \frac{\mathbf{y}_k + \mathbf{x}}{\|\mathbf{y}_k + \mathbf{x}\|} = \lim_{k\to\infty} \frac{\mathbf{y}_k}{\|\mathbf{y}_k + \mathbf{x}\|} + \lim_{k\to\infty} \frac{\mathbf{x}}{\|\mathbf{y}_k + \mathbf{x}\|} \\
&= \lim_{k\to\infty} \frac{\mathbf{y}_k}{\|\mathbf{y}_k\|} \cdot \lim_{k\to\infty} \frac{\|\mathbf{y}_k\|}{\|\mathbf{y}_k + \mathbf{x}\|} = \lim_{k\to\infty} \frac{\mathbf{y}_k}{\|\mathbf{y}_k\|}
\end{aligned}
$$

Let $p_k = \max\{0,\ k - \|\mathbf{x}\|\}$. It follows that:

$$\bigcap_{k\geq 0} \Gamma(D^{p_k}) = \bigcap_{k\geq 0} \Gamma(D^k) = \mathcal{A}(D).$$

Also, as $\mathbf{y}_k + \mathbf{x} \in (D + \{\mathbf{x}\})^k$, we have $k \leq \|\mathbf{y}_k + \mathbf{x}\| \leq \|\mathbf{y}_k\| + \|\mathbf{x}\|$ so that $\|\mathbf{y}_k\| \geq k - \|\mathbf{x}\| \geq p_k$, that is, $\mathbf{y}_k \in D^{p_k}$.

In summary,

$$\lim_{k\to\infty} \frac{\mathbf{y}_k}{\|\mathbf{y}_k\|} = \mathbf{y}, \quad \frac{\mathbf{y}_k}{\|\mathbf{y}_k\|} \in \Gamma(D^{p_k}) \ \forall\, k \in \mathbb{R}_+.$$

Now suppose, for the sake of contradiction, that $\mathbf{y} \notin \bigcap_{k\geq 0} \Gamma(D^{p_k})$. Then, there exists $k_0 \geq 0$ such that $\mathbf{y} \notin \Gamma(D^{p_{k_0}})$, that is closed. Hence, for some $\varepsilon > 0$ we have that $B(\mathbf{y}, \varepsilon) \cap \Gamma(D^{p_{k_0}}) = \emptyset$ (where $B(\mathbf{y}, \varepsilon)$ is a ball of center $\mathbf{y}$ and radius ε). Furthermore, for $k \geq k_0$, $\Gamma(D^{p_k}) \subset \Gamma(D^{p_{k_0}})$, so that $B(\mathbf{y}, \varepsilon) \cap \Gamma(D^{p_k}) = \emptyset$ for all $k \geq k_0$. As $\mathbf{y} = \lim_{k\to\infty} \frac{\mathbf{y}_k}{\|\mathbf{y}_k\|}$, for this $\varepsilon > 0$ there exists k_1 such that, for all $k \geq k_1$, $\frac{\mathbf{y}_k}{\|\mathbf{y}_k\|} \in B(\mathbf{y}, \varepsilon)$. Letting $k \geq \max\{k_0, k_1\}$ we have:

$$\frac{\mathbf{y}_k}{\|\mathbf{y}_k\|} \in B(\mathbf{y}, \varepsilon) \cap \Gamma(D^{p_k}) \ ,$$

that is a contradiction. Therefore, $\mathbf{y} \in \mathcal{A}(D)$.

We have already shown that $\mathcal{A}(D + \{\mathbf{x}\}) \subset \mathcal{A}(D)$, for all $\mathbf{x} \in \mathbb{R}^n$, all $D \subset \mathbb{R}^n$. Applying now this result to the set $(D + \{\mathbf{x}\}) \subset \mathbb{R}^n$ and the point $-\mathbf{x} \in \mathbb{R}^n$, we get $\mathcal{A}(D) = \mathcal{A}((D + \{\mathbf{x}\}) - \{\mathbf{x}\}) \subset \mathcal{A}(D + \{\mathbf{x}\})$. Therefore, $\mathcal{A}(D + \{\mathbf{x}\}) = \mathcal{A}(D)$.

(vi) Let D, T be non-empty sets in $\mathbb{R}^n$. We can write $D + T = \bigcup_{t \in T} (D + \{\mathbf{t}\})$ and apply properties (iv) and (v) above, so that:

$$\mathcal{A}(D + T) = \mathcal{A}\left[\bigcup_{t \in T}(D + \{\mathbf{t}\})\right] \supset \mathcal{A}(D + \{\mathbf{t'}\}) = \mathcal{A}(D), \ \ \forall \mathbf{t'} \in T$$

(vii) Let $B(\mathbf{0}, k) = \{\mathbf{x} \in \mathbb{R}^n \ / \ \| \mathbf{x} \| < k\}$, and call $B^c(\mathbf{0}, k)$ the complementary set $\mathbb{R}^n - B(\mathbf{0}, k)$. We can write then $D^k = D \bigcap B^c(\mathbf{0}, k)$.

For $D, T \subset \mathbb{R}^n$ we have:

$$\begin{aligned} D^k \bigcup T^k &= [D \bigcap B^c(\mathbf{0}, k)] \bigcup [T \bigcap B^c(\mathbf{0}, k)] \\ &= [D \bigcup T] \bigcap B^c(\mathbf{0}, k) = [D \bigcup T]^k \end{aligned}$$

Hence, $\Gamma(D^k \bigcup T^k) = \Gamma[(D \bigcup T)^k]$. As $D^k, T^k \subset D^k \bigcup T^k$, it follows that $\Gamma(D^k), \Gamma(T^k) \subset \Gamma(D^k \bigcup T^k)$, so that:

$$\Gamma(D^k) \bigcup \Gamma(T^k) \subset \Gamma(D^k \bigcup T^k) = \Gamma[(D \bigcup T)^k].$$

Now taking intersections for all $k \geq 0$,

$$\mathcal{A}(D) \bigcup \mathcal{A}(T) \subset \mathcal{A}(D \bigcup T)$$

Let $\mathbf{y} \in \mathcal{A}(D \bigcup T)$, with $\mathbf{y} \neq \mathbf{0}$. Reasoning as in the former cases, we can find a sequence $\mathbf{y}_k \in (D \bigcup T)^k = D^k \bigcup T^k$ such that $\mathbf{y} = \lim_{k \to \infty} \frac{\mathbf{y}_k}{\|\mathbf{y}_k\|}$. Therefore, for infinite terms either $\mathbf{y}_k \in D^k$ or $\mathbf{y}_k \in T^k$, so that, proceeding as in part (v) above, we conclude that $\mathbf{y} \in \mathcal{A}(D)$ or $\mathbf{y} \in \mathcal{A}(T)$, respectively. This means that $\mathbf{y} \in \mathcal{A}(D) \bigcup \mathcal{A}(T)$.

(viii) Let $D, T \subset \mathbb{R}^n$, with D bounded. If T is also bounded the result is trivial. Assuming that T is not bounded, we shall see first that $\mathcal{A}(D \times T) \subset \{\mathbf{0}\} \times \mathcal{A}(T)$.

Let $\mathbf{y} \in \mathcal{A}(D \times T)$, with $\mathbf{y} \neq \mathbf{0}$. Without loss of generality take $\| \mathbf{y} \| = 1$; reasoning as above, we can find a sequence $\mathbf{x}_k = (\mathbf{d}_k, \mathbf{t}_k)$ in $(D \times T)^k$, for all $k \in \mathbb{N}$, such that:

$$\lim_{k \to \infty} \frac{\mathbf{x}_k}{\| \mathbf{x}_k \|} = \mathbf{y}$$

(where $\mathbf{y} = (\mathbf{y}_1, \mathbf{y}_2)$, with $\mathbf{y}_1 \in D$, $\mathbf{y}_2 \in T$).

As D is bounded and $\| \mathbf{x}_k \| \to \infty$, it follows that $\lim_{k \to \infty} \frac{\mathbf{d}_k}{\|\mathbf{x}_k\|} = 0$. Hence,

$$\mathbf{y} = \lim_{k \to \infty} \left[\frac{1}{\| \mathbf{x}_k \|} (\mathbf{d}_k, \mathbf{t}_k) \right] = \left[\lim_{k \to \infty} \frac{\mathbf{d}_k}{\| \mathbf{x}_k \|}, \ \lim_{k \to \infty} \frac{\mathbf{t}_k}{\| \mathbf{x}_k \|} \right] = (0, \mathbf{y}_2)$$

where

$$\mathbf{y}_2 = \lim_{k \to \infty} \frac{\mathbf{t}_k}{\| \mathbf{x}_k \|} = \lim_{k \to \infty} \frac{\mathbf{t}_k}{\| \mathbf{t}_k \|}$$

because D is bounded. Therefore, $\mathbf{y}_2 \in \mathcal{A}(T)$ and $\mathbf{y} = (0, \mathbf{y}_2)$ is a point in $\{0\} \times \mathcal{A}(T)$. This proves that $\mathcal{A}(D \times T) \subset \{0\} \times \mathcal{A}(T)$ when D is bounded.

Let now $\mathbf{y} = (0, \mathbf{y}_2)$ be a point in $\{0\} \times \mathcal{A}(T)$ with $\| \mathbf{y} \| = 1$. Because $\| \mathbf{y} \| = \| \mathbf{y}_2 \|$ and $\mathbf{y}_2 \in \mathcal{A}(T)$ we can write $\mathbf{y}_2 = \lim \frac{\mathbf{t}_k}{\|\mathbf{t}_k\|}$ with $\mathbf{t}_k \in T^k$. Now taking $\mathbf{x}_k = (0, \mathbf{t}_k)$, $\| \mathbf{x}_k \| = \| \mathbf{t}_k \|$, we have:

$$(0, \mathbf{y}_2) = \lim_{k \to \infty} \frac{\mathbf{x}_k}{\| \mathbf{x}_k \|} = \mathbf{y}$$

with $\mathbf{x}_k \in (\{0\} \times T)^k$, $\mathbf{t}_k \in T^k$. Hence $\mathbf{y} \in \mathcal{A}(\{0\} \times T)$, and we have shown that $\{0\} \times \mathcal{A}(T) = \mathcal{A}(\{0\} \times T)$.

Take again $\mathbf{y} = (0, \mathbf{y}_2) \in \{0\} \times \mathcal{A}(T)$. As D is bounded, there exists $k_0 \in \mathbb{R}$ such that $\| d \| \leq k_0$, $\forall d \in D$. As $\mathbf{y}_2 \in \mathcal{A}(T)$ we have $\mathbf{y}_2 = \lim_k \frac{\mathbf{t}_k}{\|\mathbf{t}_k\|}$ with $\mathbf{t}_k \in T^k$. We can choose $\mathbf{y}_k = (\mathbf{d}_k, \mathbf{t}_k) \in (D \times T)^k$ such that $\mathbf{y} = \lim_k \frac{(\mathbf{d}_k, \mathbf{t}_k)}{\|\mathbf{y}_k\|}$, because $\lim_k \frac{\mathbf{d}_k}{\|\mathbf{y}_k\|} = 0$ and $\| \mathbf{y}_k \| \geq \| \mathbf{t}_k \| \geq k$.

Therefore $\mathbf{y} \in \mathcal{A}(D \times T)$ and we have also shown that $\{0\} \times \mathcal{A}(T) \subset \mathcal{A}(D \times T)$, when D is bounded.

(ix) Let $D \subset \mathbb{R}^{n_1}$, $T \subset \mathbb{R}^{n_2}$ and call $B^i(0, k)$ the ball with center 0 and radius k in $\mathbb{R}^{n_i}$, for $i = 1, 2$. Then,

$$\mathcal{A}(D \times T) = \mathcal{A}\left(\left[D^k \bigcup \left[D \bigcap B^1(0, k) \right] \right] \times \left[T^{k'} \bigcup \left[T \bigcap B^2(0, k) \right] \right] \right)$$

$$= \mathcal{A}\left(D^k \times T^{k'} \right) \bigcup \left(\left[D \bigcap B^1(0, k) \right] \times T^{k'} \right) \bigcup \left[D^k \times \left[T \bigcap B_k^2(0) \right] \right] \bigcup \left[\left[D \bigcap B^1(0, k) \right] \times \left[T \bigcap B_k^2(0) \right] \right]$$

and, applying property (vii),

$$= \mathcal{A}\left(D^k \times T^{k'} \right) \bigcup \mathcal{A}\left[\left(D \bigcap B^1(0, k) \right) \times T^{k'} \right] \bigcup$$
$$\mathcal{A}\left[D^k \times \left(T \bigcap B^2(0, k) \right) \right] \bigcup \mathcal{A}\left[D \bigcap B^1(0, k) \right] \times \left[T \bigcap B^2(0, k) \right]$$

As the sets $D \bigcap B^1(0,k)$ and $T \bigcap B^2(0,k)$ are bounded, we can apply property (viii) and write:

$$= \mathcal{A}\left(D^k \times T^{k'}\right) \bigcup \mathcal{A}(D^k \times \{\mathbf{0}\}) \bigcup \{\mathbf{0}\}$$

Moreover, as $D^k \times T^{k'} = (\{\mathbf{0}\} \times T^{k'}) + (D^k \times \{\mathbf{0}\})$, it follows from property (vi) that $\mathcal{A}(\{\mathbf{0}\} \times T^{k'}) \subset \mathcal{A}[(\{\mathbf{0}\} \times T^{k'}) + (D^k \times \{\mathbf{0}\})] = \mathcal{A}(D^k \times T^{k'})$. Similarly, $\mathcal{A}(D^k \times \{\mathbf{0}\}) \subset \mathcal{A}(D^k \times T^{k'})$.

Developing still the equalities above, we can write:

$$\mathcal{A}\left(D^k \times T^{k'}\right) \bigcup \mathcal{A}\left(\{\mathbf{0}\} \times T^{k'}\right) \bigcup \mathcal{A}(D^k \times \{\mathbf{0}\}) \bigcup \{\mathbf{0}\} \subset \mathcal{A}(D^k \times T^{k'})$$

$$\subset \mathcal{A}\left[\Gamma\left(D^k\right) \times \Gamma\left(T^{k'}\right)\right] \subset \Gamma(D^k) \times \Gamma(T^{k'}) \qquad \forall \ k, k' \geq 0.$$

(we have used property (iii) in the last step, because $\Gamma(D^k)$, $\Gamma(T^{k'})$ are closed convex sets that contain the origin).

So far we have shown that $\mathcal{A}(D \times T) \subset \Gamma(D^k) \times \Gamma(T^{k'})$ for all $k, k' \geq 0$. Taking now intersections for all $k, k' \geq 0$ we conclude:

$$\mathcal{A}(D \times T) \subset \bigcap_{k,k' \geq 0} \left[\Gamma\left(D^k\right) \times \Gamma\left(T^{k'}\right)\right] = \bigcap_{k \geq 0} \Gamma(D^k) \times \bigcap_{k' \geq 0} \Gamma(T^{k'})$$

$$= \mathcal{A}(D) \times \mathcal{A}(T)$$

(x) Let $\{D_i\}_{i \in I} \subset \mathbb{R}^n$ with $\bigcap_{i \in I} \mathcal{A}(D_i) = \{\mathbf{0}\}$. Suppose that $\bigcap_{i \in I} D_i$ is not bounded, that is, $\left[\bigcap_{i \in I} D_i\right]^k \neq \emptyset$ for all $k \geq 0$. Let $\mathbf{y}_k \in \left[\bigcap_{i \in I} D_i\right]^k$; then, $\mathbf{y}_k \in D_i$ for all $i \in I$, and $\|\mathbf{y}_k\| \geq k$, so that $\mathbf{y}_k \in D_i^k$ for all $i \in I$, all $k \geq 0$. Thus,

$$\frac{\mathbf{y}_k}{\|\mathbf{y}_k\|} \in \Gamma(D_i^k), \ \forall i \in I, \ \forall k \geq 0$$

and

$$\frac{\mathbf{y}_k}{\|\mathbf{y}_k\|} \in \Gamma(D_i^k) \bigcap B(\mathbf{0},1) \ \forall k \geq 0, \ \forall i \in I$$

By compactness we can find a convergence subsequence:

$$\left\{\frac{\mathbf{y}_{k'}}{\|\mathbf{y}_{k'}\|}\right\}_{k' \in Q} : Q \subset \mathbb{N}$$

so that $\lim_{k' \to \infty} \frac{\mathbf{y}_{k'}}{\|\mathbf{y}_{k'}\|} = \mathbf{y}$. Because $\mathbf{y} \in \Gamma(D_i^k) \ \forall k \geq 0, \ \forall i \in I$, it follows that $\mathbf{y} \in \bigcap_{k \geq 0} \Gamma(D_i^k)$ for all $i \in I$, that is, $\mathbf{y} \in \mathcal{A}(D_i)$ for all $i \in I$. As $\|\mathbf{y}\| = 1$, we have found a point $\mathbf{y} \neq \mathbf{0}$ such that $\mathbf{y} \in \bigcap_{i \in I} \mathcal{A}(D_i)$, against the assumption.

Q.e.d.

12.2   Closed sums

Consider the following definition, relative to a collection of cones:

Definition 12.2 *A family $\{C_i\}_{i=1}^r$ of cones with vertex zero in $\mathbb{R}^n$ is **positively semi-independent** if, for any collection of points $\{x_i\}_{i=1}^r$ with $x_i \in C_i$ for all i, $\sum_{i=1}^r x_i = 0$ implies $x_i = 0$ for all i.*

From a geometrical point of view, this property means that these sets do not contain vectors in opposite directions. The next figures illustrate this fact for two cones. Figure (b) shows two cones that are positively semi-independent, whereas figure (a) shows two cones without this property.

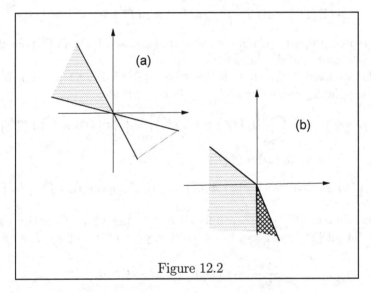

(a)

(b)

Figure 12.2

The following result illustrates the usefulness of asymptotic cones, and the strength of the positive semi-independence property:

Theorem 12.2 *Let $\{D_i\}_{i=1}^r$ be a family of closed subsets of $\mathbb{R}^n$, and let $\mathcal{A}(D_1), \mathcal{A}(D_2), ..., \mathcal{A}(D_r)$ be the corresponding asymptotic cones. If the family $\{\mathcal{A}(D_i)\}_{i=1}^r$ is positively semi-independent, the set $D = \sum_{i=1}^r D_i$ is closed in $\mathbb{R}^n$.*

Proof. It suffices to prove the result for the case of two sets.

Let $D_1, D_2 \subset \mathbb{R}^n$ be closed and such that $\mathcal{A}(D_1), \mathcal{A}(D_2)$ are positively semi-independent. To see that $D = D_1 + D_2$ is closed in $\mathbb{R}^n$, we have to show that for any convergent sequence $\{z_k\} \subset D$, with $\lim_{k \to \infty} z_k = z$, the limit point $\mathbf{z}$ belongs to D. Note that, by definition, $\mathbf{z}_k = \mathbf{x}_k + \mathbf{y}_k$, with $\mathbf{x}_k \in D_1$, $\mathbf{y}_k \in D_2$.

Two cases are to be considered. The first one is that in which one of the sequences, $\mathbf{x}_k$ or $\mathbf{y}_k$, is bounded. The second one is that in which both sequences are unbounded.

(i) Suppose first that $\{\mathbf{x}_k\}$ is bounded. Hence, it contains a convergent subsequence $\{\mathbf{x}_{ks}\}$ such that $\lim \mathbf{x}_{ks} = \mathbf{x}$. As this sequence is in the closed set D_1, $\mathbf{x} \in D_1$. The corresponding subsequence $\{\mathbf{x}_{k_s} + \mathbf{y}_{k_s}\}$ in $\{\mathbf{z}_k\}$ is convergent, as $\{\mathbf{z}_k\}$ is convergent. Therefore, $\{\mathbf{y}_{k_s}\}$ will also be a convergent sequence, with $\lim \mathbf{y}_{k_s} = \mathbf{y} \in D_2$ (because D_2 is closed). Moreover, $\lim(\mathbf{x}_{ks} + \mathbf{y}_{ks}) = \lim_{k \to \infty} \mathbf{z}_k = \mathbf{z}$, and, by the uniqueness of the limit, $\mathbf{z} = \mathbf{x} + \mathbf{y} \in D_1 + D_2 = D$. Hence in this case D is closed.

(ii) Now suppose $\{\mathbf{x}_k\}$, $\{\mathbf{y}_k\}$ are unbounded sequences, in spite of the fact that $\{\mathbf{z}_k\}$ is bounded. We shall see that this contradicts the assumption that $\mathcal{A}(D_1)$, $\mathcal{A}(D_2)$ are positively semi-independent.

(iia) Let us first show that there are sequences $\{\mathbf{x}_k^*\} \subset \mathcal{A}(D_1)$, $\{\mathbf{y}_k^*\} \subset \mathcal{A}(D_2)$ such that each one is divergent in norm, whereas the sum is bounded in norm.

As $\{\mathbf{x}_k\}$ is not bounded in norm, it contains a divergent subsequence $\{\mathbf{x}_{k_s}\}$ that goes through non-bounded directions in D_1. As $\mathcal{A}(D_1)$ contains all such unbounded directions, there exists a sequence $\{\mathbf{x}_{ks}^*\} \subset \mathcal{A}(D_1)$ such that $\| \mathbf{x}_{k_s}^* \| = \| \mathbf{x}_{k_s} \|$ so that the distance between these two sequences is bounded; namely, there exists a number N_1 such that for all $k_s > N_1$ the elements of $\{\mathbf{x}_{k_s}\}$ are in the unbounded directions of D_1. Let d_1 denote the maximum distance between these two sequences; then,

$$k_s > N_1 \implies \| \mathbf{x}_{k_s} - \mathbf{x}_{k_s}^* \| \leq d_1$$

By the same argument with respect to $\{\mathbf{y}_{k_s}\}$, there exists $\{\mathbf{y}_{ks}^*\} \subset \mathcal{A}(D_2)$ and numbers N_2, d_2 such that:

$$k_s > N_2 \implies \| \mathbf{y}_{k_s} - \mathbf{y}_{k_s}^* \| \leq d_2$$

with $\| \mathbf{y}_{k_s} \| = \| \mathbf{y}_{k_s}^* \|$.

Furthermore, as $\{\mathbf{x}_{k_s} + \mathbf{y}_{k_s}\}$ converges, there exists N_3 such that for all $k_s \geq N_3$, $\| \mathbf{x}_{ks} + \mathbf{y}_{ks} \| \leq \alpha$, for some $\alpha \in \mathbb{R}_+$.

Letting $N_0 = \max\{N_1, N_2, N_3\}$ and taking $k_s \geq N_0$ we have:

$$\| \mathbf{x}_{k_s}^* + \mathbf{y}_{k_s}^* \| = \| \mathbf{x}_{k_s}^* - \mathbf{x}_{k_s} + \mathbf{x}_{k_s} + \mathbf{y}_{k_s} + \mathbf{y}_{k_s}^* - \mathbf{y}_{k_s} \|$$

$$\leq \| \mathbf{x}_{k_s}^* - \mathbf{x}_{k_s} \| + \| \mathbf{x}_{k_s} + \mathbf{y}_{k_s} \| + \| \mathbf{y}_{k_s}^* - \mathbf{y}_{k_s} \|$$
$$\leq d_1 + d_2 + \alpha = \mu$$

Therefore, the sequence $\{\mathbf{x}^*_{k_s} + \mathbf{y}^*_{k_s}\}$ is bounded.

(iib) We shall see next that there are sequences $\{\alpha_k\}$, $\{\beta_k\}$ in $\mathcal{A}(D_1) \cap B(\mathbf{0}, 1)$ and $\mathcal{A}(D_2) \cap B(\mathbf{0}, 1)$, respectively, such that their sum converges to zero.

Let

$$\alpha_{k_s} = \frac{\mathbf{x}^*_{k_s}}{\| \mathbf{x}^*_{k_s} \|}, \quad \beta_{k_s} = \frac{\mathbf{y}^*_{k_s}}{\| \mathbf{y}^*_{k_s} \|}$$

that are clearly in $\mathcal{A}(D_1)$ and $\mathcal{A}(D_2)$, respectively. To make notation simpler we rename these sequences as $\{\alpha_k\}$, $\{\beta_k\}$. Observe that the sequences $\{\mathbf{x}^*_k\}$, $\{\mathbf{y}^*_k\}$ are not bounded, so that they are different from zero from some k onwards. Moreover,

$$\| \alpha_k + \beta_k \| = \left\| \frac{\mathbf{x}^*_k}{\| \mathbf{x}^*_k \|} + \frac{\mathbf{y}^*_k}{\| \mathbf{y}^*_k \|} \right\| = \left\| \frac{\mathbf{x}^*_k \| \mathbf{y}^*_k \| + \| \mathbf{x}^*_k \| \mathbf{y}^*_k}{\| \mathbf{x}^*_k \| \| \mathbf{y}^*_k \|} \right\|$$

$$= \left\| \frac{\mathbf{x}^*_k \| \mathbf{y}^*_k \| + \mathbf{y}^*_k \| \mathbf{y}^*_k \| - \mathbf{y}^*_k \| \mathbf{y}^*_k \| + \| \mathbf{x}^*_k \| \mathbf{y}^*_k}{\| \mathbf{x}^*_k \| \| \mathbf{y}^*_k \|} \right\|$$

$$= \left\| \frac{\| \mathbf{y}^*_k \| [\mathbf{x}^*_k + \mathbf{y}^*_k] + \mathbf{y}^*_k [\| \mathbf{x}^*_k \| - \| \mathbf{y}^*_k \|]}{\| \mathbf{x}^*_k \| \| \mathbf{y}^*_k \|} \right\|$$

$$\leq \left\| \frac{\mathbf{x}^*_k + \mathbf{y}^*_k}{\| \mathbf{x}^*_k \|} \right\| + \left\| \frac{\mathbf{y}^*_k}{\| \mathbf{y}^*_k \|} \frac{\| \mathbf{x}^*_k \| - \| \mathbf{y}^*_k \|}{\| \mathbf{x}^*_k \|} \right\| \leq$$

$$\leq 2 \left\| \frac{\mathbf{x}^*_k + \mathbf{y}^*_k}{\mathbf{x}^*_k} \right\| \to 0$$

(where $\left\{ \frac{\mathbf{x}^*_k + \mathbf{y}^*_k}{\mathbf{x}^*_k} \right\} \to 0$ because is the quotient between a bounded sequence and an unbounded one. As $\{\alpha_k\} \subset \mathcal{A}(D_1) \cap B(\mathbf{0}, 1)$, a compact set, there exists a subsequence $\{\alpha_{k_s}\}$, with $\lim_s \alpha_{k_s} = \alpha \in \mathcal{A}(D_1) \cap B(\mathbf{0}, 1)$. Similarly for $\{\beta_k\}$, $\lim_s \beta_{k_s} = \beta \mathcal{A}(D_2) \cap B(\mathbf{0}, 1)$.[2]

Therefore,

$$\lim_{s \to \infty} (\alpha_{k_s} + \beta_{k_s}) = \lim_{s \to \infty} (\alpha_k + \beta_k) = 0,$$

$$\lim_{s \to \infty} (\alpha_{k_s} + \beta_{k_s}) = \alpha + \beta$$

Hence, $\alpha + \beta = 0$. Moreover, $\alpha \in \mathcal{A}(D_1) \cap B(\mathbf{0}, 1)$ and $\beta \in \mathcal{A}(D_2) \cap B(\mathbf{0}, 1)$, so that $\| \alpha \| = \| \beta \| = 1$.

We conclude then that there exist points $\alpha \in \mathcal{A}(D_1)$, $\beta \in \mathcal{A}(D_2)$, with $\alpha \neq 0$, $\beta \neq 0$ and $\alpha + \beta = 0$. But this contradicts the assumption that $\mathcal{A}(D_2)$, $\mathcal{A}(D_2)$ are positively semi-independent.

---

[2] We can choose these subsequences with the same indexes k_s because there exist $\lim_s (\alpha_{k_s} + \beta_{k_s})$ and $\lim_s \alpha_{k_s}$, so that the algebra of limits implies that $\lim_s \beta_{k_s}$ also exists.

Therefore, case 2 cannot occur and $D = D_1 + D_2$ turns out to be a closed set. $\boxed{\text{Q.e.d.}}$

Remark 12.1 *An immediate consequence of this theorem is that the sum of a finite number of compact sets is compact.*

12.3 Structural properties of the economy

Let us recall here that, for a given economy E, an allocation is a point $\left[(\mathbf{x}_i)_{i=1}^m, (\mathbf{y}_j)_{j=1}^n\right]$ in $\Pi_{i=1}^m X_i \times \Pi_{j=1}^n Y_j$, and that the set of feasible allocations is given by:

$$\Omega \equiv \left\{ [(\mathbf{x}_i)_{i=1}^m, (\mathbf{y}_j)_{j=1}^n] \in \prod_{i=1}^m X_i \times \prod_{j=1}^n Y_j \ / \ \sum_{i=1}^m \mathbf{x}_i - \omega \le \sum_{j=1}^n \mathbf{y}_j \right\}$$

The projections of Ω on X_i, Y_j give us the ith consumer's set of attainable consumptions, and the jth firm's set of attainable production plans, respectively.

We discuss in this section the closedness of the aggregate consumption and production sets, and the compactness of the set Ω of attainable allocations.

12.3.1 The closedness of aggregate production and consumption sets

The following results give us the key properties of the aggregate consumption and production sets.

Proposition 12.1 *Let $X = \sum_{i=1}^m X_i$, where $X_i \subset \mathbb{R}^\ell$ is closed and bounded from below, for all $i = 1, 2, ..., m$. Then the aggregate consumption set X is closed in $\mathbb{R}^\ell$.*

Proof. By Theorem 12.2, it suffices to prove that the asymptotic cones $\{\mathcal{A}(X_i)\}_{i=1}^m$ are positively semi-independent.

By assumption, for all $i = 1, 2, ..., m$, there exists $\mathbf{c}_i \in \mathbb{R}^\ell$ such that $\mathbf{x}_i - \mathbf{c}_i \ge 0$, for all $\mathbf{x}_i \in X_i$. Then, $X_i \subset \{\mathbf{c}_i\} + \mathbb{R}_+^\ell$. From (iii), (v) and (vi) of Theorem 12.1, it follows that $\mathcal{A}(X_i) \subset \mathcal{A}(\{\mathbf{c}_i\} + \mathbb{R}_+^\ell) = \mathcal{A}(\mathbb{R}_+^\ell) = \mathbb{R}_+^\ell$, for all i. Then, $\sum_{i=1}^m \mathbf{z}_i = \mathbf{0}$ with $\mathbf{z}_i \in \mathcal{A}(X_i)$ implies $\mathbf{z}_i = \mathbf{0}$ for all i (because all these vectors are points in $\mathbb{R}_+^\ell$). Therefore, the asymptotic cones $\{\mathcal{A}(X_i)\}_{i=1}^m$ are positively semi-independent. $\boxed{\text{Q.e.d.}}$

Proposition 12.2 *Let* $Y = \sum_{j=1}^{n} Y_j$, *where* $Y_j \subset \mathbb{R}^\ell$ *is a closed set for all* j. *If* $\mathcal{A}(Y) \bigcap \mathcal{A}(-Y) = \{0\}$ *then* Y *is closed in* $\mathbb{R}^\ell$.

Proof. Here again it is sufficient to prove that the cones $\{\mathcal{A}(Y_j)\}_{j=1}^{n}$ are positively semi-independent.

Let $\sum_{j=1}^{n} \mathbf{y}_j = 0$ with $\mathbf{y}_j \in \mathcal{A}(Y_j)$ for all j, and suppose that there exists t such that $\mathbf{y}_t \neq 0$. Then, $\sum_{j \neq t} \mathbf{y}_j = -\mathbf{y}_t$. As $\mathbf{0} \in \mathcal{A}(Y_t)$, it follows that $\sum_{j \neq t} \mathbf{y}_j \in \mathcal{A}(Y)$, or, equivalently, $-\mathbf{y}_t \in \mathcal{A}(Y)$. But we know that $\mathbf{y}_t \in \mathcal{A}(Y)$ as well, because $\mathbf{y}_t = \mathbf{y}_t + 0 + 0 + \ldots + 0 \in \mathcal{A}(Y)$ (as $\mathbf{0} \in \mathcal{A}(Y_j)$ for all j). Therefore, we have found points $\mathbf{y}$ and $-\mathbf{y}$, different from zero, that are in $\mathcal{A}(Y)$, against the assumption. $\boxed{\text{Q.e.d.}}$

Corollary 12.1 *Let* $Y = \sum_{j=1}^{n} Y_j$, *where* $Y_j \subset \mathbb{R}^\ell$ *is a closed convex set such that* $\mathbf{0} \in Y_j$, *for all* j. *If* $Y \bigcap (-Y) = \{0\}$ *then* Y *is closed in* $\mathbb{R}^\ell$.

Proof. By (iii) of Theorem 5.1, $\mathcal{A}(Y_j) \subset Y_j$. Hence, $Y \bigcap (-Y) = \{0\}$ implies that $\mathcal{A}(Y) \bigcap \mathcal{A}(-Y) = \{0\}$. Proposition 5.2 gives us the desired result. $\boxed{\text{Q.e.d.}}$

12.3.2 The compactness of the set of attainable allocations

Consider the following preliminary result, that is interesting on its own, in order to analyze the key properties of the set Ω of attainable allocations:

Proposition 12.3 *(i) Let* $Y \subset \mathbb{R}^\ell$ *be such that* $\mathcal{A}(Y) \bigcap \mathbb{R}_+^\ell = \{0\}$. *Then, for any* $\mathbf{c} \in \mathbb{R}^\ell$ *the set* $Y(\mathbf{c}) = \{\mathbf{y} \in Y \ / \ \mathbf{y} \geq \mathbf{c}\}$ *is bounded.*

(ii) Let $X, Y \subset \mathbb{R}^\ell$ *be such that* X *is bounded from below and* $\mathcal{A}(Y) \bigcap \mathbb{R}_+^\ell = \{0\}$. *Then, the set* $G = \{(\mathbf{x}, \mathbf{y}) \in X \times Y \ / \ \mathbf{x} \leq \mathbf{y}\}$ *is bounded. If, moreover,* X *and* Y *are closed, then* G *is compact.*

Proof. (i) As $Y(\mathbf{c})$ is bounded from below, reasoning as in Proposition 12.1 we conclude that $\mathcal{A}[Y(\mathbf{c})] \subset \mathbb{R}_+^\ell$. Moreover, by (iv) of Theorem 12.1 we know that $Y(\mathbf{c}) \subset Y$ implies that $\mathcal{A}[Y(\mathbf{c})] \subset \mathcal{A}(Y)$. Hence, $\mathcal{A}[Y(\mathbf{c})] \subset \mathcal{A}(Y) \bigcap \mathbb{R}_+^\ell$. But $\mathcal{A}(Y) \bigcap \mathbb{R}_+^\ell = \{0\}$, by assumption, so that $\mathcal{A}[Y(\mathbf{c})] = \{0\}$, that is, $Y(\mathbf{c})$ is bounded [(ii) of Theorem 12.1].

(ii) By assumption, there exists $\mathbf{c} \in \mathbb{R}^\ell$ such that $\mathbf{c} \leq \mathbf{x}$ for all $\mathbf{x} \in X$. Now define $Y(\mathbf{c}) = \{\mathbf{y} \in Y \ / \ \mathbf{y} \geq \mathbf{c}\}$. By (i) $Y(\mathbf{c})$ is bounded, so that there exists $\overline{\mathbf{y}} \in \mathbb{R}^\ell$ such that $\overline{\mathbf{y}} \geq \mathbf{y}$, for all $\mathbf{y} \in Y(\mathbf{c})$. Let now $X(\overline{\mathbf{y}}) = \{\mathbf{x} \in X \ / \ \mathbf{x} \leq \overline{\mathbf{y}}\}$. Clearly $X(\overline{\mathbf{y}})$ is bounded. Moreover, as $G \subset X(\overline{\mathbf{y}}) \times Y(\mathbf{c})$ it follows from

(iv) and (ix) of Theorem 12.1 that $\mathcal{A}(G) \subset \mathcal{A}[X(\overline{\mathbf{y}})] \times \mathcal{A}[Y(\mathbf{c})] \subset \{\mathbf{0}\} \times \{\mathbf{0}\}$. Hence G is bounded. When these sets are also closed, G is compact. $\boxed{\textbf{Q.e.d.}}$

Part (i) of Proposition 12.3 says that when a production set satisfies $\mathcal{A}(Y) \bigcap \mathbb{R}_+^\ell = \{\mathbf{0}\}$, then bounded inputs imply bounded outputs. Note that $-\mathbb{R}_+^\ell \subset Y$ and $\mathcal{A}(Y) \cap \mathcal{A}(-Y) = \{\mathbf{0}\}$ imply $\mathcal{A}(Y) \bigcap \mathbb{R}_+^\ell = \{\mathbf{0}\}$, because $-\mathbb{R}_+^\ell \subset Y$ implies $-\mathbb{R}_+^\ell \subset \mathcal{A}(Y)$. More specifically, when Y is closed and convex, with $-\mathbb{R}_+^\ell \subset Y$, and $Y \bigcap (-Y) = \{\mathbf{0}\}$, it follows that $\mathcal{A}(Y) \bigcap \mathbb{R}_+^\ell = \{\mathbf{0}\}$. This is so because in that case $Y \cap \mathbb{R}_+^\ell = \{\mathbf{0}\}$ and $\mathcal{A}(Y) \subset Y$.

Part (ii) establishes that the set of aggregate production and consumption plans that are feasible is bounded, when $\mathcal{A}(Y) \bigcap \mathbb{R}_+^\ell = \{\mathbf{0}\}$ and X is bounded from below. The following theorem is actually a consequence of this result:

Theorem 12.3 *Let* $X = \sum_{i=1}^m X_i$, *where* $X_i \subset \mathbb{R}^\ell$ *is bounded from below for all* i, *and let* $Y = \sum_{j=1}^n Y_j$, *where* $Y_j \subset \mathbb{R}^\ell$ *for all* j, *and* $\mathcal{A}(Y) \bigcap \mathbb{R}_+^\ell = \{\mathbf{0}\}$. *Then the set of feasible allocations* $\Omega = \{[(\mathbf{x}_i), (\mathbf{y}_j)] \in \Pi_{i=1}^m X_i \times \Pi_{j=1}^n Y_j$ *such that* $\sum_{i=1}^m \mathbf{x}_i \le \sum_{j=1}^n \mathbf{y}_j + \omega\}$ *is bounded. If, furthermore, all* X_i *and all* Y_j *are closed, then* Ω *is compact.*

Proof. As every X_i is bounded from below, there exists a point in $\mathbf{c} \in -\mathbb{R}_+^\ell$ such that, for all points $[(\mathbf{x}_i), (\mathbf{y}_j)]$ in Ω, $\mathbf{c} \le \sum_{i=1}^m \mathbf{x}_i \le \sum_{j=1}^n \mathbf{y}_j + \omega$. Let $Y(\mathbf{c}') = \{\mathbf{y} \in Y \ / \ \mathbf{y} \ge \mathbf{c}'\}$, where $\mathbf{c}' = \mathbf{c} - \omega$. This is a bounded set, according to Proposition 12.3. Call $Y_j(\mathbf{c}')$ to the set of points $\mathbf{y}_j \in Y_j$ such that $\mathbf{y}_j + \sum_{h \neq j} \mathbf{y}_h \ge \mathbf{c}'$, for some $(\mathbf{y}_h)_{h \neq j} \in \Pi_{h \neq j} Y_h$. As $Y(\mathbf{c}') = \sum_{j=1}^n Y_j(\mathbf{c}')$, (vi) of Theorem 12.1 implies that $\mathcal{A}[Y_j(\mathbf{c}')] \subset \mathcal{A}[Y(\mathbf{c}')]$, so that each $Y_j(\mathbf{c}')$ is bounded.

Let now $\overline{\mathbf{y}}$ be a point in $\mathbb{R}^\ell$ such that $\overline{\mathbf{y}} \ge \mathbf{y}$ for all $\mathbf{y} \in Y(\mathbf{c})$, and consider the set $X(\overline{\mathbf{y}}) = \{\mathbf{x} \in X \ / \ \mathbf{x} \le \overline{\mathbf{y}}\}$. As X is bounded from below, by assumption, $X(\overline{\mathbf{y}})$ is bounded. Proceeding as before, call $X_i(\overline{\mathbf{y}})$ to the set of points $\mathbf{x}_i \in X_i$ such that $\mathbf{x}_i + \sum_{g \neq i} \mathbf{x}_g \le \overline{\mathbf{y}}$, for some $(\mathbf{x}_g)_{g \neq i}$ in $\Pi_{g \neq i} X_g$. As $X(\overline{\mathbf{y}}) = \sum_{i=1}^m X_i(\overline{\mathbf{y}})$, it follows that $\mathcal{A}[X_i(\overline{\mathbf{y}})] \subset \mathcal{A}[Y(\overline{\mathbf{y}})]$, so that $X_i(\overline{\mathbf{y}})$ is bounded.

As $\Omega \subset \Pi_{j=1}^n Y_j(\mathbf{c}') \times \Pi_{i=1}^m X_i(\overline{\mathbf{y}})$, (iv) and (ix) of Theorem 12.1 imply that Ω is bounded. If, moreover, all consumption and production sets are closed, then Ω is compact. $\boxed{\textbf{Q.e.d.}}$

Remark 12.2 *Note that when* $\omega \in X$ *and* $\mathbf{0} \in Y$ *we can also ensure that* Ω *is non-empty (because in this case we can choose* $(\mathbf{x}_i)_{i=1}^m$ *such that* $\sum_{i=1}^m \mathbf{x}_i = \omega$, *and* $(\mathbf{y}_j)_{j=1}^n$ *such that* $\sum_{j=1}^n \mathbf{y}_j = \mathbf{0}$).

12.4 References to the literature

This chapter is essentially a self-contained exposition of the corresponding results in sections 1.9, 3.3, 4.3 and 5.4 of Debreu (1959). The first section is based on the works of Carmen Herrero (1982) and Walter Trockel (1991). Section 2 contains a minor extension of these results, that allows to dispense with the convexity of production sets. For a further discussion see Cornet (1988b).

Bibliography

[1] Alós, C. & Ania, A. B. (1997), Tarifas en Dos Partes, **mimeo**, University of Alicante.

[2] Alós, C. & Villar, A. (1995), Clarke Cones and Marginal Pricing: An Exposition of the Key Results, **mimeo**, University of Alicante.

[3] Arrow, K.J. (1974), General Economic Equilibrium: Purpose, Analytic Techniques, Collective Choice, **American Economic Review**, 64 : 253-272.

[4] Arrow, K.J. & Debreu, G. (1954), Existence of Equilibrium for a Competitive Economy, **Econometrica**, 22 : 265–290.

[5] Arrow, K.J. & Enthoven, A.C. (1961), Quasi-Concave Programming, **Econometrica**, 29 : 779-800.

[6] Arrow, K.J. & Hahn, F.H. (1971), **General Competitive Analysis**, Holden Day, San Francisco.

[7] Arrow, K.J., Hurwicz, L. & Uzawa, H. (1961), Constraint Qualifications in Maximization Problems, **Naval Research Logistics Quarterly**, 8 : 175-186.

[8] Aumann, R.J. & Shapley, L.S. (1974), **Values of Nonatomic Games**, Princeton University Press, Princeton, New Jersey.

[9] Barten, A.P. & Böhm, V. (1982), Consumer Theory, Chapter 9 in K.J. Arrow & M.D. Intriligator (Eds.), **Handbook of Mathematical Economics**, vol. II, North-Holland, Amsterdam, 1982.

[10] Baumol, W.J., Bailey, E.E. & Willig, R.D. (1977), Weak Invisible Hand Theorems on the Sustainability of Prices in a Multiproduct Monopoly, **American Economic Review**, 67 : 350-365.

[11] Bazaraa, M.S. & Shetty, C.M. (1979), **Nonlinear Programming**, John Wiley, New York.

[12] Beato, P. (1982), The Existence of Marginal Cost Pricing Equilibria with Increasing Returns, **Quarterly Journal of Economics**, 389 : 669-688.

[13] Beato, P. & Mas-Colell, A. (1983), Gestion au Côut Marginal et Efficacité de la Production Aggregé: un Example, **Annales de L'INSEE**, 51 : 39-46.

[14] Beato, P. & Mas-Colell, A. (1985), On Marginal Cost Pricing with Given Tax-Subsidy Rules, **Journal of Economic Theory**, 37 : 356-365.

[15] Benassy, J.P. (1991), Monopolistic Competition, in W. Hildenbrand and H. Sonnenschein (Eds.), **Handbook of Mathematical Economics (vol. IV)**, North-Holland, Amsterdam, 1991.

[16] Bergstrom, T.C. (1970), A "Scandinavian Consensus" Solution for Efficient Income Distribution among Nonmalevolent Consumers, **Journal of Economic Theory**, 2 : 383-398.

[17] Berman, A. & Plemmons, R.J. (1979), **Nonnegative Matrices in Mathematical Sciences**, Academic Press, New York.

[18] Bidard, Ch. (1991), **Prix, Reproduction, Rareté**, Dunod, Paris.

[19] Billera, L.J. & Heath, D.C. (1982), Allocation of Shared Costs: A Set of Axioms Yielding a Unique Procedure, **Mathematics of Operations Research**, 30 : 32-39.

[20] Billera, L.J., Heath, D.C. & Raanan, J. (1978), Internal Telephone Billing Rates -A Novel Application of Non-Atomic Game Theory, **Mathematics of Operations Research** 26 : 956-965.

[21] Bobzin, H. (1998), **Indivisibilities. Microeconomic Theory with respect to Indivisible Goods and Factors**, Physica-Verlag, Heidelberg.

[22] Böhm, V.(1986), Existence of Equilibria with Price Regulation, in W. Hildenbrand & A. Mas-Colell (Eds.), **Contributions to Mathematical Economics. Essays in Honor of Gerard Debreu**, North-Holland, Amsterdam, 1986.

[23] Boiteaux, M. (1956), Sur la Gestion des Monopoles Publiques Astreints à l'Equilibre Budgétaire, **Econometrica**, 24 : 22-44.

[24] Bonnisseau, J.M., (1988), On Two Existence Results of Equilibria in Economies with Increasing Returns, **Journal of Mathematical Economics**, 17 : 193-207.

[25] Bonnisseau, J.M. (1991), Existence of Equilibria in Presence of Increasing Returns: A Synthesis, *Laboratoire d'Econométrie*, working paper n° 328.

[26] Bonnisseau, J.M. & Cornet, B. (1988a), Existence of Equilibria when Firms follow Bounded Losses Pricing Rules, **Journal of Mathematical Economics**, 17 : 119-147.

[27] Bonnisseau, J.M. & Cornet, B. (1988b), Valuation Equilibrium and Pareto Optimum in Non-Convex Economies, **Journal of Mathematical Economics**, 17 : 293-308.

[28] Bonnisseau, J.M. & Cornet, B. (1990a), Existence of Marginal Cost Pricing Equilibria in Economies with Several Nonconvex Firms, **Econometrica**, 58 : 661-682.

[29] Bonnisseau, J.M. & Cornet, B. (1990b), Existence of Marginal Cost Pricing Equilibria: The Nonsmooth Case, **International Economic Review**, 31 : 685-708.

[30] Border, K.C. (1985), **Fixed Point Theorems with Applications to Economics and Game Theory**, Cambridge University Press, Cambridge.

[31] Bös, D. (1987), Public Sector Pricing, Chapter 3 in A.J. Auerbach and M. Feldstein (Eds.), **Handbook of Public Economics**, North-Holland, Amsterdam, 1987.

[32] Brown, D.J. (1991), Equilibrium Analysis with Nonconvex Technologies, Ch. 36 in W. Hildenbrand & H. Sonnenschein (Eds.), **Handbook of Mathematical Economics (vol. IV)**, North-Holland, Amsterdam, 1991.

[33] Brown, D.J. & Heal, G.M. (1979), Equity, Efficiency and Increasing Returns, **Review of Economic Studies**, 46 : 571–585.

[34] Brown, D.J. & Heal, G.M. (1982), Existence, Local Uniqueness and Optimality of a Marginal Pricing Equilibrium with Increasing Returns, Social Science Working Paper 415, California Institute of Technology.

[35] Brown, D.J. & Heal, G.M. (1983), The Optimality of Regulated Pricing: A General Equilibrium Analysis, in C. Aliprantis and O. Burkinshaw (eds.), **Advances in Equilibrium Theory**, Springer-Verlag, Berlin, 1983.

[36] Brown, D.J., Heal, G., Khan, M.A. & Vohra, R. (1986), On a General Existence Theorem for Marginal Cost Pricing Equilibria, **Journal of Economic Theory**, 38 : 371-379.

[37] Brown, D.J., Heller, W.J. & Starr, R.M. (1992), Two-Part Marginal Cost Pricing Equilibria: Existence and Efficiency, **Journal of Economic Theory**, 57 : 52-72.

[38] Buchanan, J.M. & Yoon, Y.J. (1994), **The Return to Increasing Returns**, The University of Michigan Press, Ann Arbor.

[39] Calsamiglia, X. (1977), Decentralised Resource Allocation and Increasing Returns, **Journal of Economic Theory**, 14 : 263-283.

[40] Chipman, J.S. (1970), External Economies of Scale and Competitive Equilibrium, **Quarterly Journal of Economics**, 84 : 347-385.

[41] Clarke, F. (1975), Generalized Gradients and Applications, **Transactions of the American Mathematical Society**, 205 : 247-262.

[42] Clarke, F. (1983), **Optimization and Nonsmooth Analysis**, New York, Wiley.

[43] Coase, R.H. (1946), The Marginal Cost Controversy, **Economica**, 13 : 169–189.

[44] Corchón, L. (1988), Cost-Prices with Variable Returns, **Metroeconomica**, 40 : 93-99.

[45] Corchón, L. (1994), Fixed Prices and Quality Signals, **Mathematical Social Sciences**, 27 : 49-58.

[46] Cornet, B. (1986), The Second Welfare Theorem in Nonconvex Economies, C.O.R.E. Discussion Paper 8630, Université Catolique de Louvain.

[47] Cornet, B. (1988a), General Equilibrium Theory and Increasing Returns, **Journal of Mathematical Economics**, 17 : 103-118.

[48] Cornet, B. (1988b), Topological Properties of the Attainable Set in a Non-Convex Production Economy, **Journal of Mathematical Economics**, 17 : 275–292.

[49] Cornet, B. (1990), Existence of Equilibria in Economies with Increasing Returns, in B. Cornet & H. Tulkens (Eds.), **Contributions to Economics and Operations Research: The XXth Anniversary of the C.O.R.E.**, The MIT Press, Cambridge Ma., 1990.

[50] Cornwall, R. (1984), **Introduction to the Use of General Equilibrium Analysis**, North-Holland, Amsterdam.

[51] Deaton, A. & Muellbauer, J. (1980), **Economics and Consumer Behavior**, Cambridge University Press, Cambridge.

[52] Debreu, G. (1952), A Social Equilibrium Existence Theorem, **Proceedings of the National Academy of Sciences**, 38 : 886-893.

[53] Debreu, G. (1959), **Theory of Value**, Wiley, New York.

[54] Debreu, G. (1962), New Concepts and Techniques for Equilibrium Analysis, **International Economic Review**, 3 : 257–273.

[55] Debreu, G. (1982), Existence of Competitive Equilibrium. Chapter 15 in Arrow & Intriligator. (Eds.), 1982-86.

[56] Debreu, G (1984), Economic Theory in the Mathematical Mode, **American Economic Review,** 267-278.

[57] Debreu, G. & Herstein, I.N. (1953), Nonnegative Square Matrices, **Econometrica**, 21: 597-607.

[58] Debreu, G. & Scarf, H. (1963), A Limit Theorem on the Core of an Economy, **International Economic Review**, 4 : 234–246.

[59] Dehez, P. (1988), Rendements d'Echelle Croissants et Equilibre Generale, **Revue d'Economie Politique**, 98 : 765-800.

[60] Dehez, P. & Drèze, J. (1988a), Competitive Equilibria with Quantity-Taking Producers and Increasing Returns to Scale, **Journal of Mathematical Economics**, 17 : 209-230.

[61] Dehez, P. &Drèze, J. (1988b), Distributive Production Sets and Equilibria with Increasing Returns, **Journal of Mathematical Economics**, 17 : 231-248.

[62] Demsetz, H. (1968), Why Regulate Utilities?, **Journal of Law and Economics**, 11 : 55–65.

[63] Diamantaras, D. & Gilles. R.P. (1996), The Pure Theory of Public Goods: Efficiency, Decentralization and the Core, **International Economic Review**, 37 : 851–860.

[64] Diamantaras, D., Gilles. R.P. & Scotchmer, S. (1996), Decentralization of Pareto Optima in Economies with Public Projects, Nonessential private goods and Convex Costs, **Economic Theory**, 8 : 555–564.

[65] Diamantaras, D. & Wilkie, S. (1994), A Generalization of Kaneko's Ratio Equilibrium to Economies with Private and Public Goods, **Journal of Economic Theory**, 62 : 499-512.

[66] Dierker, E. (1986), When does Marginal Cost Pricing Lead to Pareto Efficiency?, **Zeitschrift für Nationalökonomie**, Supl. 5 : 41–66.

[67] Dierker, E., Guesnerie, R. & Neufeind, W. (1985), General Equilibrium where some Firms follow Special Pricing Rules, **Econometrica**, 53 : 1369-1393.

[68] Dierker, E. & Neufeind, W. (1988), Quantity Guided Price Setting, **Journal of Mathematical Economics**, 17 : 249–259.

[69] Dieudonné, J. (1969), **Foundations of Modern Analysis**, Academic Press Inc., New York.

[70] Dixit, A. & Stiglitz. J. (1977), Monopolistic Competition and Product Diversity, **American Economic Review**, 76 : 297–308.

[71] Drèze, J.H. & Hagen, K. (1978), Choice of Product Quality: Equilibrium and Efficiency, **Econometrica**, 46 : 493-513.

[72] Dupuit, J. (1844), De la Mesure de l'Utilité des Travaux Publics, **Annales de Ponts et Chaussées**, 2nd series, 8. Translated in **International Economic Papers**, 2 : 83–110, 1952.

[73] Edlin A.S.& Epelbaum, M. (1993), Two-Part Marginal Cost Sharing Equilibria with n Firms: Sufficient Conditions for Existence and Optimality, **International Economic Review**, 34 : 903–922.

[74] Edlin, A.S. Epelbaum, M. & Heller, W.P. (1998), Is Perfect Price Discrimination Really Efficient?: Welfare and Existence in General Equilibrium, **Econometrica**, 66 : 987–922.

[75] Fitzroy, F.R. (1974), Monopolistic Equilibrium, Non-Convexity and Inverse Demand, **Journal of Economic Theory**, 7 : 1-16.

[76] Florenzano, M. (1981), **L'Equilibre Economique General Transitif et Intransitif: Problèmes d'Existence**, Editions du CNRS, Paris.

[77] Foley, D. (1967), Resource Allocation and the Public Sector, **Yale Economic Essays**, 7 : 45-98.

[78] Fujimoto, T., Herrero, C. & Villar, A. (1985), A Sensitivity Analysis in a Nonlinear Leontief Model, **Journal of Economics**, 45 : 67–71.

[79] Gabsewicz, J.J. & Vial, J.P. (1972), Oligopoly "à la Cournot" in General Equilibrium Analysis, **Journal of Economic Theory**, 4 : 381-400.

[80] Gale, D. (1960), **The Theory of Linear Economic Models**, McGraw Hill, New York.

[81] Ginés, M. (1996), Core Selections in Economies with Increasing Returns and Public Goods, **mimeo**, University of Alicante.

[82] Greenberg, J. & Shitovitz, B. (1984), Aumann-Shapley Prices and Scarf Social Equilibrium, **Journal of Economic Theory**, 34 : 380-382.

[83] Guesnerie, R. (1975), Pareto Optimality in Nonconvex Economies, **Econometrica**, 43 : 1–29.

[84] Guesnerie, R. (1980), **Modèles de l'Economie Publique**, Monographie du Séminaire d'Econometrie, Editions du CNRS, Paris.

[85] Guesnerie, R. (1990), First-Best Allocation of Resources with Nonconvexities in Production, in B. Cornet & H. Tulkens (Eds.), **Contributions to Economics and Operations Research: The XXth Anniversary of the C.O.R.E.**, The MIT Press, Cambridge Ma., 1990.

[86] Hammond, P. & Villar, A. (1998), Efficiency with Non-Convexities: Extending the 'Scandinavian Consensus' Approaches, **The Scandinavian Journal of Economics**, 100 : 11-32.

[87] Hammond, P. & Villar, A. (1999a), Valuation Equilibrium Revisited, in A. Alkan, R. Aliprantis & N.C. Yannelis (eds.), **Current Trends in Economics**, Springer-Verlag, 1999.

[88] Hammond, P. & Villar, A. (1999b), Valuation Equilibrium with Increasing Returns, **mimeo**, University of Alicante.

[89] Hart S. & Mas-Colell, A. (1989), Potential Value and Consistency, **Econometrica**, 57 : 589-614.

[90] Heal, G. (ed.) (1999), **The Economics of Increasing Returns**, Edward Elgar (in press).

[91] Henderson, J.M. & Quandt, R.E. (1980), **Microeoconomic Theory. A Mathematical Approach**, Third Ed., McGraw Hill, London.

[92] Herrero, C. (1982), Sobre la Compacidad de los Conjuntos Alcanzables de Producción y Consumo, **Estadística Española**, nº 96 : 63-68.

[93] Herrero, C. & Villar, A. (1988a), A Characterization of Economies with the Non-substitution Property, **Economics Letters,** 26 : 147–152.

[94] Herrero, C. & Villar, A. (1988b), General Equilibrium in a Nonlinear Leontief Framework, **The Manchester School**, 56 : 159-166.

[95] Hildenbrand, W. (1968), The Core of an Economy with a Measure Space of Economic Agents, **Review of Economic Studies**, 35 : 443–452.

[96] Hildenbrand, W. & Kirman, A. (1988), **Equilibrium Analysis**, North-Holland, Amsterdam.

[97] Hotelling, H.S. (1938), The General Welfare in Relation to Taxation and of Railway and Utility Rates, **Econometrica**, 6 : 242–269.

[98] Ichiishi, T. (1993), **The Cooperative Nature of the Firm**, Cambridge University Press, Cambridge.

[99] Ichiishi, T. & Quinzii, M. (1983), Decentralization for the Core of a Production Economy with Increasing Returns, **International Economic Review**, 24 : 397-412.

[100] Johansen, L. (1963), Some Notes on the Lindahl Theory of Determination of Public Expenditures, **International Economic Review**, 4 : 346-358.

[101] Johnson, Ch. R. (1983), Sign Patterns of Non-negative Inverse Matrices, **Linear Algebra and Its Applications**, 55 : 69–80.

[102] Jouini, E. (1988), A Remark on Clarke's Normal Cone and the Marginal Cost Pricing Rule, **Journal of Mathematical Economics**, 17 : 309-315.

[103] Kamiya, K. (1988), Existence and Uniqueness of Equilibria with Increasing Returns, **Journal of Mathematical Economics**, 17 : 149-178.

[104] Kamiya, K. (1995), Optimal Public Utility Pricing: A General Equilibrium Analysis, **Journal of Economic Theory**, 66 : 548-572.

[105] Kaneko, M. (1977), The Ratio Equilibrium and a Voting Game in a Public Goods Economy, **Journal of Economic Theory**, 16 : 123-136.

[106] Khan, M. A. & Vohra, R. (1987), An Extension of the Second Welfare Theorem to Economies with Nonconvexities, **Quarterly Journal of Economics**, 102 : 223-241.

[107] Koopmans, T.C. (1957), **Three Essays on the State of Economic Science**, McGraw-Hill, New York.

[108] Kuhn, H.W. & Tucker, A.W. (1951), Nonlinear Programming, in J. Neyman (Ed.), **Proceedings of the Second Berkeley Symposium on Mathematical Statistics and Probability**, University of California Press, Berkeley, 1951.

[109] Leontief, W.W. (1941), **The Structure of the American Economy 1919–1929**, Harvard University Press, Cambridge Ma.

[110] Leontief, W.W. (1966), **Input-Output Economics**, Oxford University Press, New York.

[111] Lindahl, E. (1919), **Die Gerechtigkeit der Besteuerung: Eine Analyse der Steuerprinzipen auf der Grundlage der Grenznutzentheorie**, Gleerup and H. Ohlsson, Lund.

[112] Llinares, J.V. (1998), Unified Treatment of the Problem of the Existence of Maximal Elements in Binary Relations, **Journal of Mathematical Economics**, 29 : 285-302.

[113] MacKinnon, J.G. (1979), Computing Equilibria with Increasing Returns, **European Economic Review**, 12 : 1-16.

[114] Makowski, L. (1980a), A Characterization of Perfectly Competitive Economies with Production, **Journal of Economic Theory,** 22 : 208–221.

[115] Makowski, L. (1980b), Perfect Competition, the Profit Criterion, and the Organization of Economic Activity, **Journal of Economic Theory,** 22 : 222–242.

[116] Makowski, L. & Ostroy, J.M. (1995), Appropriation and Efficiency: A Revision of the First Theorem of Welfare Economics, **American Economic Review**, 85 : 808–827.

[117] Malinvaud, E. (1969), **Leçons de Théorie Microeconomique**, Dunod, Paris.

[118] Malinvaud, E. (1972), **Lectures on Microeoconomic Theory**, North-Holland, Amsterdam.

[119] Mantel, R. (1979), Equilibrio con Rendimientos Crecientes a Escala, **Anales de la Asociación Argentina de Economía Política**, 1 : 271-283.

[120] Marshall, A. (1890), **Principles of Economics**, Macmillan, London.

[121] Mas-Colell, A. (1974), An Equilibrium Existence Theorem without Complete or Transitive Preferences, **Journal of Mathematical Economics**, 1 : 237-246.

[122] Mas-Colell, A. (1980), Efficiency and Decentralization in the Pure Theory of Public Goods, **Quarterly Journal of Economics**, 94 : 625-641.

[123] Mas-Colell, A. (1987), **Lecciones sobre la Teoría del Equilibrio con Rendimientos Crecientes**, Segundas Lecciones Germn Berncer, Valencia, Generalitat Valenciana.

[124] Mas-Colell, A. & Silvestre, J. (1989), Cost-Share Equilibria: A Lindahlian Approach, **Journal of Economic Theory**, 47 : 239-256.

[125] Mas-Colell, Whinston & Green (1995), **Microeconomic Theory**, Oxford University Press, New York.

[126] McKenzie, L. W. (1959), On the Existence of General Equilibrium for a Competitive Market, **Econometrica**, 27 : 54–71.

[127] Meek, R. (1962), **The Economics of Physiocracry**, George Allen & Unwin, London.

[128] Milleron, J.C. (1972), Theory of Value with Public Goods: A Survey, **Journal of Economic Theory**, 5 : 419-477.

[129] Mirman, L.J., Samet, D. & Tauman, Y. (1983), An Axiomatic Approach to the Allocation of a Fixed Cost Through Prices, **Bell Journal of Economics**, 14 : 139-151.

[130] Mirman L.J. & Tauman, Y. (1982), Demand Compatible Equitable Cost Sharing Prices, **Mathematics of Operations Research**, 7 : 40-56.

[131] Mirman, L.J., Tauman, Y. & Zang, I. (1985), Supportability, Sustainability, and Subsidy-Free Prices, **Rand Journal of Economics**, 16 : 114-126.

[132] Mirman, L.J., Tauman, Y. & Zang, I. (1986), Ramsey Prices, Average Cost Prices and Price Sustainability, **International Journal of Industrial Organization**, 4 : 1-18.

[133] Moré, J.J. (1974), Classes of Functions and Feasibility Conditions in Nonlinear Complementarity Problems, **Mathematical Programming**, 6 : 327–338.

[134] Moriguchi, C. (1996), Two-part Marginal Cost Pricing in a Pure Fixed Cost Economy, **Journal of Mathematical Economics**, 26 : 363–385.

[135] Morishima, M. (1964), **Equilibrium, Stability and Growth**, Oxford University Press, Oxford.

[136] Moulin, H. (1988), **Axioms of Cooperative Decision Making**, Cambridge University Press, Cambridge.

[137] Nadiri, M.I. (1982), Producers Theory, Chapter 10 in K.J. Arrow & M.D. Intriligator (Eds.), **Handbook of Mathematical Economics**, vol. II, North-Holland, Amsterdam, 1982.

[138] Negishi, T. (1961), Monopolistic Competition and General Equilibrium, **Review of Economic Studies**, 28 : 196-201.

[139] Nikaido, H. (1972), **Introduction to Sets and Mappings in Modern Economics**, North-Holland, Amsterdam.

[140] Ostroy, J.M. (1980), The Non-Surplus Conditions as a Characterization of Perfectly Competitive Equilibrium, **Journal of Economic Theory,** 22 : 183–207.

[141] Ostroy, J. (1984) A Reformulation of the Marginal Productivity Theory of Distribution, **Econometrica**, 52 : 599–630.

[142] Panzar, J.C. & Willig, R.D. (1977), Free Entry and the Sustainability of Natural Monopoly, **Bell Journal of Economics**, 8 : 1-22.

[143] Pasinetti, L. (1975), **Lezioni di Teoria della Produzione**, Il Mulino, Bologna.

[144] Peris, J.E. & Villar, A. (1993), Linear Joint-Production Models, **Economic Theory**, 3 : 735–742.

[145] Quinzii, M. (1982), An Existence Theorem for the Core of a Production Economy with Increasing Returns, **Journal of Economic Theory**, 28 : 32-50.

[146] Quinzii, M. (1991), Efficiency of Marginal Pricing Equilibria, in W. Brock and M. Majumdar (Eds.), **Equilibrium and Dynamics: Essays in Honor of David Gale**, MacMillan, New York, 1991.

[147] Quinzii, M. (1992), **Increasing Returns and Efficiency**, Oxford University Press, New York.

[148] Ramsey, F. (1927), A Contribution of the Theory of Taxation, **The Economic Journal**, 37 : 47-61.

[149] Reichert, J. (1986), **Strategic Market Behavior**, Ph.D. Dissertation, Yale University.

[150] Roberts, J. & Sonnenschein, H. (1977), On the Foundations of the Theory of Monopolistic Competition, **Econometrica**, 45 : 101-113.

[151] Rockafellar, R.T. (1970), **Convex Analysis**, Princeton University Press, Princeton.

[152] Romer, P.M. (1990), Endogenous Technical Change, **Journal of Political Economy**, 98 : S71–S102.

[153] Ruggles, N. (1949), The Welfare Basis of the Marginal Cost Pricing Principle, **Review of Economic Studies**, 17 : 29-46.

[154] Ruggles, N. (1950), Recent Developments in the Theory of Marginal Cost Pricing, **Review of Economic Studies**, 17 : 107-126.

[155] Samet, D. & Tauman, Y. (1982), The Determination of Marginal Cost Prices under a Set of Axioms, **Econometrica**, 50 : 895-910.

[156] Say, J.B. (1826), **Traité d'Economie Politique**, 5th ed. Chez Rapilly, Paris.

[157] Scarf, H.E. (1986), Notes on the Core of a Productive Economy, in W. Hildenbrand & A. Mas-Colell (Eds.), **Contributions to Mathematical Economics. Essays in Honor of Gerard Debreu**, North-Holland, Amsterdam, 1986.

[158] Schmeidler, D. (1971), A Condition for the Completeness of Partial Preference Relations, **Econometrica**, 39 : 403-404.

[159] Sen, A.K. (1970), **Collective Choice and Social Welfare**, Holden Day, San Francisco.

[160] Shafer, W.J. (1974), The Nontransitive Consumer, **Econometrica**, 42 : 913-919.

[161] Shafer, W.J. & Sonnenschein, H. (1975), Equilibrium in Abstract Economies without Ordered Preferences, **Journal of Mathematical Economics**, 2 : 345-348.

[162] Sharkey, W.W. (1979), Existence of a Core where there are Increasing Returns, **Econometrica**, 47 : 869-876.

[163] Sharkey, W.W. (1980), **The Theory of Natural Monopoly**, Cambridge University Press, Cambridge.

[164] Sharkey, W.W. (1989), Game Theoretic Modelling of Increasing Returns to Scale, **Games and Economic Behavior**, 1 : 370-431.

[165] Silvestre, J. (1977), General Monopolistic Equilibrium under Non-Convexity, **International Economic Review**, 18 : 425-434.

[166] Silvestre, J. (1978), Increasing Returns in General Non-Competitive Analysis, **Econometrica**, 46 : 397-402.

[167] Sraffa, P. (1926), The Laws of Returns under Competitive Conditions, **The Economic Journal**, 26 : 535-550.

[168] Sraffa, P. (1960), **Production of Commodities by Means of Commodities**, Cambridge University Press, Cambridge.

[169] Starr, R.M. (1996), **General Equilibrium Theory. An Introduction**, Cambridge University Press, Cambridge.

[170] Suzumura, K. (1983), **Rational Choice, Collective Decisions and Social Welfare**, Cambridge University Press, Cambridge.

[171] Takayama, A. (1985), **Mathematical Economics**, 2nd.Ed., Cambridge University Press, Cambridge.

[172] Ten Raa, T. (1983), Supportability and Anonymous Equity, **Journal of Economic Theory**, 31:176-181.

[173] Trockel, W. (1991), "Über Asymptotische Kegel" **mimeo**.

[174] Varian, H. (1992), **Microeconomic Analysis,** 3rd. ed., W.W. Norton, New York.

[175] Vega-Redondo, F. (1987), Efficiency and Nonlinear Pricing in Nonconvex Environments with Externalities: A generalization of the Lindahl Equilibrium Concept, **Journal of Economic Theory**, 41 : 54-67.

[176] Villar, A. (1991), A General Equilibrium Model with Increasing Returns, **Revista Española de Economía**, 8 : 1–15.

[177] Villar, A. (1992), **Operator Theorems with Applications to Distributive Problems and Equilibrium Models**, Springer-Verlag, Berlin.

[178] Villar, A. (1994), Equilibrium with Nonconvex Technologies, **Economic Theory**, 4 : 629–638.

[179] Villar, A. (1996), **General Equilibrium with Increasing Returns**, Springer-Verlag, Berlin.

[180] Villar, A. (1999a), **Lecciones de Microeconomía**, A. Bosch Editor, Barcelona.

[181] Villar, A. (1999b), Competitive Pricing in Economies with Non-convex Production Sets, **Optimization**, forthcoming.

[182] Villar, A. (1999c), Equilibrium in Semimonotone Market Games, **mimeo**, University of Alicante.

[183] Vohra, R. (1988a), On the Existence of Equilibria in a Model with Increasing Returns, **Journal of Mathematical Economics**, 17 : 179-192.

[184] Vohra, R. (1988b), Optimal Regulation under Fixed Rules for Income Distribution, **Journal of Economic Theory**, 45 : 65-84.

[185] Vohra, R. (1990), On the Inefficiency of Two-Part Tariffs, **Review of Economic Studies**, 57 : 415-438.

[186] Vohra, R. (1991), Efficient Resource Allocation under Increasing Returns, Stanford Institute for Theoretical Economics, Tech. Rep. no.18.

[187] Vohra, R. (1992), Marginal Cost Pricing under Bounded Increasing Returns, **Econometrica**, 60 : 859-876.

[188] Walker, M. (1977), On the Existence of Maximal Elements, **Journal of Economic Theory**, 16 : 470-474.

[189] Wicksell, K. (1896), Ein Neues Prinzip der Gerechten Besteuerung, **Finanztheorische Untersuchungen**, iv–vi, 76–87 and 101–159.

[190] Young, A. (1928), Increasing Returns and Economic Progress, **The Economic Journal**, 38 : 527-540.

Index